International Law and Security in Indo-Pacific

This book uses an interdisciplinary approach to discuss international law and conflict in the Indo-Pacific region, covering topics such as maritime security, climate change and international relations.

Detailing how international relations and particular state interests govern regional and global partnerships, the book provides suggestions for the future of the Indo-Pacific region. Exploring how conflict within the region has international repercussions, topics covered include the role of South-East Asian countries, and the role of statehood of small islands in Oceania. Detailing harmonization of laws and policies in the context of international security and maritime law, the book focuses on the impact of climate change and other topical issues such as cyber security and the protection of cultural identity.

The book will be of interest to researchers in the field of international law, law of the sea, international relations and security.

Dr. Joanna Siekiera is an expert in international law, NATO consultant, trainer, and educator. She currently works as the Assistant Professor at the War Studies University in Warsaw, Poland. She is also a fellow at the U.S. Marine Corps University in Quantico and supports various military institutions as a legal SME and course facilitator.

International Law and Security in Indo-Pacific

Strategic Design for the Region

Edited by Joanna Siekiera

Routledge
Taylor & Francis Group
LONDON AND NEW YORK

First published 2026
by Routledge
4 Park Square, Milton Park, Abingdon, Oxon OX14 4RN

and by Routledge
605 Third Avenue, New York, NY 10158

Routledge is an imprint of the Taylor & Francis Group, an informa business

British Library Cataloguing-in-Publication Data
A catalogue record for this book is available from the British Library

ISBN: 978-1-032-89211-5 (hbk)
ISBN: 978-1-032-90010-0 (pbk)
ISBN: 978-1-003-54575-0 (ebk)

DOI: 10.4324/9781003545750

Typeset in Times New Roman
by Apex CoVantage, LLC

Contents

Contributors

Helen Barbosa, a Cape Verdean, works in water and climate adaptation, focusing in Small Island Developing States (SIDS). Her current research explores Nature-Based Solutions, including in the Baltic region and Eastern Europe. She has worked nationally and internationally in the WASH sector. Helen holds an M.Sc. in Environmental Sciences from Eötvös Loránd University, Hungary, and an advanced M.Sc. in Water Resources Management from IHE Delft, Netherlands. She has partnered with various organizations to implement climate and water projects for SIDS, including Pacific islands.

Pooja Bhatt is an associate professor at Jindal School of International Affairs, Jindal Global University, India. She is the author of *Nine-Dash Line: Deciphering the South China Sea Conundrum* (republished by Routledge June 2024; Knowledge World 2020). Previously, she worked as a consultant with the Policy Planning & Research division, Ministry of External Affairs, India. Pooja received her doctoral degree from the School of International Studies, Jawaharlal Nehru University, New Delhi, in 2021. She also holds a diploma in the United Nations Convention on the Law of the Seas (UNCLOS) from Yeosu Academy, Korea Maritime Institute.

Soojeong Choi served as a senior researcher in South Korea at a governmental institute for 12 years. She was strongly involved and consulted as a legal analyst in international negotiations on the law of the sea as a negotiator for the Korean Government (the Republic of Korea) in the United Nations and the Regional Fisheries Management Organizations. She participated in a team that made a roadmap for co-fishing areas in the Northern Limit Line between North and South Korea. Her PhD studies focus on dispute settlements on marine territories and negotiations on international fishing rights on the high seas.

Amparo Pamela Fabe is a faculty member of the National Police College and the Philippine Public Safety College. She helped draft Republic Act 11479, known as the Philippine's Anti-Terrorism Act of 2020, particularly the section on penalizing the material support for terrorism. Her expertise covers maritime domain awareness, terrorism financing and economic statecraft. She was a Senior

Consultant of the European Union Delegation to Indonesia/Brunei Darussalam on Anti-Money Laundering and Countering Terrorist Financing. Her research studies are featured in CRC Press, Routledge, Palgrave Macmillan, Brill and Springer. She mentors Philippine public safety officers.

Jacob Galbreath was born in Naples, Italy. Commissioned in the United States Navy in 2003, he is qualified in Submarine and Information Warfare with over seven years at sea aboard multiple ships in the Far East. He served in NATO Training Mission – Afghanistan in Kabul, which entailed resourcing, training and oversight of all IT networks for Afghan security and police forces. At CCD-COE, as the Strategy Branch Lead, he oversaw cyberspace strategy and policy from 2021 to 2023. Currently CDR Galbreath (OF-4 USA N) conducts Fleet Experimentation as part of the Naval Warfare Development Center, Norfolk, Virginia, USA.

Colonel (Retired) Jeffry A. Hollman last served as the Chief, Mission Assurance Division (J-34), Headquarters United States Indo-Pacific Command, Camp H.M. Smith, Hawaii. There he was responsible for establishing policies and procedures to implement Anti-Terrorism (AT), Critical Infrastructure Protection (CIP), and Performance, Readiness & Integration (PR&I) across the Asia-Pacific, enabling DoD activities to mitigate risk to personnel and resources. Prior to that assignment, Colonel (Retired) Hollman served as the Chief of Security Forces at Headquarters Pacific Air Forces. As a career Security Forces officer, he has held a variety of leadership positions, both in command and headquarters assignments. Colonel (Retired) Hollman was commissioned in 1995 through the Officer Training School at Maxwell AFB, AL. Prior to his commissioning, he spent eight years in the United States Marine Corps Reserve as an enlisted Motor Transport Platoon Sergeant.

Bagus Jatmiko is an Indonesian Navy commander who is currently pursuing his doctoral degree in the Information Sciences department at Naval Postgraduate School, Monterey, California. He has experience in both academic and practical aspects, particularly related to his duty as an operational officer of the Indonesian Navy. Moreover, he is a seasoned officer at many levels of the military, particularly the Navy. His interests are in the issues of strategic and regional defense and security, particularly in the maritime domain, such as maritime domain awareness, information operation and warfare, cyber security and defense and network-centric warfare.

Joseph Tshilomb Jonathan, PhD Candidate at the Business School of the University of Winchester, England. He is currently a research scholar in Global Business Studies, focusing on aspects of research lying at the intersection of Seabed Mining and preservation of Biodiversity in maritime areas beyond national jurisdictions. He has been engaged in actions towards the protection of High Seas Biodiversity. This project has been initiated by The Marine Conservation Institute's Action Center in Seattle, United States.

William Liffick is a former U.S. Coast Guard Officer renowned for his work in maritime counterterrorism and intelligence. William spent his military career in special operations combatting terrorism and transnational crime. William holds a MA in International Relations and Global Security and other certificates from the U.S. Naval War College, NATO, and Texas A&M Bush School of International Affairs. He is a recurring speaker at the NATO School Oberammergau teaching Maritime Counter Terrorism and a contributing author to NATO's Counter Terrorism Reference Curriculum. William currently is a founder of Littoral Dynamics LLC, a training and maritime security company.

Adina Masalbekova is a researcher specializing in China's foreign policy and Central Asia. She holds an ML in Political Theory from East China Normal University and is currently affiliated with the University of Central Asia and N-OST. She previously worked with the OSCE Academy and CESS Groningen and contributed to research at institutions such as SASS, ANU, GPG, and USIP. Her research covers topics such as China's health diplomacy, tech transfer in the Global South, EU-China foreign policies in Central Asia, cultural diplomacy, social media perceptions, and Chinese FDI in the region.

Cleo Paskal is a journalist and works now as a non-resident senior fellow at Foundation for Defense of Democracy focusing on the Indo-Pacific region, in particular, the Pacific Islands and India. She has testified before the U.S. Congress, regularly lectures and moderates for seminars for the U.S. military, and has taught at defense colleges in the United States, United Kingdom, India, Canada, and Oman. From 2006 to 2022, she was an associate fellow at Chatham House, London, where, among other responsibilities, she was research lead on the multi-year futures project "Perspectives on Strategic Shifts in the Indo-Pacific 2019–2024."

Brandon Quinones is a specialist in maritime security and critical infrastructure resiliency, specializing in hybrid warfare against peer adversaries. Starting his career as an intelligence officer in the United States Marine Corps, Brandon then worked several years with Fortune 100 companies to upgrade their security capabilities. Brandon is now the Co-Founder of Littoral Dynamics, a maritime security consulting firm. With an MBA in Risk, Compliance, and Anti-Money Laundering, Brandon authored NATO's 2024 Counter Threat Financing Module and serves as a guest instructor at NATO School Oberammergau, teaching courses on Counter Terrorist Financing and Critical Infrastructure Resiliency.

Luke Shabro is the founder and CEO of Divergent Futures Consulting. He is a futurist, threat analyst, writer, and U.S. Navy veteran. He has worked as a futures consultant and author for the NATO Stability Policing Centre of Excellence. Mr. Shabro is a graduate of Old Dominion University and Virginia Tech.

Joan Andrea Toledo is a board member of the Indo-Pacific Alliance Corp., a Philippine company that does defense research and policy studies in the Indo-Pacific. She was a Senior Consultant of the European Union Delegation to Indonesia/Brunei Darussalam on Anti-Money Laundering and Countering Terrorist

Financing. She has also worked as a Preventing/Countering Violent Extremism Consultant of the Armed Forces of the Philippines and the Philippine National Police specializing in child combatants and women involved in conflict.

Juan Pablo Toro, executive director, AthenaLab think tank; Member of the Advisory Council on Foreign Policy, Ministry of Foreign Affairs – Chile; Senior associate fellow of the Royal United Services Institute; Adjunct assistant professor of the Faculty of Communications of the Catholic University and columnist for El Mercurio newspaper. He holds an MA in Political Science and a BA in Journalism from the Catholic University of Chile, and studies National and International Security from Harvard Kennedy School (US); Center for Hemispheric Defense and Studies (US), ITAM (México). Author of book chapters, articles in specialized magazines and press reports.

Wade Turvold, Captain (Ret.), U.S. Navy, Dean, Admissions and Business Operations of the Daniel K. Inouye Asia-Pacific Center for Security Studies (APCSS) in Hawaii, Honolulu. He joined APSCC after a 30-year career in the U.S. Navy. Mr. Turvold graduated with Merit from the U.S. Naval Academy in Annapolis, Maryland, in 1989 where he earned a Bachelor of Science Degree. He graduated with Distinction from the U.S. Naval War College in Newport, Rhode Island, in 2000 where he earned a Master of Arts degree. He completed numerous deployments throughout his career to the Indo-Pacific region, the Middle East, and to Europe. Mr. Turvold participated in combat operations in Somalia, Kosovo, Iraq, Afghanistan and the Philippines.

Simran Walia is pursuing a PhD in Japanese Studies under the Centre for East Asian Studies from Jawaharlal Nehru University, New Delhi, India. She has completed her M.Phil. Her research interests include Japanese politics and foreign policy, East Asia's foreign policy and Indo-Pacific Dynamics.

John Wasko is a corporate and industrial publisher for major private sector companies and public utilities in American Samoa. Since 1990, over his cumulative span of 40 years in the publishing industry, John has had a direct input in more than five hundred million dollars in economic and infrastructure growth in American Samoa. John leads two community projects; universal home health care for all American Samoa residents and development of a Electric Battery critical mineral receiving. He holds a Bachelor of Arts degree in Germanic Languages and Literature, as well as Modern European History from the Indiana University Bloomington.

Lidia M. Wisniewska is an international educator, evaluator and International Doctor of Science in Education from the University of Granada, Spain. Born in Poland, she is currently based in Paris. She is a research professor at the CENTRUM Catholic Graduate Business School & Pontifical Catholic University of Peru, Lima. She is the president of SIETAR Poland. She conducted international, interdisciplinary doctoral research across the Faculty of Education, University of Granada, Spain, Chonnam National University in South Korea, Sorbonne University in France and Michigan University, USA. Her expertise spans evaluation of internationalization of education and interdependencies between interculturalism.

Cho Wong retired from his managing director position in the global hotel distribution industry. He worked for Supranational Hotels and Pegasus Solutions (UK), as well as Four Oceans (Beijing). In the nineties, Cho served as General Manager for a new Sino-British joint venture factory (Kunming, China). Prior to that, he spent four years in Singapore establishing a regional sales office for a UK packaging company. After graduation, Cho worked as a consultant, assisting European companies in pursuing power generation, airport, and metro projects in China during the country's early stages of opening up to foreign investment.

Ryszard Zalski has been living in Taiwan for 23 years. He majored in German politics and International Relations from the University of Warsaw. He began researching a PhD thesis with the Polish Academy of Sciences and continued in Taiwan. From 2022–2024, he had a weekly show called Studio Taipei on the national radio station. He runs a YouTube channel, Studio Asia (@studio_asia), in English and comments on Asian affairs for Polish media. He publishes on international portals on politics and security in Asia. You can follow him on X under @r_zalski.

Dariusz Zdziech is a historian, founder and chairman of the Australia, New Zealand and Oceania Research Association (ANZORA) and "Poland helps Poland" Foundation. He currently works as an assistant professor at the Institute of Cultural Studies and Journalism at the Ignatianum University in Cracow, Poland. He specializes in migration of Poles to the Antipodes, international relations in the Pacific region, national history and tourism of the Pacific countries. He served as the Policy Assistant of the New Zealand Embassy in 2011–2014, as well as the Kiribati Expert to the Polish Ministry of the Environment in 2013.

Junhua Zhang used to be a professor of political science at the Zhejiang University (ZJU) and Shanghai Jiao Tong University (SJTU) in China. After his retirement, he now acts as a senior associate at the European Institute for Asian Studies and parallel expert at the Geopolitical Intelligence Service (GIS). He has been a columnist for the Neuer Zürcher Zeitung (NZZ, Switzerland), Tagesspiegel (Germany). He worked as a political scientist at universities in, among others, Germany, France, Canada, Israel and Russia.

Foreword

*Joanna Siekiera**

This monograph underlines the monumental role of the Indo-Pacific region for the global relations – at the level of international law and international security, as well as between states, organizations, and other local and large-scale arrangements. Undeniably we live in the Pacific century, where whatever happens (or does not happen) amongst the entities localized between the two Oceans – the Indian Ocean and the Pacific Ocean – immensely affects other continents and their inhabitants. The key reasons for that – demography, economic growth, and political struggle for more devoted spheres of influence – have been previously researched in many academic books.[1] What is novel in this monograph is the multidimensional, interdisciplinary, and indeed pragmatic approach to the problem; not only what is taking place now in the *Indo-Pac* but actually what is the strategic design for this region, as seen by researchers from various environments, professional and educational backgrounds, countries, and fields of expertise.

What then is the strategic design? As the 21st century continues to bring about old tragedies, like state rivalry, wars, diseases and pandemics, unemployment, and socio-economic tribulations across the globe, we must not only look at those problems from an individual's perspective, but in fact go beyond and tackle the big-picture, norm-based, logistical, organizational, and cultural problems. We, as

* Assistant Professor, War Studies University, Poland; Fellow, Krulak Center, Marine Corps University, USA

1 The Editor herself has been popularizing the Indo-Pacific region through her work, both academic, as a legal advisor, and as an educator all around the world. See: J. Siekiera, Law and Rising Seas: Navigating Ocean Change, in: J. Minnich (ed.), *The Indo-Pacific Mosaic: Comprehensive Security Cooperation in the Indo-Pacific*, Asia-Pacific Center for Security Studies, Honolulu 2025; J. Siekiera, The Indo-Pacific Geopolitics and Security Relevance for NATO – Alliance Pivots from the Euro-Atlantic Towards Great Power Competition, in: S. Romaniuk (ed.), *The Palgrave Handbook of Geopolitics and Security in the Indo-Pacific*, Palgrave Macmillan, London 2024; J. Siekiera, *Polityka regionalna na Pacyfiku Połu-dniowym* [Regional Policy in the South Pacific], Warsaw University Press, Warsaw 2021; M. Sprengel, J. Siekiera, J. Eska-Mikołajewska, *Państwowość, gospodarka i bezpieczeństwo Nowej Zelandii – historia i współczesność* [New Zealand's Statehood, Security and Economics – History and Present], Polish Economic Society, Poznań 2020; A. Kandzia-Poździał, J. Siekiera (eds.), *Australia w XX i XXI w.: Polityka, historia i kultura* [Australia in 20th and 21st Century: Politics, History and Culture], University of Silesia Press, Katowice 2016.

human beings, each one representing our own sets of experiences and areas of responsibility within time and space, have a natural ability to start new movements. This movement is to design a new practice. However, not just *design* for the pure sense of designing, creating, making something new, but *design to build a bridge to better futures* – keeping in mind that whatever happens in the Indo-Pacific sooner or later affects us in Europe, the Americas, Africa, and Asia. Such a future-oriented practice can effectively shape mindsets of those who can and in fact should generate change – politicians, businessmen, military leaders, heads of social organizations, researchers, activists, and last but not least – all of us.

Finally, how does the strategic design differ from its older counterpart – the traditional design? The strategic design takes into account public policy, economic, and demographic constraints, shortages of and demands for natural resources and assets (like human capital), and ultimately understands the role of culture and law (including customary law and soft law), as well as the great power competition between the largest, middle, and smallest of this world. To understand, scrutinize, reshape, and suggest new solutions one cannot focus only on a particular dimension or discipline in the 21st-century world. And the Indo-Pacific is just the most vibrant, alarming, and compact region we are privileged to explore.

After publishing two previous monographs on the Indo-Pacific,[2] the Editor returns with the third collection of essays in the *International Law and Security in Indo-Pacific: Strategic Design for the Region*. The book is divided into three subsections: "Multidimensional competition and cooperation," "Actors shaping the Indo-Pacific region presence and future," and "International arrangements."

The 20 chapters were written with great passion, deep care, and careful consideration towards what is happening now in *Indo-Pac*, and what has yet to be done in order to secure a peaceful, stable, and prosperous region for the current and future generations. The authors assembled gathered in this book come from or work in American Samoa, Canada, Chile, China, the Democratic Republic of the Congo, France, Germany, Poland, India, Indonesia, Kyrgyzstan, the Philippines, the Republic of Korea, Sweden, Taiwan, the United Kingdom, and the United States. They are academics, military active duty and veterans, journalists and publicists, entrepreneurs and cultural activists. They specialize in law, security, intercultural studies, history, diplomacy, political science, strategic studies, risk assessment, environmental sciences, geology, and oceanography.

The Editor encourages all readers to embrace the concept of how complex, multifaceted, and intertwined the region of Indo-Pacific is, and that there are no easy or permanent solutions to the 21st-century problems for the inhabitants of Oceania, Southeast Asia, and the coasts of both Americas. *International Law and Security in Indo-Pacific: Strategic Design for the Region* is a humble attempt to help the

2 J. Siekiera (ed.), *21st Century as the Pacific Century: Culture and Security of Oceania States in Great Power Competition*, Warsaw University Press, Warsaw 2023; J. Siekiera (ed.), *Security in Indo-Pacific and Development of Oceania: Commonwealth's Presence in the Region*, Elipsa, Warszawa 2022.

readers understand the true dilemmas, cold calculations, and rational choices that the region's leaders and ordinary citizens have to tackle every day. Knowing is the first step to helping. Helping is the first step to **making this world a slightly better place** – a motto to which all the authors and the Editor are committed.

Warsaw, November 2024

Dr. Joanna Siekiera

Introduction

*Wade Turvold**

The Indo-Pacific region is a complex tapestry of populations, cultures, climates, and events. These features all conspire to create a dynamic geopolitical condition within the backdrop of the world's two great oceans that shape the Indo-Pacific as a maritime region. The future lies in the Indo-Pacific as the global center of population, commerce, trade, finance, and development. Yet despite the region's growth as the world's economic engine, it is more at risk of conflict than ever. The world's maritime region is full of paradox and danger.

The expanse is home to most of the world's population as well as dynamic demographic shifts. The world's largest ocean is named for peace and yet is home to unheralded strategic competition. International law is largely derived from the customary law of the sea, yet rapid changes in climate, technology, as well as evolving constructivist conceptions of the region, will necessarily bring changes to the laws that govern the sea and therefore the region. The security and stability of the Indo-Pacific will consequently be created by those who best understand it because they will be best positioned to keep the uneasy peace.

This volume is positioned to engender comprehension and enable us to act to fulfill the promise of the Asian Century and deter conflict. The challenges are manifold. The presence of competition from state actors is foremost among the perils to peace and stability. China is a revisionist power that seeks to upend the rules-based international order and establish a hierarchical order in the region with itself at the top of the hierarchy. Russia, with three-fourths of its landmass in Asia, is a revanchist power that has chosen to use force in an attempt to subsume its European neighbors and similarly destabilize the Indo-Pacific. And North Korea is the burgeoning nuclear power that is lamentably becoming more connected with Russia and China. Together, these autocratic states produce a formidable security challenge. Adding to the complexity, climate change remains an existential threat to the Pacific Islands and low-lying areas in much of the region. Furthermore, transnational crime is growing in new and nefarious ways. There remains great hope, however, despite these threats.

* Captain, U.S. Navy (Ret.), Dean of Admissions and Business Operations, Asia-Pacific Center for Security Studies, Honolulu, USA

The democracies and likeminded states are cooperating within both traditional and new associations that bolster the security structure of the region and build deterrence against conflict. Technology is being equally pursued by all parties to the competition but the democracies, with their open and inclusive societies, will likely maintain the advantage. The increasingly aligned and determined democratic states, and the security structures they are producing, collectively form a unique constellation of stakeholders that will prove effective if they can remain united in the face of competition. Accountability accompanies the democratic values they aspire to embrace.

The Indo-Pacific region is therefore a maritime concept that has emerged as the world's demographic, economic, and strategic center of gravity. The current rules-based international order that underpins the Indo-Pacific's function is essential to its future and simultaneously under great threat. The focus of this book on international law and security is therefore both timely and necessary to mature our understanding, refine the vision, and empower generation of the strategic design that will enable peace and prosperity to prevail. As the sea demands accountability, so must we of ourselves, our governments, and our institutions. Happy reading!

Captain Wade Turvold (Ret.),
Dean of the Asia-Pacific Center for Security Studies

Preface

*Cleo Paskal**

The Indo-Pacific had been transformed in the eighty years since the end of World War Two. Some of the world's most (India) and least (Nauru, Tuvalu) populous countries won independence. Great powers of the 20th century receded. Global economic centers of gravity shifted from the Atlantic to the Indo-Pacific. In some ways, this is a harkening back to the pre-colonial era, when much of the world's GDP was generated in the region and political power was more dispersed.

Geography shaped the region's history. Linked by the seas, the people of the Indo-Pacific have long traded far and wide and nurtured some of the best navigators the world has ever seen. As far back as 4000 to 5000 years ago, the spread of Austronesian languages from Madagascar to Rapa Nui (Easter Island) hints at waves of movement in the region.

Those same seas also brought invaders, empires and war. A person in Saipan today may have had a great-grandmother who lived under Spanish rule, a grandmother who lived under German rule, a mother who lived under Japanese rule and who is now, themselves, an American.

While geography has shaped the history of the Indo-Pacific, geography is changing. Advances in telecommunications and mass travel expand horizons. Countries now need to think vertically as well – from deep sea to space. And the physical world itself is transforming, through the construction of artificial islands, unprecedented concentrations of populations and a changing environment.

The Indo-Pacific is fluid – in more ways than one. And the systems that have kept a fragile peace for many over the past eight decades are under severe stress. The People's Republic of China (PRC) is building the largest peacetime navy the world has ever seen, is trying to gain influence if not control of multilateral organizations and trade, and PRC-linked organized crime is interlaced with resource extraction, drug distribution and human trafficking across the region – affecting daily life for millions. Beijing seems to be determined to fundamentally reshape the Indo-Pacific on its own terms. Meanwhile, the United States, Japan, India and others are actively assessing their roles in the region, Taiwan is under constant

* Senior Fellow for the Indo-Pacific, Foundation for Defense of Democracies, USA; Fellow, Confederation of Defence Associations Institute, Canada

threat and Pacific Island countries are fighting for economic development and sovereignty.

There is a complexity of moving parts in Indo-Pacific security, currently held together largely by a stretched-thin rule of law. Every time the law is broken, and it goes unpunished – for example, with China's repeated illegal assaults on Philippines – the law weakens. If the law fails, the fallback is politics. And if politics fails, we are that much closer to war.

This is why this book is so timely. Not only do the authors bring a wide range of expertise in the various moving parts of the legal and security structures, they come from a wide range of countries, including some that have seen extraordinary change in the past few decades, and who know what it means to live under communism. They are not complacent about how fast things can change for better, and the worst. While the geography of the Indo-Pacific may have shaped its history, understanding what's at stake can help us shape its future. This book goes a long way towards accomplishing that.

Ms. Cleo Paskal
Foundation for Defense of Democracies;
Confederation of Defence Associations Institute

Part I

Multidimensional Competition and Cooperation

1 Law Enforcement

The Key to Stability in the Indo-Pacific?

*William Liffick and Brandon Quinones**

1. Introduction

The Indo-Pacific is comprised of 40 separate and unique nations with over 4 billion people, making it the most populated region in the world. Currently sitting well above $45 trillion in economic activity including immense natural resources, the Indo-Pacific region is rapidly growing.[1] These resources and sovereignty are necessary for the continued development of the region, granting stability and prosperity over time.[2] Due to its size, population, and demand for natural resources, understanding and enforcing maritime law is a necessity. Maritime law enforcement in the Indo-Pacific plays a vital role in ensuring regional stability and sustainability. The Law of the Sea protects developing and established nations by providing legal protection for natural resources and protects national sovereignty. In 2021, Asia remained the world's leading maritime cargo handling center with 40% of total trade between Asia, the United States, and Europe making Indo-Pacific regional stability a global issue. Maritime boundaries or legal borders are the backbone of international maritime law. Maritime boundaries establish sovereignty and clear borders by providing a framework for respectful interactions that promote international stability.[3] These legal borders protect vast amounts of natural resources and can be the key to a nation's prosperity or demise. Because of the importance and significant effects of maritime boundaries, there have been and will continue to be maritime disputes.[4] National pride, sovereignty, and economic prosperity

* Littoral Dynamics LLC

1 Government of Canada. "Canada's Indo-Pacific Strategy." Last modified September 3, 2024. https://www.international.gc.ca/transparency-transparence/indo-pacific-indo-pacifique/index.aspx?lang=eng.

2 United Nations Conference on Trade and Development. *Review of Maritime Transport 2022: Facts and Figures on Asia and the Pacific*. Geneva, Switzerland: United Nations, November 29, 2022, UNCTAD/PRESS/IN/2022/003. https://unctad.org/press-material/unctads-review-maritime-transport-2022-facts-and-figures-asia-and-pacific.

3 United States Department of State. "U.S. Maritime Boundaries: Agreements and Treaties." Accessed September 26, 2024. https://www.state.gov/u-s-maritime-boundaries-agreements-and-treaties/.

4 Khalfaoui, Anna, and Constantinos Yiallourides. "Maritime Disputes and Disputed Seabed Resources in the African Continent." In *Routledge Handbook of Energy Law*, 1st ed. Routledge, 2020. https://doi.org/10.4324/9780429450891.

DOI: 10.4324/9781003545750-2

are the root causes of these conflicts.[5] If these disagreements go unresolved, tensions rise, and the chance for inter-state conflict increases in the region. During these boundary disputes, crime and grey-zone operations flourish, contributing to the international tension and the destabilization of the region.[6] Enforcing international maritime boundaries using law enforcement avenues helps to restabilize the Indo-Pacific. This is not a regional issue, but an issue that will affect and impact the rest of the world.

The United Nations Convention on the Law of the Seas (UNCLOS) forms the foundation of maritime law. If it is not enforced or abided in conjunction with local laws, it can compromise international trade and invite conflict into the region, jeopardizing global security. Law enforcement administering and maintaining internationally recognized maritime boundaries and laws could be the key to regaining stability, de-escalating regional tension, and ensuring the prosperity of the Indo-Pacific.

2. UNCLOS

UNCLOS is an international treaty that governs the rights and responsibilities of nations to use the world's oceans and is the foundation for maritime law enforcement and agreed upon international maritime boundaries. The treaty addresses the use of regional waters, defining territorial waters, sea lanes, rites of passage, and maritime resource management/claim.[7] The United Nations Convention aims to balance the interests of competing global powers with the rights of other states and international entities in the maritime environment.

The origins of UNCLOS can be traced back to the early 20th century. Prior to UNCLOS, the legal governing framework of the oceans was governed by a patchwork of treaties and customary international laws.[8] Due to disputes over territorial seas, fishing zones, and continental shelves, old maritime laws were unraveling, leading to conflicts throughout the world, to include the "Cod War" between Iceland and the United Kingdom.

5 Rogoff, Martin A. "An Overview of Existing Maritime Boundary Disputes and Recommendations for Their Settlement." *Ocean and Coastal Law Journal* 15 (2010). http://digitalcommons.mainelaw.maine.edu/oclj/vol15/iss2/11.

6 Phayal, Anup, Aaron Gold, and Brandon Prins. "Interstate Hostility and Maritime Crime: Evidence from South East Asia." *Marine Policy* 143 (2022): 105134. https://doi.org/10.1016/j.marpol.2022.105134.

7 United States Navy Judge Advocate General's Corps. "The Convention on the Law of the Sea." Accessed September 19, 2024. https://www.jag.navy.mil/national-security/law-of-the-sea/#:~:text=The%20United%20Nations%20Convention%20on,essential%20navigation%20and%20overflight%20rights.

8 Treves, Tullio. "United Nations Convention on the Law of the Sea." Montego Bay, December 10, 1982. United Nations Audiovisual Library of International Law. https://legal.un.org/avl/ha/uncls/uncls.html#:~:text=It%20was%20necessary%20because%20of,extracted%20from%20the%20nodules%2C%20etc.

Iceland and United Kingdom came to conflict over fishing rights in 1952 because of a lack of international regulations which relied on 15th-century laws.[9] Iceland rejected the historical territorial claims of the United Kingdom and claimed sovereignty over their own waters. It took over 20 years for the two nations to come to an agreement. The conflict was resolved when the United Kingdom withdrew their claim to rights to the region. This situation prompted extensive diplomatic efforts, particularly by countries with long coastlines, to push for a broad reform of maritime law that would address issues comprehensively. The Geneva Conventions on the Law of the Sea in 1958 represented the initial step; however, they were limited in scope, coverage, and enforcement capabilities. UNCLOS aimed to prevent a chaotic rush among countries to grab valuable resources from the deep seabed, which were declared as the "common heritage of mankind."[10] Over time, UNCLOS expanded from just deep seabed management to a complete overhaul of maritime law.

The United Nations convened the First United Nations Conference on the Law of the Sea (UNCLOS I) in 1958, which resulted in four treaties. These treaties, however, did not resolve disputes between conflicting states nor did they provide a comprehensive legal regime and understanding regarding the navigation and territorial claims of maritime resources and commerce.[11] This convention was followed by the Second United Nations Conference on the Law of the Sea (UNCLOS II) in 1960, which addressed some of the remaining issues but ultimately fell short of creating a universally accepted framework. Defining the territorial sea limit, continental shelf considerations, high seas regulations, dispute regulation measures, and new maritime technologies were unaddressed issues.[12]

The need for a more defined and inclusive legal framework developed in the Third United Nations Conference on the Law of the Sea (UNCLOS III), which met between 1973 and 1982. The third conference was tasked with addressing outstanding issues and building on the work of previous conferences. After negotiations, UNCLOS III produced the current version of the Convention, which was adopted in 1982 and entered into force on November 16, 1994.[13]

9 Thompson, Jeremy. "The Second Anglo-Icelandic Cod War (1972–73): Analysis of a Modern Sea Dispute and Implications for the South China Sea." *Naval War College Review* 75, no. 2 (2022): 123–69. https://www.jstor.org/stable/48732041.

10 Treves, Tullio. "United Nations Convention on the Law of the Sea." Montego Bay, December 10, 1982. Audiovisual Library of International Law. Last updated July 2008. https://legal.un.org/avl/ha/uncls/uncls.html.

11 Pedrozo, Raul (Pete). "Reflecting on UNCLOS Forty Years Later: What Worked, What Failed." *International Law Studies* 99 (2022): 874. https://digital-commons.usnwc.edu/cgi/viewcontent.cgi?article=3033&context=ils.

12 Second United Nations Conference on the Law of the Sea. Geneva, March 17–April 26, 1960. Codification Division Publications, Diplomatic Conferences. United Nations Office of Legal Affairs. Accessed September 22, 2024. https://legal.un.org/diplomaticconferences/1960_los/.

13 Oceans of the Law of the Sea, United Nations. "The United Nations Convention on the Law of the Sea: A Historical Perspective." Last updated May 16, 2024. https://www.un.org/Depts/los/convention_agreements/convention_historical_perspective.htm.

3. Key Provisions from UNCLOS

Territorial Sea and Contiguous Zone: The definition of a state's territorial sea is defined as extending up to 12 nautical miles from the baseline of a coastal state. Within this zone, the coastal state has sovereignty, which includes control over the air space and the seabed below the surface. Past territorial waters of 12 nautical miles, states can claim a contiguous zone extending up to 24 nautical miles from the baseline, where they can enforce laws related to customs, immigration, and pollution.[14]

Exclusive Economic Zone (EEZ): The EEZ extends 200 nautical miles from the baseline mean tide from the state's shores. Within this zone, a coastal state has jurisdictional rights to explore and exploit maritime resources (fisheries, offshore oil, rare earth minerals, etc.), in the water column and on and under the seabed. These rights include jurisdictional legal coverage over the establishment and use of artificial islands, installations, and structures.[15]

Continental Shelf: The Convention establishes the rights of states over their continental shelf, which extends beyond the territorial sea to the outer edge of the continental margin or 200 nautical miles from the baseline, whichever is greater. States have rights to explore and exploit natural resources on the continental shelf. They also have the right to enforce state laws and regulations to protect those resources from outside entity resource exploitation, but only if the continental shelf is in their EEZ.[16]

International Seabed Authority: The Authority was established to regulate mineral-related activities in the international seabed area, ensuring that these activities are conducted for the benefit of mankind. It oversees the exploration and exploitation of the deep-sea bed, which is considered the "common heritage of mankind."[17]

4. Dispute Resolution

UNCLOS includes provisions for the peaceful settlement of disputes related to the interpretation and application of the Convention. It establishes several mechanisms, including the International Tribunal for the Law of the Sea (ITLOS), the International Court of Justice (ICJ), and arbitration tribunals.[18] These mechanisms

14 United Nations Division for Ocean Affairs and the Law of the Sea. "Territorial Sea and Contiguous Zone." Accessed September 22, 2024. https://www.un.org/Depts/los/convention_agreements/texts/unclos/part2.htm.

15 United Nations Division for Ocean Affairs and the Law of the Sea. "Exclusive Economic Zone." Accessed September 22, 2024. https://www.un.org/Depts/los/convention_agreements/texts/unclos/part5.htm.

16 United Nations Division for Ocean Affairs and the Law of the Sea. "Continental Shelf." https://www.un.org/Depts/los/convention_agreements/texts/unclos/part6.htm.

17 International Seabed Authority. "About Us." Accessed September 23, 2024. https://www.isa.org.jm/about.

18 International Tribunal for the Law of the Sea. "About ITLOS." Accessed September 23, 2024. https://www.itlos.org/.

were used to resolve a maritime dispute between Norway and Russia on historical fishing areas. On September 27, 2010, Norway and Russia signed a historic treaty that established the maritime boundary between their respective territories in the Barents Sea and the Arctic Ocean. The treaty provided for the fair sharing of resources in the area and included provisions for joint resource management/ enforcement, cooperation on environmental protection, and resource exploitation. This agreement demonstrates the effective use of UNCLOS provisions to resolve maritime disputes through negotiation and mutual agreement, avoiding potential military conflict.[19]

5. Impact and Significance

UNCLOS is a major step forward for international maritime law. It provides a comprehensive legal framework that has been widely adopted by over 160 parties to the Convention as of 2024.[20] It has facilitated international cooperation on marine issues, contributed to the conservation of marine biodiversity, and promoted the sustainable use of ocean resources. However, despite the ratification of this treaty, 15 UN Member States and one UN Observer State did not ratify or sign the UNCLOS treaty, including Andorra, Eritrea, Holy See (United Nations Observer State), Israel, Kazakhstan, Kyrgyzstan, Peru, San Marino, South Sudan, Syria, Tajikistan, Turkey, Turkmenistan, Uzbekistan, Venezuela, and (most notably) the United States of America. Every UN member and UN Observer country in the Indo-Pacific has signed and ratified UNCLOS, with the exception of the United States.[21]

The United States' decision not to adopt or ratify UNCLOS came during the Ronald Reagan Administration, when the treaty was first ratified in 1982. The United States was deeply involved in the UNCLOS negotiations to create a comprehensive treaty on the world's oceans, aiming to ensure fair use and benefit from resources like deep-sea minerals. By April of that year, a draft agreement was adopted, but the United States found that the treaties related to deep-sea mining were problematic for their perspectives on free trade. The United States felt these rules could hinder future exploration and development of deep-sea resources, and that the decision-making process did not fairly represent their interests. Additionally, the United States was concerned about a non-approval amendment process and other issues like technology transfer. As a result, the United States decided

19 Norwegian Ministry of Foreign Affairs. "Agreement Between the Kingdom of Norway and the Russian Federation Concerning Maritime Delimitation and Cooperation in the Barents Sea and the Arctic Ocean." September 27, 2010. https://www.regjeringen.no/en/topics/foreign-affairs/international-law/innsikt_delelinje/treaty_background/id614274/.

20 "United Nations Convention on the Law of the Sea." Montego Bay, December 10, 1982. Registration, November 16, 1994, No. 31363. Signatories: 157. Parties: 170. https://treaties.un.org/pages/ViewDetailsIII.aspx?src=TREATY&mtdsg_no=XXI-6&chapter=21&Temp=mtdsg3&clang=_en.

21 United Nations Division for Ocean Affairs and the Law of the Sea. "Chronological Lists of Ratifications of Accessions and Successions to the Convention and the Related Agreements." January 8, 2010. https://www.un.org/Depts/los/reference_files/chronological_lists_of_ratifications.htm.

not to sign the final version of the convention[22] and chose to participate only in the parts of the agreement that align with innocent passage (freedom of navigation), territorial integrity, and resource management of fisheries.[23]

The Convention's provisions have been instrumental in addressing conflicts over maritime boundaries and resource exploitation, helping to maintain international order and stability in maritime affairs. They serve as a foundation for ongoing discussions and developments in maritime law and policy. The case between Australia and the Russian Federation regarding illegal fishing and law enforcement of territorial waters is a poignant example. The dispute arose after the Royal Australian Navy detained the Russian fishing vessel *Volga* on February 7, 2002, for violating Australian fishing regulations in Australia's EEZ. The Russian Federation requested the vessel's release by filing an application with ITLOS under Article 292 of UNCLOS, which deals with the prompt release of vessels detained for alleged violations, even if that vessel is being charged with violating local state laws and policies. On December 23, 2002, the ITLOS issued its judgment in the case of the *Volga* (Russian Federation v. Australia).

The Tribunal unanimously found that it had jurisdiction to address the application and that the application itself was admissible. The central issue was whether the bond required by Australia for the vessel's release was reasonable, since Australia demanded a bond of AU$1,920,000. Australia argued it was necessary to ensure compliance with Australian laws and international obligations, considering the value of the vessel and its equipment, as well as the seriousness of the alleged offense of illegal fishing in Australia's EEZ.

The Tribunal's judgment, passed by a majority of 19 to 2, concluded that the bond demanded by Australia was not reasonable in the context of Article 73, paragraph 2 of UNCLOS, which requires that a bond for the release of a vessel be both reasonable and not excessively burdensome. While recognizing Australia's concerns about illegal fishing and local fish stock depletion, the Tribunal emphasized that its role was to evaluate the reasonableness of the bond, not to judge the underlying environmental issues.

The Tribunal's decision mandated Australia to release the *Volga* upon the posting of a bond or other security, reflecting a careful balance between respecting national regulations and upholding international legal standards for prompt release of detained vessels.[24] Russia, by utilizing ITLOS, illustrated how international disputes can be handled diplomatically and without the need for military involvement, creating regional cooperation and unity under international maritime law.

22 "Statement on United States Actions Concerning the Conference on the Law of the Sea." July 9, 1982. Ronald Reagan Presidential Library. Accessed September 16, 2024. https://www.reaganlibrary.gov/archives/speech/statement-united-states-actions-concerning-conference-law-sea.

23 Congressional Research Service. "United Nations Convention on the Law of the Sea (UNCLOS): Living Resources Provisions." Updated July 15, 2024. CRS Report R47744. https://crsreports.congress.gov/product/pdf/R/R47744.

24 International Tribunal for the Law of the Sea. "Press Release ITLOS/Press 75, December 23, 2002." https://www.itlos.org/en/main/cases/list-of-cases/case-no-11/#c7177.

UNCLOS has provided internationally recognized boundaries for maritime operations in the Indo-Pacific. However, as the region develops, these maritime boundaries and agreements have been violated or ignored by regional powers taking advantage of smaller, less developed nations, resulting in major territorial disputes and heightened tensions. This chaos has allowed piracy, illegal fishing, and criminal operations to thrive in contested waters.[25]

For countries that disregard UNCLOS or misinterpret its provisions, the potential for military conflict escalates. For example, when a country vacates a contested maritime zone, claims and regional dominance do not automatically transfer to another country; rather, the zone remains unclaimed if no physical presence exists. Thus, countries with robust naval capabilities can assert their dominance or exploit natural resources in these disputed waters. To maintain rights and de facto control, states frequently engage in naval patrolling, resource extraction, and enforcement of maritime laws. Without a third-party mediator or a multinational political treaty like UNCLOS, these activities can lead to escalated tensions and clashes between military vessels, state-controlled ships, and civilian boats, including maritime militias and fishing vessels.[26]

6. Impacts of Maritime Boundaries and Illegal Fishing

Maritime boundaries set the foundation for establishing laws and regulations that protect natural resources to be used for the local populous. Fish are a depleting natural resource suffering from overfishing due to minimal law enforcement oversite of maritime boundaries, poor nation-state fishing regulations, and new fishing technology.[27] Nations like Australia and Indonesia have been attacking this problem by deploying law enforcement capabilities to apply these laws and are working together to protect their own natural resources.

The enforcement of fishing regulations in Australia relies on its law enforcement agencies, including the Australian Border Force (ABF) and the Australian Fisheries Management Authority (AFMA). These agencies are instrumental in implementing fishing laws in accordance with UNCLOS. They conduct regular patrols, carry out inspections, and impose penalties for illegal fishing activities within Australia's EEZ.[28] Under UNCLOS Article 73, Australia is legally empowered to impose fines

25 Prins, Brandon, Anup Phayal, and Aaron Gold, "Fights Over Marine Boundaries Are Creating Safe Zones for Pirates: New Research Reveals How Contested Waters Have Become Maritime Hot Spots." *The Washington Post*, August 5, 2021. https://www.washingtonpost.com/politics/2021/08/05/fights-over-marine-boundaries-are-creating-safe-zones-pirates/.

26 Bowers, Ian. "Escalation at Sea." *Naval War College Review* 71, no. 4 (2018): 45–66. https://www.jstor.org/stable/26607089.

27 Hunt, Colin. "Economic Globalisation Impacts on Pacific Marine Resources." *Marine Policy* 27, no. 1 (2003): 79–85. https://doi.org/10.1016/S0308-597X(02)00055-6.

28 Australian Government, Australian Fisheries Management Authority. "Enforcement Operations." Accessed September 26, 2024. https://www.afma.gov.au/fisheries-management/international-fisheries-management/enforcement-operations.

and bail on captured vessels, but imprisonment is not permitted as a penalty unless stipulated by a specific bilateral agreement.[29] Additionally, Article 73, paragraph 4 requires that any detention of foreign fishing vessels be promptly communicated to the vessel's flag state, providing details of the actions taken and penalties imposed.[30]

In addressing cross-border fishing issues, Australia collaborates closely with Indonesia through agreements such as the Lombok Treaty of 2006, which established the Indonesia-Australia Fisheries Surveillance Forum (IAFSF). These agreements facilitate regular meetings, joint patrols, and mutual support in enforcement efforts. The IAFSF is crucial for coordinating responses to illegal fishing, sharing resources, and leveraging expertise. This bilateral partnership has significantly improved monitoring and led to a marked reduction in illegal fishing incidents, demonstrating the effectiveness of their coordinated approach.[31]

The collaboration between Australia and Indonesia has been enhanced by regional frameworks such as the Regional Plan of Action (RPOA), which made significant progress in combatting illegal fishing in a historically difficult region.[32] Both nations have effectively reduced criminal activities while fostering a cooperative relationship by adhering to UNCLOS provisions and coordinating enforcement strategies. This collaborative approach underscores a non-escalatory method of conflict resolution, promotes sustainable fishing practices, and aligns with international standards, thereby bolstering regional maritime security.[33] International collaboration is essential to tackling the complicated issues of maritime boundaries. In addition to this cooperation, however, a nation-state must strengthen their own law enforcement fusion and enforcement.

The Philippines actively promote cooperation amongst its government agencies to enhance law enforcement and tackle emerging maritime security threats such as piracy, maritime terrorism, border disputes, transnational crime, and illegal, unreported, and unregulated (IUU) fishing. This inter-agency approach is evident by numerous agreements and partnerships between key agencies including the Philippine Coast Guard (PCG), the Bureau of Customs (BUCUS), and the Bureau of Fisheries and Aquatic Resources (BFAR). The PCG's collaboration with BUCUS

29 United Nations Convention on the Laws of the Sea (UNCLOS). 1982, Art. 73, para. 3. https://www.un.org/depts/los/convention_agreements/texts/unclos/unclos_e.pdf.

30 United Nations Convention on the Laws of the Sea (UNCLOS). 1982, Art. 73, para. 4. https://www.un.org/depts/los/convention_agreements/texts/unclos/unclos_e.pdf.

31 Safitri, Diva Aisya, Gladis Tazaka Mustaqim, and Kania Dewi. "The Implementation of International Law on the Enforcement of Illegal Fishing in the Border Area Between Indonesia and Australia." https://www.researchgate.net/publication/348734752_THE_IMPLEMENTATION_OF_INTERNATIONAL_LAW_ON_THE_ENFORCEMENT_OF_ILLEGAL_FISHING_IN_THE_BORDER_AREA_BETWEEN_INDONESIA_AND_AUSTRALIA.

32 Australian Government, Department of Agriculture, Fisheries and Forestry. "Steps Australia Has Taken to Address Illegal Fishing." Accessed September 26, 2024. https://www.agriculture.gov.au/agriculture-land/fisheries/iuu/illegal-fishing.

33 Budiyanti, Mauly Dini, and Arfin Sudirman. "Implementasi RPOA-IUU di Kawasan Asia Tenggara." *Jurnal Hubungan Internasional*, Tahun XII, no. 2 (Juli–December 2019). https://www.researchgate.net/publication/342553501_Implementasi_RPOA-IUU_di_Kawasan_Asia_Tenggara.

focuses on combating smuggling, while its agreement with BFAR addresses anti-illegal fishing operations. The PCG's broader coordination efforts are demonstrated through its involvement with the National Law Enforcement Coordinating Committee and other committees, underscoring its role in integrating strategies across various agencies to effectively address specific maritime challenges.[34]

7. Beyond Illegal Fishing and the Importance of International Cooperation

In addition to national efforts, the Philippines has significantly strengthened its maritime security through interagency collaboration in anti-illegal drugs operations. The Interagency Counternarcotics Operations Network (ICON), which includes the Philippine Drug Enforcement Agency (PDEA) and the Philippine National Police (PNP), serves as a central hub for intelligence and coordination in drug enforcement. The PCG has played a crucial role in drug interdiction, executing successful operations that have led to the seizure of substantial amounts of illegal drugs and the arrest of suspects. This interagency collaboration highlights a unified approach to combating the drug trade, demonstrating how the PCG and its partners work together to address multifaceted security issues.[35]

On the international front, the Philippines has bolstered maritime security through active participation in regional and global initiatives. The PCG collaborates with Association of Southeast Asian Nations (ASEAN) countries and engages in exercises such as Cooperation Afloat Readiness and Training (CARAT) and the Southeast Asia Cooperation against Terrorism (SEACAT) to address regional maritime threats.[36] Additionally, the Philippines is involved in the Coastal Surveillance (CWS) initiative with the United States and Australia, which aims to enhance maritime domain awareness and border security. The country plays a key role in the Regional Cooperation Agreement on Combating Piracy and Armed Robbery against ships in Asia (ReCAAP), where the PCG serves as the focal point in the ReCAAP Information Sharing Centre (ReCAAP-ISC). These international collaborations underscore the Philippines' strategic commitment to addressing maritime

34 "Philippine Agencies Work Together to Enhance National Inter-Agency Coordination and Information Sharing on Securing Safe Seas." *European External Action*, December 1, 2023. https://www.eeas.europa.eu/delegations/philippines/philippine-agencies-work-together-enhance-national-inter-agency-coordination-and-information-sharing_en?s=176.

35 Monje, Teresa Guia R. *Maritime Enforcement in the Philippines: Issues and Challenges*. The United Nations-Nippon Foundation Fellowship Programme 2012–2013. New York: Division for Ocean Affairs and the Law of the Sea, Office of Legal Affairs, The United Nations, 2012. https://www.un.org/oceancapacity/sites/www.un.org.oceancapacity/files/monje_-_un_nippon_paper_aprl_9_final.pdf.

36 U.S. Indo-Pacific Command. "ASEAN-US Maritime Exercise Begins in Thailand." September 3, 2019, by Courtesy of LGWP Logistics Group Western Pacific. https://www.pacom.mil/Media/News/News-Article-View/Article/1950814/.

crime and security challenges through a combination of national coordination and global partnerships.[37]

Even with the major strides that the Philippines has made with international law enforcement, interagency cooperation, and external international joint operations, they still struggle with maritime boundaries. Chinese proxies and military vessels, transnational criminal organizations, and terrorist groups are operating in Philippine maritime areas exploiting its natural resources and citizens to expand their control of disputed maritime zones – stressing the importance of the need to invest in interagency and partner-nation law enforcement collaboration in disputed maritime areas.[38]

8. Challenges to Maritime Boundaries

Grey-zone operations refer to activities that take place between peace and war, involving a range of tactics that fall short of conventional military conflict.[39] Grey-zone activities often challenge maritime boundaries. China's strategy for asserting control over disputed maritime territories, particularly in the South China Sea and Taiwan Strait, illustrates a complex, multifaceted approach, often described as a grey-zone strategy. China's strategy integrates maritime militia confrontations, coast guard enforcement, and strategic military intimidation, allowing it to exert significant control over contested waters, deter foreign interference, and manage regional tensions without escalating into overt military conflict with the United States or other nations within the region.[40]

China claims the South China Sea based on its "nine-dash line," which overlap with the Philippines, Vietnam, Malaysia, and Brunei territorial claims. The 2016 Permanent Court of Arbitration ruling invalidated China's expansive claims under UNCLOS. Despite this, China has rejected the ruling, asserting its "indisputable sovereignty" and has maintained an aggressive posture in the region.[41]

37 Monje, Teresa Guia R. *Maritime Enforcement in the Philippines: Issues and Challenges*. The United Nations-Nippon Foundation Fellowship Programme 2012–2013. New York: Division for Ocean Affairs and the Law of the Sea, Office of Legal Affairs, The United Nations, 2012. https://www.un.org/oceancapacity/sites/www.un.org.oceancapacity/files/monje_-_un_nippon_paper_aprl_9_final.pdf.

38 Mahadzir, Dzirhan. "Philippine Forces Spot 48 Chinese Fishing Vessels Guarded by Warships in Its EEZ." U.S. Naval Institute, July 7, 2023. https://news.usni.org/2023/07/07/philippine-forces-spots-48-chinese-fishing-vessels-guarded-by-warships-in-its-eez.

39 Goldrick, James. "Grey Zone Operations and the Maritime Domain." 2018. Accessed September 19, 2024. https://ethz.ch/content/dam/ethz/special-interest/gess/cis/center-for-securities-studies/resources/docs/ASPI_SR%20131%20Grey%20zone%20operations.pdf.

40 Kennedy, Conor M., and Andrew S. Erickson. "China Maritime Report No. 1: China's Third Sea Force, the People's Armed Forces Maritime Militia: Tethered to the PLA." Accessed September 26, 2024. https://digital-commons.usnwc.edu/cmsi-maritime-reports/1/.

41 Campbell, Caitlin, and Nargiza Salidjanova. "South China Sea Arbitration Ruling: What Happened and What's Next?" U.S.-China Economic and Security Review Commission, July 12, 2016. Accessed September 26, 2024. https://www.uscc.gov/research/south-china-sea-arbitration-ruling-what-happened-and-whats-next.

China's large-scale land reclamation projects in the Spratly Islands, beginning around 2013, aimed to bolster its territorial claims. These artificial islands, including Mischief Reef, Subi Reef, and Fiery Cross Reef, were developed with various facilities and infrastructure. By May 2015, concerns about the potential militarization of these islands were confirmed when China deployed surface-to-air missiles and advanced radar systems. The militarization of these islands has since included airstrips, naval facilities, and radar installations, transforming them into strategic military outposts.[42] These developments have allowed China to project power across the South China Sea, and enforce its claims more assertively, further complicating regional dynamics.

Following the construction of the artificial islands, China has significantly escalated its military activities in the South China Sea and Taiwan Strait.[43] Extensive military exercises, including live-fire drills and the deployment of advanced naval and air assets, have demonstrated China's growing military capabilities and readiness to assert its claims. The commissioning of the *Fujian* aircraft carrier in June 2022, equipped with a catapult launch system, marks another significant enhancement in China's Naval capabilities.[44] Frequent air and naval patrols by China, involving aggressive maneuvers and interceptions of foreign vessels, reflect its broader strategy to assert control and challenge rival powers, particularly the United States.[45] This rivalry creates global tensions that threaten regional security and heighten the potential for a global military conflict.

9. Furthering Military Escalation

Nations with power tend to abide by their own national laws over other country's national laws. However, when there is a disconnect between two nation's internal laws and international law, tension and conflict can ensue. The United States has conducted Freedom of Navigation Operations (FONOPs) with United States Naval warships to challenge China's maritime boundary claims. For instance, a FONOP near Mischief Reef in January 2017, reaffirmed the waters' international status.[46] These operations aim to uphold the principle of free navigation and

42 Asia Maritime Transparency Initiative. "The Asia Maritime Transparency Initiative and the Center for Strategic and International Studies." 2024. Accessed September 19, 2024. https://amti.csis.org/island-tracker/china/#Spratly%20Islands.

43 Easton, Ian. "Challenges Facing Taiwan in the South China Sea." Virginia: Project 2049, 2016. Accessed September 19, 2024. https://project2049.net/wp-content/uploads/2018/04/P2049_Easton_Challenges-Facing_Taiwan-in-the_South-China-Sea_101716.pdf.

44 Dahm, J. Michael, and Peter W. Singer. "China's Latest Aircraft Carrier Is Much More Than a Big Ship: Along with Technical and Operational Advances, the Fujian Represents a Response to 19th-Century Humiliation." *Defense One*, June 6, 2024. Accessed September 19, 2024. https://www.defenseone.com/ideas/2024/06/chinas-latest-aircraft-carrier-much-more-big-ship/397188/.

45 Cardenas, Nicky C. "Military Competition Between the United States and China in the South China Sea: A Critical Analysis." December 18, 2020. https://doi.org/10.36304/ExpwMCUP.2020.07.

46 Standifer, Cid. "Updated: A Brief History of U.S. Freedom of Navigation Operations in the South China Sea." U.S. Naval Institute, May 29, 2017. Updated July 2, 2017. https://news.usni.org/2017/05/29/brief-history-us-freedom-navigation-operations-south-china-sea.

counter China's unilateral restrictions. China, in turn, has framed these FONOPs as aggressive and unjustified, using information operations to depict them as threats to regional peace.[47] In response, China has intensified its naval and coast guard activities, using these operations to demonstrate its resolve and capability to protect its claimed interests. FONOPs by the United States Military vessels and its allies have been met with international scrutiny.

The United States utilizes the concept and legal permission of innocent passage to deter aggression and show the rest of the world that it has the right to sail its warships where it pleases within the framework of international law. Innocent passage is a valid claim, but when a warship is utilized as a method of deterrence or force projection, is it innocent in its passage? In 2021, India claimed that the United States had violated national laws when the USS *John Paul Jones* transited through Indian EEZs. India requires all warships transiting on innocent passage provide notice to the Indian Government before transiting.[48] The United States and India both recognize UNCLOS of 1982's provision on 'innocent passage,' and the United States asserted that it was following international laws. While international law may stand, violating Indian laws shows disregard for Indian policy, creating regional tension. Both India and China have more restrictive laws for innocent passage and the United States routinely disregards these claims. While the United States is correct in the interpretation of international law, by disregarding and violating national laws with China and India, it is creating a rift diplomatically. The United States needs to recognize that these are shows of force and deterrence by allowing military warships to conduct such patrols, which could be seen as inflammatory. If the United States continues to conduct FONOPS under innocent passage, it could escalate regional tensions and call into question if the United States is indeed "innocent" in its intentions.[49]

Military escalation is a dangerous game to play. The presence of a warship sends an aggressive message. Shows of force and deterrence are only exacerbating tensions that exist in the region. The intent of military vessels in the area can easily be misinterpreted and cause a military response. A military response could turn into conflict, as seen in 1988 with the Black Sea "Bump." In 1978 the United States sent the cruiser USS *Yorktown* into the Black Sea to project force and exercise the international right of innocent passage. The Soviet Union, at the time, was trying to enforce their rights to territorial seas and required foreign warships to sail within approved sea lanes. The United States did not recognize these sea lanes and

47 Panda, Ankit. "China Condemns US FONOP Near Mischief Reef in the South China Sea." *The Diplomat*, March 25, 2018. https://thediplomat.com/2018/03/china-condemns-us-fonop-near-mischief-reef-in-the-south-china-sea/.

48 Snehesh, Alex Philip. "US Navy Ship Violates Indian Law as It Sails Through Exclusive Zone in 'Messaging to China'." *The Print*, April 9, 2021. https://theprint.in/defence/us-navy-ship-violates-indian-law-as-it-sails-through-exclusive-zone-in-messaging-to-china/636880.

49 Bianco, Christine, Zenel Garcia, and Bibek Chand. "What Is Innocent? Freedom of Navigation Versus Coastal States' Rights in the Law of the Sea." *Ocean Development and International Law* 54, no. 3 (2023): 349–74. https://doi.org/10.1080/00908320.2023.2267406.

was undermining Soviet Laws in favor of international regulations. Today, this would be seen as a FONOP, which is routinely conducted. The Soviet Union did not adhere to the international law of innocent passage and only recognized predetermined sea lanes. The Soviet Union sent out a Mirka class frigate to "bump" or push the USS *Yorktown* back into international waters. This conflict was later resolved through diplomatic means but had the potential of erupting into a kinetic conflict during a time of tension.[50] Military vessels are, by their nature, aggressive. This gives the edge to coast guard or law enforcement vessels, which are much less threatening and help bring stability and regional cooperation.

10. Understanding the Role of Maritime Law Enforcement

Coast guards and navies are inherently different in their role. Law enforcement maritime assets, such as coast guard vessels, have been used in the past to bring a de-escalating presence to areas of high tension. Coast guard vessels are seen as less provocative than naval warships as they have a different purpose than a warship.[51] Coast guard vessels can conduct fisheries patrols, search and rescue operations, and promote regional stability through enforcing international and national laws. In a traditional role, coast guards can de-escalate and improve international relations if they are utilized as a neutral law enforcement instrument.

While a naval warship can be utilized to conduct humanitarian missions, it is not what they are built to do – warships are built for war. Coast guards are inherently built to support the domestic population or act as a national instrument to enforce international laws and to deliver international aid. In 2008, the United States Coast Guard in tandem with a United States Naval warship was able to deliver aid to Georgia during "Operation Assured Delivery." Russia accused the United States of delivering military weapons and support. Russian Foreign Ministry official Andrei Nesterenko did not believe that a United States Naval warship could carry large amounts of humanitarian supplies, but instead it was for the purpose of delivering military supplies stating, "[i]t is unlikely that warships of this class can deliver humanitarian aid in great quantities."[52] This reinforces the reality that warships send an aggressive message, while coast guard vessels send a more neutral or even peaceful message.

After the passage of UNCLOS, the rights and responsibilities of smaller nations in the Indo-Pacific grew. Now nations have exclusive rights to their own EEZs. These rights also include the added responsibility of maintaining their waters. Pollution, fishing, other economic and environmental concerns were now being

50 Aceves, William J. "Diplomacy at Sea: U.S. Freedom of Navigation Operations in the Black Sea." *Naval War College Review* 46, no. 2 (1993): 59–79. http://www.jstor.org/stable/44642450.

51 Guilfoyle, Douglas, and Edward Sing Yue Chan. "Lawships or Warships? Coast Guards as Agents of (in)Stability in the Pacific and South and East China Sea." *Marine Policy* 140 (2022): 105048. https://doi.org/10.1016/j.marpol.2022.105048.

52 Gutterman, Steve. "US Warship to Georgian Port Partly Held by Russia." Associated Press, September 5, 2008. Archived from the original on September 7, 2008.

discussed. UNCLOS acted as a catalyst for the development of coast guards by nations like Bangladesh, Japan, Vietnam, and the Philippines.[53] These coast guards have been instrumental at regulating fisheries, deterring piracy, and maintaining international maritime boundaries.

Law enforcement presence can help deter and confront piracy and attacks on commercial shipping, which are global issues. Piracy thrives in regions with disputed maritime boundaries.[54] Today, with the attacks in the Red Sea, the world is seeing how vulnerable commercial shipping can be when faced with non-state actors. After a successful attack in a shipping lane, commercial vessels will need to be rerouted, insurance for the crew and ship will rise, and this price increase will be passed on to the consumer, impacting the global economy. Law enforcement can maintain and enforce maritime boundaries and provide intelligence on regional piracy as well as target the crime of piracy – bringing stability and safety for commercial vessels transiting the area.

Japan has taken a leading role in voicing their opinions on the need for increased maritime security in the Indo-Pacific. Japan recognizes the need for an established and universally recognized international maritime law which supports freedom of navigation and free trade. In 2023, Japan launched an updated free and open Indo-Pacific plan, which highlighted the need for the Indo-Pacific region to develop plans that support the culture and politics of the region. This plan stresses the need for de-escalation and the importance of avoiding the use of force or coercion.[55] Japan realizes the need for increased security cooperation and the importance of maintaining and clarifying international maritime law. Japan's vision needs the involvement of law enforcement assets to enforce and maintain security. It is vitally important that these law enforcement arms do not operate in a vacuum but communicate with each other.

Communication among stakeholders in the region needs to occur frequently. In 2000, the Japanese Coast Guard initiated The North Pacific Coast Guard Forum, which consists of Canada, Russia, the United States, Japan, China, and South Korea and is a great example of international cooperation and communication. Japan initiated this forum to share information and to combat the rising criminal threats in the North Pacific. The forum has six areas of focus: combatting illegal trafficking, combined operations, emergency response, fisheries enforcement, information exchange, and maritime security. This forum increases the visibility between nations and allows for open communication. The forum enables joint exercises and operations between nations. The North Pacific Coast Guard Forum has had success in catching illegal driftnet fishing as well as forming and performing joint

53 Bateman, Sam. "Coast Guards: New Forces for Regional Order and Security." *Asia-Pacific Issues*, no. 65 (2003): 1. https://www.sciencedirect.com/science/article/abs/pii/S0308597X22000951.

54 Prins, Brandon, Anup Phayal, and Aaron Gold. "Where Are Today's Piracy Hotspots?" *The Washington Post*, August 5, 2021. https://www.washingtonpost.com/politics/2021/08/05/fights-over-marine-boundaries-are-creating-safe-zones-pirates/.

55 Nishino, Junya. "Japan's New Plan for a 'Free and Open Indo-Pacific' and Its Challenges." *Asia Policy* 18, no. 3 (July 2023): 17–25. https://muse.jhu.edu/article/903860.

law enforcement patrols.[56] Bi-lateral and multi-lateral agreements are important to have in place before an incident occurs. If there is a process or procedure in place when an international law is violated, there is a sequence of events that takes place which are agnostic towards the violating nation and not motivated by race, nationality, or politics. This ensures that the laws and agreements will not be weaponized to attack or weaken a targeted group, but rather shows how these laws and regulations are enforced, regardless of the nation. Law enforcement mechanisms and multi-national enforcement cooperation help to reduce regional tensions and can de-escalate conflicts.

Joint coast guard patrols have been requested by the United States in 2015 in the South China Sea. This idea has been accepted as a positive step forward by the Philippines, but China has expressed negativity toward the concept.[57] These patrols could target the rising threat of piracy and illegal fishing that is present in the South China Sea. Law enforcement cooperation benefits all parties involved and by finding ways to get countries that are in a dispute over maritime boundaries into a cooperation, it could be a big step forward in establishing open communication and possibly de-escalate the current tensions. If an agreement could be reached between China and the Philippines, it could be the first step towards reconciliation between the two nations.

As maritime boundaries are being contested, leading to greater levels of crime and grey-zone operations, it is time for coast guards and law enforcement units to step up and take the stage. Actions against coast guard and law enforcement vessels are met with much greater disdain in the international community than actions toward military vessels.[58] A coast guard presence can deter China's expansionism and help to bring the international community together to reconfirm UNCLOS. Utilizing the United States Coast Guard instead of United States Naval warships for FONOPS sends a positive message of diplomacy and helps contain the perception that the United States is overextending or coercing smaller nations. Coast guard vessels acting as law enforcement assets can serve many different roles as a neutral envoy – building smaller nation maritime capabilities, deterring regional crime, and building international cooperation.

11. When Law Enforcement Goes Too Far

The social contract between law enforcement and the rest of society is founded on mutual trust, where citizens consent to be governed in exchange for protection and the maintenance of common order. This contract relies on the expectation that law

56 National Marine Fisheries Service. *2014 Report of the Secretary of Commerce to the Congress of the United States Concerning U.S. Actions Taken on Foreign Large-Scale High Seas Driftnet Fishing*, 7–9. Washington, DC: Government Printing Office, 2014.

57 Cheney-Peters, Scott. "Joint Patrols and U.S. Coast Guard Capacity." *The Asia Maritime Transparency Initiative*, April 1, 2015. https://amti.csis.org/joint-patrols-and-u-s-coast-guard-capacity/.

58 Rusling, Mathew. "Coast Guard Boosting Cooperation with Military." *National Defense* 93, no. 662 (2009): 28. http://www.jstor.org/stable/45351469.

enforcement will uphold the law fairly and justly. However, if law enforcement engages in corruption, abuses their power, or acts outside of legal boundaries – such as being militarized or acting criminally – they undermine this trust, eroding the credibility and legitimacy of the laws they enforce. When law enforcement legitimacy is compromised, it can lead to a breakdown of the social order law enforcement is trying to uphold.[59]

Chinese Coast Guard Order #3, introduced on June 15, 2024, represents a significant escalation in China's maritime strategy and a potential breakdown in China's Law Enforcement credibility. This regulation grants the Chinese Coast Guard broad authority to detain foreign vessels and individuals suspected of violating Chinese Laws within its claimed territorial waters for up to 60 days. The order's ambiguous language, including references to the contentious "nine-dash line," provides China with extensive discretion in enforcing its claims.[60] The recent collision on August 19, 2024, between a Philippine Coast Guard supply ship and a Chinese Coast Guard vessel near the Sabina Shoal, resulting in damage and injuries, highlights the aggressive enforcement of China's maritime regulations.[61]

The use of aggressive maritime militia and coast guard tactics has increased tension and instability in the South China Sea. By employing non-military assets to assert control and disrupt foreign vessels' operations, China has created an environment of uncertainty and intimidation. This has forced foreign vessels, including those from ASEAN countries and international commercial shipping, to alter their routes or avoid certain areas to prevent confrontations. The threat of detention under Order #3 exacerbates these concerns, complicating navigation and operations in the region.

China's strategy to maintain de facto control over disputed maritime territories is a delicate balance between assertiveness and diplomacy. This approach allows China to assert its dominance in the South China Sea while managing the complexities of international relations and minimizing the risks of a full-scale conflict.[62] This approach was evident during the Scarborough Shoal standoff in April 2012, when Chinese Coast Guard and maritime surveillance vessels blocked Philippine Naval

59 Tyler, Tom R. "Enhancing Police Accountability: A Report to the National Institute of Justice." *University of Illinois Law Review* 2017, no. 3 (2017): 1037–68. https://heinonline.org/HOL/LandingPage?handle=hein.journals/unilllr2017&div=64&id=&page=.

60 USINDOPACOM Joint Operational Law Team. "Topic: China Coast Guard Regulation No. 3." May 30, 2024. https://www.pacom.mil/Portals/55/Documents/Legal/J06%20TACAID%20-%20CCG%20Regulation%203%20(FINAL)%20-%20VER%202.pdf?ver=DbFQtB0oqN0l2NcJ_55HNA%3D%3D.

61 Reed, Betsy. "Chinese and Philippine Ships Collide Near Disputed Sabina Shoal in South China Sea." *The Guardian*, August 19, 2024. https://www.theguardian.com/world/article/2024/aug/19/china-philippine-ships-crash-sabina-shoal-south-china-sea.

62 Dutton, Peter A. "Conceptualizing China's Maritime Gray Zone Operations." In *Maritime Gray Zone Operations*, 19–34. Routledge, 2022. https://www.taylorfrancis.com/chapters/edit/10.4324/9781003310723-2/conceptualizing-china-maritime-gray-zone-operations-peter-duttond.

ships from accessing the shoal, which is within the Philippines' EEZ.[63] Similarly, the deployment of the Haiyang Shiyou 981 oil rig near the Paracel Islands in 2014, accompanied by aggressive actions against Vietnamese fishing boats, demonstrated China's use of non-military means to assert control.[64]

Since 2015, Chinese maritime militia, onboard Chinese fishing vessels, began harassing Philippine and Vietnamese ships near strategic features like Fiery Cross Reef and Mischief Reef. This harassment created hazardous conditions and showcased China's use of non-military means to project power and enforce its claims. The period between 2018 and 2020 saw intensified tensions around the Second Thomas Shoal, with Chinese Coast Guard vessels engaging in aggressive actions against Philippine fishing boats, reflecting China's broader strategy to assert and consolidate its claims.[65]

Violations of the law enforcement social contract have also been seen with Western Nations. In September 2017, Jamaican citizen Robert Weir and his crew were lost at sea after a storm during a fishing trip near Morant Cays, mistakenly drifting towards Haiti instead of Jamaica. They were intercepted by the United States Coast Guard, who boarded their boat, searched for drugs (no drugs were found using an ion-scan and physical drug search), and detained the men for over a month under questionable conditions.[66]

The United States Coast Guard's actions were conducted under the Maritime Drug Law Enforcement Act (MDLEA), which allows them to combat drug smuggling on the high seas, even without direct connection to the United States. However, the Weir v. The United States court case highlights the significant legal and constitutional questions regarding the extent of the United States Coast Guard authority to conduct operations in international waters. Especially since Weir and his crew had no ties to the United States and were not engaged in activities directed against the United States.[67]

After a month, the men were transferred to the United States Drug Enforcement Administration and charged with drug trafficking. Those charges were dropped due to no clear evidence of drug trafficking. Instead, they plead guilty to lying about

63 Morris, Lyle J., Michael J. Mazarr, Jeffrey W. Hornung, Stephanie Pezard, Anika Binnendijk, and Marta Kepe. "Gaining Competitive Advantage in the Gray Zone: Response Options for Coercive Aggression Below the Threshold of Major War." Research Report. RAND Corporation, June 27, 2019. https://www.rand.org/pubs/research_reports/RR2942.html.

64 Fook, Lye Liang, and Hoang Ha Hop. "Vietnam's Responses to China's Maritime Assertiveness in the South China Sea." Singapore, August 31, 2018. https://www.iseas.edu.sg/wp-content/uploads/pdfs/ISEAS_Perspective_2018_50@50.pdf.

65 Chang, Agnes, and Hannah Beech. "Fleets of Force: How China Strong-Armed Its Way into Dominating the South China Sea." *The New York Times*, November 16, 2023. https://www.nytimes.com/interactive/2023/11/16/world/asia/south-china-sea-ships.html.

66 BIA Cases by Biahelp. "Weir v. United States of America." January 15, 2021. https://biahelp.com/weir-v-united-states-of-america/.

67 Watt, Steven M., David Cole, and Aaron Madrid Aksoz. "The Coast Guard Destroyed Their Livelihoods: Will the Supreme Court Hear Their Case?" ACLU, March 23, 2022. https://www.aclu.org/news/human-rights/the-coast-guard-destroyed-their-livelihoods-will-the-supreme-court-hear-their-case.

their destination to a Coast Guard Officer (the crew said they were going to Jamaica, but drifted toward Haiti), resulting in a 10-month prison sentence. After a year, they were released to Jamaica.

Weir's case had been brought to the United States Supreme Court to challenge the United States Government's authority to criminalize actions on the high seas that lack a connection to the United States. The argument centered on historical legal principles, asserting that the United States Congress can only legislate on such matters if there is a clear nexus to the United States. The lower court's ruling, which allowed broad authority to prosecute any high seas conduct, is seen as a misinterpretation of both constitutional intent and Supreme Court precedent.[68]

The United States' defendant legal arguments cited various maritime cases questioning military or national security decisions to suggest that there are no clear judicial standards to adjudicate this case. They referenced Wu Tien Li-Shou v. United States, where the plaintiff sued for damages after the United States Navy accidentally killed her husband and sank his ship during an anti-piracy operation. The court deemed this case "non-justiciable," meaning it could not be decided by the courts due to its involvement with military operations and national security complexities.[69]

The United States' defendants stated that this case is comparable, arguing that determining negligence would require delving into military decisions that are typically outside judicial review. However, the distinction is that the operations conducted by the United States Coast Guard fall under law enforcement rather than military actions, suggesting that different legal standards should apply. This differentiation is crucial for evaluating whether judicial intervention is appropriate regarding the United States Coast Guard's actions against Weir, his crew, and others in the same predicament. The United States Supreme Court ruled in Weir's favor, paying Weir and his crew compensation in 2024.[70]

12. Conclusion

UNCLOS and the acceptance of international law are the foundation for maritime stability. Stability and maritime security in the Indo-Pacific is a global issue which must have a regional investment by all nations involved. Regional law enforcement cooperation has been proven to de-escalate conflict and regional tension. Coast guards can be instrumental in providing a neutral force focused on maintaining the peace while preventing international crime. Law enforcement mechanisms, when

68 *Weir v. United States*, 518 F. Supp. 3d 1 (D.D.C. 2021). United States District Court for the District of Columbia in Admiralty, January 15, 2021. https://casetext.com/case/weir-v-united-states-21.

69 *Wu Tien Li-Shou v. United States*, No. 14–1338 (4th Cir. January 23, 2015). United States Court of Appeals, Fourth Circuit. https://casetext.com/case/li-shou-v-united-states-1#p178.

70 ACLU District of Columbia. "Weir v. United States – Challenging Inhumane Detention Conditions and Property Destruction by U.S. Coast Guard." Accessed September 25, 2024. https://www.acludc.org/en/cases/weir-v-united-states-challenging-inhumane-detention-conditions-and-property-destruction-us.

put into action, must maintain their integrity by operating within their legal authority and jurisdiction.

International laws are often improperly executed due to a lack of political will, resources, and a strong legal framework, highlighting the need for effective national and international laws to support these instruments. It is essential to define key terms clearly, as their ambiguity can be exploited by nation-states for their own interests. Law enforcement in the maritime environment requires legal checks and balances to ensure fair treatment, including bi-lateral agreements, judicial oversight, and a common social agreement that all citizens follow. Nation-states should always have a voice regarding their citizens operating in international waters, especially in cases where 'other than grave crimes' have been committed.[71] Additionally, when drafting international and national laws on extradition, it is critical to ensure these laws are not weaponized against individuals based on religion, race, nationality, or political beliefs. Equitable punishments should be prioritized to prevent extradition from being obstructed by differing legal standards, ensuring that justice is served fairly without discrimination,[72] no matter which nation's law enforcement is enforcing the law.

Loose maritime boundaries and disruptions to commercial shipping in the Indo-Pacific will have devastating impacts on the global economy. If international maritime laws and boundaries are not recognized and enforced by law enforcement entities, the potential for military conflict amongst the world's strongest military powers increases. However, dangerous military interactions between nation-states in the region can be avoided through international coordination and law enforcement cooperation. Law enforcement entities, like coast guards, serve as essential enforcement and informational tools that hold nations accountable, without resorting to military action.

The ongoing tensions in the South China Sea, exacerbated by great power competition between the United States and China, has heightened sensitivities of military presence in the region. While law enforcement may not be the perfect solution to avoid military conflict, it does provide a middle ground by de-escalating tensions, delivering humanitarian aid, enforcing maritime boundaries, and deterring piracy. Nations need to use law enforcement vessels for law enforcement purposes, and not as grey-zone instruments of force projection. When this happens, global tensions will continue to rise, and international dialogue will be strained. To maintain peace and encourage diplomacy, it is essential that law enforcement assets remain true to their law enforcement roles. Law enforcement could be the key to stability in the Indo-Pacific, creating a safer and prosperous maritime environment while avoiding military escalation and conflict.

71 Center for Justice and Accountability. "Universal Jurisdiction." Accessed September 25, 2024. https://cja.org/what-we-do/litigation/legal-strategy/universal-jurisdiction/#:~:text=International%20law%20recognizes%20that%20certain,crimes%2C%20genocide%2C%20and%20torture.

72 Jha, Aditya, and Ritu Raj. "Critical Analysis of International Laws on Maritime Crimes with Special Emphasis on Interstate Cooperation." Centre for Maritime Law, September 29, 2021. National Law University Odisha. https://cmlnluo.law.blog/2021/09/29/critical-analysis-of-international-laws-on-maritime-crimes-with-special-emphasis-on-interstate-cooperation/.

2 Formation of a Multipolar World in a Context of Authoritarianism

*Junhua Zhang**

1. Introduction

The BRICS summit in Kazan in late October last year was a historic event, symbolizing formally the advent of the multipolar world and the decline of the US-dominated unipolar world, as reported by the Polish media outlet Myśl Polska on October 30th, 2024.[1] The report stated that the West tried to isolate Russia for three years, but the plan failed completely. Some 35 countries supported Russia's position at the summit, which was also attended by UN Secretary General Antonio Guterres and representatives of many other international organizations.

In a sense, the so-called multilevel world has become just one way for the authoritarian camp to strengthen its power against the democracies. The authoritarian leaders like Putin and Xi Jinping understand that many countries in the world do not want to take a clear line between authoritarianism and democracy, and therefore the term "multipolar world" is far more acceptable than the term of direct confrontation with the democratic camp. In reality, however, there are two main forces at work in the world today. Each side is trying to expand its own influence. One is the democratic camp, dominated by the market economy and democratic ideas, while the other is characterized by the rule of the strongman, represented by mixed economies (mostly crony capitalism). It adorns itself with pretty and pleasant rhetorics.

The Polish media coverage of the 16th BRICS Summit reflects the views of a number of right-wing groups and individuals in democratic countries regarding the current world situation. As for the authoritarian camp, led by China and Russia, it sees the existing Western-dominated international order as broken, and the so-called new order, which they themselves are creating but in fact have not yet established, as a given fact, or as something that will certainly be replaced by the new order in near future.[2]

* Senior associate of the European Institute for Asian Studies, Expert at the Geopolitical Intelligence Service (GIS) on Eurasian region.

1 Myśl Polska, 30 October 2024, *BRICS po szczycie w Rosji*, https://myslpolska.info/2024/10/30/brics-po-szczycie-w-rosji/.

2 Bernard Orr, Guy Faulconbridge and Andrew Osborn, Putin and Xi Pledge a New Era and Condemn the United States, *Reuters*, 17 May 2024.

DOI: 10.4324/9781003545750-3

Nevertheless, pandits on global political developments do recognize that the threat to the democratic camp posed by authoritarianism exists eminently. Unlike the Cold War of the past, the forces of totalitarianism and authoritarianism have reached a point where they can play openly with the forces of democracy, and the Cold War of the past has been replaced by the Hot War of today. The war in Ukraine is the most striking example of a typical game between two camps.

In order to understand the structure of this so-called multipolar world and its future trends, it is necessary to analyze the history of its emergence and the process of its development regarding the authoritarian camp. To do so, it is necessary to examine the following issues.

1) How did the democratic camp become complacent after the fall of the Soviet Union?
2) And what harm did this complacency bring to subsequent developments?
3) Why did the democracies neglect to take steps to prevent the revival of the authoritarianism that seemed possible a decade ago?
4) How many tools do the democratic countries have to fight against the growing authoritarian forces, particularly against the backdrop that democracy itself is also suffering from division?
5) Will the multipolar world move towards a more democratic or a more authoritarian world in the future?

Methodologically, this chapter attempts to exam the trajectory of the authoritarian camp's development from a historical review. At the same time, it will apply a perspective of comparative politics to make the trend of the development of the world understandable.

2. Complacency Among the Elites of Democracies

The fall of the Soviet Union in 1991 marked a dramatic change that many political scientists did not anticipate. The changes in the Soviet Union also led to changes in the entire global communist camp. The political bloc that was supposed to confront and compete with the Western democratic camp disappeared all of a sudden. Although the process of transformation to a market economy and democratic rule of law, both in the Soviet Union and in other so-called socialist countries in Eastern Europe, turned out to be very difficult. But since the economies of the democracies at the time were out of the upswing, it was a great incentive for those countries that followed the Western examples.

The sudden fall of a huge rival (the USSR) was a never-before-seen incentive for the leading elites of the democracies, who then began to rely too much on their political imagination. A typical example is Francis Fukuyama's book *The End of History and the Last Man* in 1992 The book takes the victory of democracy as a natural result of human political development, thinking that no authoritarianism or centralization will be able to fight against democracy in the future, and that it is the inevitable trend of human beings to crave for democracy and the free market.

Fukuyama also represents the thinking of the leading elites of many democratic countries, that democracy and capitalism and market economy are an ideal and natural pair. Therefore, the fall of the Soviet Union also equals the victory of the market economy.[3]

While the democratic leading elites were so engrossed in this atmosphere of triumph, they often forgot that the transition from the former state-controlled economy to a market economy is far from being as smooth and easy as Western pundits would like to think, and all the more so when the former nomenclature structure is still in place. This is the tragedy that Russia experienced in the era of President Yeltsin in the 1990s. The terms "democracy" and "market economy" later became synonyms for the Russian people cursing those who were relying on their privileges to enrich themselves in a greedy and brutal way. Thus, the hope for a strongman, rather than the desire for a democratic leader, became the inevitable outcome of the bitter transition of the late 1990s in Russia.

3. Backslide of Globalization on the Democracies

While the leading elites of the democracies are celebrating the arrival of the "the end of history", another unpleasant development is unfolding: that is, the gradual separation of capital from the democracies. According to the theories of the democratic elites[4] at that time, the world had now become "flat," that is, capital can flow everywhere, and this flow is also conducive to the expansion of democracy because of the aforementioned affinity between democracy and contemporary capitalism. As a result, various so-called transformation theories have emerged.[5] Many see the influence of the market economy and the flow of capital and diffusion of technology (i.e., globalization) as the way for a country to move from poverty to wealth and the way for a middle class to emerge, and as the authoritarian countries (mostly those that are welcoming Western capital and technology) interacted with the democratically developed countries that exported capital and technology, the former were able to produce a transformation at the political and social levels. This is what the German proverb *Wandel durch Handel* (change via trade) means.

While this idea seems to have become the consensus of Western leaders around 2000, the German government seems to be even more convinced of the inevitability of its transition among recipient countries such as China. It was these consensuses that led to the impetus for the Western democratic camp to push hard for China's accession to the World Trade Organization. Interestingly, China's authoritarian leaders, who seem to be more astute than those who dominated the transition during Russia's Yeltsin period, have skillfully exploited that Western expectation of China, and with promises that they didn't actually want to keep or only

3 Francis Fukuyama, 1992, *The End of History and the Last Man*, Free Press.

4 Carnegie Council, 2005, *The World Is Flat: A Brief History of the Twenty-First Century*, https://www.carnegiecouncil.org.

5 Vivienne Shue, 2003, *Globalization and Democratization in Asia*, Routledge, pp. 4–8.

partially were able to fulfill, they passed through successfully the approval process to become a member of the World Trade Organization.

If anything, the flow of capital from the Western world to China before 2000 was a positive benefit, thus bringing reciprocity to the bilateral working class. The flow of capital after China's accession to the WTO, however, has led to a gradual loss of guidance ability of capital by Western governments, especially European democracies, which have even become dependent on China's manufacturing industry.[6] Although the cost of living seems to be a little lower for the working class in the West due to the massive importation of goods from China, the balance of production and consumption, which was relatively stable in the democracies, has been upset by the so-called globalization. In other words, the flow of capital and technology has brought superficial satisfaction to the Western working class, i.e., a seemingly lower cost of living, in reality, they have become real losers. Because their bosses have moved the jobs that were theirs to much cheaper and harder-working but not less technically competent countries, such as China, and the so-called developed countries in the West are slowly hollowing out their industries, democracies have less and less room to use the capital as a card to influence other countries.

At the same time, however, the leaders of the democracies are not aware of this. They continue to dream of transforming authoritarian countries, such as China. It is under the influence of this optimism that the governments and capitals of the developed countries seem to turn a blind eye to China's use of improper means to acquire Western technology.

In other words, the marriage of democracy and capital that the original democratic elites appreciated has finally become a kind of nostalgia for the good old days. Worse still, the capital doesn't seem to care much about whether it is cooperating with authoritarianism or democracies.[7]

It is all these reasons that made China advance swiftly from a poor country to the number two economy in the world, a country with the largest manufacturing sector in the world, through decades of very targeted efforts.

4. The Miscalculation of the Obama Administration

Xi Jinping's rise to power in 2013 marked the decisive time interval of re-emergence of the world's authoritarian camp. This rise could originally have been entirely prevented. However, because the elites of democracies still continued to be under the influence of Fukuyama's thinking and are unable to abandon their illusions, they have overlooked Xi's potential.

Xi Jinping is one of the more mediocre of the CCP leaders in terms of intellectuality. His knowledge structure is not as good as Mao Zedong, who had a more

6 Joachim Ragnitz, 2020, *Strukturwandel nach Entindustrialisierung* (The Structural Transition After the De-Industrialisation), Bundeszentrale für Politische Bildung.

7 Wolfgang Merkel, 2023, Democracy and Capitalism Are Forcibly Married, *The Review of Democracy*, https://revdem.ceu.edu/2023/01/27/wolfgang-merkel-democracy-and-capitalism-are-forcibly-married/.

in-depth study of ancient Chinese literature and was able to apply it skillfully to the war affairs he was waging against his enemies. Xi also lacks the charisma of Mao and Deng Xiaoping, and his understanding of the world more rudimentary than that of any of the CCP leaders because he was of the generation of China's Cultural Revolution, which prevented him from obtaining normal schooling. But he resembles Mao Zedong as a man of ambition and with enough energy and skills in the party's power struggle.[8] His great goal is to lead China to become the strongest country in the world. At the same time, he vows to ensure that China's red color (the communism) would remain unchanged during his term. Finally, he determined that the Taiwan issue must be resolved during his tenure. Perhaps he knew from the beginning that it would take time to achieve these goals, and it became clear that the informal rule set by Deng Xiaoping, that each top party leader could not stay in office for longer than 10 years, would hinder him from successfully achieving his goals. So, he took the risk of amending the Constitution in his second term, thus legitimizing his tenure beyond 10 years.[9]

5. "Building a New Type of Great Power Relationship"

When Xi Jinping first came to power in 2013, he decided that China must continue to ride on the coattails of the West and take advantage of their generosity in technology transfers and investments, so he focused his attention on the leaders of the most developed countries. Around 2013, he strongly advocated what he called "a new type of great power relationship" with the United States, in which Beijing would work with the U.S. to build China into the largest economy and industrial vanguard with the help of the West.[10] Xi's thinking at that time was actually in line with the Chinese intellectual elite, namely that Russia represented a backward economy and was not a role model for China. Only the technology and management of the United States and other Western countries was what China needed.

Unfortunately, the Obama administration, as well as the political elites in Europe, did not echo Xi Jinping's call. Partly, Western governments were probably getting tired of China's hitchhiking on technology and capital, so the Obama administration was not thrilled about Xi Jinping's initiative. On the contrary, Western democratic elites were still under the impression that the world's capital is on the side of democracy, that democracies are also in control of the world's best technology, and that authoritarian countries are as certain to beg and plead before democracies as a beggar.

The reality tells us that the opposite might be true: Thousands of Chinese undergraduates, graduate students, and doctoral students were studying in the United

8 Alfred L. Chan, 2022, *Xi Jinping: Political Career, Governance, and Leadership, 1953–2018*, Oxford University Press.

9 Eerishika Pankaj, 2020, *Xi Jinping and Constitutional Revisions in China*, Institute for Security and Development Policy.

10 Ren Xiao, 2013, *Modeling a "New Type of Great Power Relations": A Chinese Viewpoint*, The Asan Forum.

States and other Western countries in what today seem to be sensitive technological disciplines, and many of them have official Chinese backgrounds. They have been playing an enormous role in China's later development. At the same time, China skillfully used its official control over everything in China (land, labor, etc.) to induce Western capital to gain access to the Chinese market, but only if it contributed its own technology, especially sensitive technology. China's manufacturing sector grew so rapidly under the example of the West that the term "factory of the world" became synonymous with China.

6. Russia, China's Affinity

The Obama administration in 2015 could have taken advantage of Xi Jinping's initiative to, on the one hand, avoid or minimize China's free-riding on sensitive technologies, but on the other hand, through clever maneuvers, make it possible to steer China toward the "peaceful coexistence" that the democratic camp should have expected, rather than toward transformation. This is because transition takes a long time in a country like China. But the U.S. government at the time defied Xi's call for "a new two great power relationship".

This kind of ignorance brought frustration to Xi and made him readjust his search for potential partners. Thus, Russia became the target as substitute for the USA. This was despite the fact that China's elites were not in favor of this approach at first. A think tank at Tsinghua University even submitted a study in 2013 on the matter, telling Xi Jinping that cooperation with Russia was an unwise choice. But Xi, at that time, had already made a firm decision to deal with Russia under Putin as a strategic partner of China. Therefore, he simply labeled the report as "nonsense".[11]

Several factors determined Xi's choice of Russia. First, Xi sees today's Russia as the successor to the Soviet Union, which Xi sees as a symbol of the red socialist world (not unlike Mao's perception in his later life). The efforts of Putin-led Russia to rebuild the "Russian world"[12] are understood by Xi as an effort to at least partially revive the spirit of the Soviet Union. The fact that Putin is not at all interested in the so-called Red (i.e., socialism in Xi's sense of the word) does not make Xi uncomfortable with being close to Putin. Second, there are a number of areas of Russia's military industry that are enviable role models for China. Finally, Russia can provide China with endless resources once it makes up with Russia.

This chapter will not go into detail about how Putin induced the Russians under his leadership to turn toward China. Yet one thing is certain: Xi Jinping and Putin hit it off from the moment they met. More importantly, the war in Ukraine in 2022

11 RFA, 2024, *Xi Jinping Criticized "Nonsense" on a Report* (习近平在一份报告上批示"废话"), https://www.wenxuecity.com/news/2022/12/14/12022211.html.

12 Anatolii Babynskyi, 2022, *'Russkiy Mir' – The 'Russian World' Meets Ukrainian Politics and Vatican Diplomacy, Religious Information Service of Ukraine*, https://risu.ua/en/russkiy-mir-the-russian-world-meets-ukrainian-politics-and-vatican-diplomacy_n126775.

has forced Putin to drop what were the last few guardrails of defense against China. To ensure the success of his war on Ukraine, he decided to open up his market completely to China and involve the Chinese in the exploitation of resources. Xi Jinping has indeed lived up to Putin's expectations by providing full support to Russia during the war in Ukraine, not only in terms of finance, but also in terms of military industry and trade. In other words, Putin's war was simply unsustainable without China's full support. Right now, Russia's military industry seems much stronger than that of the European countries combined.[13]

7. Choices in a Time of the "Hot War"

While the world was in a Cold War before the fall of the Soviet Union, the authoritarian camp after 2022 has become so powerful that it can directly engage democracies in a "Hot War" that is far from over. But the "marriage" of Moscow and Beijing has had an impact on the world that is unparalleled in history. One is a country with a vast territory blessed with immense natural gas, oil, and all types of rare resources, while the other is the country with the world's largest manufacturing industry, as well as the one that has absorbed the West's technology most effectively.

If today's war in Ukraine, even with Trump's return to the White House, is likely to end with Ukraine being humiliated, the European countries can only do something to make Ukraine "lose with dignity". Then, another part of the Hot War will follow. That is, Xi Jinping's seizure of Taiwan by force will create another headache for the Western democracies. Siezing Taiwan forcefully, because of its geography, will not necessarily be easier than the war in Ukraine, which in turn will have a knock-on effect on world trade and the world economy as a whole.

Trump's return to power illustrates the bankruptcy of the Western democratic elite's narrative and is a resounding slap in the face of the Western democratic elite's "end-of-history" complacency, overconfidence, and inability to predict tense developments. This chapter is not intended to discuss whether the Trump administration can transform the fact that China is number one in manufacturing and whether it can make America strong again by regaining its industries. His ascension to power has at least added a good deal of uncertainty within the democratic camp, even though his term is only four years long. But these uncertainties, in turn, are likely to create disadvantages for the democratic camp to confront and compete with the authoritarian camp.

13 Oleksandr V. Danylyuk and Jack Watling, 2024, *Winning the Industrial War Comparing Russia, Europe and Ukraine, 2022–24*, https://static.rusi.org/winning-the-industrial-war-comparing-russia-europe-ukraine-2022-24.pdf, 1) China and Russia: Toward an alternate financial system, 2) Russia turns to China to develop its Far East, 3) The burgeoning China-Russia axis. Geopolitical Intelligence Service (GIS).

8. Conclusions

The multipolarity of the world should be understood as a process of global democratization. However, behind this term appear the confrontation and competition between the democratic camp and the authoritarian camp, and this confrontation has moved from the stage of polemics to the stage of a Hot War. Ironically, the authoritarian camp seems better prepared for and more confident of winning this Hot War.

Rather than the inevitability of the formation of the authoritarian camp with Russia and China as the main players and Iran and North Korea as the assistants, it is the arrogance of the democratic elites and their stubborn and unrealistic design of the future that has led to the fortuitous "marriage" of Russia and China. And it is this fortuitous union that has brought about stagnation and regression in the development of democracy in the world today. It has even caused irreparable damage within democracies such as the United States. It may take one or more generations of effort to recoup and rectify this loss.

If we are based on Kantian optimism,[14] we believe that the vast majority of the world's people still aspire to democracy and freedom, and that they are the inevitable trend of world development. But if these ideas of democracy and freedom are really to take root among the populations of various countries, it will obviously take longer than people in the 1990s thought. This is because the Western democratic elites after the fall of the Soviet Union have unfortunately missed the chance and thus deprived a number of regions of the opportunity to expand steadily.

References

Ferdows, Mir A., 2009, *Internationale Politik*, Bayerische Landeszentrale für Politische Bildung (ed.), Bayerische Staatsregierung, A111.

Fukuyama, Francis, 2011, *The Origins of Political Order*, Farrar, Straus and Groux, New York.

Fukuyama, Francis, 2014, *Political Order and Political Decay*, Farrar, Straus and Groux, New York.

Gilpin, Robert, 2001, *Global Political Economy*, Princeton University Press, Princeton and Oxford.

Kaiser, Karl and Hans-Peter Schwarz (eds.), 1995, *Die Neue Weltpolitik*, Bundeszentrale für Politische Bildung.

Nye, Jr., Joseph S., 2011, *The Future of Power*, BBS, New York.

14 Immanuel Kant, 2016, *Zum ewigen Frieden – Ein philosophischer Entwurf*, Publishing House Hoffenburg, pp. 10–20.

3 The Duality of Strategy in the Indo-Pacific

Balancing Competition and Readiness

*Luke Shabro**

I. Introduction: The Strategic Paradox in the Indo-Pacific

On the morning of August 18th, 2024, two Chinese Coast Guard (CCG) vessels violently collided with two Philippine Coast Guard (PCG) vessels near Escoda Shoal in the South China Sea, quickly escalating tensions between Manila and Beijing.[1] Less than a week later, over 30 People's Liberation Army (PLA) aircraft were flying in Taiwan's Air Defense Identification Zone (ADIZ) and 12 People's Liberation Army Navy (PLAN) vessels were sailing in the waters around Taiwan in an aggressive reaction to Taiwanese President Lai Ching-te's visit to Kinmen Island that commemorated the Second Taiwan Strait Crisis.[2]

As these events unfolded, both of which had the potential to escalate into crisis or conflict, the U.S. Navy had no aircraft carriers stationed in the Western Pacific or forward-deployed in Japan – something that hadn't happened in nearly ten years. Despite recent debate about the combat value of aircraft carriers in the face of the U.S.' pacing threat's growing anti-access/area denial (A2/AD) capability and capacity growth, the lack of presence of the U.S.' most visible hard power tool is highly concerning when tensions in the Taiwan Strait are potentially more escalated than they have been since the Third Taiwan Strait Crisis. Faced with crises and commitments worldwide – from responding to Russian aggression in Eastern Europe to countering Iranian provocations in the Gulf – the U.S. Navy is stretched thin, deploying its limited number of carriers to meet immediate security needs across multiple theaters. As a result, the Indo-Pacific, arguably the most strategically critical region for countering China's rise, was left without the presence of a U.S. carrier, a key instrument of power projection and deterrence.

* U.S. Navy Veteran; Futurist, Writer.

1 A.M. Lariosa, *China Coast Guard Rams Philippine Cutters Near Disputed South China Sea Shoals* (19.08.2024), "USNI News": https://news.usni.org/2024/08/19/china-coast-guard-rams-philippine-cutters-near-disputed-south-china-sea-shoals.

2 F. Hamacher and A. Wang, *On Frontline Island, Taiwan President Rejects China's Rule for Freedom* (23.08.2024), "Reuters": https://www.reuters.com/world/asia-pacific/frontline-island-taiwan-president-rejects-chinas-rule-freedom-2024-08-23/.

DOI: 10.4324/9781003545750-4

This real-life scenario is emblematic of increasing friction between two critical areas for the United States: competition and readiness. While competition and readiness are commonly intertwined, each represents a unique objective that can occasionally lead to contrasting strategic requirements. However, embracing a duality in strategy allows for a balanced approach that can serve both masters – competition and readiness – by blending assertive action with sustained preparedness.

The Indo-Pacific isn't just a region on a map; it's the arena for the 21st century's most significant global power struggles, stretching from the U.S. West Coast to the Indian Ocean. Serving as a central artery for global commerce, this vast region supports over 60% of the world's maritime trade, making chokepoints like the Strait of Malacca and the South China Sea crucial to the global economy. Beyond trade routes, the Indo-Pacific is anchored by economic hubs like Tokyo, Singapore, and Sydney, attracting major global players. China's rise as an economic powerhouse, backed by its expansive Belt and Road Initiative, has intensified regional competition, prompting the United States to strengthen alliances with Japan, India, and Australia to counterbalance China's reach and secure its own influence in this pivotal area. Then, of course, there's the ever-present threat of conflict. Taiwan sits as a flashpoint, with China asserting its claim over the island and the United States committed to Taiwan's defense. In the South China Sea, China's construction of artificial islands and military installations has set off alarms, not only among its neighbors but also with the United States, which regularly conducts Freedom of Navigation Operations (FONOPs) to challenge these claims and keep the sea lanes open.[3]

The stakes in the Indo-Pacific are high. Control over these trade routes, influence over economic centers, and the ability to manage, escalate, or deescalate potential flashpoints make this region a focal point of modern strategic competition – a place where the balance of power in the coming decades will be decided.

And yet, all the economic influence and strategic alliances in the world mean little without the hard edge of military readiness backing them up. The Indo-Pacific isn't just an arena for political maneuvering or economic deals; it's a region where the potential for actual conflict is palpable, and where readiness could be the difference between deterrence (or containment) and disaster. China's rapid military modernization, from building up its navy to advancing missile capabilities (and capacity) and cyber warfare tactics, underscores the urgency of preparedness.[4] This isn't a hypothetical chess game – China's continuous pressure campaign around Taiwan, its militarization of the South China Sea, and its pressure, from both hard and soft power, on neighboring countries are concrete signals of what's at stake.

3 *Territorial Disputes in the South China Sea* (17.09.2024), "Council on Foreign Relations: Center for Preventive Action": https://www.cfr.org/global-conflict-tracker/conflict/territorial-disputes-south-china-sea.

4 M. Xiu, *PLA Rocket Force Organization* (22.01.2022), "Air Force Air University": https://www.airuniversity.af.edu/Portals/10/CASI/documents/Research/PLARF/2022-01-05%20PLARF%20Organization%20ExecSum.pdf.

For the U.S. and its allies, maintaining military readiness in the Indo-Pacific isn't about saber-rattling; it's about ensuring that, if push comes to shove, they can respond rapidly and decisively. It's about having the right assets in place, from carrier strike groups to advanced ISR capabilities, to act fast if tensions ignite. Readiness isn't just about keeping ships and planes at the ready; it's about practicing interoperability with allies, developing resilient and adaptive logistics networks – from "tooth to tail" – that can withstand disruptions, and prepositioning critical materiel to ensure swift access when needed. Forces must be trained and capable across a range of scenarios, from humanitarian assistance to high-intensity conflict, ensuring that response capability remains robust under any conditions.[5]

In the Indo-Pacific, the balance between influence and force projection is delicate. You can talk about cooperation and diplomacy all you want, but at the end of the day, it's the ability to stand ready for conflict that keeps competitors honest. Readiness ensures that the stakes are real, that aggressors know there's a price to pay for crossing red lines, and that stability in the region has teeth behind it.

II. Finding Duality in Strategy

In the Indo-Pacific, strategy isn't a simple "either-or" choice between peace and war – it is a constant balancing act. This is the duality of strategy, where nations must juggle the art of competitive posturing with the necessity of being militarily ready at a moment's notice. Competition demands influence: establishing a presence, building alliances, shaping narratives, and showcasing both hard and soft power. But while those actions project strength, they don't necessarily prepare a country for the grind of combat if the proverbial balloon goes up. The line between competition and conflict here is razor-thin, and any misstep can tilt the balance toward open hostilities.[6] That's why military readiness must be woven into every competitive move, ensuring that if the need arises, the transition from influence to action is seamless.

A Convergent Strategy is a cohesive approach that integrates elements of competition and readiness to create a unified, balanced framework for national security and influence. It is designed to address the dual demands of geopolitical influence and military preparedness, particularly in regions of strategic importance where great power rivalry is prevalent. This strategy leverages both soft and hard power, ensuring that diplomatic, economic, and cultural initiatives are supported by a credible military posture, and vice versa.

Balancing these two demands isn't easy. On one hand, you have the need to project influence, to win hearts and minds, and to strengthen alliances through

5 M. Bremer and K. Grieco, *The Four Tyrannies of Logistical Deterrence* (08.11.2023), "Stimson Center": https://www.stimson.org/2023/the-four-tyrannies-of-logistical-deterrence/.

6 M. Pomerleau, *To Be Ready for Conflict, Army Leader Urges Focus on Information Space in 'Competition'* (03.07.2024), "DefenseScoop": https://defensescoop.com/2024/07/03/to-be-ready-for-conflict-army-leader-urges-focus-information-space-competition/.

diplomatic and economic means. On the other hand, there's the very real requirement to be prepared for a fast-moving, high-stakes military confrontation. The same assets and personnel involved in regional engagements, humanitarian aid, and joint exercises must be able to shift gears in a heartbeat to respond to aggression. This dual-purpose approach doesn't just apply to physical assets – it's a mindset.

Leaders, policymakers, and commanders need to operate with an understanding that every act of influence must be backed by the latent power of rapid response and decisive force.

The duality of strategy isn't about choosing competition over readiness or vice versa; it's about threading both into a coherent approach that serves national interests on multiple levels. A show of strength that's purely symbolic is hollow, but a military presence without the soft power to back it up is provocative, unsustainable, and often leads to ambiguous and confused narratives. True strategy in the Indo-Pacific means operating on both fronts at once, reinforcing influence with readiness and readiness with influence, creating a posture that keeps adversaries guessing and allies reassured. This is a delicate dance, one that requires constant adjustment and a clear understanding that in this region, competition and readiness aren't just parallel efforts – they are two sides of the same coin.

III. Strategic Equilibrium: U.S. and Allied Approaches to Competition and Readiness

The purpose of this chapter is to examine how the United States and its critical allies navigate the delicate duality of competition and readiness in the Indo-Pacific, especially under the intense pressure of great power rivalry with China and explore the potential of embracing a Convergent Strategy. This isn't just a theoretical balancing act – it's an urgent, strategic challenge that requires a coordinated approach among nations with shared interests and overlapping, yet distinct, priorities. Together, the U.S. and its allies – countries like Japan, Australia, South Korea, and others – must assert their influence, deter aggression, and prepare for the possibility of rapid, large-scale conflict.

For the U.S., competition in the Indo-Pacific goes beyond economic maneuvers or showcasing military might; it's about establishing a credible, resilient presence that reassures allies and deters adversaries. But competition alone isn't enough. To be effective, this influence must be grounded in real readiness – the capability and capacity to respond quickly and decisively if tensions turn to conflict. For U.S. allies, this balance is just as crucial. They contribute to regional stability and amplify U.S. influence, but they also face the challenge of maintaining their own security autonomy while depending on the strength of the U.S. commitment. Each ally has its own strategic interests, yet all recognize that being unprepared would be a costly gamble in the face of China's growing capabilities.

This chapter explores how the United States, in close coordination with its allies, can work to achieve this balance and embrace a Convergent Strategy. We'll look at how allies like Japan and Australia bolster the regional security architecture, adding both depth and deterrence to the U.S. presence, while navigating their own balancing acts between competition and readiness. By examining the approaches of the U.S. and its partners, this chapter aims to reveal the nuanced strategies and complex trade-offs involved in maintaining influence and staying prepared in a region where the contest for dominance is unrelenting, and the stakes could not be higher.

IV. Understanding the Elements of Competition in the Indo-Pacific

Soft Power and Economic Influence

Competition in the Indo-Pacific isn't just about military strength; it's a battle over economic influence and soft power. Countries in the region need more than defense pacts – they need economic opportunities and infrastructure support. Both the U.S. and China understand this, embedding soft power into their strategies to shape regional alliances.

China's Belt and Road Initiative (BRI) exemplifies this approach. Through infrastructure projects and loans, China has cultivated economic dependencies across Asia and beyond, securing strategic assets like ports and railways. These projects, while promoting growth, often tie recipient nations closer to China, subtly advancing Beijing's ambitions. For China, this isn't about immediate control but gradually shaping the Indo-Pacific's economic landscape to reinforce its strategic goals.[7]

The U.S., meanwhile, has countered with initiatives like the Indo-Pacific Economic Framework (IPEF) to provide alternatives to BRI.[8] This approach underscores transparency, sovereignty, and fair trade, offering partner nations pathways to development without sacrificing autonomy. In places like the Philippines and Vietnam, the U.S. invests in projects ranging from digital infrastructure to clean energy, reinforcing ties while respecting local sovereignty. Australia, Japan, and the U.S. have also collaborated to support Pacific Island nations, countering China's growing influence in these smaller, strategically vital states.

Political and Diplomatic Maneuvering

Diplomatic agility is as crucial as military strength in the Indo-Pacific, where nations like Japan, India, and Association of Southeast Asian Nations (ASEAN) members carefully navigate ties with both the U.S. and China. Each has its unique priorities but shares a core objective: maintaining sovereignty amid great power competition.

Japan, closely allied with the U.S., benefits from its security umbrella yet carefully manages its relationship with China through economic engagement and

7 J. McBride, N. Berman, and A. Chatzky, *China's Massive Belt and Road Initiative* (02.02.2023), "Council on Foreign Relations": https://www.cfr.org/backgrounder/chinas-massive-belt-and-road-initiative.

8 C.S. Cimino-Isaacs, K. Kitamura, and M. Manyin, *Indo-Pacific Economic Framework for Prosperity (IPEF)* (22.07.2024), "Congressional Research Service": https://www.cfr.org/backgrounder/chinas-massive-belt-and-road-initiative.

diplomatic channels. India pursues a policy of strategic autonomy, partnering with the U.S. and others while maintaining trade and defense ties with Russia and dialogue with China. ASEAN states strive for neutrality, creating platforms like the ASEAN Regional Forum to maintain balanced relationships with major powers while avoiding entanglement.[9]

Military Posturing and Presence

The Indo-Pacific's military landscape is a stage for power projection, with both the U.S. and China reinforcing their influence through strategic positioning and joint exercises. China's militarization of the South China Sea – building outposts with airstrips, missiles, and radars – sends a clear message of its intent to secure its claimed territory. The U.S. counters with Freedom of Navigation Operations (FONOPs) and bolstered alliances, emphasizing a commitment to regional stability and the principle of open seas. Joint exercises and security agreements enhance interoperability and reinforce alliances, ensuring that both nations' presence in the region remains unmistakable.

Impact on Regional Powers

For smaller Indo-Pacific nations, the stakes are high. Countries like Vietnam and the Philippines balance economic dependence on China with security ties to the U.S., crafting strategies that protect their interests without binding them to any single power. Meanwhile, Pacific Island nations, vulnerable to climate change and economic pressures, weigh Chinese investment against the potential long-term consequences for their sovereignty.[10]

In the Indo-Pacific, every diplomatic decision, investment, and alliance is a calculated move in a broader game of influence. These nations are not mere bystanders; they're active participants, shaping their own paths amid the tug-of-war between the U.S. and China.

V. The Imperative of Military Readiness in a Volatile Region

Readiness in the Indo-Pacific Context

In the Indo-Pacific, readiness isn't just about keeping forces in shape; it's a constant state of being prepared for sudden crises. The region's volatility demands that the U.S. and its allies can respond swiftly and seamlessly, integrating capabilities

9 *ASEAN and China: Past, Present, Future* (24.11.2018), "National University of Singapore: Centre for International Law": https://cil.nus.edu.sg/publication/asean-and-china-past-present-future/.

10 T.F. Lynch, J. Przystup, and P. Saunders, *The Indo-Pacific Competitive Space: China's Vision and the Post-World War II American Order* (04.11.2020), "National Defense University": https://ndupress.ndu.edu/Media/News/News-Article-View/Article/2404551/9-the-indo-pacific-competitive-space-chinas-vision-and-the-postworld-war-ii-ame/.

across alliances. Readiness here means forces are strategically positioned, fully supplied, and backed by a robust logistics network that can overcome vast distances and respond at a moment's notice. Alliances are key to this readiness, transforming joint exercises into practiced coordination that stands ready to counter any aggressive move with speed and unity.

Challenges Unique to the Region

The Indo-Pacific presents unique hurdles. Spanning vast distances, it requires logistical resilience, with forward bases, refueling assets, and supply chains to support sustained operations. Territorial disputes, particularly in the South China Sea, create flashpoints that require a constant, cautious presence – enough to deter aggression without sparking unnecessary escalation. Adding to this complexity are hybrid threats, like China's maritime militia and cyber tactics, which blur the lines between peace and conflict. Readiness here means more than just traditional military preparation; it demands capabilities that can counter gray-zone actions and unconventional threats.

Evolving Threat Landscape

The Indo-Pacific's threat landscape is dynamic, with new forms of warfare challenging traditional military responses. Asymmetric tactics from actors like North Korea, pervasive cyber operations from China, and the rise of hypersonic technology demand adaptable strategies. In this environment, static readiness isn't enough. The U.S. and its allies must stay agile, prepared not only for known threats but for emerging ones – whether they come in the form of cyber disruptions, missile tests, or hypersonic strikes that leave no room for delay.

In the Indo-Pacific, staying prepared means staying adaptable, ready to meet a constantly shifting set of challenges head-on.

VI. The Trade-offs between Competition and Readiness

Resource Allocation Dilemmas

In the Indo-Pacific, competition isn't limited to military posturing; it extends to economic and diplomatic engagement. However, each dollar spent on soft power is a dollar diverted from military readiness. Investments like the Indo-Pacific Economic Framework (IPEF) or partnerships with Vietnam and the Pacific Islands offer strategic alternatives to China's Belt and Road Initiative, but they stretch already-tight military budgets. Diplomatic and cultural initiatives build long-term influence but lack immediate returns in defense capability. Balancing these priorities is crucial – underfunding either risks ceding influence or compromising preparedness. The challenge is to support both competition and readiness without sacrificing one for the other.

Strategic Messaging vs. Tactical Preparedness

Projecting strength in the Indo-Pacific is essential, but it must also be underpinned by genuine readiness. Freedom of Navigation Operations (FONOPs) in the South China Sea and carrier deployments signal U.S. resolve but strain resources, potentially reducing combat readiness. Tactical preparedness – training, maintenance, and force readiness – requires focus but can be overshadowed by high-profile deterrent actions and demands from other theaters. Striking a balance is key: show too much without substance, and adversaries may call the bluff; focus solely on readiness without visible deterrence, and allies might question U.S. commitment. The goal is to ensure that every demonstration of strength reflects true capability.

Flashpoints in the Taiwan Strait and South China Sea

The Taiwan Strait and South China Sea are high-stakes arenas where U.S. resolve and readiness are constantly tested. Support for Taiwan and FONOPs challenge China's territorial claims, but they demand significant resources, risking overextension. Each maneuver – whether arms sales to Taiwan or naval patrols in and around the Taiwan Strait – sends signals that could provoke miscalculation, potentially triggering conflict. These flashpoints underscore the delicate balance between deterring aggression and preserving readiness. In these tense environments, a single misstep could escalate rapidly, making it crucial for the U.S. and its allies to carefully manage both competition and preparation to avoid unintended crises.

VII. Case Studies: Dual Strategy Approaches by Key Indo-Pacific Powers

The balance of competition and readiness in the Indo-Pacific is a complex game, with each country navigating it based on their unique interests, resources, and threats. From the United States to Japan, the Philippines, and ASEAN nations, each player in the region adopts a dual strategy that reflects its own strategic objectives, while acknowledging the realities of a landscape shaped by the looming presence of both the U.S. and China. These case studies illustrate how different Indo-Pacific powers manage the balance between influence and preparedness, each crafting an approach that suits their role and stakes in the region.

United States: Balancing Diplomacy, Economic Initiatives, and Military Presence

For the United States, maintaining a strategic foothold in the Indo-Pacific hinges on a balanced blend of diplomacy, economic investment, and a credible military presence. Economic initiatives like the Indo-Pacific Economic Framework (IPEF) and infrastructure projects offer essential alternatives to China's Belt and Road Initiative, strengthening regional partnerships.

However, economic outreach alone cannot sustain influence without the assurance of military readiness. This is where Operation Pathways plays a pivotal role, enhancing U.S. commitment to security and stability through forward-positioned assets and robust joint exercises.

Operation Pathways, formerly Pacific Pathways, is central to this dual strategy. Through dynamic employment of Army pre-positioned stocks, comprehensive sustainment, and medical support capabilities, the operation ensures that U.S. forces remain agile, adaptable, and ready to respond to crises. Exercises within Operation Pathways, such as those involving sustainment and medical support, strengthen interoperability with regional allies, sending a clear message of support and reinforcing collective defense. This operational framework allows the U.S. to continuously test and demonstrate readiness without overextending forces, aligning military presence with diplomatic and economic commitments.[11]

However, balancing this strategy remains a challenge. Lean too much into diplomacy and economic initiatives, and the deterrent power of a credible military presence could erode. Overemphasize forward deployment, and resources may be stretched thin, especially with competing priorities across other global regions. Each carrier deployment, every Freedom of Navigation Operation (FONOP), and every exercise under Operation Pathways serves as both a deterrent signal and a reaffirmation of U.S. support for regional allies. Behind the scenes, this delicate balance between influence and readiness ensures that the U.S. maintains a posture of sustained commitment while keeping forces prepared for any contingency.

Japan: Economic Investment Paired with Defensive Strengthening

Japan's approach in the Indo-Pacific is shaped by its unique position as both an economic powerhouse and a frontline state facing the realities of an assertive China and a volatile North Korea. Japan wields considerable economic influence across the region, investing in infrastructure projects in Southeast Asia and promoting development initiatives that align with its strategic goals. Japan's soft power influence extends beyond mere economics; it actively engages in diplomatic efforts, advocating for a "Free and Open Indo-Pacific" and bolstering relations with countries wary of Chinese expansionism.[12]

On the defense side, Japan is no longer a passive player. It has increased its defense budget significantly, embarked on a major modernization of its Self-Defense Forces, and taken steps to amend its post-war stance on collective security. With new capabilities, from advanced missile defense systems to amphibious rapid deployment brigades, Japan is preparing for potential scenarios where it

11 E. Johnson, and M. Yore, *Operation Pathways: Dynamic Employment of Army Pre-Position Stock Tested in the Indo-Pacific* (02.05.2023), "U.S. Army": https://www.army.mil/article/265891/operation_pathways_dynamic_employment_of_army_pre_position_stock_tested_in_the_indo_pacific.

12 *New Plan for a "Free and Open Indo-Pacific* (01.03.2023), "Japanese Ministry of Foreign Affairs": https://www.mofa.go.jp/files/100477660.pdf.

might need to act swiftly.[13] This dual strategy of economic engagement paired with defensive strengthening allows Japan to build regional goodwill while sending a clear message: it will defend itself and support allies if pushed. For Japan, the balance lies in projecting influence without being perceived as overly aggressive, all while maintaining a state of readiness that fits its role in the region.

The Philippines: A Balancing Act of Strategic Partnerships and Military Modernization

The Philippines is acutely aware of the strategic chessboard it sits on, particularly as China ramps up its activities in the South China Sea. For years, the Philippines has had to balance economic ties with China – an essential trading partner and investor – against its security reliance on the United States. The Duterte administration took a softer stance on China, welcoming economic cooperation, but recent shifts in leadership have brought the security relationship with the U.S. back into sharper focus. Joint exercises, renewed defense agreements, and access to Philippine bases for U.S. forces have all been part of this recalibration.[14]

But the Philippines isn't just leaning on the U.S. to carry the weight. It has undertaken its own military modernization, focusing on naval and air assets that could be critical in any potential South China Sea skirmishes. By investing in missile systems, fast-attack craft, and coastal defense, the Philippines is building capabilities that enable it to defend its territorial waters, while reinforcing its commitments to regional stability.[15] The Philippines' dual strategy involves threading the needle – strengthening ties with the U.S. for deterrence while maintaining enough flexibility to engage with China on economic terms when needed.

ASEAN Nations: Economic Dependence on China, Defense Cooperation with the U.S.

The ASEAN bloc – made up of ten Southeast Asian nations – is navigating one of the trickiest dual strategies in the region. Individually, these countries rely heavily on China for trade and investment. China is ASEAN's largest trading partner, and Chinese infrastructure projects provide essential development support in places like Cambodia, Laos, and Myanmar. For many ASEAN countries, economic dependence on China is an inescapable reality, one that ties their economic futures to Beijing's continued prosperity.

13 S.A. Smith, *How Japan Is Doubling Down on Its Military Power* (20.12.2022), "Council on Foreign Relations": https://www.cfr.org/article/how-japan-doubling-down-its-military-power.

14 G.B. Poling, *The Transformation of the U.S.-Philippines Alliance* (02.02.2023), "Center for Strategic & International Studies": https://www.csis.org/analysis/transformation-us-philippines-alliance.

15 J. Guild, *The Philippines' $35 Billion Military Modernization Plan, Explained* (17.05.2024), "The Diplomat": https://thediplomat.com/2024/05/the-philippines-35-billion-military-modernization-plan-explained/.

Yet, ASEAN nations are also wary of China's assertiveness, particularly in the South China Sea, where several members have overlapping claims with Beijing. To counterbalance China's influence, ASEAN countries have deepened security cooperation with the United States and other Quad nations, participating in joint training exercises, maritime patrols, and even signing defense agreements. This strategy allows them to bolster their security without directly antagonizing China, maintaining a stance that's collaborative but cautious. For ASEAN, the challenge is clear: engage with China economically but avoid getting drawn into its sphere of influence. The balance they seek is one of neutrality backed by security partnerships that ensure they don't have to face any regional threats alone.

Each of these Indo-Pacific powers tries to employ dual strategies tailored to its unique geopolitical challenges. For the United States, Japan, the Philippines, and the ASEAN nations, the balance between competition and readiness isn't a one-size-fits-all solution. It's a constantly shifting equation, adjusted by the realities on the ground and the pressures of a region where influence is hard-won, and readiness is the ultimate backstop.

VIII. The Role of Emerging Technologies in Competition and Readiness

Emerging and disruptive technology is reshaping both competition and readiness in the Indo-Pacific. Cyber capabilities, AI, and dual-use technologies aren't just tools; they're strategic assets that amplify influence and defense alike.

Cyber and Information Warfare

Cyber operations have become core to Indo-Pacific competition. Beyond defending networks, cyber capabilities are wielded to project influence and destabilize adversaries without a shot fired. China, for instance, uses cyber campaigns to manipulate media, erode trust in institutions, and weaken alliances. For the U.S. and allies, robust cyber defenses are crucial to safeguard critical infrastructure, ensuring readiness even amidst cyber offensives.[16]

AI and Autonomous Systems

AI is a game-changer, enhancing both intelligence gathering and real-time responsiveness. AI-driven systems – from autonomous drones to decision-making algorithms – allow faster and more precise actions in both competition and conflict. For the U.S. and its partners, AI ensures agility and speed in a high-stakes region where every second counts.

16 V. Atkins, *To Combat Chinese Cyber Threats, the US Must Spearhead a New Indo-Pacific Intelligence Coalition* (27.02.2024), "Atlantic Council": https://www.atlanticcouncil.org/blogs/new-atlanticist/to-combat-chinese-cyber-threats-the-us-must-spearhead-a-new-indo-pacific-intelligence-coalition/.

Dual-Use Technologies

Dual-use tech, like space assets and 5G, blurs the line between civilian and military applications. These systems enhance economic growth and military capability simultaneously. Secure 5G networks, for example, support digital infrastructure while protecting against espionage, strengthening both economic and security postures. But they can also have large threat surfaces.[17]

In the Indo-Pacific, emerging technologies aren't optional; they're essential. Mastering these tools defines a nation's ability to influence, deter, and defend, marking the line between security and vulnerability in this evolving landscape.

IX. Strategic Implications for Future Conflict Scenarios

Balancing competition and readiness pose unique challenges as tensions rise in the Indo-Pacific. A Convergent Strategy shapes how nations respond to crises, manage alliances, and navigate potential escalation, with each signal carrying significant weight.

Crisis Response under Dual Strategy Constraints

The Convergent Strategy approach can enhance crisis response by maintaining forward presence and reinforced alliances, but it also risks stretching resources thin. When U.S. forces are committed to signaling strength, redeploying them swiftly in a crisis becomes challenging. Allies like Japan and Australia, while supportive in principle, may hesitate if they perceive the U.S. focus as more symbolic than prepared. A Convergent Strategy requires every deployment and decision to balance immediate action with sustained alliance trust and force readiness.

Potential Escalation Paths

A finely tuned Convergent Strategy can deter adversaries and reassure allies, but misaligned or overly aggressive signals risk escalation. Actions intended to deter could be misinterpreted as preparatory moves for conflict, triggering a preemptive response. Similarly, allies concerned about overstretched U.S. capabilities may act unilaterally, complicating coordination. Here, the Convergent Strategy can either prevent or inadvertently spark escalation, depending on how actions are perceived across the region.

Scenarios of Miscalculation

The Indo-Pacific's high-stakes environment amplifies the risk of miscalculation. Signals meant as competitive posturing can easily be misread as conflict

17 N. Berman, L. Maizland, and A. Chatzky, *Is China's Huawei a Threat to U.S. National Security?* (08.02.2023), "Council on Foreign Relations": https://www.cfr.org/backgrounder/chinas-huawei-threat-us-national-security.

preparations. A routine exercise or diplomatic visit near contested areas could be viewed as provocative, sparking unintended escalation. For example, a U.S. show of support near disputed waters could prompt China to mobilize, creating a cycle of escalation neither intended. This constant risk underscores the need for calibrated actions, recognizing that the same signals meant to stabilize could inadvertently ignite conflict.

In a region where the line between competition and conflict is thin, each strategic move must be carefully measured. The Convergent Strategy of influence and readiness can keep the peace, but only if the signals it sends are clear and consistent, avoiding the very misjudgments it seeks to prevent.

X. Policy Recommendations for Implementing a Convergent Strategy

A Convergent Strategy in the Indo-Pacific requires a unified approach that integrates diplomatic, economic, and military efforts to enhance both influence and readiness. By aligning these elements, policymakers can maximize impact, prevent resource strain, and strengthen regional stability. The following recommendations provide concrete actions for operationalizing this strategy.

1. Synchronize Diplomatic, Economic, and Military Goals

- Prioritize Dual-Use Infrastructure Projects: When selecting international development projects, prioritize investments that serve both economic and security purposes. For example, funding port and airfield upgrades in partner countries can enhance regional trade and simultaneously support military logistics in a crisis.
- Design Integrated Initiatives: Ensure that each diplomatic mission, trade agreement, or development initiative reinforces security goals. For instance, agreements with nations like the Philippines and Vietnam should incorporate provisions for joint exercises, access to bases, or logistical support in exchange for economic or development aid.
- Measure Return on Investment (ROI) in Both Influence and Readiness: Establish metrics that assess both the soft power benefits and defense implications of economic and diplomatic initiatives. By evaluating projects based on their contributions to influence and operational readiness, decision-makers can better allocate resources.

2. Create Joint Interagency Task Forces for Convergent Strategy Oversight

- Form Dedicated Task Forces: Establish interagency task forces specifically tasked with overseeing the Convergent Strategy's implementation, ensuring that diplomatic, economic, and defense actions support one another. These teams should meet regularly to align objectives and identify any gaps in influence-readiness integration.

- Embed Defense Representatives in Economic and Diplomatic Planning: Include defense experts in economic and diplomatic planning sessions to advise on projects that have strategic military value, ensuring alignment across initiatives.
- Institutionalize Cross-Agency Communication Channels: Develop secure, cross-agency communication channels that facilitate real-time information sharing and coordination on Indo-Pacific initiatives. This ensures that diplomatic and economic engagements are informed by defense priorities and vice versa.

3. Enhance Regional Cooperation and Transparent Engagements

- Establish Regional Intelligence-Sharing Networks: Strengthen regional stability by expanding intelligence-sharing networks with allies and partners, focusing on maritime security, cyber threats, and hybrid warfare. These networks can support a unified response to threats and reduce the risk of miscalculations in contested areas.
- Conduct Routine, Small-Scale Exercises: Implement a schedule of frequent, lower-profile joint exercises with allies to build operational familiarity without the resource strain of large-scale drills. These exercises maintain readiness and send a continuous signal of commitment without overextending assets.
- Use Confidence-Building Measures to Mitigate Escalation Risks: Develop clear protocols with allies and regional actors on responses to incidents in disputed areas. Confidence-building measures, like hotlines or joint monitoring agreements, can help prevent unintended escalations by fostering transparency.

4. Institutionalize Rapid Innovation to Stay Ahead of Emerging Threats

- Invest in Rapid Innovation Teams: Establish specialized teams focused on fast-tracking the development and deployment of technologies that serve both competitive and readiness goals, such as cybersecurity tools, autonomous reconnaissance drones, and AI-driven analysis platforms.
- Conduct Regular Scenario-Based Wargames: Implement wargaming exercises that simulate the latest threat scenarios, from cyber incursions to hybrid warfare tactics, allowing policymakers to test and refine the Convergent Strategy under realistic conditions. These wargames should directly inform adjustments in resource allocation and operational tactics.
- Develop a Strategic Reserve of Emerging Technologies: Create a reserve fund specifically for rapidly implementing emerging technologies that bolster both influence and readiness. This allows policymakers to quickly adapt to sudden changes in the regional security landscape without waiting for budget cycles.

5. Establish Clear, Measurable Success Criteria for Convergent Strategy

- Set Benchmarks for Influence and Readiness: Define specific, quantifiable targets for both influence-building (e.g., number of trade agreements, diplomatic missions) and readiness (e.g., response times, allied interoperability) to evaluate the Convergent Strategy's effectiveness.

- Conduct Quarterly Reviews: Perform quarterly reviews to assess progress against these benchmarks, adjusting the approach based on recent developments and emerging threats in the Indo-Pacific.
- Incorporate Feedback Loops: Solicit regular feedback from allies, regional partners, and interagency teams to ensure that the Convergent Strategy remains responsive and relevant to evolving dynamics. Continuous feedback will help policymakers course-correct and optimize the strategy.

5. Conclusion: The Strategic Imperative of Convergent Balance

The Indo-Pacific is a critical arena where competition and readiness collide, demanding a strategy that deftly balances influence with preparedness. This chapter has highlighted the importance of a Convergent Strategy, integrating alliance-building, economic engagement, and military capability to counter adversarial ambitions while ensuring rapid response and resilience. For the United States and its allies, mastering this balance is essential for navigating the complexities of this volatile region.

The stakes go beyond immediate gains. A strategy that leans too heavily on competition risks escalation and resource strain, while an overemphasis on readiness forfeits opportunities for enduring influence. To secure a stable and favorable Indo-Pacific, policymakers must commit to a strategy that weaves together both elements – each reinforcing the other, creating a robust and adaptive foundation for long-term peace and influence.

The call to action is clear and urgent: policymakers, military leaders, and diplomatic actors of the U.S. and its allies in the Indo-Pacific must embrace a Convergent Strategy. This requires breaking down silos across diplomatic, economic, and military realms, fostering interagency coordination to ensure that every act of influence is backed by credible defense. It means building transparency and cooperation mechanisms to reduce miscalculation risks and embracing emerging technologies that empower both competition and deterrence. Above all, it requires a mindset shift, recognizing that competition and readiness are not separate forces but complementary tools that, when aligned, provide unparalleled strategic depth.

In the Indo-Pacific, the margin for error is slim, and the repercussions of missteps are profound. A Convergent Strategy is not just a choice – it is an imperative. This approach enables the U.S. and its allies to project strength wisely, cultivate alliances without fostering dependency, and prepare as rigorously for peace as for potential conflict. The time to act is now; the choices made today will define the regional order and global stability for generations to come.

4 Why is Framing Partnership Crucial for Addressing Food and Water Security Challenges in the Pacific? A Perspective Beyond Knowledge Transfer on Water Operator Partnerships

*Helen Barbosa**

1. Introduction

In this chapter, the Pacific region is referred to as Pacific Island Countries (PICs). It is well known that PICs face a unique set of challenges when it comes to ensuring food and water security. These countries are particularly vulnerable to the effects of climate change, resource depletion, and population growth.[1] The Pacific region's diverse biophysical condition such as climate and geography pose a great challenge to the water and food sector, significantly impacting the overall economic development. Public water utilities have historically been the entity responsible for the provision of water supply sought to respond to diverse development sectors. But public water utilities in the developing countries have always been characterised [by] "low rates of cost recovery, low productivity, and ultimately low service quality and coverage".[2] What aggravates water utility performance specifically in the Pacific is the highly diverse biophysical conditions characterised by the small size of most nations, combined with remote or isolated communities spread over vast distances increasing costs and creating obstacles for the reliable and affordable transportation of goods, delivery of services, and market access.[3] These elements impact the water sector, pose a great challenge to food security, and threaten water security. Specifically, over the last decade, Fiji has been experiencing some major

* PhD Candidate, Water Management and Governance, Södertörn University, Sweden

1 T. Regina Souter et al., Strengthening rural community water safety planning in Pacific Island countries: Evidence and lessons from Solomon Islands, Vanuatu, and Fiji, *Journal of Water and Health*, 2024, 22(3), 467–486.

2 See S. Spronk, Water and sanitation utilities in the global South: Re-centering the debate on efficiency, *Review of Radical Political Economics*, 2010, 42(2), 157.

3 W. Helen, Demography, migration and conflict in the Pacific, *Journal of Peace Research*, 2005, 42(4), 435–454. See also, new published book A. Dansie et al., *The Water, Energy, and Food Security Nexus in Asia and the Pacific*, United Nations Educational, Scientific and Cultural Organization, UNESCO, 2024, https://link.springer.com/book/10.1007/978-3-031-25463-5, where water security, on water, food and energy nexus being aggravated due to the geographical and natural characteristics.

DOI: 10.4324/9781003545750-5

climatic events that have either disrupted provision of service or completely damaged water and wastewater assets. These events often cause wastewater overflow into the local agricultural lands and fauna and pose a health hazard for the surrounding communities. The cost of a quick fix and permanent solution ran into the millions.[4]

The responsibility for water provision has gradually shifted from being solely government-run to incorporating various forms of partnerships. However, adhering to partnership agreements has several practical implications. First of all, the implications extend beyond mere financial obligations. Second, the partnership often entails a complex reconfiguration of power dynamics and knowledge interaction processes. Third, if the partnership is not structured with a strong emphasis on inclusive knowledge exchange, local staff are relegated to passive roles, existing expertise is undervalued, and their input is overlooked both within and outside the utility context.

2. Partnerships to Achieve Sustainable Development Goals

The recent progress report by UN-Water[5] highlights that the global target of 6.5 to implement integrated water resources management at all levels (100%), including through transboundary cooperation, is inappropriate. The report says that the implementation level is lower and emphasises that efforts need to be doubled. Amidst biophysical limitation and the pressure to achieve the SDG targets, the regions only see themselves relying heavily on aid and external actors.[6]

To address the dismal performance of public water utilities,[7] many developing countries began to adhere to the concept of partnerships in their diverse forms. Among other forms, Public Private Partnership (PPP) is prominent within Water Utilities, which has increasingly received widespread support across the political spectrum including policy makers, officials, and local communities.[8] However,

4 See the more updated annual report from the Water Authority of Fiji, 2017. The report emphasises the complexities around water supply system and distribution and the urgency for external partners to intervene.

5 United Nations Educational, Scientific and Cultural Organization, *The United Nations World Water Development Report: Valuing Water*, UNESCO, 2021, https://unesdoc.unesco.org/ark:/48223/pf0000375724. The report identified partnerships as essential for accelerating progress in water for all.

6 D. M. Taylor & S. Middleby, Aid is not development: The true character of Pacific aid, *Development Policy Review*, 2023, 41(S2), e12745, https://doi.org/10.1111/dpr.12745.

7 M. Rusca & K. Schwartz, The paradox of cost recovery in heterogeneous municipal water supply systems: Ensuring inclusiveness or exacerbating inequalities? *Habitat International*, 2018, 73, 101–108, https://doi.org/10.1016/j.habitatint.2017.03.002.

8 See G. P. Coppel & K. Schwartz, Water operator partnerships as a model to achieve the millennium development goals for water supply? Lessons from four cities in Mozambique, *Water SA*, 2011, 37(4), 575–584; R. W. McQuaid, The theory of partnership: Why have partnerships? in: *Public-Private Partnerships: Theory and Practice in International Perspective*, Routledge, 2000, pp. 27–53. These authors are critical on the role of partnership and for what it serves.

PPP has been disappointing due to persisting incoherence between social goals to achieve water for all and the utility financial goals.[9] As a response to this (quasi) irreconcilable goal, one of the increasing forms of partnership that has been promoted across the world is Water Operator Partnership (WOP) for its non-profit and mentorship character.[10]

While WOPs and other forms of partnership have been advocated by organisations like the International Water Association and UN-HABITAT, useful for countries that are off track with Sustainable Development Goals 6 targets, many questions around partnership dimensions and how it is framed in a context of power play remain in debate. This is especially relevant when the receiver is in a lower power capacity and often "desperate" to start the collaboration.

While partnerships are associated with many positive languages such as trust and win-win, scholars began to challenge the term "partnership".[11] Atkinson argues that these terms are not neutral but are constructs of power and examines their meaning within official discourse in shaping a particular result. In joining a partnership agreement, it is critical whether knowledge is transferred or translated into the reality.[12] These are a few examples of literature that understand that while partnership might be beneficial, it can also obscure more complex realities and power dynamics. As put by Pollit and Hupe and referred to as a magic concept,[13] terms such as partnership are often attractive and serve to dilute potential trade-offs and concerns with power dynamic and structure. In this vein, the central questions of this chapter are: Why is a framing partnership crucial? And what are the practice of WOPs for water supply and security?

To address these questions, I draw from the practical experience of working with water utilities either in a position of the recipient, or facilitating the development of partnership and networks in the SIDS region. During this period, I had the chance to discuss with key WOP recipients and implementors (e.g., in Malawi). In addition to my personal experience, I interviewed key water utility staff of the Fiji

9 See A. S. Boakye-Ansah, Unravelling pro-poor water services: What does it mean and why is it so popular? *Journal of Water, Sanitation and Hygiene for Development*, 2019, 9(2), 187–197.

10 See S. Pascual et al., What counts as 'results' in capacity development partnerships between water operators? A multi-path approach toward accountability, adaptation and learning, *Water Policy*, 2013, 15(S2), 242–266.

11 See R. Atkinson, Discourses of partnership and empowerment in contemporary British urban regeneration, *Urban Studies*, 1999, 36(1), 59–72; H. Johnson & G. Wilson, North-South/South-North partnerships: Closing the 'mutuality gap', *Public Administration and Development*, 2006, 26(1), 71–80; D. Robinson, T. Hewitt, & J. Harriss, Why inter-organisational relationships matter, in: *Managing Development: Understanding Inter-Organizational Relationships*, London: Sage, 2000. These authors highlight that "partnership" can often obscure the true complexity of relationships, where power, interests, and resources are distributed unequally and vary significantly in their organisation. As such, it needs to be critically examined.

12 F. Mukhtarov, Rethinking the travel of ideas: Policy translation in the water sector, *Policy & Politics*, 2014, 42(1), 71–88.

13 C. Pollitt & P. Hupe, Talking about government: The role of magic concepts, *Public Management Review*, 2011, 13(5), 641–658.

Water Utility. The interviews were carried out in the period between May 2024 to October 2024. This example brings practical experience of how WOP manifested in practice with the water utility staff in Fiji.

3. The Surge of Interest in Partnerships

The public-private partnerships (PPPs) in the water sector start to gain prominence from the 1980s and 1990s, championed by international development banks, bilateral donors, and water sector professionals advocating for increased private sector involvement in water service provision. This has gained importance, both in developed as well as in developing countries.[14] But more emphasis has been placed on developing countries to catch up with development goals. Often, we see Western organisations such as Partners for Water (The Netherlands) or The Netherlands Enterprise Agency (RVO), through different models of partnership such public-private partnership (PPP) or Water Operator Partnership (WOP) playing in this space. The involvement of external partners was expected to bring efficiency gains, depoliticise the water sector, and attract investment.[15] Although it has multiple definitions, partnership is often defined as an agreement between two or more partners/actors to share knowledge, skills, and responsibilities in order to achieve, through synergy, a common objective, a better position, and/or economies of scale. It is argued that partnership is a positive feature that is based on ideas of dialogue, reciprocity, trust, equality, and sharing different values, knowledges, and practices to realise mutually beneficial processes and outcomes.[16] These partnerships operate in similar ways and share the same goals, involving different types of partners. Partnerships offer a range of setups that are different from services provided solely by government agencies, completely privatised services, or community-based services. The idea is that these partnerships, which can include the government, private sector, and sometimes the community, are better suited to handle the complicated challenges (developing) countries face in providing water services.

4. Involvement of Public-Private Partnership in the Water Sector for Water Security

Despite the ongoing controversy around the practical challenges that lie in private sector involvement[17] (e.g., power dynamics, accountability, and social impacts),

14 G. Teisman & E. Klijn, Partnership arrangements: Governmental rhetoric or governance scheme? *Public Administration Review*, 2003, 62(2), 197–205; C. Kelly, Measuring the performance of partnerships: Why, what, how, when? *Geography Compass*, 2012, 6(3), 149–162.

15 See S. Graas, J. Bos, A. Figueres, & T. Adegoke, *Partnerships in the Water and Sanitation Sector*, International Water and Sanitation Centre, 2007.

16 B. E. Evans, J. McMahon, & K. Caplan, *The Partnership Paperchase: Structuring Partnership Agreements in Water and Sanitation in Low-income Communities*, 2005, https://eprints.whiterose.ac.uk/42857/.

17 D. Hall & E. Lobina, Public sector alternatives to water supply and sewerage privatization: Case studies, *International Journal of Water Resources Development*, 2000, 16(1), 35–55.

the concept of partnership has been consistently associated largely with positive outcomes. The term "partnership" has two interesting features that highlight the importance of words and discourses around it. First, it stresses that private sector involvement does not exclude the public sector or consumers from involvement in the water services sector. Even if private sector involvement is increased, roles and responsibilities of public and community organisations remain equal. Secondly, the term represents a more acceptable and friendly term than blunt "privatization" promoting trust between parts.[18] Despite initial optimism, the implementation of public-private partnership (PPPs) remains debatable. In practice these complementary roles are challenged by diverse socio-politico elements. As such, in recent years, enthusiasm for private sector involvement in the water supply and sanitation sector has declined due to unresolved conflicts between social and financial objectives, marking a shift away from the once heavily promoted model.

5. The Time for Water Operator Partnership

The development of Water Operator Partnerships (WOP) stages and practice framework draws upon several theoretical streams, integrating insights from capacity development,[19] organisational change,[20] organisational development,[21] knowledge transfer,[22] and partnership theory.[23] These theoretical foundations provide a comprehensive approach to understanding and implementing effective partnerships. While these are rich literature, few literatures explicitly analyse WOP in the Pacific on how they manifest in practice. There are Pascual Sanz et al. 2013, which analysed the case of capacity development partnerships in Malawi using Vitens Evides International. Also, another case is the analysis of WOP as potential model that can be scaled up (Coppel and Schwartz, 2011). These literatures are sceptical about the way WOP success is measured and sustained. The authors observed that besides the practical constraints that the interventions face, it also requires significant time and both sides' engagement to actually address to the goals of water operator performance gains as the partnership's agreement are short-term. Although these are important points, WOP continues to be practiced.[24] It presents

18 R. Franceys, GATS, 'privatization' and institutional development for urban water provision: Future postponed? *Progress in Development Studies*, 2008, 8(1), 45–58.

19 G. Alaerts & J. M. Kaspersma, Progress and challenges in knowledge and capacity development, *Capacity Development for Improved Water Management*, 2009, 3(2009), 3–30.

20 J. B. Cullen, J. L. Johnson, & T. Sakano, Success through commitment and trust: The soft side of strategic alliance management, *Journal of World Business*, 2000, 35(3), 223–240.

21 D. Waddell, A. Creed, T. G. Cummings, & C. G. Worley, *Organisational Change: Development and Transformation*, Cengage AU, 2019.

22 S. L. Hoe, Tacit knowledge, Nonaka and Takeuchi SECI model and informal knowledge processes, *International Journal of Organization Theory & Behavior*, 2006, 9(4), 490–502.

23 R. W. McQuaid, The theory of partnership: Why have partnerships? in: *Public-Private Partnerships: Theory and Practice in International Perspective*, Routledge, 2000, pp. 27–53.

24 After the 2006 Hashimoto Action Plan, WOP was recommended as a beneficial mechanism to enhance global efforts in achieving the Millennium Development Goal targets for water and sanitation.

a more nuanced alternative to the blunt terms "privatisation" and "public-private partnership". Essentially, WOP are non-profit collaborations between two or more water and/or sanitation operators, aimed at enhancing their capacity to sustainably deliver quality services to all. In this framework there is a mentor and a mentee. Mentor typically refers to an organisation or individual that are professionally more experienced in the field of water resources management and governance. Mentees, in the other hand, are less experienced water utility organisations or individuals receiving the capacity building programs from mentors.[25]

A number of features makes WOP attractive.

- Mostly funded through grants and decentralised cooperation and development funding mechanisms;
- In-kind contribution from partners;
- The partnership is mostly regulated through light contractual forms – agreements;
- Relational and long-term instead of short-term and ad hoc;
- Developing the capacity of local staff to improve performance, not doing it for them, with emphasis on learning for improved performance;
- Inducing lasting change that takes into account social, environmental, and financial considerations;
- Partnerships take place between peer service providers, be they operators, utilities, or municipal departments;
- WOPs are not to be used for money-making purposes. The costs of WOPs that need to be recovered should be done so on a cost-recovery basis only.

6. Example of WOP in Practice

Based on my experiences on partnership implementation in developing countries (Cabo Verde and Malawi), it is often highlighted by the operational working staff that partnerships built are merely a form to check the formal boxes of the international organisation's agendas. It is often mentioned that there are few rooms to actually bring real concerns and needs as the implementers have already prescribed forms for which ways the program will be applied. This means that the implementors have upfront the working tools (e.g. leak detector, software programs such as QGIS, SCADA, Primavera, and working routines to be used at the utility). Often, after project completion, the company has no intention or financial capacity to keep up with the internal training, working routine, or the software licenses. Due to this inconsistency, the working staff goes back to their working culture – minimum digitalisation or operating on minimum requirements due to a shortage of resources.

25 See https://gwopa.org/ for more descriptions and Mentor/Mentees activities.

6.1 The Case Water Utility of Fiji and WOP

In 2017, a training programme framed within WOP took place. It was facilitated by Sydney Water and Climate Risk under the framework of Climate Change Adaptation sponsored by the Asian Development Bank (ADB). It was a three-week programme over 12 months. The first master class training was carried out in Sydney, Australia, in February 2017 while the second master class training was held in Fiji in June 2017, and the final Master Class Training in October 2017. In 2023, another experience related to WOP happened between water utilities in Fiji and Japan. The WOP was in the form of technical training for maintenance works. The capacity developments and trainings were targeted to middle-level management. A more recent WOP was done between Pacific islands led by Water Utility of Fiji. Water Utility of Fiji is the mentor in the Pacific region, as it is considered a reference point in managing their water supply. When it partners with overseas organisations like SUEZ, it takes on the role of a mentee.

From these experiences, it was highlighted by the utility staffs that the exchange facilitated by WOP activities inspires actions to establish working automatisation, new water infrastructures, and management plans. One practical example is the elaboration of a catchment management plan that was never done before at the Water Utility of Fiji. However, a number of aspects highlighted by them suggest the deviations between how WOP is framed with how it practically manifested.

First, the often-encompassing goals of WOP have a relatively short term to actually be operationalised in practice. The capacity development, which is often the focus, in reality needs more time to be done and followed up over time. In reality, after the capacity building activity ends, there is no accountability for those who took the training whether it is being practiced or not. As put by the stakeholder engagement leader, "there was training to develop climate change adaption plan. A draft was compiled in 2018–2019 . . . but after seven years, the utility still does not have an approved and practical climate change adaptation plan".[26] Also, many times the advanced technologies suggested by mentors are not financially attainable. As expressed by the engagement expert, "all that happened, the staff are impressed by advanced technologies, and they return to tell the tale and over time it is forgotten".

Second, WOPs largely serve to showcase best practices. In showcasing best practices, many daily working challenges are hidden, not aligning with the Pacific islands water utilities problems. This point is explained by the stakeholder expert, demonstrating that often Water Utility of Fiji hosts learning training for other Pacific islands: "we hosted Vanuatu and Salomon Island to learn from our utility, but we are the one proposing learning goals". The person continues, "the learning expeditions are programmed to show the 'glittering' aspects of the utility rather than the 'dirt' or the reality on the ground". Many capacity development activities

26 Interview by the author, Engagement stakeholder leader October 2024.

that happen between Pacific islands water utilities or capacity building between Pacific islands with overseeing (e.g. New Caledonia) are not aligned with the daily problem of operating water utilities. As put by the operational staff, "the contract is often done within high-level management that that are not aware of the real problems or don't want to actually tell the real situation".[27] This happens because the same people are participating, excluding the lower level of working staff (plumbers, maintenance team, etc.). Participants are engineers or members of high-level management. According to those responsible for leading the learning process between parties, the exclusion of lower-level working staff in the process of WOP leads to a disconnect to the everyday operational working issues of the utilities. The training is supposed to be passed on to operational staff, but in practice it rarely happens. When it happens, the presentation is limited. As put by the individual responsible for the learning, "often there is a training of one week or one month, but the presentation takes 40 minutes to end".[28] Internally, the utility conducts a consultation process with the lower-level working staff to get the priorities and insights from the ground. However, the priorities list does not reflect on the strategic planning or to the capacity building agenda.[29] In complementing this point, the water governance expert adds, "the operational staff that actually knows what the needs are kept out of these conversations".

Third, the different understanding and perceptions of what WOP means differs according to the working field and perhaps depending on the situatedness knowledge and worldviews of each member staff. For example, it was expressed by one interviewee that "they come to earn money which could be done by nationals".[30] This highlights the notion that WOP is for the profit base while it is framed as based on recovery cost of the water utility.

7. Analysis and Conclusion

What is the Problem with WOP in Practice?

The natural fragilities of small islands have put PICs in the spotlight for aid, partnerships to advance SDG 6 (access to water for all), and climate-related issues. Although WOP is deemed to be based on ideas of dialogue, reciprocity, trust, equality, and sharing different values, knowledges, and practices to realise mutually beneficial processes and outcomes, in practice, there are experiences of unequal recognition of knowledge and power dynamic. This unequal relation is often tied back to the type of status/influence each mentor or mentee has in shaping the technology or governance expertise.

Rarely do the mentees question how that particular partnership is to manifest in practice. Or how parties are situated in the process, what can be shared and

27 Interview made by the author to operational worker July 2024, online.
28 Interview made by the author, water governance expert 2024, online.
29 Interview made by the author, water utility staff 2024, online.
30 Interview made by the author to GIS officer 13 July 2024, online.

what cannot, how discussions take shape, and who is included or excluded from decision-making venues and processes.[31] On the one hand, the mentees who are expectant of improving the actual situation to a better state are less concerned with differences, the role that partnership can play in the capacity building process, or a realistic assessment of the strengths and limitations of the particular approach. Who would deny a partnership or a capacity training that is portrayed as win-win?

A critique of the WOP begins by challenging the idealistic assumption that partners within a partnership inherently play complementary roles, a notion often based on the belief that differences between partners serve as a foundational rationale for their collaboration. However, such idealised "definitions" are recognised as exercises in power. Based on experiences with capacity building through WOP, it suggests that the process often perpetuates and reinforces existing inequalities within water utilities by determining who is deemed eligible to participate in such training. Middle-level management consistently participates, while lower-level staff are frequently excluded. The principles of WOP often disguise underlying power imbalances and exclusionary practices. Furthermore, this case underscores the highly unequal power dynamics involved in capacity building and training, where mentors hold significant influence over the learning goals of mentees, shaping both the methods and the outcomes. This inherent inequality is deemed crucial to be interrogated. It is imperative to scrutinise what the term "capacity building" in the context of WOP truly signifies and how it materialises in practice, especially in light of the existing practice of partnership. As aptly observed,[32] "the language of partnership often masks a complex reality, which is that relationships take many different forms, and that these vary widely in terms of the ways in which power, interests, substance . . . are organised".

As recently emphasised in a thought-provoking article, there is a need to look at the importance of partnership that goes beyond the plain contractual agreements that takes place in the context of aid/capacity building in the Pacific region. It highlights the need for genuine collaboration and meaningful engagement between donors, intermediaries, and Pacific recipients to ensure that all the efforts are effective and responsive to actual needs, rather than solely checkbox activities of involved parties.

Strategic Design of Partnership Beyond Knowledge Transfer

While WOPs have been widely implemented across developing countries to improve the water sector, both their strategic design and practical implementation remain questionable. Experiences reveal a significant gap between WOP theory and practice, with the conceptual model often being attractive in theory but one-directional in reality. Knowledge is frequently transferred rather than translated into the local

31 F. Mukhtarov, Reflexivity, positionality and normativity in the ethnography of policy translation, in: *World Politics in Translation*, Routledge, 2017, p. 18.

32 D. Robinson, T. Hewitt, & J. Harriss, Why inter-organisational relationships matter, in: *Managing Development: Understanding Inter-Organizational Relationships*, London: Sage, 2000, p. 13.

context, and the fit of development of skills, tools, and everyday management practices tends to play a secondary role in mentor and mentee engagement.

Practical examples demonstrate that the goals envisioned by WOPs are often unattainable, primarily due to limited timeframes and capacity-building efforts that focus narrowly on high-level management. This emphasis on completing planned activities within set deadlines undermines long-term assimilation and practical implementation of knowledge, highlighting the need for a more inclusive approach to capacity building.

A more effective strategic design for WOPs requires adopting a reflexive approach that recognises the knowledge interactions occurring in the everyday work of water utilities. This approach must consider the sociocultural and governance complexities of these environments and allow the necessary time for real change to take root. Crucially, it should engage operational staff to avoid one-sided knowledge transfer and encourage active participation across all levels.

References

Alaerts, G., & Kaspersma, J. M., Progress and challenges in knowledge and capacity development. *Capacity Development for Improved Water Management*, 2009, 3(2009), 3–30.

Atkinson, R., Discourses of partnership and empowerment in contemporary British urban regeneration. *Urban Studies*, 1999, 36(1), 59–72. https://doi.org/10.1080/0042098993736.

Cherlet, J., *Tracing the Emergence and Deployment of the "Integrated Water Resources Management" Paradigm*, 12th EASA Biennial Conference, Proceedings, 2012. http://hdl.handle.net/1854/LU-2964994.

Coppel, G. P., & Schwartz, K., Water operator partnerships as a model to achieve the millenium development goals for water supply? Lessons from four cities in Mozambique. *Water SA*, 2011, 37(4), Article 4. https://doi.org/10.4314/wsa.v37i4.17.

Cullen, J. B., Johnson, J. L., & Sakano, T., Success through commitment and trust: The soft side of strategic alliance management. *Journal of World Business*, 2000, 35(3), 223–240.

Dansie, A. et al., *The Water, Energy, and Food Security Nexus in Asia and the Pacific*. United Nations Educational, Scientific and Cultural Organization, UNESCO, 2024. https://link.springer.com/book/10.1007/978-3-031-25463-5.

Evans, B. E., McMahon, J., & Caplan, K., *The Partnership Paperchase: Structuring Partnership Agreements in Water and Sanitation in Low-Income Communities*, 2005. https://eprints.whiterose.ac.uk/42857/.

Franceys, R., GATS, 'Privatization' and institutional development for urban water provision: Future postponed? *Progress in Development Studies*, 2008, 8(1), 45–58.

Graas, S., Bos, J. J., Figueres, A., & Adegoke, T., *Partnerships in the Water and Sanitation Sector*. International Water and Sanitation Centre, 2007.

Harriss, J., Working together: The principles and practice of co-operation and partnership. In: D. Robinson, T. Hewitt, & J. Harriss (eds) *Managing Development: Understanding Inter-Organizational Relationships*. London: Sage Publications Ltd., 2000, pp. 225–242.

Hoe, S. L., Tacit knowledge, Nonaka and Takeuchi SECI model and informal knowledge processes. *International Journal of Organization Theory & Behavior*, 2006, 9(4), 490–502.

Johnson, H., & Wilson, G., North-South/South-North partnerships: Closing the 'mutuality gap'. *Public Administration and Development*, 2006, 26(1), 71–80.

Kelly, C., Measuring the performance of partnerships: Why, what, how, when? *Geography Compass*, 2012, 6(3), 149–162.

Lobina, E., & Hall, D., Public sector alternatives to water supply and sewerage privatization: Case studies. *International Journal of Water Resources Development*, 2006, 16(1), 35–55.

McQuaid, R. W., The theory of partnership: Why have partnerships? In: *Public-Private Partnerships: Theory and Practice in International Perspective*. Routledge, 2000, pp. 9–35.

Mukhtarov, F., Reflexivity, Positionality and Normativity in the Ethnography of Policy Translation. In: *World Politics in Translation*. Routledge, 2017.

Pascual Sanz, M. et al., What counts as 'results' in capacity development partnerships between water operators? A multi-path approach toward accountability, adaptation and learning. *Water Policy*, 2013, 15, 242–266.

Pollitt, C., & Hupe, P., Talking about government: The role of magic concepts. *Public Management Review*, 2011, 13(5), 641–658. https://doi.org/10.1080/14719037.2010.532963.

Rusca, M., & Schwartz, K., The paradox of cost recovery in heterogeneous municipal water supply systems: Ensuring inclusiveness or exacerbating inequalities? *Habitat International*, 2018, 73, 101–108. https://doi.org/10.1016/j.habitatint.2017.03.002.

Souter, R. T., Ruuska, D., Pene, S., Benjamin, C., Funubo, S., Beal, C. D., Sanderson, R., Batikawai, S., Ravai, A., Antoinette-Wickham, T., Rankin, T., Peter, L., Molitambe, H., Theophile, G., Shrestha, S., Kotra, K. K., Bugoro, H., Panda, N., Deo, V., & Love, M., Strengthening rural community water safety planning in Pacific Island countries: Evidence and lessons from Solomon Islands, Vanuatu, and Fiji. *Journal of Water and Health*, 2024, 22(3), 467–486. https://doi.org/10.2166/wh.2024.144.

Spronk, S., Water and sanitation utilities in the global South: Re-centering the debate on efficiency. *Review of Radical Political Economics*, 2010, 42(2), 156–174.

Taylor, D. M., & Middleby, S., Aid is not development: The true character of Pacific aid. *Development Policy Review*, 2023, 41(S2), e12745. https://doi.org/10.1111/dpr.12745.

Teisman, G., & Klijn, E., Partnership arrangements: Governmental rhetoric or governance scheme? *Public Administration Review*, 2003, 62(2), 197–205.

UN-Water, *Summary Progress Update 2021: SDG 6—Water and Sanitation for All*, 2021. https://www.unwater.org/sites/default/files/app/uploads/2021/12/SDG-6-Summary-Progress-Update-2021_Version-July-2021a.pdf.

Waddell, D., Creed, A., Cummings, T. G., & Worley, C. G., *Organisational Change: Development and Transformation*. Cengage AU, 2019.

WAF, *Water Authority of Fiji, Annual Report 2017*. https://www.parliament.gov.fj/wp-content/uploads/2022/06/19-Water-Authority-of-Fiji-2017-Annual-Report.pdf.

5 Cultural Dimensions of Oceania

Between the Past and Future, West and East

*Dariusz Zdziech**

1. Introduction

In the minds of the inhabitants of today's "Global North", mainly Europe, the Middle East and North America, since ancient times there have been attempts to scientifically prove the existence of the legendary *Terra Australis Incognita.*[1] Aristotle in the 4th century BC believed that the land masses in the northern hemisphere must be balanced by the masses of land in the southern hemisphere. Ptolemy thought similarly in the 2nd century AD, drawing the boundaries of the Indian Ocean. His scientific treatises were extremely important for later Byzantine, Western European and Islamic science.[2] In the Middle Ages, the traveler Marco Polo claimed to have seen Locac[3] (Southern Land) full of gold, unknown animals and idolaters. It was only the era of great geographical discoveries, the Portuguese expeditions to the Moluccas, the Spanish discoveries in Central America and especially the Magellan-Elcano expedition (1519–1522), that confirmed the Europeans' theories about the lands located in the Pacific Ocean. At that time, the countries of East and Southeast Asia had already had long-term contacts with the cultures of Oceania.[4]

* Institute of Cultural Studies and Journalism; Ignatianum University in Cracow, Poland

1 "The unknown land of the south" in Latin. Its existence was already suspected by Roman cartographers, such as Pomponius Mela, around 43 AD published the work *De situ orbis* (also called De Chorographia), and philosophers, like Marcus Tullius Cicero, in the book *Somnium Scipionis*, written in 52 AD, being the sixth book of the work *De res publica.*

2 Claudius Ptolemy (c. 100 – c. 170 AD) born in Egypt, of Greek origin, an astronomer, geographer, mathematician. Author of the eight-volume treatise *Geography*, containing all the knowledge of the world known in the 2nd century AD. Additionally, it contained 26 maps of the globe known at that time. J.L. Berggren, A. Jones, *Ptolemy's Geography: An Annotated Translation of the Theoretical Chapters*, Princeton University Press, 2000.

3 Locac (according to other scientists Lochac, or Locach) could be the areas of present-day Cambodia, Thailand, Indonesia or even Australia, yet is most likely the areas located far to the Southeast of China, P. Wheatley, Lochac Revisited (1969), *Oriens Extremus*, Volume 16, Issue 1, pp. 85–110.

4 This is not about Gavin Menzies' theory from the book *1421: The Year China Discovered America*, but about trade contacts between Asian merchants and the inhabitants of Micronesia and Melanesia. J.D. Conroy, Melanesia in the Trade of the Malay Archipelago, in: *Exchange and Markets in Early Economic Development: Informal Economy in the Three New Guineas*, New York, Oxford: Berghahn Books, 2023, pp. 26–33.

DOI: 10.4324/9781003545750-6

The theme of new lands to trade with greatly absorbed Dutch sailors and merchants who were exploring the waters around New Holland (present-day Australia), Staaten Landt (present-day New Zealand) and the huge island of New Guinea.[5] The following centuries observed the domination by French and British ships in the Indo-Pacific.[6] In the second half of the 18th century, James Cook, described by Charles Darwin as the man who added the hemisphere to European knowledge,[7] tried to define the last unexplored boundaries of the Pacific Ocean, in pursuit of the mythical *Terra Australis Incognita*. Unfortunately, his conclusions postponed for another half century the discovery of the last continent bordering the Pacific – Antarctica.[8]

The second half of the 19th century saw the increasingly bold entry of Germany, the United States and Japan into Oceania, particularly in the region of Micronesia. After World War I, Japan's influence in the region developed rapidly, although not as spectacularly as the United States, which in the 20th century expanded its network of influence over almost the entire Pacific Ocean, at the expense of European powers and Japan. Since the end of World War II, the strong US economy has provided the islands of Oceania with a relative sense of stability and security.[9]

The first part of the introduction to this chapter showed how the West came to know Oceania, but it was not the West but in fact the East that first colonized it, and its descendants created the cultures of Micronesia, Melanesia and Polynesia. Contrary to the theories of Thor Heyerdahl,[10] genetic studies of the inhabitants of Oceania clearly indicate that the ancestors of the current Pacific islanders came to these areas from Asia.[11] The first people arrived in New Guinea and Australia over 65,000 years ago, and according to current scientific knowledge, the settlement of Micronesia, by travelers coming from what is now Taiwan, Hong Kong and Southeast Asia, dates back only a few thousand years.[12] Various causes, including overpopulation, wars, diseases, but also those of plants and animals, tropical

5 J. Tenbruggencate, *Dutch Pacific Voyages of Discovery*, Bridge House Press, 2018.

6 J. Dunmore, *French Explorers in the Pacific, Vol. I: The Eighteenth Century*, Oxford: Oxford University Press, 1965; J. Dunmore, *French Explorers in the Pacific, Vol. 2: The Nineteenth Century*, Oxford: Oxford University Press, 1969.

7 C.R. Darwin, *Journal of Researches into the Natural History and Geology of the countries Visited During the Voyage of H.M.S. Beagle Round the World*, London, 1845, p. 501.

8 J. Cook, *A Voyage to the Pacific Ocean Undertaken, by the Command of His Majesty for Making Discoveries in the Northern Hemisphere*, London, 1784, vol. 1, p. XXVII.

9 J. Siekiera, The Role of the United States in the South Pacific at the Turn of the 20th and 21st Centuries (March 2020), *Journal of Oriental Scientific Research (JOSR)*, Volume 12, Issue 1, p. 26.

10 V. Melander, David's Weapon of Mass Destruction: The Reception of Thor Heyerdahl's 'Kon-Tiki Theory' (2019), *Bulletin of the History of Archaeology*, Volume 29, Issue 1, p. 6.

11 M. Kayser, et al., Melanesian and Asian Origins of Polynesians: mtDNA and Y Chromosome Gradients Across the Pacific (November 2006), *Molecular Biology and Evolution*, Volume 23, Issue 11, pp. 2234–2244; J.N. Wilford, Pacific Islanders' Ancestry Emerges in Genetic Study (18.01.2008), *The New York Times*.

12 B. Shaw, et al., Frontier Lapita Interaction with Resident Papuan Populations Set the Stage for Initial Peopling of the Pacific (2022), *Nature Ecology & Evolution*, Volume 6, pp. 802–812; D. Olivier, *Polynesia in Early Historic Times*, Honolulu: Bess Press, 2002.

cyclones, eruptions of numerous in the Pacific Ring of Fire volcanoes, but also related earthquakes and tsunamis, forced the people of Oceania to further explore the Pacific – eastwards, all the way to the Americas.[13]

2. Cultures of Oceania – Unity, Sharing, Cooperation, Integrating Processes

The lack of knowledge by former inhabitants of the "Global North" about the cultures of the Oceania region does not mean that, in those vast areas there were no valuable and wonderful cultures of people who had a completely different perspective on the world around them than Europeans and other Westerners. One of the most important differences in the perception of Oceania by the natives and the new colonizers was, and still is the ocean. For centuries, the water has been mainly an obstacle for people from the "Global North". Rivers, lakes, wetlands, seas, oceans were perceived as an obstacle that must be overcome on the way to another island, peninsula or continent. In addition, the water, in the form of seas and rivers, is most often the border separating one country from another, which is after all best seen on maps.

For the inhabitants of the Pacific, it is land (usually an island) that limits: the number of crops, the number of animals that can be fed, and consequently the number of people it can support. For the cultures of Oceania, water represents freedom, it is a highway to any other island and its specific resources. Naturally, you need to have knowledge of how to travel via water. Attention to one's own culture promotes maintenance and development of knowledge on how to effectively navigate usage of shades of blue, the temperature of sea currents, the movement of waves, knowledge of ornithology, but also astronomy. Knowledge, rooted in your own culture, must not be lost for any, even the most colorful culture from the East or the West. In the cultures of the Pacific, a lack of knowledge of where you come from, or where you sail from does not allow you to get anywhere, or even return home.[14]

The ocean enables discovery: new areas, new plants and animals that will help make life easier, safer and cheaper. This struggle with the power of the ocean while on a small boat motivates the creation of innovative construction solutions, using the forces of nature for our purposes, without harming our planet – known today as green technologies.[15]

13 L. Wade, Polynesians Steering by the Stars Met Native Americans Long Before Europeans Arrived (08.07.2020), *Science*, Volume 369; C. McFadden, et al., Temporal Trends in the Colonisation of the Pacific: Palaeodemographic Insights (2021), *Journal of World Prehistory*, Volume 34, pp. 47–73.

14 D. Lewis, *We, the Navigators: The Ancient Art of Landfinding in the Pacific* (Second Edition), Honolulu: University of Hawaii, 1994; K. Oatley, Pacific Arts of Navigation (1973), *Nature*, Volume 245, pp. 273–274; B. Finney, *Piailug Mau (1932–2010)*, Pacific Islander Biography, National Centre of Biography, Australian National University.

15 R. Taonui, Canoe Navigation – Waka –Canoes, in: *Te Ara – the Encyclopedia of New Zealand*: https://teara.govt.nz/en/canoe-navigation/page-1 (access 31.10.2024).

Access to water also ensures equality as everyone can enjoy it and swim in it, as well as look for food and transport cargo and people from one place to another. In Oceanic culture, catches were divided among all the inhabitants of the island, regardless of whether someone from their family could send their representative to fish. This is not about someone cheating someone and getting food without work. In the culture of Tuvalu, this is called *Falepili* (also written as *fale pili*), or taking care of neighbors, or those who came from another island, as if they were family.[16] Among the inhabitants of Oceania, the elderly who did not have children and could not send them to a specific task were not abandoned or left to their own devices. They contributed to the island community in a different way, with their knowledge, giving of their many years of experience, teaching the next generations. By focusing on what unites in this way, they achieve a strong and prosperous society.

Oceanic societies have a fractious relationship with world powers. There is a lack of respect from dominant world powers for cultures that originated hundreds of years ago in the Indo-Pacific region. In many cases the people of Oceania have left their beliefs, customs and philosophies behind because they are flawed according to world. Traditional culture has been replaced by those of arrivals from other parts of the world, despite also being flawed. Now they are realizing that not everything that is new, such as plastic, is a miracle of modern innovation.[17]

That said, what does connect the cultures of the East and West with Oceania is water. Water is life, both fresh water – needed for drinking and watering plants, and salt water – full of crustaceans, fish, seals and whales, whose meat, shells and bones have many uses in local cultures.[18]

The legal-political-societal fight to protect the Pacific, to solve the problem of its pollution, overfishing, etc. also unites the cultures of Oceania. Protection of the natural environment is an extremely important topic for the inhabitants of the islands of Oceania, and successful environmental protection is a high priority for the cultures of Melanesia, Micronesia and Polynesia. Respect for the land and the fight to improve the climate and above all, protection of the ocean, from plastic litter and overfishing, are priorities for the islanders of the Pacific.[19] The inhabitants of Oceania are fighting to improve the health of the ocean alongside large economies of the East and West and local organizations. They are promoting their own culture, knowledge and experience in protecting the ocean, going out into the

16 T. Kitara, T. Suliman, Fale Pili: A Tuvaluan Perspective on Mobility Justice (2024), *Applied Mobilities*, Volume 9, Issue 2–3; The Department of Foreign Affairs and Trade, *Australia-Tuvalu Falepili Union Factsheet*: https://www.dfat.gov.au/geo/tuvalu/australia-tuvalu-falepili-union (access 31.10.2024).

17 S. Freinkel, *Plastic: A Toxic Love Story*, Boston, New York: Houghton Mifflin Harcourt, 2011; D. Hohn, *Mobby Duck*, Penguin, 2012.

18 A.L. Kaeppler, *The Pacific Arts of Polynesia & Micronesia*, Oxford, New York: Oxford University Press, 2008.

19 S. Fleming, These Pacific Islands Have an Innovative Scheme to Prevent Overfishing in Their Waters (21.06.2021), *World Economic Forum*: https://www.weforum.org/agenda/2021/06/subsidized-fishing-man-made-tragedy/ (access 31.10.2024).

world, joining the voices of other small island communities of the world, within the Alliance of Small Island States (AOSIS), which was established in 1990. This organization, as stated on its official website, represents the interests of the 39 small island and low-lying coastal developing states in international climate change, sustainable development negotiations and processes. As a voice for the vulnerable, its mandate is amplifying marginalized voices and advocating for these countries' interests. AOSIS, like the countries it represents, is a relatively small organization that, on the global stage, often punches far above its weight, negotiating historic global commitments to cut greenhouse gas emissions, among other achievements.[20]

The influence of the Pacific people on this international organization is significant, as evidenced by the election of the Samoan representative as the current president of AOSIS.[21] The smallest countries are already leading the world in this matter, showing the largest economies their failings in caring for the environment. The cultures of Oceania greatly value water, and they express this by leading by example. For example, in 2009 Palau was the first country in the world to transform its exclusive economic zones (EEZ) into a Shark Sanctuary[22] and the Palau National Marine Sanctuary (PNMS).[23]

Similar decisions have been made by other countries in Oceania, showing that the smallest and the least wealthy are able to give something back to the Earth, while the wealthiest fight for every bit of land and sea.[24] Additionally, through the protection of the natural environment, voices from Pacific nations are entering the global debate, such as the Tanaloa Dialogue, which was organized by Fiji[25] during COP 23, or the cooperation between Australia and Tuvalu as part of the Falepili Union.[26]

20 Alliance of Small Island States, *About – Chair of AOSIS*: https://www.aosis.org/about/chair-of-aosis/ (access 31.10.2024).

21 Alliance of Small Island States, *About – Chair of AOSIS*: https://www.aosis.org/about/chair-of-aosis/ (access 31.10.2024).

22 Palau Soultrips, *World's First Shark Sanctuary*: https://palau.co/conservation-sustainability/world-s-first-shark-sanctuary/ (access 31.10.2024).

23 The Stanford Center for Ocean Solutions, *The Palau National Marine Sanctuary*: https://oceansolutions.stanford.edu/key-initiatives/sustainable-ocean-economies/palau-national-marine-sanctuary (access 31.10.2024).

24 J.M. Foster, Pacific Islands Band Together on a Shark Sanctuary (04.08.2011), *The New York Times*: https://archive.nytimes.com/green.blogs.nytimes.com/2011/08/04/pacific-islands-band-together-on-a-shark-sanctuary/ (access 31.10.2024).

25 United Nations Climate Change, *2018 Talanoa Dialogue Platform:* https://unfccc.int/process-and-meetings/the-paris-agreement/the-paris-agreement/2018-talanoa-dialogue-platform; Cities and regions in the UNFCCC Process, *Cities and Regions Talanoa Dialogues*: https://www.cities-and-regions.org/talanoa/ (access 31.10.2024).

26 T. Kitara, C. Farbotko, *Tuvalu, Australia, and the Falepili Union*, Australian Institute of International Affairs: https://www.internationalaffairs.org.au/australianoutlook/tuvalu-australia-and-the-falepili-union/; Prime Minister of Australia, *Entry into Force of Historic Australia-Tuvalu Falepili Union*, https://www.pm.gov.au/media/entry-force-historic-australia-tuvalu-falepili-union (access 31.10.2024).

Today, in Oceania, 19th-century nationalism is giving way to large international corporations, whose shareholders are rivals from the conservative East and the liberal West. Opportunities provided by stripping the ocean of fish and underwater mining are a great test for the people of Oceania. They must decide what is more important: quick money or the long-term protected environment in which they live. At the same time they must also decide if their children can continue to live and prosper in Oceana, or if they will be displaced by rising water levels, lack of food from the ocean, destruction of their lands by nuclear weapons tests (the example of the Bikini Atolls, Mururoa), extraction of raw materials on land (mostly in Nauru, Makatea, West Papua, Australia, New Caledonia, Bougainville). Or will their homes be underwater in the future, as the authorities of the Marshall Islands loudly declare:

> The world needs to ensure that the high seas seabed is not stripped of its unique biodiversity before we even document it. Without a clear-eyed scientific understanding of impacts and risks – the world's oceans are too fragile to turn into a speculative experiment. The Marshall Islands joins the growing chorus applying a precautionary approach towards high seas mining, at least until there is adequate and meaningful agreement at the International Seabed Authority on binding environmental measures and the mining code.[27]

In the introduction, it was mentioned that the ancestors of the inhabitants of Oceania came from the East. They gave rise to the cultures of Melanesia, Micronesia and Polynesia, which are widely spread across the Pacific. Currently, the people of these subregions recognize the political weakness of their microstates, but they are also aware of their cultural heritage. As a result, they are uniting forces to have a greater influence on the larger economies of the West and the East. This unity of Oceania's cultures did not suddenly resurface in the 20th century. It was and is still being built through various means, such as economy, sports, politics, culture, tradition, religion and even film. But this a recent phenomenon and until the end of World War II, the division of the Oceania islands between the greatest powers of the world at that time was clear.[28]

In the following years, worldwide decolonization movements awakened the national consciousness of the islanders. Two years after the end of the Pacific War, in 1947, Australia, France, the Netherlands, New Zealand, the USA and Great Britain established an organization in Canberra with the aim of promoting the

27 Pacific Islands Forum, *Remarks: RMI President Heine Delivers Statemen to UNGA79* (26.09.2024): https://forumsec.org/publications/remarks-rmi-president-heine-delivers-statemen-unga79 (access 31.10.2024).

28 F.J. West, S. Foster, *Pacific Islands Colonial Rule*, Encyclopedia Britannica, 09.09.2024; J. Fraenkel, Pacific Islands and New Zealand – Colonial Control in the Pacific, in: *Te Ara – the Encyclopedia of New Zealand*, https://teara.govt.nz/en/interactive/36846/colonial-control-in-the-pacific (access 31.10.2024); S.R. Fischer, *A History of the Pacific Islands*, New York: Palgrave, 2002.

economic and social welfare and advancement of the peoples in the region.[29] Its principals gave it the name *South Pacific Commission*, which was renamed Pacific Community in 1997, with the mission: "To advance all Pacific peoples' rights and well-being through science and knowledge, guided by our deep understanding of Blue Pacific contexts and cultures".[30]

A significant gesture by the founding states was the establishment of the headquarters of this organization in 1949 not in Canberra, Wellington or Sydney, but in the Melanesian Noumea, the main city of New Caledonia. Over the years, this organization has avoided participating in matters of politics, defense and security but has taken the lead for development aid, social and economic matters, including health and education. SPC, still used by some as its old acronym, has often been referred to as a non-political technical assistance agency. This basic assistance in various aspects of the lives of the inhabitants of Oceania allowed them to adapt more quickly to the global standards set by the "Global North".[31] Initially, the organization collected all materials relating to the cultures of Oceania on a large scale. According to the National Library of Australia, in 1951 the Research Council of the South Pacific Commission determined that the Commission should collect and copy manuscripts, dictionaries, textbooks and other linguistic material and place them in repositories in the metropolitan countries. The National Library was one of the nominated repositories, and it began receiving microfilms in 1953. The project lapsed in 1958.[32] Such projects brought together the people of Oceania through discovery of their forgotten history and culture. SPC subsequently became a place where new ideas for economic growth and cooperation among the people of Oceania flourished.

In this context, the importance of physical culture, especially sport, is often overlooked. Sport played an important part in the process of uniting the inhabitants of Oceania, thanks to the South Pacific Games (SPG), which brought together the region's population as an opportunity to represent their island or tribe. The idea for the games in 1959 came from Dr. Abdul Habib Sahu Khan, Fiji's representative at the SPC. The first Games were held four years later, in Suva. Their goal, apart from the promotion of sport, was "to create friendship and brotherhood among the Pacific".[33] The Fiji Games were attended by 646 athletes, including 130 women. They represented the following countries and territories: British Solomon Islands, Fiji, Nauru, Niue, New Caledonia, New Hebrides (now Vanuatu), Papua New Guinea, French Polynesia, American Samoa, Western Samoa (known as Samoa

29 Pacific Community, *About Us: History*: https://www.spc.int/about-us/history (access 31.10.2024).

30 Pacific Community, *About Us: History*: https://www.spc.int/about-us/history (access 31.10.2024).

31 National Library of Australia, *South Pacific Commission: History, Aims and Activities*, Noumea, 1996: https://nla.gov.au/nla.obj-3283302344/view?partId=nla.obj-3283313079#page/n74/mode/1up (access 31.10.2024).

32 National Library of Australia, *South Pacific Commission*: https://www.nla.gov.au/collections/guide-selected-collections/south-pacific-commission (access 31.10.2024).

33 Samoa News, *Pacific Games: How It All Began 60 Years Ago* (29.09.2023), https://www.samoanews.com/local-news/pacific-games-how-it-all-began-60-years-ago (access 31.10.2024).

since 1997), Tonga, the Cook Islands, and the Elis and Gilbert Islands (today the separate countries of Tuvalu and Kiribati). The quality of the fields, swimming pools, other sports grounds and infrastructure for spectators were a challenge, but so was the issue of flags and anthems as representation of nationhood. This was because at that time only Tonga and Western Samoa were independent.[34] In order to avoid flying the flags and playing the anthems of Great Britain and France, who were the two pre-eminent colonial powers, the organizers instructed the island territories to come with their own flags and anthems. This is how many Pacific islands began their journey to identify, understand and slowly embrace their independence. In addition, this helped differentiate Melanesian culture, through the use of separate flags and anthems, from Papua New Guinea from that of the Solomon Islands, or the Polynesian culture of the inhabitants of Western Samoa from those who came from American Samoa. Initially, the Games were organized every three years, and now they are held every four years. As these sports competitions developed and the islanders became more aware of their own cultures, the sports which were represented at SPG, such as swimming, sailing and surfing, grew to include double-hulled boat races (outrigger boats since 1995), which were extremely popular before the European colonization of the region.[35]

The SPG, which has been known as the Pacific Games since 2007 and which hosts approximately 5,000 athletes, coaches and doctors from 24 countries and territories located in the Pacific,[36] has a huge organizational cost. The smallest countries and territories of Oceania cannot afford to organize such a large event. For this reason, since 1981, the South Pacific Mini Games (now Pacific Mini Games) have been organized in smaller countries and territories such as Palau or the Wallis and Futuna Islands.[37]

A completely separate organization from the Pacific Community (formerly SPC) is the South Pacific Forum, which was founded in 1971 with its headquarters in Suva. Despite changing its name in 1999 to the Pacific Island Forum (PIF), the organization still emphasizes:

> Our ambition is for a region where all Pacific peoples benefit from our Forum Leaders working together to safeguard, secure, and progress the Blue Pacific Continent. Where we achieve regional priorities through a united and cohesive political leadership supported by the Pacific Islands Forum

34 Samoa News, *Pacific Games: How It All Began 60 Years Ago* (29.09.2023), https://www.samoanews.com/local-news/pacific-games-how-it-all-began-60-years-ago (access 31.10.2024).

35 E. Doran, Outrigger Ages (1974), *The Journal of the Polynesian Society*, Volume 83, Issue 2, pp. 130–140; B.A. Beheim, A.V. Bell, Inheritance, Ecology and the Evolution of the Canoes of East Oceania (23.02. 2011), *Proceedings of the Royal Society B*, Volume 278, Issue 1721.

36 R.D. Picazo, The Pacific Games Concluded with New Caledonia as the Clear Winner, (03.12.2023), *Inside the Games*: https://www.insidethegames.biz/articles/1142791/sol2023-concluded-new-caledonia-winner (access 31.10.2024).

37 Z.K. Goh, Pacific Games: From 1963 to 2023 – a Brief History (13.11.2023), *Olympics*: https://olympics.com/en/news/pacific-games-from-1963-to-2023-a-brief-history (access 31.10.2024).

> and a responsive regional architecture that aligns to the region's priorities and values. A region where our Partners recognise and respect our collective approach as the Blue Pacific Continent.[38]

It is a political organization that unites the people of Oceania, ensuring security and social integration in the region, strengthening the role of Pacific cultures in global discourse.[39]

An extremely important achievement of the people of Oceania in the 1970s was the creation of The Festival of Pacific Arts and Culture (FestPAC), also known today as the Pacific Arts Festival. The first one was held in the capital of Fiji in 1972 and sought to promote the preservation of culture. It wished to highlight the "Fight against the disappearance of traditional arts in most Pacific countries. Protect them from being submerged by other cultural influences. Start a process of preservation and development of the various local arts forms".[40] Its main goal is to stop the erosion of traditional skills, including dances and songs, originating from the cultures of Oceania by promoting them at a festival held every four years in a different country or dependent territory located on the islands of the Pacific Ocean. Additionally, the Pacific Arts Festival is not only a great place to share one's own culture, but also for cultural exchange between the inhabitants of the newly separate territories of Oceania. The Festival itself is not a competition with prizes, but rather a promotion of native culture, an exchange of experiences between artists proud of representing their island, as well as the audience who come to the event. It unites and strengthens the identity of the inhabitants of Oceania, but also allows for the appreciation of the value of Pacific cultures. Free admission to all events during the Festival helps to increase the number of viewers and thus to disseminate knowledge about the cultures of Oceania more widely among people who no longer remember these traditions. This gives them the opportunity to reintegrate with the culture of their ancestors and represent it in the world.[41]

As Dr. Karen Stevenson, a lecturer at the Oceania Centre for Arts, Cultures and Pacific Studies at the University of the South Pacific in Fiji, notes: the "festival is now about maintaining and providing a venue for innovation and the integration of one's culture into modern day society".[42] The most recent FestPAC took place in 2024 in Hawaii. Over two thousand artists participated and were watched by over

38 Pacific Island Forum, *Political Leadership and Regionalism*: https://forumsec.org/political-leadership-and-regionalism (access 31.10.2024).

39 I. Frazer, J. Bryant-Tokalau (eds.), *Redefining the Pacific? Regionalism Past, Present and Future*, London: Routledge, 2006.

40 South Pacific Commission, *1972 Festival of Pacific Arts, Fiji Islands*: https://web.archive.org/web/20050223000541/http://www.spc.int/culture/festival_72.htm (access 31.10.2024).

41 Pacific Community, *Festival of Pacific Arts and Culture*: https://www.spc.int/festival-of-pacific-arts-and-culture (access 31.10.2024).

42 Radio New Zealand, *Return of Cultural Artefacts Hailed as Way to Grow Economy* (20.07.2012): https://www.rnz.co.nz/international/pacific-news/206054/return-of-cultural-artefacts-hailed-as-way-to-grow-economy (access 31.10.2024).

half a million people.[43] FestPAC integrates the entire Pacific Island region through culture, but it has also had an impact on the processes that integrate the cultures of individual islands, such as the Tapati Festival on Rapa Nui,[44] individual territories – Heiva I Tahiti in French Polynesia,[45] or entire regions – the Pasifika Festival in New Zealand, which mainly brings together Polynesian people.[46]

The influence of the Pacific Arts Festival in 1972 can be seen in one of Oceania's most significant cultural milestones: the first voyage of the traditional Polynesian double-hulled seafaring vessel Hokule'a in 1976. Founded in Hawaii in 1973 with a mission to cultivate the art and science of traditional Polynesian sailing, the Polynesian Voyaging Society built a traditional double-hulled vessel without navigational devices developed by European civilization. Using only the ancient navigational knowledge of the Oceanians, the Hokule'a sailed from Honolulu, Hawaii to Papeete, French Polynesia, celebrating the heritage and the great knowledge, experience and wisdom of pre-colonial Pacific cultures. In 1985–87, Hokule'a reached Aotearoa (the Maori name for New Zealand), and in 1999, it reached the third tip of the Polynesian triangle, the island of Rapa Nui.[47] Hokule'a became a symbol of the pride of the people of Oceania in their ancestral culture: the same culture that the West and the East considered insignificant and viewed as destined to be forgotten.[48]

The old Oceania religions and the faith that arrived with the first missionaries were significantly different. Yet, the vast majority of the society of the Oceania islands still cannot imagine life without faith, which is solemnly celebrated on Sundays, especially in the Cook Islands, Tonga or Samoa.[49] Other, more secular

43 Island Business, *FestPAC 2024: Fight Against the Extinction of Pacific People* (13.06.2024): https://islandsbusiness.com/news-break/festpac-2024-fight-against-the-extinction-of-pacific-people/; The Garden Island, *Festpac Draws 500000 Attendees in World's Largest Pacific Islander Celebration* (18.06.2024): https://www.thegardenisland.com/2024/06/18/lifestyles/festpac-draws-500000-attendees-in-worlds-largest-pacific-islander-celebration/; FestPac Hawaii, *About the Festival*, https://www.festpachawaii.org/about (access 31.10.2024).

44 Chile Travel, *All About the Tapati 2024 on Rapa Nui*: https://www.chile.travel/en/events/all-about-the-tapati-2024-on-rapa-nui/ (access 31.10.2024).

45 J.C. Shigetomi, *Heiva I Tahiti l'histoire*: https://www.heiva.org/fr/heiva-i-tahiti-lhistoire/ (access 31.10.2024).

46 Discover Auckland, *Festival Pasifika History*: https://www.aucklandnz.com/pasifika/history (access 31.10.2024).

47 Polynesian Voyaging Society, *History:* https://hokulea.com/history/ (access 31.10.2024).

48 There are many examples of colonizers displacing indigenous cultures from what is now the "Global North". From Taiwanese Aborigines, through Japanese influence in Micronesia and Melanesia, through European missionaries and traders, to American landowners in Samoa and Hawaii.

49 Parliament Cook Islands, *Public Holidays*: https://parliament.gov.ck/wp-content/uploads/2022/05/Public-Holidays-Amdt-No.−17.pdf; Ministry of Internal Affairs Government of the Cook Islands, *Employment Relations Fact Sheet*: https://www.intaff.gov.ck/wp-content/uploads/2020/07/Public-Holidays-20140501.pdf; US Department of State, *2023 Report on International Religious Freedom: Tonga*, https://www.state.gov/reports/2023-report-on-international-religious-freedom/tonga/; National Park of American Samoa, *Fa'asamoa – the Samoan Way:* https://www.nps.gov/npsa/learn/historyculture/faasamoa.htm; Samoa Travel, *Sundays in Samoa*: https://www.samoa.travel/pagepreview/sundays-in-samoa (access 31.10.2024).

islands of Oceania, such as Hawaii or New Zealand, are moving away from Christianity, looking for old cults, or leaving religion en masse.[50] The activities of missionaries should not be overlooked either, because their work, in addition to pushing out elements of old cultures that were not supported by the colonizers, helped to preserve local languages and history by writing them down and studying local customs or objects. Thanks to this, they have survived to this day and can now be developed at many universities in the Pacific, promoting the culture of Oceania among visitors from all over the world.[51] In addition to basic information about the local cultures of Oceania, university centers, museums and associations also play a significant role in discovering the old heritage of the islanders.[52]

In the 21st century, music and film art appeal more strongly to the younger generation. It is through longer (classical) or shorter (clips) film materials that the culture of Oceania reaches audiences beyond the proud inhabitants of Oceania. Thanks to film festivals such as The International Oceanian Documentary Film Festival (FIFO), which has existed since 2004, one of the main goals of which is to "promote Oceania and show it to the world",[53] or the Pasifika Film Fest (PFF),[54] established in 2013, but also thanks to films such as: *Whale Rider*, *Once were Warriors*, *Mr. Pip*, *Tanna*, *Orator* or *Moana* (*Vaiana*) with music by the band Te Vaka, and even Next Goal Wins.[55]

In the 1980s, the heirs of the cultures of Oceania came to understand that it was the colonizers who, in accordance with the ancient principle of *divide et impera* (divide and rule), divided them into Melanesians, Micronesians and Polynesians, and into smaller states and territories that have been officially using Spanish, German, Japanese and, above all, French and English for centuries, and in the process losing their own languages that are carriers of their old cultures over time. The next stage of the return to unity of the inhabitants of Melanesia, Micronesia and Polynesia began in 1986, when the Melanesian Spearhead Group (MSG) was formed at an

50 Stats NZ, *Losing Our Religion*: https://www.stats.govt.nz/news/losing-our-religion (access 31.10.2024).

51 Founded by Mormons, the Polynesian Culture Centre (PCC) has been providing visitors from around the world with basic information about Polynesia since its founding in 1963. Polynesian Cultural Center, *Purpose and History of Polynesian Cultural Center*: https://www.polynesia.com/history (access 31.10.2024).

52 Pacific Islands University, *About Us*: https://www.piu.edu/about-piu/; Bishop Museum in Honolulu, *About Us*: https://www.bishopmuseum.org/about/; Pacific Islands Museum Association, *PIMA*: https://www.facebook.com/profile.php?id=100064354254871; Pacific Arts Association, *About the Pacific Arts Association*: https://pacificarts.org/about-paa/ (access 31.10.2024).

53 FIFO, The International Oceanian Documentary Film Festival, *Our Goals*: https://www.fifotahiti.com/en/presentation/ (access 31.10.2024).

54 The Pasifika Film Fest, *About Us*: https://www.pasifikafilmfest.com/about-us (access 31.10.2024).

55 H. Lutukefu et al., 13 Pacific Islander Movies That Showcase the Richness and Diversity of Pasifika Cinema (27.05.2021), *Rotten Tomatoes News*, https://editorial.rottentomatoes.com/article/pacific-islander-movies-that-showcase-the-richness-and-diversity-of-pasifika-cinema/; K.F. Schmidt, 7 Essential Pacific Films to Add to Your Queue, from "Once Were Warriors" to "Vai" (21.05.2021), *Sundance*: https://www.sundance.org/blogs/special-edition/essential-pacific-films-watchlist/ (access 31.10.2024).

informal meeting. It is the first organization to connect states and dependent territories through their ancient common culture. Its goal is to develop a stronger cultural, social and economic identity in the region by strengthening the bonds between the people and communities of Melanesia. It is also a common voice of the entire group of Melanesians; established during the leaders' summits, it also has political functions, taking care of weaker members; at the same time it has a stronger mandate in talks in the Pacific with the great economies of the East and West.[56]

Following the example of Melanesia, whose model has proven successful over the years, the cultures of Micronesia in 2003 established a common position for the entire group at the semi-annual Micronesian Chief Executives Summits, which in recent years transformed into the Micronesia Presidents' Summit (MPS).[57]

The last cultural region of Oceania to follow the example of the Melanesians and Micronesians were the Polynesians, who formed the Polynesian Leaders Group (PLG) in 2011.[58] As the originator of the PLG, the then-Prime Minister of Samoa, stated:

> the goal and mission of this Polynesian alliance are to work together to seek a future for our Polynesian people and countries. The Polynesian Leaders Group (PLG) is an international governmental cooperation group bringing together eight independent or self-governing island nations and territories in Polynesia. As the various countries come together to share their governmental affairs, the PLG provides an opportunity to engage and educate each other on issues that present the most challenges within their respective countries. Issues such as education, culture and language, environmental conservation (climate change), healthcare, and regional economics. These discussions intend to provide a vehicle that strengthens the partnerships between all island nations of Polynesia.[59]

The youngest of the three subregional organizations still has a lot to do, from establishing a permanent seat of the PLG secretariat to attempts to include the Maori from New Zealand, the Hawaiians and the inhabitants of Rapa Nui from the three corners of the Polynesian triangle in its activities. Certainly, the MSG, MPS and PLG are an attempt to break through the voice of the smaller islands of Oceania

56 Melanesian Spearhead Group Secretariat, *About MSG*: https://msgsec.info/about-msg/ (access 31.10.2024).

57 Island Times, *Micronesian Countries Ink MOU to Institutionalize MPS* (26.02.2019): https://islandtimes.org/micronesian-countries-ink-mou-to-institutionalize-mps/ (access 31.10.2024).

58 M.H. Ilailo, *Polynesian Leaders Group formed in Samoa, Regional Sub-Group Is Samoa PM's 'Dream Come True'*, Pacific Islands Report: https://web.archive.org/web/20160305012809/http://archives.pireport.org/archive/2011/November/11-21-01.htm; I. Iati, *Pacific Regionalism and the Polynesian Leaders Group*, Te Herenga Waka-Victoria University of Wellington, Journal contribution (2017): https://openaccess.wgtn.ac.nz/articles/journal_contribution/Pacific_Regionalism_and_the_Polynesian_Leaders_Group/20486499?file=36671724 (access 31.10.2024).

59 American Samoa Governor, *PLG 2021: Building Resilience in Times of Uncertainty* (21.01.2021), https://www.americansamoa.gov/plg (access 31.10.2024).

over the voice of the stronger countries of the region, such as Australia and New Zealand.

Returning to their roots is not easy for the peoples of Oceania. Armed conflicts in the Pacific continue to exist to this day (coups in Fiji, fighting in the Solomon Islands, Bougainville, Western New Guinea, and currently in New Caledonia). During several conflicts in the region, sending stabilization forces from neighboring countries with a similar culture helped to resolve the conflict more quickly, through greater acceptance of external forces by the natives. An example is the Regional Assistance Mission to the Solomon Islands "Helpem Fren".[60] There are also problems in Oceania that are harder to counteract related to the fight for independence.[61] In the modern global village, the rivalry between powers is no longer limited to the influence of only regional players, but encompasses the entire world, an example of which is the support of the Baku Initiative Group for the independence aspirations of the Kanaks in New Caledonia.[62] Both the East and the West are struggling to support their interests on the islands of Oceania, but the question is whether these external players want to help the locals or themselves more.

Rivalry between the East and the West for influence over the people of Oceania continues. This is illustrated by attempts to pull the countries of the region to the East or the West by helping to train the police of the island countries in the Pacific.[63] It can also be seen through the construction of runways, administrative buildings, hospitals or ports on the Pacific islands that the powers of the East and West continue to approach the people of Oceania from a position of paternity and not fraternity. Both then and now, the lack of respect for the cultures of Oceania by the world's economic powers does not allow them to better understand the islanders and their culture.

Oceania is also a place of games between the powers, considering the massive, illegal migration of the immigrant population which, numerically outnumbering

60 M. Wesley, *Helpem Fren: Australia and the Regional Assistance Mission to Solomon Islands 2003–2017*, Melbourne: Melbourne University Press, 2023.

61 M. Ghaedi, Pacific Islands That Are Still Colonized (25.05 2024), *Deutsche Welle*: https://www.dw.com/en/last-colonies-pacific-islands-still-owned-by-other-nations/a-69176707 (access 31.10.2024).

62 Eurasianet, *Azerbaijan: Baku Denying French Accusations of Meddling in New Caledonia*: https://eurasianet.org/azerbaijan-baku-denying-french-accusations-of-meddling-in-new-caledonia; A. Farhadova, *France Accuses Azerbaijan of Supporting Riots in New Caledonia*, OC Media: https://oc-media.org/france-accuses-azerbaijan-of-supporting-riots-in-new-caledonia/ (access 31.10.2024).

63 S. Dziedzic, Pacific Island Police Ministers, Delegates Enter High-Level Security Talks with China in Beijing, *ABC News*: https://www.abc.net.au/news/2023-12-11/pacific-islands-police-ministers-security-talks-beijing/103213960; S. Dziedzic, Pacific Islands Leaders Endorse Regional Policing Initiative in Strategic Victory for Australia, *ABC News*: https://www.abc.net.au/news/2024-08-28/vanuatu-melanesia-officials-warn-policing-could-block-china/104277614; M. Kapu, Chinese Security Delegation Visits Tonga to Provide Police 'Assistance' Ahead of Pacific Islands Forum, *ABC News*: https://www.abc.net.au/news/2024-04-04/china-security-group-in-tonga-ahead-of-pacific-islands-forum/103665524.

the local population on smaller islands, threatens the local culture.[64] New technologies and tourism also have a huge impact on the development of local cultures. In order to achieve prosperity, the islanders often sacrifice their values and space, carefully adapting to the requirements of tourists from the East or the West, making their country dependent on the whims of the politics of world powers.[65]

As time passes, the "Global North" is learning about the cultures of Oceania, as well as its successes and problems and genuine attempts to help the islanders become noticeable. They appear to not just be alms from the rich to the poor but increasingly illustrate a certain kind of respect from the East and the West towards the cultures of the Pacific.[66] Exhibitions of Oceania cultures shown in Asia, the United States and Europe are becoming more frequent and larger.[67] Larger film studios began to create productions showing Oceanic culture in an increasingly positive light. All of this is indeed a step in the right direction, and attempts are being made to understand the Oceania cultures as they are, without Westerners' lenses.

In the 21st century, the "Global North" is moving beyond stereotypes about Oceania, leaning more (and more respectfully) towards the knowledge and experience of the peoples of Melanesia, Micronesia and Polynesia. Despite this, there are still examples of powers from the East and West viewing the Pacific Islands as a

64 Migration Data Portal, *Migration Data in Oceania*: https://www.migrationdataportal.org/regional-data-overview/oceania; Cultural Survival Quarterly, *Oceania, Islands, Land, People* (16.03.2010): https://www.culturalsurvival.org/publications/cultural-survival-quarterly/oceania-islands-land-people (access 31.10.2024).

65 T. Tuuhia, V. Harrison, Paradise Cost: The Pacific Islands Changing the Future of Tourism (12.12.2023), *The Guardian*, https://www.theguardian.com/world/2023/dec/12/pacific-islands-tourism-the-price-of-paradise; A, Movano, R. Scheyvens, *Resistance to Mega-Tourism Is Rising in the South Pacific – but Will Governments Put Words into Action?* The Global Sustainable Tourism Council, https://www.gstcouncil.org/resistance-to-mega-tourism-is-rising-in-the-south-pacific/ (access 31.10.2024).

66 V. Naidu, Development Assistance Challenges, in: M. Powels (ed.), *Pacific Future*, Canberra: Pandanus Books, 2006, pp. 142–157; World Bank Group, *World Bank Significantly Steps Up Assistance to the Pacific Islands and Papua New Guinea* (14. 02.2023): https://www.worldbank.org/en/news/press-release/2023/02/15/world-bank-significantly-steps-up-assistance-to-the-pacific-islands-and-papua-new-guinea; World Health Organization, *Pacific Islands Countries (Donors)*: https://iris.who.int/bitstream/handle/10665/136831/ccsbrief_pci_en.pdf?sequence=1&isAllowed=y (access 31.10.2024).

67 E. Kjellgren, *Oceania: Art of the Pacific Islands in the Metropolitan Museum of Art*, The Metropolitan Museum of Art: https://www.metmuseum.org/met-publications/oceania-art-of-the-pacific-islands-in-the-metropolitan-museum-of-art; The Embassy of the Kingdom of Tonga in China, Culture and Tourism Exhibition in South Pacific Countries (31.05.2018): http://www.tongaembassycn.gov.to/en/media-room/press-releases/157-culture-and-tourism-exhibition-in-south-pacific-countries; X. Yi, *Exhibition Exploring the Art of Oceania Opens in Shanghai* (18.06.2019): *China Daily*: https://www.chinadaily.com.cn/a/201906/18/WS5d083cf1a3103dbf14328cb4.html (access 31.10.2024).

place to be subjugated and made financially dependent, rather than as a peer partner in conversation.[68]

In order for the "Global North", both the West and the East, to understand the cultures of Oceania, something the Maoris call Tikanga is indeed needed. It is translated as social knowledge of culture.[69] It requires silence, humility, patience and work, and thanks to it, those who come to these areas have the opportunity to fully understand and participate in the culture of the Blue Continent. What needs to be emphasized here is the fact that there are no deeply rooted nationalisms among the peoples of Oceania. These countries were the last in the world to gain independence after the period of colonization and, with varying results, are still trying to adapt to the requirements of the Western world's notion of sovereignty. Oceania is indeed the people of the culture of the Blue Continent who take care of each other, unless someone from the outside whispers in their ears that, for a fee, one of them can be more important, richer and have a better life than the others. The ancient maxim *divide and rule* is currently reaping its harvest in the Indo-Pacific. Will the cure be the wisdom drawn from the culture of the inhabitants of Oceania, or has the knowledge of the region's ancestors already been forgotten and the recipe for the cure has escaped the minds of the guardians of the region's culture?[70]

3. Conclusions

Even today, the difference in the perception of water distinguishes the inhabitants of the "Global North" from the cultures of the Oceania region. The name Indo-Pacific, like Oceania, very clearly indicates what area we are talking about. The heart of this region is not the land area at all, but indeed the maritime area. The ocean gives life, work, potential, innovation, and it has proved that it is a significant factor in world politics, economy and security. Continuing with the theme of water, one can perceive the world through the prism of the half empty-half full glass and pay attention mainly to what divides, to deficiencies, dysfunctions, showing that water is bad because it takes away land, island, place, country.

Oceania's cultures currently have a great role to play in world history. They must show their own value and that it is worth appreciating the glass half full perspective. They should show the richest of this world that the common good of the islands' inhabitants has always been more important than the good of one or the other group. Instead of competing for dominance in the area of these two beautiful

68 Radio New Zealand, *Palau Govt Asks Japan and US for Help After China Crackdown* (28.07.2018): https://www.rnz.co.nz/international/pacific-news/362852/palau-govt-asks-japan-and-us-for-help-after-china-crackdown; D. Dingwall, *Pacific Island Nations Hope to Lure China's Tourists with a Promise of 'Purity' as Travellers Return to the Skies* (07.09.2024), *ABC News*: https://www.abc.net.au/news/2024-09-08/chinese-tourism-in-the-pacific-palau-fiji-vanuatu/104311298 (access 31.10.2024).

69 University of Otago, *Societal Lore (tikanga) in Māori Culture:* https://www.otago.ac.nz/maori/world/tikanga/lore (access 31.10.2024).

70 G.A.L. Hunkin, F.L.F. Mayer, Language and Culture Loss in the Pacific, in: M. Powels (ed.), *Pacific Future*, Canberra: Pandanus Books, 2006, pp. 63–71.

oceans – the Indian Ocean and the Pacific Ocean – it is worth appreciating their existence and potential, as well as the values from which we can all learn. As the Minister of Foreign Affairs and Trade of New Zealand said during the United Nations General Debate of the Seventy-Ninth Session:

> We small states need today's superpowers to talk more, seek better understanding between them, and develop ways of compromising more. Rather than a zero-sum game, effecting better relations between today's "Great Powers" only enhances global stability, and that is what we smaller nations seek.[71]

The "Global North", if it can muster more respect for the knowledge and experiences of the peoples of Oceania, can truly learn a lot, not only from them, but from the entire Indo-Pacific population. Oceania just needs to be given space, without constant demand stemming from the "Global North" that it conforms to the demands of the East or the West, and instead be allowed to return to its own roots, to find and assert its own culture in the 21st century. As Pinky Thompson used to say,

> Before our ancestors set out to find a new island, they had to have a vision of that island over the horizon. They made a plan for achieving that vision. They prepared themselves physically and mentally and were willing to experiment, to try new things. They took risks. And on the voyage, they bound each other with aloha so they could together overcome the risks and achieve their vision. You find these same values throughout the world: seeking, planning, experimenting, taking risks and the importance of caring for each other. . . . The same principles that we used in the past are the ones that we use today and that we will use into the future. No matter what culture we are, or what race, these are values that work for us all.

Pinky's vision united past, present and future by reaffirming that traditional Polynesian values applied universally across time and space.[72]

If the "Global North" takes its eyes off of the land for a moment and focuses on water and its value, it will understand the cultures of the Blue Continent, which are a signpost for the East and the West to respect the only life-giving Blue Planet.

References

Alliance of Small Island States, *About – Chair of AOSIS*: https://www.aosis.org/about/chair-of-aosis/ (access 31.10.2024).

American Samoa Governor, *PLG 2021: Building Resilience in Times of Uncertainty* (21.01.2021), https://www.americansamoa.gov/plg (access 31.10.2024).

71 Pacific Islands Forum, *Remarks: NZ DPM Peters Delivers UNGA79 Statement* (27.09.2024), https://forumsec.org/publications/remarks-nz-dpm-peters-delivers-unga79-statement (access 31.10.2024).

72 Polynesian Voyaging Society, *Our Vision*: https://hokulea.com/about/ (access 31.10.2024).

Beheim B.A., Bell A.V., Inheritance, Ecology and the Evolution of the Canoes of East Oceania (23.02. 2011), *Proceedings of the Royal Society B*, Volume 278, Issue 1721.

Berggren J.L., Jones A., *Ptolemy's Geography: An Annotated Translation of the Theoretical Chapters*, Princeton University Press, 2000.

BishopMuseum in Honolulu, *About Us*: https://www.bishopmuseum.org/about/ (access 31.10.2024).

Chile Travel, *All About the Tapati 2024 on Rapa Nui*: https://www.chile.travel/en/events/all-about-the-tapati-2024-on-rapa-nui/ (access 31.10.2024).

Cities and Regions in the UNFCCC Process, *Cities and Regions Talanoa Dialogues*: https://www.cities-and-regions.org/talanoa/ (access 31.10.2024).

Conroy J.D., Melanesia in the Trade of the Malay Archipelago, in: *Exchange and Markets in Early Economic Development: Informal Economy in the Three New Guineas*, New York, Oxford: Berghahn Books, 2023.

Cook J., *A Voyage to the Pacific Ocean Undertaken, by the Command of His Majesty for Making Discoveries in the Northern Hemisphere*, London, 1784, vol. 1.

Cultural Survival Quarterly, *Oceania, Islands, Land, People* (16.03.2010): https://www.culturalsurvival.org/publications/cultural-survival-quarterly/oceania-islands-land-people (access 31.10.2024).

Darwin C.R., *Journal of Researches into the Natural History and Geology of the Countries Visited During the Voyage of H.M.S. Beagle Round the World*, London, 1845.

The Department of Foreign Affairs and Trade, *Australia-Tuvalu Falepili Union Factsheet*: https://www.dfat.gov.au/geo/tuvalu/australia-tuvalu-falepili-union (access 31.10.2024).

Dingwall D., Pacific Island Nations Hope to Lure China's Tourists with a Promise of 'Purity' as Travellers Return to the Skies (07.09.2024), *ABC News*: https://www.abc.net.au/news/2024-09-08/chinese-tourism-in-the-pacific-palau-fiji-vanuatu/104311298 (access 31.10.2024).

Discover Auckland, *Festival Pasifika History*: https://www.aucklandnz.com/pasifika/history (access 31.10.2024).

Doran E., Outrigger Ages (1974), *The Journal of the Polynesian Society*, Volume 83, Issue 2.

Dunmore J., *French Explorers in the Pacific, Vol. I: The Eighteenth Century*, Oxford: Oxford University Press, 1965.

Dunmore J., *French Explorers in the Pacific, Vol. 2: The Nineteenth Century*, Oxford: Oxford University Press, 1969.

Dziedzic S., Pacific Islands Leaders Endorse Regional Policing Initiative in Strategic Victory for Australia, *ABC News*: https://www.abc.net.au/news/2024-08-28/vanuatu-melanesia-officials-warn-policing-could-block-china/104277614 (access 31.10.2024).

Dziedzic S., Pacific Islands Police Ministers, Delegates Enter High-Level Security Talks with China in Beijing, *ABC News*: https://www.abc.net.au/news/2023-12-11/pacific-islands-police-ministers-security-talks-beijing/103213960 (access 31.10.2024).

The Embassy of the Kingdom of Tonga in China, *Culture and Tourism Exhibition in South Pacific Countries* (31.05.2018): http://www.tongaembassycn.gov.to/en/media-room/press-releases/157-culture-and-tourism-exhibition-in-south-pacific-countries (access 31.10.2024).

Eurasianet, *Azerbaijan: Baku Denying French Accusations of Meddling in New Caledonia*: https://eurasianet.org/azerbaijan-baku-denying-french-accusations-of-meddling-in-new-caledonia (access 31.10.2024).

Farhadova A., France Accuses Azerbaijan of Supporting Riots in New Caledonia, *OC Media*: https://oc-media.org/france-accuses-azerbaijan-of-supporting-riots-in-new-caledonia/ (access 31.10.2024).

FestPac Hawaii, *About the Festival* (20.07.2012): https://www.festpachawaii.org/about (access 31.10.2024).

FIFO, The International Oceanian Documentary Film Festival, *Our Goals*, https://www.fifotahiti.com/en/presentation/ (access 31.10.2024).

Finney B., *Piailug Mau (1932–2010)*, Pacific Islander Biography, National Centre of Biography, Australian National University.

Fischer S.R., *A History of the Pacific Islands*, New York: Palgrave, 2002.

Fleming S., These Pacific Islands Have an Innovative Scheme to Prevent Overfishing in Their Waters (21.06.2021), *Word Economic Forum*: https://www.weforum.org/agenda/2021/06/subsidized-fishing-man-made-tragedy/ (access 31.10.2024).

Foster J.M., Pacific Islands Band Together on a Shark Sanctuary (04.08.2011), *The New York Times*: https://archive.nytimes.com/green.blogs.nytimes.com/2011/08/04/pacific-islands-band-together-on-a-shark-sanctuary/ (access 31.10.2024).

Fraenkel J., Pacific Islands and New Zealand – Colonial Control in the Pacific, *Te Ara – the Encyclopedia of New Zealand*: https://teara.govt.nz/en/interactive/36846/colonial-control-in-the-pacific (access 31.10.2024).

Frazer I., Bryant-Tokalau J. (eds.), *Redefining the Pacific? Regionalism Past, Present and Future*, London: Routledge, 2006.

Freinkel S., *Plastic: A Toxic Love Story*, Boston, New York: Houghton Mifflin Harcourt, 2011.

The Garden Island, *Festpac Draws 500000 Attendees in World's Largest Pacific Islander Celebration* (18.06. 2024): https://www.thegardenisland.com/2024/06/18/lifestyles/festpac-draws-500000-attendees-in-worlds-largest-pacific-islander-celebration/ (access 31.10.2024).

Ghaedi M., Pacific Islands That Are Still Colonized (25.05 2024), *Deutsche Welle*: https://www.dw.com/en/last-colonies-pacific-islands-still-owned-by-other-nations/a-69176707 (access 31.10.2024).

Goh Z.K., Pacific Games: From 1963 to 2023 – a Brief History (13.11.2023), *Olympics*: https://olympics.com/en/news/pacific-games-from-1963-to-2023-a-brief-history (access 31.10.2024).

Hohn D., *Mobby Duck*, Penguin, 2012.

Hunkin G.A.L., Mayer F.L.F., Language and Culture Loss in the Pacific, in: M. Powels (ed.), *Pacific Future*, Canberra: Pandanus Books, 2006.

Iati, I., *Pacific Regionalism and the Polynesian Leaders Group*, Te Herenga Waka-Victoria University of Wellington, Journal contribution (2017): https://openaccess.wgtn.ac.nz/articles/journal_contribution/Pacific_Regionalism_and_the_Polynesian_Leaders_Group/20486499?file=36671724 (access 31.10.2024).

Ilailo M.H., *Polynesian Leaders Group Formed in Samoa, Regional Sub-Group Is Samoa PM's 'Dream Come True'*, Pacific Islands Report: https://web.archive.org/web/20160305012809/http://archives.pireport.org/archive/2011/November/11-21-01.htm (access 31.10.2024).

Island Business, *FestPAC 2024: Fight Against the Extinction of Pacific People* (13.06.2024): https://islandsbusiness.com/news-break/festpac-2024-fight-against-the-extinction-of-pacific-people/ (access 31.10.2024).

Island Times, *Micronesian Countries Ink MOU to Institutionalize MPS* (26.02.2019), https://islandtimes.org/micronesian-countries-ink-mou-to-institutionalize-mps/ (access 31.10.2024).

Kaeppler A.L., *The Pacific Arts of Polynesia & Micronesia*, Oxford, New York: Oxford University Press, 2008.

Kapu M., Chinese Security Delegation Visits Tonga to Provide Police 'Assistance' Ahead of Pacific Islands Forum, *ABC News*: https://www.abc.net.au/news/2024-04-04/china-security-group-in-tonga-ahead-of-pacific-islands-forum/103665524 (access 31.10.2024).

Kayser M., et al., Melanesian and Asian Origins of Polynesians: mtDNA and Y Chromosome Gradients Across the Pacific (November 2006), *Molecular Biology and Evolution*, Volume 23, Issue 11.

Kitara T., Farbotko C., *Tuvalu, Australia, and the Falepili Union*, Australian Institute of International Affairs: https://www.internationalaffairs.org.au/australianoutlook/tuvalu-australia-and-the-falepili-union/ (access 31.10.2024).

Kitara T., Suliman T., Fale Pili: A Tuvaluan Perspective on Mobility Justice (2024), *Applied Mobilities*, Volume 9, Issue 2–3.

Kjellgren E., *Oceania: Art of the Pacific Islands in The Metropolitan Museum of Art*, The Metropolitan Museum of Art: https://www.metmuseum.org/met-publications/oceania-art-of-the-pacific-islands-in-the-metropolitan-museum-of-art (access 31.10.2024).

Lewis D., *We, the Navigators: The Ancient Art of Landfinding in the Pacific* (Second Edition), Honolulu: University of Hawaii, 1994.

Lutukefu H., et al., 13 Pacific Islander Movies That Showcase the Richness and Diversity of Pasifika Cinema (27.05.2021), *Rotten Tomatoes News*: https://editorial.rottentomatoes.com/article/pacific-islander-movies-that-showcase-the-richness-and-diversity-of-pasifika-cinema/ (access 31.10.2024).

McFadden C., et al., Temporal Trends in the Colonisation of the Pacific: Palaeodemographic Insights (2021), *Journal of World Prehistory*, Volume 34.

Melander V., David's Weapon of Mass Destruction: The Reception of Thor Heyerdahl's 'Kon-Tiki Theory' (2019), *Bulletin of the History of Archaeology*, Volume 29, Issue 1.

Melanesian Spearhead Group Secretariat, *About MSG*: https://msgsec.info/about-msg/ (access 31.10.2024).

Migration Data Portal, *Migration Data in Oceania*: https://www.migrationdataportal.org/regional-data-overview/oceania (access 31.10.2024).

Ministry of Internal Affairs Government of the Cook Islands, *Employment Relations Fact Sheet*: https://www.intaff.gov.ck/wp-content/uploads/2020/07/Public-Holidays-20140501.pdf (access 31.10.2024).

Movano A., Scheyvens R., *Resistance to Mega-Tourism Is Rising in the South Pacific – but Will Governments Put Words into Action?* The Global Sustainable Tourism Council: https://www.gstcouncil.org/resistance-to-mega-tourism-is-rising-in-the-south-pacific/ (access 31.10.2024).

Naidu V., Development Assistance Challenges, in: M. Powels (ed.), *Pacific Future*, Canberra: Pandanus Books, 2006.

National Library of Australia, *South Pacific Commission*: https://www.nla.gov.au/collections/guide-selected-collections/south-pacific-commission (access 31.10.2024).

National Library of Australia, *South Pacific Commission: History, Aims and Activities*, Noumea, 1996: https://nla.gov.au/nla.obj-3283302344/view?partId=nla.obj-3283313079#page/n74/mode/1up (access 31.10.2024).

National Park of American Samoa, *Fa'asamoa – the Samoan Way:* https://www.nps.gov/npsa/learn/historyculture/faasamoa.htm (access 31.10.2024).

Oatley K., Pacific Arts of Navigation (1973), *Nature*, Volume 245.

Olivier D., *Polynesia in Early Historic Times*, Honolulu: Bess Press, 2002.

Pacific Arts Association, *About the Pacific Arts Association*: https://pacificarts.org/about-paa/ (access 31.10.2024).

Pacific Community, *About Us: History*: https://www.spc.int/about-us/history (access 31.10.2024).

Pacific Community, *Festival of Pacific Arts and Culture*: https://www.spc.int/festival-of-pacific-arts-and-culture (access 31.10.2024).

Pacific Island Forum, *Political Leadership and Regionalism*: https://forumsec.org/political-leadership-and-regionalism (access 31.10.2024).

Pacific Islands Forum, *Remarks: NZ DPM Peters Delivers UNGA79 Statement* (27.09.2024): https://forumsec.org/publications/remarks-nz-dpm-peters-delivers-unga79-statement (access 31.10.2024).

Pacific Islands Forum, *Remarks: RMI President Heine Delivers Statemen to UNGA79* (26.09.2024): https://forumsec.org/publications/remarks-rmi-president-heine-delivers-statemen-unga79 (access 31.10.2024).

Pacific Islands Museum Association, *PIMA*: https://www.facebook.com/profile.php?id=100064354254871 (access 31.10.2024).
Pacific Islands University, *About Us*: https://www.piu.edu/about-piu/ (access 31.10.2024).
Palau Soultrips, *World's First Shark Sanctuary*: https://palau.co/conservation-sustainability/world-s-first-shark-sanctuary/ (access 31.10.2024).
Parliament Cook Islands, *Public Holidays*: https://parliament.gov.ck/wp-content/uploads/2022/05/Public-Holidays-Amdt-No.-17.pdf (access 31.10.2024).
The Pasifika Film Fest, *About Us*: https://www.pasifikafilmfest.com/about-us (access 31.10.2024).
Picazo R.D., The Pacific Games Concluded with New Caledonia as the Clear Winner (03.12.2023), *Inside the Games*: https://www.insidethegames.biz/articles/1142791/sol2023-concluded-new-caledonia-winner (access 31.10.2024).
Polynesian Cultural Center, *Purpose and History of Polynesian Cultural Center*: https://www.polynesia.com/history (access 31.10.2024).
Polynesian Voyaging Society, *History:* https://hokulea.com/history/ (access 31.10.2024).
Polynesian Voyaging Society, *Our Vision*: https://hokulea.com/about/ (access 31.10.2024).
Prime Minister of Australia, *Entry into Force of Historic Australia-Tuvalu Falepili Union*, https://www.pm.gov.au/media/entry-force-historic-australia-tuvalu-falepili-union (access 31.10.2024).
Radio New Zealand, *Palau Govt Asks Japan and US for Help After China Crackdown* (28.07.2018), https://www.rnz.co.nz/international/pacific-news/362852/palau-govt-asks-japan-and-us-for-help-after-china-crackdown (access 31.10.2024).
Radio New Zealand, *Return of Cultural Artefacts Hailed as Way to Grow Economy* (20.07.2012): https://www.rnz.co.nz/international/pacific-news/206054/return-of-cultural-artefacts-hailed-as-way-to-grow-economy (access 31.10.2024).
Samoa News, *Pacific Games: How It All Began 60 Years Ago* (29.09.2023): https://www.samoanews.com/local-news/pacific-games-how-it-all-began-60-years-ago (access 31.10.2024).
Samoa Travel, *Sundays in Samoa*: https://www.samoa.travel/pagepreview/sundays-in-samoa (access 31.10.2024).
Schmidt K.F., 7 Essential Pacific Films to Add to Your Queue, from "Once Were Warriors" to "Vai" (21.05.2021), *Sundance*: https://www.sundance.org/blogs/special-edition/essential-pacific-films-watchlist/ (access 31.10.2024).
Shaw B., et al., Frontier Lapita Interaction with Resident Papuan Populations Set the Stage for Initial Peopling of the Pacific (2022), *Nature Ecology & Evolution*, Volume 6.
Shigetomi J.C., *Heiva I Tahiti l'histoire*: https://www.heiva.org/fr/heiva-i-tahiti-lhistoire/ (access 31.10.2024).
Siekiera J., The Role of the United States in the South Pacific at the Turn of the 20th and 21st Centuries (March 2020), *Journal of Oriental Scientific Research (JOSR)*, Volume 12, Issue 1.
South Pacific Commission, *1972 Festival of Pacific Arts, Fiji Islands*: https://web.archive.org/web/20050223000541/http://www.spc.int/culture/festival_72.htm (access 31.10.2024).
The Stanford Center for Ocean Solutions, *The Palau National Marine Sanctuary*: https://oceansolutions.stanford.edu/key-initiatives/sustainable-ocean-economies/palau-national-marine-sanctuary (access 31.10.2024).
Stats NZ, *Losing Our Religion*: https://www.stats.govt.nz/news/losing-our-religion (access 31.10.2024).
Taonui R., Canoe Navigation – Waka –Canoes, in: *Te Ara – the Encyclopedia of New Zealand*: https://teara.govt.nz/en/canoe-navigation/page-1 (access 31.10.2024).
Tenbruggencate J., *Dutch Pacific Voyages of Discovery*, Bridge House Press, 2018.
Tuuhia T., Harrison V., Paradise Cost: The Pacific Islands Changing the Future of Tourism (12.12.2023), *The Guardian*: https://www.theguardian.com/world/2023/dec/12/pacific-islands-tourism-the-price-of-paradise (access 31.10.2024).

United Nations Climate Change, *2018 Talanoa Dialogue Platform:* https://unfccc.int/process-and-meetings/the-paris-agreement/the-paris-agreement/2018-talanoa-dialogue-platform (access 31.10.2024).

University of Otago, *Societal Lore (tikanga) in Māori Culture*: https://www.otago.ac.nz/maori/world/tikanga/lore (access 31.10.2024).

US Department of State, *2023 Report on International Religious Freedom: Tonga*: https://www.state.gov/reports/2023-report-on-international-religious-freedom/tonga/ (access 31.10.2024).

Wade L., Polynesians Steering by the Stars Met Native Americans Long Before Europeans Arrived (08.07.2020), *Science*, Volume 369.

Wesley M., *Helpem Fren: Australia and the Regional Assistance Mission to Solomon Islands 2003–2017*, Melbourne: Melbourne University Press, 2023.

West F.J., Foster S., *Pacific Islands Colonial Rule*, Encyclopedia Britannica, 09.09.2024.

Wheatley P., Lochac Revisited (1969), *Oriens Extremus*, Volume 16, Issue 1.

Wilford J.N., Pacific Islanders' Ancestry Emerges in Genetic Study (18.01.2008), *The New York Times*.

World Bank Group, *World Bank Significantly Steps Up Assistance to the Pacific Islands and Papua New Guinea* (14. 02.2023): https://www.worldbank.org/en/news/press-release/2023/02/15/world-bank-significantly-steps-up-assistance-to-the-pacific-islands-and-papua-new-guinea (access 31.10.2024).

World Health Organization, *Pacific Islands Countries (Donors)*: https://iris.who.int/bitstream/handle/10665/136831/ccsbrief_pci_en.pdf?sequence=1&isAllowed=y (access 31.10.2024).

Yi X., Exhibition Exploring the Art of Oceania Opens in Shanghai (18.06.2019), *China Daily*: https://www.chinadaily.com.cn/a/201906/18/WS5d083cf1a3103dbf14328cb4.html (access 31.10.2024).

6 Understanding the Cyber Terrain

Global Solutions for Stability in the Pacific

*Jacob Galbreath**

1. Introduction

Many people think of cyberspace as an abstract idea of various applications (apps), hosted by large corporations with few physical components. The current NATO definition is "Cyberspace is not limited to, but at its core consists of, a computerized environment, artificially constructed and constantly under development."[1] Cyberspace differs from the other domains, as the "terrain" is not limited to the usual geographical lines and borders easily understood in the air, land, and sea as established and recognized by various laws, agreements, treaties, and warfare.[2] For cyberspace over the last few years, many nations are attempting to exert their sovereignty over what they deem as their segments of cyberspace along physically recognized borders. But there are often unclear determinations and delineations of what is sovereign data in transit, between government and civilian use, or who has authority or responsibility between governing bodies.

As we further come to understand this new domain called cyberspace, nations and organizations will continue to use it to conduct various types of cyber actions in order to achieve their objectives and influence results in the physical world, as clearly evidenced by the latest Russo-Ukrainian War started in 2021. While cyberspace is unique, it cannot be removed from the traditional domains of air, land, and sea. However, its uses are unique, and existing policy and laws continue to struggle in application within the cyber domain. Cyberspace must be seen as more than an app store and services provided by software vendors. Instead, it should be understood to be an integrated hybrid apparatus (or simply, a system-of-system) fundamental to the resilience of our modern infrastructure and society. The terrain and activities of cyberspace are understandably different from the traditional domains of air, land, and sea; however, they all have something in common: the people.

* Cmdr., United States Navy, Naval Warfare Development Center, Norfolk, Virginia, USA. The views expressed in the article do not necessarily represent the views of the agency or the United States.

1 Introducing cyberspace operations, in: NATO Standardization Office, Introducing Cyberspace Operations, in: *NATO Allied Joint Doctrine for Cyberspace Operations*, NSO, 2020.

2 Meeting of the North Atlantic Council in Warsaw 8–9.07.2016, *Warsaw Summit Communiqué*, Warsaw, 09.07.2016.

DOI: 10.4324/9781003545750-7

From a societal and governing perspective, the question is whether the existing laws, rules, regulations, authorities, and precedence designed in a territorial context are as relevant to the cyberspace domain, and if not, what should they be. Cyberspace does not yet have agreed upon international or historic norms, codes of conduct, or even common understanding of definition and scope across the world, and often, even within our own nations and organizations.

In this chapter we will look at a very small sample of recent cyber attacks, a simple dossier of representative cyber actors, and a snapshot of the recent significant cyberspace activities, thus providing context of what the cyber terrain is and to begin to understand the scope of leading issues in cyberspace today.

2. An (Extremely) Small Sample of Recent Cyber Attacks in the Indo-Pacific

November 2022, Vanuatu

> Hackers attack servers of the Government of Vanuatu affecting those services to their nation for over a week.[3]

November 2023, Philippines

> Chinese hackers compromised Philippine government networks. Beginning in August 2023, hackers used phishing emails to embed malicious code into their target's systems to establish command-and-control and spy on their target's activities.[4]

November 2023, Australia

> DP World Australia, one of the country's largest ports operators, said on Tuesday hackers had accessed files containing personal details of employees after a cyber incident early this month forced it to suspend operations for three days.[5]

June 2024, Indonesia

> Hackers deployed ransomware in Indonesia's national data center which briefly disrupted a variety of immigration services, including immigration

3 Mao F., *Vanuatu: Hackers Strand Pacific Island Government for Over a Week* (17.11.2022) "BBC News World Asia": https://www.bbc.com/news/world-asia-63632129

4 Reuters, *Philippines Wards Off Cyber Attacks from China-Based Hackers* (05.02.2024) "Asia Pacific Data Privacy": https://www.reuters.com/world/asia-pacific/philippines-wards-off-cyber-attacks-china-based-hackers-2024-02-05/

5 Reuters, *DP World Says Hackers Stole Australian Ports Employee Data* (27.11.2023) "Technology Cybersecurity": https://www.reuters.com/technology/cybersecurity/dp-world-says-hackers-stole-australian-ports-employee-data-2023-11-28/

document management services at airports, and deleted information that was not backed up. The attack prompted Indonesia's Director General of Informatics Applications at the Communications and Informatics Ministry to resign and initiate a nation-wide audit of Indonesia's national data centers.[6]

March 2024, Palau

The government of Palau accused Chinese hackers of stealing over 20,000 government documents shortly after the island nation signed a 20-year economic and security deal with the United States in March 2024. Palau's president said this was the first major attack on government records that the island has seen.[7,8]

These cyberattacks are just a minuscule snapshot of what is occurring in cyberspace at any given moment. Some of the most common methods malicious cyber actors use to perpetuate their crimes are as follows.

Distributed Denial of Service (DDoS) Attacks

One of the oldest and still most prolific types of cyber attacks are Distributed Denial of Service (DDoS) attacks. Denial of Service (DoS) attacks use various types of data packets to flood a server with bogus requests to initiate communication. A more modern and advanced take is the DDoS attack, which distributes the source of the attack to many, often thousands, of points which work together to overwhelm network security firewall algorithms that may be resilient to DoS attacks. While as sophisticated as having a crowd of shoppers blocking a shop's door, this type of attack is still fairly effective in interrupting services and causing operational interruptions to government and businesses. As apps have moved to the cloud, so too have DDoS attacks. Advances in this method utilize modern cloud resources and more advanced bots. In more recent years, "DDoS-for-hire" has seen a 20% increase from 2022, whereas a person, company, or government may purchase this type of attack for as little as USD$5 and measured as high as several Terabits per second.[9,10]

6 Reuters, *Cyber Attack Compromised Indonesia Data Centre, Ransom Sought* (24.06.2024) "Technology Cybersecurity": https://www.reuters.com/technology/cybersecurity/cyber-attack-compromised-indonesia-data-centre-ransom-sought-reports-antara-2024-06-24/

7 Agence France Presse, *Palau Confirms 'Major' Cyberattack, Points to China* (05.06.2024) "Barron's News": https://www.barrons.com/news/palau-confirms-major-cyberattack-points-to-chinese-state-actors-2caedc3c

8 Lloyd R., *China 'Hacked Pacific Nation to Punish It for Backing Taiwan'* (05.06.2024) "The Sunday Times World Asia": https://www.thetimes.com/world/asia/article/china-hacked-pacific-nation-to-punish-it-for-backing-taiwan-l9hfb7nf0

9 Microsoft, *Microsoft Digital Defense Report 2023* (03.11.2024) "Microsoft Security Insider": https://www.microsoft.com/en-us/security/security-insider/microsoft-digital-defense-report-2023

10 1 000 000 000 000 bits, or approximately 125 copies of the entire Encyclopedia Britannica, per second.

Ransomware

IBM defines ransomware as "a type of malware that holds data and devices hostage until a ransom is paid".[11] Bad actors use ransomware as a tool to steal data that they will then return when payment is received. Ransomware attacks are the third most common cyberattack method, accounting for ten percent of all data breaches. The emergence of cryptocurrency has been attributed to the rise in popularity of ransomware attacks, as it simplifies the ransom payment. Data shows that globally there were 6,670 ransomware incidents in 2023, which was a 73 percent increase from 2022. Ransomware payments also made a new record, totaling over one billion US dollars.[12] Ransomware attacks can cause far more than lost revenue. For example, the inability to access electronic health records in hospitals can disrupt care delivery, cause appointments and procedures to be canceled, and force ambulances to travel to other facilities.[13]

Cyberattacks on Critical Infrastructure

Some of the most potentially devastating cyber attacks are those that involve attacks on Critical Infrastructure. Critical Infrastructure is defined by United States National Institute of Standards and Technology as

> System and assets, whether physical or virtual, so vital . . . that the incapacity or destruction of such systems and assets would have a debilitating impact on security, national economic security, national public health or safety, or any combination of those matters.[14]

Some examples of critical infrastructure that are vulnerable to cyber attacks are the "energy grid" (power generation and electricity transport), public transportation (including both air and sea traffic), public services, telecommunications, and manufacturing of critical resources, e.g. food, water, and housing. A well-known attack on critical infrastructure was the May 2021 attack on the Colonial Oil Pipeline in North America, which forced Colonial Oil Industries to shut down its network,

11 Kosinski M., *What Is Ransomware?* (04.06.2024) "IBM Topics": https://www.ibm.com/topics/ransomware

12 Grossman T., Smith T., *2023 RTF Global Ransomware Incident Map: Attacks Increase by 73%, Big Game Hunting Appears to Surge* (26.09.2024) "IST Future of Digital Security Blog": https://securityandtechnology.org/blog/2023-rtf-global-ransomware-incident-map/#:~:text=Global%20Ransomware%20Incidents&text=In%202023%2C%20the%20data%20shows,2023%20in%20the%20above%20graph

13 Olsen E., *Healthcare Is an 'Easy Victim' for Ransomware Attacks: How Hospitals Can Mitigate the Damage* (18.07.2024) "HealthCareDive News": https://www.healthcaredive.com/news/how-hospitals-can-mitigate-ransomware-attacks-healthcare/719751/#:~:text=Ransomware%2C%20a%20type%20of%20malware,to%20travel%20to%20other%20facilities

14 National Institute of Standards and Technology, Appendix B, in: *NIST Special Publication 800–30 Version 1*, NIST, 2012, p. B-3.

leaving huge swaths of the United States East Coast without gas and causing gas prices to rise across the entire nation.[15] Another example are the devastating malware attacks on Ukraine's power grid, which seriously compromised Ukraine's physical infrastructure in the early stages of the current Russo-Ukrainian War.[16] The energy sectors are not the only infrastructure at risk. In the maritime industry,

> (c)yber attacks on the maritime industry's operational technology (OT) systems have grown by at least 900% over the last 3 years, with some port operations being knocked out for days or even weeks, according to the maritime cybersecurity company Naval Dome.[17]

As we have seen, cyberattacks can be multidimensional, and the methods may include DDoS, ransomware, or attacks directly on critical infrastructure. The next section will be a brief glimpse at two common types of cyber perpetrators.

3. Cyber Actors

There are so many structures, rationales, goals, funding, and designs of cyber groups on the global stage that it would take another book to scratch the surface of the discussion. Existing knowledge of these various groups tend to center on objective knowledge and data analytics, but in reality, relationships of the individuals involved, their evolving skills, and opportunistic (or mandated) goals add a dynamic that makes organizing the topic immediately outdated. For the sake of this section, we will simply define two groups: (1) state-sponsored cyber teams, that are contracted, work for, or are temporarily aligned to government direction and tasking and (2) non-state-sponsored cyber teams, which tend to focus on financial gain through ransoming information, social activism, or selling their services to governments or corporations. Due to the obscurity of networking technology, governmental and corporate public affairs, and the lack of sharing of information, regulation, or enforcement, the true nature of how prolific or severe cyber actors' effects on a day-to-day basis cannot be well understood with today's policies and technical structure. Adding more confusion, many governments and corporations in the cyber security field use various methodologies to define as well as name these obscure and dynamic groups.

15 Easterly J., Fanning T., *The Attack on Colonial Pipeline: What We've Learned & What We've Done Over the Past Two Years* (07.05.2023) "Cybersecurity & Infrastructure Security Agency Blog": https://www.cisa.gov/news-events/news/attack-colonial-pipeline-what-weve-learned-what-weve-done-over-past-two-years

16 Cerf E., *Ukraine Blackouts Caused by Malware Attacks Warn Against Evolving Cybersecurity Threats to the Physical World* (17.05.2024) "UC Santa Cruz Newscenter": https://news.ucsc.edu/2024/05/ukraine-cybersecurity.html

17 Alexander J., George M., Buck G., Griffin J., *Cyber Attacks on Navy Port Supply Operations* (03.11.2024) "Booz Allen Hamilton Perspectives": https://www.boozallen.com/markets/defense/indo-pacific/cyberattacks-on-navy-port-supply-operations.html

A somewhat popular state-sponsored group that focuses effort primarily in the Indo-Pacific is United States Air Force Designation Advanced Persistent Threat (APT) 40[18,19,20] which as of 2016 seems tied to reinforcing China's Belt-and-Road initiative.[21] A brief list of tactics and exploits that have been attributed to this group are:

- Quick to identify and employ novel proof-of-concept exploitations of new vulnerabilities
- Continuously reconnoitering networks in targeted countries networks to look for known vulnerabilities that have not been secured or patched and end-of-life devices that likely no longer are maintained by the vendor
- Acquires domains that appear to be legitimate
- Acquired or created new email and social media accounts for social engineering exploitation, to include spear phishing
- Use vulnerabilities to gain (higher-level administrator) access to then download tools, create backdoors, and obscure presence

An example of a non-state-sponsored cyber criminal organization is one known as RansomHouse[22,23] which uses tactics of data exfiltration and researching vulnerabilities in order to extort money from their victims. Some of the attacks they have claimed responsibility for include a November 2022 attack on Keralty, a multinational healthcare organization. Keralty provides healthcare for over six million patients in hospitals and medical centers in the U.S., Europe, Latin America, and Asia. The attack on Keralty directly impacted patients, with people waiting in line for 12 hours or more to receive medical care. The group also are attributed to bringing the government of Vanuatu to a standstill in December 2022. RansomHouse stole 3.2 Terabytes of data and disabled the websites of Vanuatu's parliament, police, and prime minister's office, which also took down the island's database of hospitals and schools. While the identities or national origins of RansomHouse are unknown, their goal is simple financial gain. On the RansomHouse Telegram

18 Gingham Typhoon (Microsoft), Kryptonite Panda (Crowdstrike), Bronze Mohawk (Secureworks), Leviathan (Proofpoint), and many more . . .

19 Cybersecurity & Infrastructure Security Agency, *People's Republic of China (PRC) Ministry of State Security APT40 Tradecraft in Action* (08.07.2024) "Cybersecurity Advisory": https://www.cisa.gov/news-events/cybersecurity-advisories/aa24-190a

20 MITRE, *Leviathan* (03.11.2024) "Groups": https://attack.mitre.org/groups/G0065/

21 Plan F., Fraser N., O'Leary J., Cannon V., Read B., *APT40: Examining a China-Nexus Espionage Actor* (04.03.2019) "Mandiant Threat Intelligence": https://cloud.google.com/blog/topics/threat-intelligence/apt40-examining-a-china-nexus-espionage-actor/

22 Noone G., *Vanuatu Is Showing Small Nations How to Resist Big Cyberattacks* (28.04.2023) "TechMonitor Focus": https://www.techmonitor.ai/focus/vanuatu-is-showing-small-nations-how-to-resist-big-cyberattacks/

23 Avertium, *Everything You Need to Know About the Data Extortion Group Ransom House* (31.01.2023) "Threat Reports": https://www.avertium.com/resources/threat-reports/everything-about-data-extortion-group-ransomhouse

channel, they have overtly stated that they don't want to "mix business with politics or work with radical hacktivists or espionage groups."

4. The Current Cyber Terrain

We need to define a common set of terms, not just of what cyberspace is, but also terms that are becoming more common in the industry and government, which then will help us better understand the complexities of what constitutes the cyber terrain. Despite the current lack of a common international understanding, many nations and entities are scrambling to assert some sort of order in the cyberterrain. So, what definition of cyberspace do we use? A quick internet search returns many, often conflicting, ideas. The US National Institute of Standards and Technology (NIST) defines cyberspace as "a global domain within the information environment consisting of the interdependent network of information systems infrastructures including the internet, telecommunications networks, computer systems, and embedded processors and controllers,"[24] while Merriam-Webster simply defines cyberspace as "the online world of computer networks and especially the internet."[25]

Internationally, the state of regional and global standards, definitions, regulations, and policies are as disjointed as can be expected. Yet, there is finally movement as the UN General Assembly has put forth a draft policy for Cybercrime on the 7th of August in 2024 after more than 20 years of dithering.[26]

In the Pacific region, the island nation of Fiji took steps back in 2017 (updated in 2024)[27] to begin implementing a cybersecurity strategy, by adopting both a five-year and a 20-year National Development Plan that placed cyber safety and fighting cybercrime as of paramount importance. In February of 2021, Fiji passed the "Cybercrime Act of 2021," which aimed to protect its people against cyber offenses.[28]

Interestingly, regional coalitions such as the Association of Southeast Asian Nations (ASEAN) released their Cybersecurity Cooperation Strategy 2021–2025,[29] where the 10-nation bloc recognized that "Cybersecurity is a key enabler of the economic progress and betterment of living standards in the digital economy,"

24 National Institute of Standards and Technology, Appendix B, in: *NIST Special Publication 800–30 Version 1*, NIST, 2012, p. B-3.

25 Merriam-Webster, *Merriam-Webster.com Dictionary* (24.10.2024) "Cyberspace": https://www.merriam-webster.com/dictionary/cyberspace

26 UN Office of Drugs and Crime, *United Nations: Member States Finalize a New Cybercrime Convention* (09.08.2024) "Press Release": https://www.unodc.org/unodc/en/frontpage/2024/August/united-nations_-member-states-finalize-a-new-cybercrime-convention.html

27 Government of the Republic of Fiji, *Fiji National Development Plan 2025–2029 and Vision 2050*, Ministry of Finance, Strategic Planning, National Development and Statistics, 2024.

28 Haniff F., Cook S., Suguturaga P., *Tackling Modern Day Extortion: The Cybercrime Act of Fiji* (09.2021) "Haniff Tuitoga Pacific News Network": https://www.haniffuitoga.com.fj/single-post/tackling-modern-day-extortion-the-cybercrime-act-of-fiji

29 Association of Southeast Asian Nations, *ASEAN Cybersecurity Cooperation Strategy (2021–2025)*, Draft, ASEN, 2022.

and the establishment of an ASEAN Cyber Emergency Response Team (CERT) to "facilitate the timely exchange of threat and attack-related information among . . . National CERTs," along with capacity building and higher awareness of cyber incidents to their member nations.

To fill the gap in the international need but lack of international consensus, there are countless Non-profit Organizations, Coalitions, and Centers attempting to bring attention to and ultimately address the policy and regulatory gaps in cyberspace. For example, in October 2024, the Center for Cybersecurity Policy and Law (a nonprofit group) announced the launch of the Digi Asia-Pacific Coalition (Digi-APAC), whose purpose is "multinational partnership that will partner with governments, businesses, and regional bodies to help shape digital and cybersecurity policy, and strengthen digital security."[30] Also, the Coalition for Cybersecurity in Asia-Pacific is an association of businesses (including, among others, Amazon Web Services and Cisco Systems) who "are working to positively shape the cybersecurity environment in Asia through policy analysis, engagement, and capacity building." The partnership analyzes cyber policy across the region, and then engages with cyber officials "to influence policy and regulation that impact markets."[31]

This apparent confusion further underscores the immediate and critical need for nations across the world to internationally come to an agreement, as free nations, on those definitions, rules, and codes of conduct so that we may operate in this global domain. We need these common understandings not just for when we are at peace, but also in times of conflict, so that we may cooperate and collaborate with others in order to maintain and enforce order.

5. Conclusions

Cyberspace is more than an abstract idea; it is a critical and essential component of modern life. While Cyberspace differs from the other domains, there must be laws, agreements, and treaties to protect and defend it. After all, we need to consider:

- How should existing national and international laws and regulations apply to these cyber incidents and actors?
- What is considered a violation of national sovereignty "in the cloud"?
- Who has ultimate sovereignty and responsibility when Russian cyber actors disrupt Ukrainian government and military information using an American satellite service provider in Polish territory?

We must universally define cyberspace and clearly delineate its lawful use. We must understand and acknowledge that nations and organizations will use cyberspace to

30 Center for Cybersecurity Policy and Law, *Center for Cybersecurity Policy and Law Launches Digi Asia-Pacific Coalition* (16.10.2024) "News Cybersecurity" https://www.centerforcybersecuritypolicy.org/insights-and-research/center-for-cybersecurity-policy-and-law-launches-digi-asia-pacific-coalition

31 The Coalition for Cybersecurity in Asia-Pacific, "About Us": https://ccapac.asia/about-us/

conduct operations in order to achieve their objectives and influence results in the physical world. Since cyberspace cannot be removed entirely from the physical domains, we must clearly understand the rules, authorities, and responsibilities of those constituent parts. Cyberspace is an integral part and fundamental to the resilience of our modern infrastructure and society.

National governments and international bodies must quickly establish, and to what extent, existing laws, rules, regulations, authorities, and precedent are relevant to cyberspace. People, organizations, and nations must view cyberspace as the integrated part of the essential human needs for modern life.

Free nations around the world must lead the way in securing cyberspace as a global resource that freely allows information exchange, trade, and the sharing of ideas. Cyberspace knows no borders or boundaries and we must act together to maintain its security to further stability, not just in the Indo-Pacific region, but globally.

References

Agence France Presse, *Palau Confirms 'Major' Cyberattack, Points to China* (05.06.2024) "Barron's News": https://www.barrons.com/news/palau-confirms-major-cyberattack-points-to-chinese-state-actors-2caedc3c

Alexander J., George M., Buck G., Griffin J., *Cyber Attacks on Navy Port Supply Operations* (03.11.2024) "Booz Allen Hamilton Perspectives": https://www.boozallen.com/markets/defense/indo-pacific/cyberattacks-on-navy-port-supply-operations.html

Association of Southeast Asian Nations, *ASEAN Cybersecurity Cooperation Strategy (2021–2025)*, Draft, ASEAN, 2022.

Avertium, *Everything You Need to Know About the Data Extortion Group Ransom House* (31.01.2023) "Threat Reports": https://www.avertium.com/resources/threat-reports/everything-about-data-extortion-group-ransomhouse

Center for Cybersecurity Policy and Law, *Center for Cybersecurity Policy and Law Launches Digi Asia-Pacific Coalition* (16.10.2024) "News Cybersecurity": https://www.centerforcybersecuritypolicy.org/insights-and-research/center-for-cybersecurity-policy-and-law-launches-digi-asia-pacific-coalition

Cerf E., *Ukraine Blackouts Caused by Malware Attacks Warn Against Evolving Cybersecurity Threats to the Physical World* (17.05.2024) "UC Santa Cruz Newscenter": https://news.ucsc.edu/2024/05/ukraine-cybersecurity.html

The Coalition for Cybersecurity in Asia-Pacific, "About Us": https://ccapac.asia/about-us/

Cybersecurity & Infrastructure Security Agency, *People's Republic of China (PRC) Ministry of State Security APT40 Tradecraft in Action* (08.07.2024) "Cybersecurity Advisory": https://www.cisa.gov/news-events/cybersecurity-advisories/aa24-190a

Easterly J., Fanning T., *The Attack on Colonial Pipeline: What We've Learned & What We've Done Over the Past Two Years* (07.05.2023) "Cybersecurity & Infrastructure Security Agency Blog": https://www.cisa.gov/news-events/news/attack-colonial-pipeline-what-weve-learned-what-weve-done-over-past-two-years

Government of the Republic of Fiji, *Fiji National Development Plan 2025–2029 and Vision 2050*, Ministry of Finance, Strategic Planning, National Development and Statistics, 2024.

Grossman T., Smith T., *2023 RTF Global Ransomware Incident Map: Attacks Increase by 73%, Big Game Hunting Appears to Surge* (26.09.2024) "IST Future of Digital Security Blog": https://securityandtechnology.org/blog/2023-rtf-global-ransomware-incident-map/#:~:text=Global%20Ransomware%20Incidents&text=In%202023%2C%20the%20data%20shows,2023%20in%20the%20above%20graph

Haniff F., Cook S., Suguturaga P., *Tackling Modern Day Extortion: The Cybercrime Act of Fiji* (09.2021) "Haniff Tuitoga Pacific News Network": https://www.haniftuitoga.com.fj/single-post/tackling-modern-day-extortion-the-cybercrime-act-of-fiji

Kosinski M., *What Is Ransomware?* (04.06.2024) "IBM Topics": https://www.ibm.com/topics/ransomware

Lloyd R., *China 'Hacked Pacific Nation to Punish It for Backing Taiwan'* (05.06.2024) "The Sunday Times World Asia": https://www.thetimes.com/world/asia/article/china-hacked-pacific-nation-to-punish-it-for-backing-taiwan-l9hfb7nf0

Mao F., *Vanuatu: Hackers Strand Pacific Island Government for Over a Week* (17.11.2022) "BBC News World Asia": https://www.bbc.com/news/world-asia-63632129

Meeting of the North Atlantic Council in Warsaw 8–9.07.2016, *Warsaw Summit Communiqué*, Warsaw, 09.07.2016.

Merriam-Webster, *Merriam-Webster.com Dictionary* (24.10.2024) "Cyberspace": https://www.merriam-webster.com/dictionary/cyberspace

Microsoft, *Microsoft Digital Defense Report 2023* (03.11.2024) "Microsoft Security Insider": https://www.microsoft.com/en-us/security/security-insider/microsoft-digital-defense-report-2023

MITRE, *Leviathan* (03.11.2024) "Groups": https://attack.mitre.org/groups/G0065/

National Institute of Standards and Technology, Appendix B, in: *NIST Special Publication 800–30 Version 1*, NIST, 2012, p. B-3.

NATO Standardization Office, Introducing Cyberspace Operations, in: *NATO Allied Joint Doctrine for Cyberspace Operations*, NSO, 2020, pp. 2, B-5.

Noone G., *Vanuatu Is Showing Small Nations How to Resist Big Cyberattacks* (28.04.2023) "TechMonitor Focus": https://www.techmonitor.ai/focus/vanuatu-is-showing-small-nations-how-to-resist-big-cyberattacks/

Olsen E., *Healthcare Is an 'Easy Victim' for Ransomware Attacks: How Hospitals Can Mitigate the Damage* (18.07.2024) "HealthCareDive News": https://www.healthcaredive.com/news/how-hospitals-can-mitigate-ransomware-attacks-healthcare/719751/#:~:text=Ransomware%2C%20a%20type%20of%20malware,to%20travel%20to%20other%20facilities

Plan F., Fraser N., O'Leary J., Cannon V., Read B., *APT40: Examining a China-Nexus Espionage Actor* (04.03.2019) "Mandiant Threat Intelligence": https://cloud.google.com/blog/topics/threat-intelligence/apt40-examining-a-china-nexus-espionage-actor/

Reuters, *Cyber Attack Compromised Indonesia Data Centre, Ransom Sought* (24.06.2024) "Technology Cybersecurity": https://www.reuters.com/technology/cybersecurity/cyber-attack-compromised-indonesia-data-centre-ransom-sought-reports-antara-2024-06-24/

Reuters, *DP World Says Hackers Stole Australian Ports Employee Data* (27.11.2023) "Technology Cybersecurity": https://www.reuters.com/technology/cybersecurity/dp-world-says-hackers-stole-australian-ports-employee-data-2023-11-28/

Reuters, *Philippines Wards Off Cyber Attacks from China-Based Hackers* (05.02.2024) "Asia Pacific Data Privacy": https://www.reuters.com/world/asia-pacific/philippines-wards-off-cyber-attacks-china-based-hackers-2024-02-05/

UN Office of Drugs and Crime, *United Nations: Member States Finalize a New Cybercrime Convention* (09.08.2024) "Press Release": https://www.unodc.org/unodc/en/frontpage/2024/August/united-nations_-member-states-finalize-a-new-cybercrime-convention.html

Part II

Actors Shaping the Indo-Pacific Region Presence and Future

7 Irregular Warfare Lessons Learned from Operation Pacific Eagle-Philippines

Amparo Pamela Fabe and Joan Andrea Toledo***

1. Introduction

The U.S. Government launched Operation Pacific Eagle-Philippines (OPE-P) in 2017 to support the Philippine government in its efforts to counter Islamic State of Iraq and Syria (ISIS) affiliates and other violent extremist organizations in the Philippines.[1] In coordination with other U.S. Government agencies, the U.S. Department of Defense (DoD) conducts counterterrorism operations under the auspices of OPE-P by, with, and through its Philippine partners. It is important to take into account the insights of retired US Army Colonel Dave Maxwell, a former commander of Joint Special Operations Task Force-Philippines, who stated that many local terrorist organizations were attracted to the narratives and messages of ISIS in order to enforce their legitimacy and win recruits, generate resources, and gain respect (OPE-P, 2020). This chapter highlights the major lessons learned from this operation, particularly in the area of engagement with partner forces and in the conduct of information operations.

2. Information Operations

Extremism takes place in all societies and takes on different faiths, ideologies and beliefs based on race religion, class and ethnicity. Violent extremism is a complicated phenomenon that consists of various structural and psychological elements.[2] The phenomenon of Terrorism and Violent Extremism is definitely shaped by many forces, and it is impacted by the response of countries towards terrorists as well as terrorist groups. The subsequent government responses are heavily influenced by domestic political issues, international terrorism incidents or trends and increasing

* Faculty Member, National Police College and Philippine Public Safety College
** Board Member, Indo-Pacific Alliance Corp and Consultant, Armed Forces of the Philippines.
1 The authors underscore the importance of enduring US-Philippine defense and security relationship amidst the geopolitical challenges in the Indo-Pacific. This work highlights the benefits of lesser-known operations of the US Department of Defense with partner countries.
2 United Nations Development Program. (2020). *Assuming the Worst: Narratives and their Impacts on Violent Extremism in South-East Asia*. Thailand: UNDP Publications Office.

DOI: 10.4324/9781003545750-9

geopolitical tensions. The Philippine governments uphold the importance of continuous vigilance and urgent action going forward.

The government policies on preventing and countering violent extremism have slowly evolved over time as the former takes in the series of suicide bombings that have occurred, and the scale, nature and surprise that was caused by the terrorist proponents of the Marawi Siege that took place in the City of Marawi, Lanao del Sur from May to October 2017. The Islamic State (IS) wanted to declare an East Asia Wilayat, or province of the caliphate, in the Philippines. The IS wanted to replicate what they had previously established in Iraq and Syria. The siege of Marawi shows that IS can co-opt local groups and undermine the sovereignty of the ASEAN (Association of Southeast Asian Nations) member states and their bilateral and regional security cooperation. The Marawi siege reflects the importance of increasing various ASEAN cooperative and collaborative mechanisms to tackle the threat posed by a build-up of IS capabilities in Southeast Asia and the need to effectively deal with home-grown extremism.[3] The Marawi Siege has left a long trail of trauma and post-traumatic stress syndrome among Filipino security forces and internally displaced residents. The Islamic State have inspired some terrorist attacks by these groups; however, they have proved to be neither very deadly nor enduring. They also supplied some form of funding. The IS provided the inspiration for the occupation of the city of Marawi in the Philippines through a loose conglomeration of supporting groups which promoted terrorism.

Table 7.1. Narratives by Islamic State-East Asia Post-Marawi Siege by Amparo Pamela Fabe and Joan Andrea Toledo.

Concept	*Islamic State-East Asia (IS-EA) – ASG-Maute Filipino Terrorists*	*Bangsamoro Islamic Freedom Fighters*	*Islamic State-East Asia Affiliated Foreign Terrorist Fighters*
A. US-Related Narratives	The US Forces are here to reinforce the oppressive policies of the Philippine government.	The US Forces assist the Armed Forces of the Philippines to arrest designated high-profile foreign terrorists.	The US Forces empower the Philippine security forces in terms of firepower, tactics and techniques, making it difficult for terrorists who are veterans of Syria to fight with them.

(*Continued*)

3 Rommel Banlaoi. (ed.), *The Marawi Siege and Its Aftermath*. London: Cambridge Scholars Publishing, UK Press, p. 1.

Table 7.1 (Continued)

Concept	*Islamic State-East Asia (IS-EA) – ASG-Maute Filipino Terrorists*	*Bangsamoro Islamic Freedom Fighters*	*Islamic State-East Asia Affiliated Foreign Terrorist Fighters*
	The US forces are present to get the natural resources which belong to the local population.	The US forces are present to get the natural resources which belong to the local population.	The US forces are present to get the natural resources which belong to the local population.
	The US forces prefer to kill the IS-EA terrorists rather than bring them to justice.	The US forces apply lethal force all the time.	The US forces prefer to kill the IS-EA terrorists rather than bring them to justice.
B. Narratives for the Philippine Audience	The IS-EA offers a stable employment and income for the Muslim youth and Muslim men.	The IS-EA affiliation brings followers closer to the dream of a caliphate.	Swearing allegiance to IS-EA will bring in financial support from the Middle East.
	The IS-EA offers paramilitary training, helping young men to protect themselves and their families.	The IS-EA gives weapons and ammunition to followers, assuring their security and those of their families.	The Muslim youth will have a better life by joining the IS-EA terrorist organization and have the opportunity to travel to Malaysia and Indonesia.
	The Philippine government does not care about the future of the Muslim youth and causes their continuous marginalization.	The Philippine government does not care about the future of the Muslim youth and causes their continuous marginalization.	The Philippine government does not care about the future of the Muslim youth and causes their continuous marginalization.
	The Islamic Caliphate will have a modern administration and offer justice for everyone.	The Islamic Caliphate will have a modern administration and offer justice for everyone.	The Islamic Caliphate will have a modern administration and offer justice for everyone.
	The IS-EA has a plethora of resources in the Middle East that can be downloaded to the Philippines and Indonesia.	The IS-EA has a plethora of resources in the Middle East that can be downloaded to the Philippines and Indonesia.	The IS-EA has a plethora of resources in the Middle East that can be downloaded to the Philippines and Indonesia.

(*Continued*)

Table 7.1 (Continued)

Concept	*Islamic State-East Asia (IS-EA) – ASG-Maute Filipino Terrorists*	*Bangsamoro Islamic Freedom Fighters*	*Islamic State-East Asia Affiliated Foreign Terrorist Fighters*
	In order to bring about the Islamic Caliphate, violence is a necessary instrument for those who will not cooperate with the terrorists.	In order to bring about the Islamic Caliphate, violence is a necessary instrument for those who will not cooperate with the terrorists.	In order to bring about the Islamic Caliphate, violence is a necessary instrument for those who will not cooperate with the terrorists.

Source: Interviews with Islamic State-East Asia terrorists, Bangsamoro Islamic Freedom Fighters terrorists and Islamic State-East Asia Affiliated Foreign Terrorist Fighters After the Marawi Siege in Lanao del Sur by Amparo Pamela Fabe and Joan Andrea Toledo, Indo-Pacific Alliance Corp, May-October 2017.

3. Discussion of IS-EA Narratives Post-Marawi Siege

The Islamic State East Asia (IS-EA) terrorists and their affiliates, the Abu Sayaff Group-Maute Group, which is funded by ISIS, focused their ongoing youth recruitment of Muslim, Christian and tribal youth primarily through the use of Facebook, WhatsApp, Telegram and Facebook Messenger after the Marawi Siege.[4] The IS-EA terrorists also spread their online radicalization efforts through several Facebook accounts featuring the aforementioned narratives spread through the major local Muslim dialects like Yakan, Maguindanaoan, Tausug, Sanguil, Iranun, Jama Mapun, Kalagan, Kalibugan, Maguindanao, Maranao, Molbog and Sama. Several FB accounts featuring IS-EA narratives were also written in Chavacano, a dialect prevalent in Zamboanga City. The primary focus of the Islamic State is Islamic radicalization. The secondary goal is to spread disinformation and misinformation against the U.S. and Philippine forces. Although the Philippine security forces are also helped by Japanese, Australian, Israeli, Bruneian and Singaporean security forces, the general narrative of the IS-EA terrorists is focused on the U.S. forces only.[5]

The series of counter-narratives and information operations that were carried out by the Philippine Army in Facebook and WhatsApp accounts through the help of the OPE-P were also conducted in the Muslim dialects. The Philippine Army information operations officers recruited Muslim social media influencers, who recruited other Muslim university students who were active and influential in social

4 AsiaTimes.Com. (February 21, 2019). "Facebook Has a Terrorism Problem in the Philippines." Available at URL: https://asiatimes.com/2019/02/facebook-has-a-terrorism-problem-in-the-philippines/.

5 Amparo Pamela Fabe and Joan Andrea Toledo. (May–October 2017). Unpublished Field Notes in Narrative Warfare.

media. These social media influencers were given the appropriate training on several occasions by Philippine Army social media experts.

4. Analysis and Lessons Learned on Information Operations

There are three main takeaways in the area of information operations. The first main takeaway is that the main impact of the U.S. and Philippine security forces was for the latter to increase and widen their online presence and radio presence after the Marawi Siege. The Armed Forces of the Philippines (AFP) and Philippine National Police Special Action Force (PNP-SAF) and the Philippine Coast Guard (PCG) decided to establish, craft and widen their counter-narratives against IS-EA terrorists to be able to reach to all the Filipino youth groups who were the most vulnerable to recruitment and violence. Specifically, university and high school teachers as well as school administrators and guidance counselors in the Lanao del Sur and Lanao del Norte provinces were tapped and encouraged to voluntarily help in the campaign for peace after the Marawi Siege and the spread of information on government projects in terms of social and economic development in conflict areas were disseminated.[6]

The second takeaway is the the U.S. and the Armed Forces were closely integrated into various post-9/11 irregular warfare campaigns that were carried out from December 2017 to June 2018.

It is important to highlight the multiple positive effects of the irregular warfare campaigns that were crafted and duly implemented. The positive specific effects they produced consisted of the reduction in the number of youths who were recruited in the succeeding months and the identification of specific Facebook and WhatsApp accounts that were constantly used by the terrorists and terrorist organizations. Additionally, another positive effect of the information operations was the diminishing network cohesion of the Islamic State-East Asia and the decreasing support from the international leadership of ISIS (ISIS-Core). Moreover, as more local terrorists were arrested, the series of information operations had a negative impact on the terrorists' internal leadership, which then impeded ISIS-EA's ability to conduct activity outside its base of operations or carry out large-scale attacks. The sustained information operations had weakened the resolve of the terrorists in the succeeding months for online radicalization and the spread of their ideology.[7]

The third key takeaway for the U.S. forces as well as the AFP was that the primary measure of success and effectiveness of the information operations units was the drastic reduction in the number of Facebook accounts, WhatsApp, Telegram and Facebook Messenger accounts linked to IS-EA terrorists that were taken down by Facebook at the request of the Philippine Government after the Marawi Siege.

6 Amparo Pamela Fabe and Joan Andrea Toledo. (May–October 2017). Unpublished Field Notes in Narrative Warfare.

7 Operation Pacific Eagle-Philippines Bulletin. (January 1, 2020–March 31, 2020), pp. 11–14.

The AFP continue monitoring all these accounts in order to ensure that the Muslim youth are protected from extremist online views.

A joint study by The Asia Foundation and Rappler concluded that Facebook has a terrorism problem in the Philippines. The study showed that young Filipinos who are residents of the southern Mindanao region were found and contacted over Facebook Messenger by anonymous Islamic State (ISIS) recruiters. The number of Filipino youths who have been recruited by the IS-EA terrorists is not confirmed. The study showed that Facebook was used to spread propaganda and increase its members within IS-EA. It concluded that most of the extremist online activities are basically opportunistic and unsophisticated and that the localized messaging focused on local grievances, which were then widely published and disseminated online.[8] An added measure of success reported by the U.S. Department of Defense officials was that ISIS's total media footprint had decreased by as much as 83 percent since its peak in 2014 and 2015. Moreover, its monthly online magazine, the Rumiyah, had not been published in 14 months.[9]

5. Engaging with Partner Forces

There are three areas of evaluation where U.S. forces can be evaluated while engaging with partner forces, the AFP, PCG and PNP-SAF. The U.S. forces face diverse challenges in the process of engaging with local forces, indigenous forces and enemy forces. The soldiers need to possess the requisite language skills, social, historical, economic and cultural knowledge of the place, and they need a good grasp of societal as well as community-based implications of ongoing military operations.

The first area of concern is to determine the best practices of the U.S. forces for engaging with allied and indigenous military, paramilitary and guerrilla forces. The Filipino military personnel have a positive perspective of the current engagement of U.S. forces, where they view the latter as showing a high level of courage, commitment and dedication. Some of the best practices of the U.S. forces for engaging with their Philippine colleagues are trust and respect in all mutual dealings focusing on counterterrorism efforts. The U.S. forces relay information that is immediately acted upon by Philippine forces due to this prevailing high level of trust and respect. In December 2019, the AFP's 33rd Infantry Battalion and 5th Special Forces Battalion engaged in heavy combat with the BIFF in Mamasapano and Shariff Aguak, two towns in central Mindanao where the BIFF has strongholds. The fighting resulted in the AFP overrunning nearly a dozen BIFF camps and killing at least seven militants. The U.S. forces trusted the report of the AFP on the number of casualties when they stated that "the general outcome was positive" and

8 The Asia Foundation/Rappler. (2018). *Understanding Violent Extremism: Messaging and Recruitment Strategies on Social Media in the Philippines*. Manila, Philippines: The Asia Foundation Publications.

9 Operation Pacific Eagle-Philippines Bulletin. (October 1, 2018–December 31, 2018), p. 12.

resulted in the removal of Bangsamoro Islamic Freedom Fighters (BIFF) elements from the area and a reduction in violent extremist organization activity. In addition, the AFP established a checkpoint in Indanan in response to reports of a planned suicide bombing in Jolo, Sulu. The terrorists started a firefight which resulted in the deaths of all three terrorists. In order to achieve a long-term impact, the U.S. forces established a Regional Counterterrorism Training Center for the Philippine government with the objective of denying terrorist groups the freedom of movement and access to terrorism financing.[10]

A second aspect of best practices is the manner of engagement of U.S. forces in adopting a continuous level of consultation and collegial decision-making approach when it comes to the launch of joint operations. Another best practice is the high level of intelligence sharing of the U.S. forces with their partner forces. For example, the USINDOPACOM described ISIS-Philippines as being in a "reorganization stage" with the capability to carry out only "small-scale attacks such as the improvised explosive devices and small-arms and ambush attacks."[11] To add, the USINDOPACOM's intelligence assessment revealed the ISIS-EA's lack of network cohesion and viable support from the international leadership of ISIS (ISIS-Core). The assessment also revealed the weaknesses of IS-EA, such as the lack of a strong internal leadership and adequate financing that has impeded ISIS-EA's ability to conduct activity outside its base of operations to carry out large-scale attacks.[12]

A third best practice is the rapid assistance given to the Philippine forces after the Marawi Siege through the establishment of the Operation Pacific Eagle-Philippines. The U.S. special operations forces provided support to the AFP, consisting of logistical support; intelligence sharing; operational planning; and intelligence, surveillance and reconnaissance. The aim of OPE-P was to help the AFP stabilize the area and prevent the southern Philippines from becoming a safe haven for terrorists.[13]

The fourth best practice is the use of technology, such as the utilization of the U.S. Marine Corps MQ-9A Reaper drones, which were transferred to a Philippine Air Force base. This drone supported intelligence-sharing efforts between the U.S. Indo-Pacific Command and the AFP, and the I Marine Expeditionary Force. The missions undertaken spanned five sorties over the South China Sea to support critical maritime domain awareness and overwatch of the Second Thomas Shoal. An Army MQ-1C Grey Eagle stationed another air base in the Southern Philippines flew over a Philippine resupply mission to BRP Sierra Madre at Second Thomas Shoal as part of the counter-terrorism missions. The Marine Unmanned Aerial Vehicle (UAV) Squadron also utilized its new Reaper unmanned aerial vehicles in several missions. The Marine Corps UAV squadron was the first to achieve initial operational capability of the service's MQ-9A Extended-Range Marine Air-Ground Task Force Unmanned Expeditionary Medium-Altitude, High-Endurance aircraft.

10 Operation Pacific Eagle-Philippines Bulletin. (October 1, 2019–December 31, 2019), pp. 15–16.
11 Operation Pacific Eagle-Philippines. (July 1, 2018–September 30, 2018), p. 18.
12 Operation Pacific Eagle-Philippines Bulletin. (July 1, 2019–September 30, 2019), p. 4.
13 Operation Pacific Eagle-Philippines Bulletin. (October 1, 2017–December 31, 2017), p. 6.

The Marines have used more capable and longer-ranged Unmanned Aerial Systems that support new concepts and missions.[14]

The fifth best practice is the continuous provision of capacity building, such as counterterrorism training for Philippine forces and legal skills training for Philippine prosecutors that were conducted jointly by the U.S. Department of Defense and U.S. Department of State. According to the USINDOPACOM, the U.S. advisors provided training to the AFP on the proper use of tactical equipment, such as night vision goggles; small intelligence, surveillance and reconnaissance (ISR) unmanned aircraft systems; and remotely operated video devices. Moreover, the AFP has requested additional U.S. training on the use of ISR assets and intelligence processing systems to seek and identify ISIS-EA terrorists (OPE-P Report July 1, 2019-October 31, 2019). Additionally, the U.S. Marines and the members of the Philippine Marine Corps participated in a U.S.-Philippine Marine Aviation Support Activity that tackled strategic issues on mutual defense, counterterrorism, humanitarian assistance and disaster relief. This particular training aimed to improve and hasten the interoperability and to upgrade the aviation capabilities of both the U.S. and Philippine forces. Lastly, on September 6, 2019, U.S. Ambassador to the Philippines Sung Kim participated in the Philippine Convention of Counterterrorism Prosecutors in Manila, which gathered 70 prosecutors as participants. U.S. Department of Justice personnel worked and cooperated with their Philippine counterparts to promote the best practices in investigating and in successfully prosecuting terrorism cases. A major objective was achieving a high conviction rate for all of the future anti-terrorism cases that will be filed in local courts.[15]

The U.S. forces also pinpoint the weaknesses of the Philippine forces and recommend implementing the appropriate intervention. According to the U.S. Special Operation Command Pacific, the Armed Forces of the Philippines' organizational infrastructure is unable to generate, process or act upon intelligence gathered from manned and unmanned aerial systems independent of U.S. support. To be able to address this specific capacity gap, the U.S. Department of Defense gave the AFP an intelligence training package, software, multiple unmanned aerial vehicle systems, tactical command posts and other equipment to increase command and control, situational awareness and operational security. Additionally, the USINDOPACOM spent US$50.1 million on contracted Intelligence Surveillance Reconnaissance (ISR) operations and US$11.8 million on U.S. Army ISR support to the Armed Forces of the Philippines in fiscal year 2019.[16]

The second factor is to determine the specific aspects of U.S. culture (both military and civilian) that kept them from better engaging with allied and indigenous forces. There are two main points for improvement. The first point is the need for humility among the U.S. forces to accept alternative viewpoints from partner

14 US Naval Institute News. (June 3, 2024). "U.S. Marine MQ-9A Reapers Now Deployed to the Philippines." p. 5.

15 Operation Pacific Eagle-Philippines Bulletin. (July 1, 2019–October 31, 2019), p. 8.

16 Operation Pacific Eagle-Philippines Bulletin. (October 1, 2018–December 31, 2018), p. 7.

forces. Diversity of opinion and perspectives is important for an increased level of engagement with the local troops. The U.S. forces commander should not interpret the non-agreement to his advice as a failure to understand on the part of the local commanders. It is just that sometimes the perspectives differ on some topics. The second point is to respect the Asian way, which focuses on adopting an indirect approach and which is done by way of suggestion instead of a straightforward presentation of one's opinion or perspective. Sometimes, if the U.S. forces commander does not understand the Asian style of management, then they will fail to detect the opinion or perspective of the Filipino commander. However, with the increasing number of Filipino officers who study in U.S. military colleges, future Filipino commanders will be better able to understand the leadership styles of the designated U.S. force commanders.

The third factor highlights the kind of partnering that needs to be done in the future with regards to the selection, training and support of U.S. advisors assigned to partner forces. There are multiple areas for improvement on the part of the U.S. advisors. There is a need for U.S. advisors to training Filipino commanders to show innovation in combat. Since urban warfare is highly unpredictable, the advisors should be able to formulate solutions taking into account the importance of necessity and expediency. The advisors need to help the Filipino commanders find localized solutions to local problems and to give strong encouragement to the troops to be creative in carrying out their respective missions.[17]

In addition, the U.S. advisors must help combat forces to be adept at using Unmanned Aerial Services (UAS); there is benefit from increasing exposure to, and understanding of, these technologies. There is a need for more U.S. advisors who are well-versed in combat shooting, battlefield fitness and small team tactics, techniques and procedures (TTPs) to achieve better success in the field. Combat shooting, urban tactics, joint fires, counter Improvised Explosive Device (CIED), urban breaching and combat trauma management training will empower the AFP, PNP-SAF and the PCG to win more rapidly in the field and to sustain fewer casualties. There is a need for U.S. advisors who can train Philippine forces in fighting as combined-arms sections, platoons, combat teams and battlegroups. Since it takes considerable time to refine TTPs and develop the trust and understanding required to fight in combined-arms teams, the U.S. advisors need to ensure that infantry and armor should train together regularly in this environment. Urban mobility training for armor and engineers should also be prioritized. The combined process of small team leadership and developing tactical acumen needs to be a fundamental line of effort.[18]

17 James Lewis. (November 27, 2018). "The Battle of Marawi: Small Team Lessons Learned for the Close Fight." Available at URL: https://cove.army.gov.au/article/battle-marawi-small-team-lessons-learned-close-fight.

18 James Lewis. (November 27, 2018). "The Battle of Marawi: Small Team Lessons Learned for the Close Fight." Available at URL: https://cove.army.gov.au/article/battle-marawi-small-team-lessons-learned-close-fight.

6. Conclusion

There are several key lessons learned by the U.S. and Armed Forces of the Philippines (AFP), the Philippine Coast Guard (PCG) and the Philippine National Police Special Action Force (PNP-SAF) in a post-Marawi Siege setting which are a valuable reference for the forces to assimilate and understand prior to the next conflict. Giving due importance and consideration to these lessons could help inform, improve, refine and perfect the current approaches to the force generation and modernization of these forces. These lessons in the area of information operations and engagement with Coalition/Partner Forces, in this case the AFP, the PCG and the PNP-SAF, have broad relevance across a number of corps and disciplines. The prevailing existential reality of conflict amongst people will compel the Army to be experts at this most difficult of environments so as to emerge victorious from the different conflict areas. There has to be continued emphasis on the importance and the development of the individual and small team skillset. The Philippine forces, which are composed of small teams, showed remarkable adaptability and innovation in solving the challenges they faced in a post-conflict environment.[19] The U.S. forces need to assimilate and understand the key lessons learned from both the information operations and engagement with Coalition/Partner forces in order to maximize their ability to operate, fight and win in the urban environment.

The United States-Philippine security relationship has been centered on bolstering deterrence as well as supporting Philippine efforts to combat terrorism since the 2000s. In 2002, U.S. and Philippine servicemen worked closely in Operation Enduring Freedom-Philippines to eliminate the threat posed by the Abu Sayyaf Group on the island of Basilan. By 2006, U.S. and Philippine forces worked together in Oplan Ultimatum to carry out decapitation strikes against the Abu Sayyaf Group leaders. The U.S. advisory and training role took a very prominent role in Operation Pacific Eagle-Philippines, and by its conclusion in 2020, the serious threat posed by terrorism decreased greatly.[20] This positive development in the form of an improved peace and ordered environment can be attributed to the joint partnership and engagement of both U.S. and Philippine forces.

Bibliography

The Asia Foundation/Rappler. (2018). *Understanding Violent Extremism: Messaging and Recruitment Strategies on Social Media in the Philippines*. Manila, Philippines: The Asia Foundation Publications.

AsiaTimes.Com. (February 21, 2019). "Facebook Has a Terrorism Problem in the Philippines." Available at URL: https://asiatimes.com/2019/02/facebook-has-a-terrorism-problem-in-the-philippines/.

19 G. Fealy. (2017). The Battle for Marawi and ISIS in South East Asia." *ASPI Strategist*, p. 4, last accessed 23 August 2018. Available at URL: https://www.aspistrategist.org.au/battle-marawi-isis-southeast-asia/https://www.aspistrategist.org.au/battle-marawi-isis-southeast-asia/.

20 The Soufan Center. (May 30, 2024). "IntelBrief: The U.S. and the Philippines Strengthen Ties as a Bulwark to Counter China." p. 5. https://thesoufancenter.org/intelbrief-2024-may-30.

Fabe, Amparo Pamela and Joan Andrea Toledo. (May–October 2017). Unpublished Field Notes in Narrative Warfare.

Fealy, G. (2017). "The Battle for Marawi and ISIS in South East Asia." *ASPI Strategist*, last accessed 23 August 2018. Available at URL: https://www.aspistrategist.org.au/battle-marawi-isis-southeast-asia/https://www.aspistrategist.org.au/battle-marawi-isis-southeast-asia/.

Lewis, James. (November 27, 2018). "The Battle of Marawi: Small Team Lessons Learned for the Close Fight." Available at URL: https://cove.army.gov.au/article/battle-marawi-small-team-lessons-learned-close-fight.

Operation Pacific Eagle-Philippines and Other Overseas Contingency Operations. (October 1, 2017–December 31, 2017). *Lead Inspector General Report to the United States Congress*. Hawaii, US: INDOPACOM Headquarters.

Operation Pacific Eagle-Philippines and Other Overseas Contingency Operations. (July 1, 2018–September 30, 2018). *Lead Inspector General Report to the United States Congress*. Hawaii, US: INDOPACOM Headquarters.

Operation Pacific Eagle-Philippines and Other Overseas Contingency Operations. (October 1, 2018–December 31, 2018). *Lead Inspector General Report to the United States Congress*. Hawaii, US: INDOPACOM Headquarters.

Operation Pacific Eagle-Philippines and Other Overseas Contingency Operations. (July 1, 2019–October 31, 2019). *Lead Inspector General Report to the United States Congress*. Hawaii, US: INDOPACOM Headquarters.

Operation Pacific Eagle-Philippines and Other Overseas Contingency Operations. (October 1, 2019–December 1, 2019). *Lead Inspector General Report to the United States Congress*. Hawaii, US: INDOPACOM Headquarters.

Operation Pacific Eagle-Philippines and Other Overseas Contingency Operations. (January 1, 2020–March 31, 2020). *Lead Inspector General Report to the United States Congress*. Hawaii, US: INDOPACOM Headquarters.

The Soufan Center. (May 30, 2024). "IntelBrief: The U.S. and the Philippines Strengthen Ties as a Bulwark to Counter China." Available at URL: https://thesoufancenter.org/intelbrief-2024-may-30/.

United Nations Development Program. (2020). *Assuming the Worst: Narratives and Their Impacts on Violent Extremism in South-East Asia*. Thailand: UNDP Publications Office.

USNI News. (June 3, 2024). "U.S. Marine MQ-9A Reapers Now Deployed to the Philippines."

8 Who Will Dive into the Crevasse? Backlash of the Russia-North Korea Defense Pact in the Communist trio of Russia-North Korea-China

*Soojeong Choi**

1. Introduction

When Russia and North Korea agreed to revamp their forgotten military assistance treaty in 1961, the rest of the world was seriously concerned about whether the agreement might be another source of instability in the Korean Peninsula. With consideration of the bomb-shed battlefield of Ukraine, Russia grabbed a new supporter to provide it with massive ammunition. However, as for the isolated State, North Korea, stricken by continuous sanctions in the United Nations Security Council (hereinafter UNSC), this would be an opportunity to escape from such difficulties. In particular, since the aid from China was not enough to relieve the scarcity and darkness in North Korea, North Korea wanted further support. However, China has taken a lukewarm attitude toward the issue of labor exports to China. North Korea needed a substantial source of money other than trade with China. In these circumstances, the interests of Russia and North Korea fell into place.

However, the aftermath is not calculated precisely. As for the relationship between North Korea and Russia, it should go back to their first bilateral agreement to ensure the peace and security of North Korea in the Korean Peninsula. The treaty needs to be comparatively analyzed compared to this new treaty in 2024. Their most crucial clause would be the "immediate military assistance" in both treaties. The reason the first military assistance treaty in 1961 was terminated should be researched to understand the background of the newly inserted "military assistance" in 2024. A comparative analysis is needed with another "military assistance" treaty between China and North Korea. By concluding another military assistance treaty in the middle of North Korea, it seems that the communist trio completed a triangle alliance for political stability in the Korean Peninsula. However, some untold restraints are preventing them from fastening their relations tightly. Their goals in the Korean Peninsula need to be elaborated to understand their delicate and complicated power dynamics. These three States have different goals when making bilateral agreements on military assistance.

Most of all, what is conspicuous is that North Korea is in the middle of these treaties to invite the two strong States into the Korean Peninsula. From both treaties,

* Ph.D. Candidate, Faculty of Law, Hamburg University

DOI: 10.4324/9781003545750-10

China bought the status quo in the Korean Peninsula with food, energy, and money. And it allowed China to take significant leverage over North Korea with almost monopolistic dominance. On the other hand, Russia also paid substantial aid to suffice the scarcity of food and energy for North Korea, even with its high technology. Finally, it was returned with the support of mass ammunition for Russian arms to fight in Ukraine. According to these two treaties, North Korea succeeded in making two sources of aid for food, energy, and money. In addition, it did not promise to stop any nuclear weapons or missile test programs. North Korea was deemed to have diplomatic success with two big States. However, the situation in the Korean peninsula depends on North Korea's follow-up skills.

2. What is the Matter in the New Defense Pact Between Russia and Korea?

Between 18 and 19 June 2024, Russian President Vladimir Putin visited Kim Jeong-un of North Korea precisely 24 years after meeting Kim Jeong-il, Kim's father, in Pyongyang in 2000.[1] During Putin's visit in July 2000, he seemingly tried to persuade Kim's father to discourage the nuclear program; however, in June 2024, he took the opposite position, helping North Korea with advanced Russian technology in developing missiles and nuclear weapon systems.[2] Indeed, he utilized the unstable nuclear tensions between North and South Korea to enhance Russian influence as a *de facto* mediator. Even though at that time, Russia was in a closer relationship with South Korea, this time, Russia decided to make closer friends with North Korea.

As for the perspective of regional peace and security in the Korean Peninsula, the issue of the nuclear program by North Korea has been a leverage source to oscillate the pendulum in terms of the projection of regional influence for any political stakes in North Korea. In this respect, the weakest post has always been for South Korea, which should desperately curb the expedition of the nuclear program and has asked Russia and China for influence at the cost of non-political interests. Before this visit in 2024, Russia seemingly took balanced distances between the two Koreas and exploited economic and political stakes with proper mitigations. However, this visit in 2024 ruined the vibe of the relationship between Russia and South Korea, which will lead to a fiasco. Russia made a treaty with North Korea as a form of a bilateral agreement, reviving the obsolete military pact in the formal Soviet Union and casting undeniable signs of a neo-cold war in the Korean peninsula. Hence, in the wake of military guarantees by Russia, North Korea can get a revamped military alliance with Russia, which will be a good source of propaganda

1 Presidential Press and Information Office, "A Russian-North Korean Summit Was Held in Pyongyang", 19 July 2000, http://en.kremlin.ru/events/president/news/38435

2 Andrew S. Bowen et al., "Russia-North Korea Relations", CRS Reports, 10 September 2024, https://crsreports.congress.gov/product/pdf/IF/IF12760

for its people to hypnotize their country to finish the nuclear program and outwit the threat of hegemonic States, like the USA.

During the visit in 2024, Russia and North Korea agreed on three things: the Comprehensive Partnership Treaty, the Agreement between the governments of North Korea and Russia on the construction of a road bridge across the Tumangang border, and the Agreement between the governments of North Korea and Russia on cooperation in health care, medical education, and science. The most noticeable one is the status of a comprehensive partnership with North Korea. Meanwhile, Russia made a 'Treaty of Friendship, Good-Neighborliness and Cooperation' with North Korea in 2000; this agreement meant a significant leap in the relationship for North Korea.[3]

3. Guarantee for Immediate Military Assistance

Then, with a review of the contents of this comprehensive partnership agreement, there are some conspicuous points: military assistance, respect for the UN system, and the attitude of non-reciprocity with third States. First, the "military assistance clause" was revamped after terminating the "Treaty of Friendship, co-operation, and mutual assistance" in 1996.[4] In comparison with "military assistance" in Soviet-DPRK in 1961,[5] the military assistance in Russia-DPRK in 2024 has two extensive procedural requirements "by Article 51 of the UN Charter" and "in accordance with the legislation of the Democratic People's Republic of Korea and the Russian Federation."[6] As well-known as the armor of Article 51 of the UN charter, many mutual defense arrangements depend on this peace and security framework.[7] This clause allows every state the inherent right of self-defense in individual or collective ways. However, it also delimits such exercises until the Security Council's necessary measures are taken. Where one party would be a

3 For example, it has a 'new era comprehensive strategic cooperative partnership' with China and a 'special and privileged strategic partnership' with India. In addition to North Korea, the countries with which Russia has a 'comprehensive strategic partnership' include Vietnam, Egypt, Mongolia, and South Africa. Russia established a 'strategic cooperative partnership' with South Korea in 2008 and added the modifier 'comprehensive' to it with North Korea.

4 North Korea and Russia have signed three treaties consecutively, which are the Treaty of Friendship, co-operation, and mutual assistance in 1961(terminated in 1996; hereinafter Soviet-DPRK Treaty in 1961), the Treaty of Friendship, good neighborliness and Cooperation in 2000, and Treaty on comprehensive strategic partnership in 2024 (hereinafter Russia-DPRK treaty in 2024). The Treaty of Friendship in 2000 will be ceased on the date of entry into force of the Treaty of Comprehensive Strategic Partnership in accordance with Article 22 of the last treaty.

5 Article 1 of Soviet-DPRK in 1961 stated as follows: "Should either of the Contracting Parties suffer **armed attack** by any State or coalition of States and thus find itself **in a state of war**, the other Contracting Party **shall immediately** extend **military and other assistance with all the means at its disposal**." UN, United Nations Treaty Collection No. 6045, https://treaties.un.org/doc/Publication/UNTS/Volume%20420/volume-420-I-6045-English.pdf

6 Article 4 of Russia-DPRK treaty in 2024.

7 Article 51 has been and can be interpreted to fit the needs of any state or group of states that want to avail themselves of collective self-defense. John S. Gibson, Article 51 of the Charter of the United Nations, *India Quarterly* 13, no. 2 (1957), 121–138.

permanent member of security councils and consistently cast a veto to take a measure to end such self-defense action, Article 51 does not work as initially intended. Individual or collective self-defense may be justified without proper stoppage when the attacked state wants to keep the self-defense measures against the armed attack. Hence, it would be fair to state that Russia, as a permanent member of the Security Council, has a key to activating Article 51 of the UN Charter concerning the Russia-DPRK treaty in 2024.[8]

Likewise, regarding the prior condition of the domestic legislature, Russian military intervention in foreign territories is known under Russian parliamentary control by Article 102–1. G of the Russian Constitution.[9] This also comes at the request of the Russian president.[10] As for immediate military assistance, even though there are some procedural limits to pulling a brake on troops expatriates to foreign States, they are purportedly dependent upon the intention of supreme power, the Russian president.

4. Contradictory Vow for the UN System

The second concerns the respect of the UN and other international organizations in the Russia-DPRK Treaty in 2024. Contradictorily, Russia and North Korea repeatedly stress the importance of the UN system for peace and stability in the world. As a permanent member of the UNSC, Russia intends to keep its duty of "serial resolutions of UNSC." However, the new Russia and North Korea treaty in 2024 contradicts the duties and obligations of the UNSC; *inter alia*, the military arms transfer from North Korea to Russia is a breach of the UNSC.[11] Before, Russia supported the resolution with five other permanent members. However, Russia is now strongly suspected of a breach of serial UNSCRs.[12]

8 John S. Gibson, Article 51 of the Charter of the United Nations, *India Quarterly* 13, no. 2 (1957). Meanwhile, this is not always a justified interpretation. When it comes to the role of "The Security Council in the Korean War (1950–1953), in the absence of the Soviet Union, the Security Council measures were passed without unanimity in accordance with United Nations Security Council Resolution (UNSCR) 82, 83, 84, 85. United Nations Command, "History of the Korean War", https://www.unc.mil/History/1950-1953-Korean-War-Active-Conflict

9 U.S.A. gov, "Russian Federation: New Rules for Special Operations Abroad (LL file No. 2007-03469)", December 2006, https://tile.loc.gov/storage-services/service/ll/llglrd/2019669411/2019669411.pdf

10 U.S.A. gov, "Russian Federation: New Rules for Special Operations Abroad (LL file No. 2007-03469)", December 2006, https://tile.loc.gov/storage-services/service/ll/llglrd/2019669411/2019669411.pdf

11 Since the first test of a nuclear weapon in October 2006, the UNSC has continuously adopted resolutions with unanimity on the prohibition of direct or indirect supply, sale, or transfer of weapons like Any battle tanks, armored combat vehicles, large-caliber artillery systems, combat aircraft, attack helicopters, warships, missiles, or missile systems to the DPRK, and after that in accordance with UNSCR 1874 in 2009 prohibited any export of weapons in the list. UN, "UNSCR 1781 and 1874", www.unscr.com

12 EEAS, "Sanctions: Joint Statement on DPRK-Russia", 31 May 2024, www.eeas.europa.eu/eeas/sanctions-joint-statement-dprk-russia_en. Australia, Canada, France, Germany, Italy, Japan, New Zealand, the Republic of Korea, the United Kingdom, the High Representative of the European Union, and the Secretary of the United States of America affirmed this joint Statement.

In particular, there is no case that a permanent member of the UNSC signs a treaty of military assistance with a State that is a sanctioned State by the UN with threats of continuous nuclear weapon tests. Aside from the military operation in Ukraine, it is the only State of Russia that took its steps forward as a peace wrecker with a rogue State, which is a target State in a series of UNSCRs. Even more, Russia voted for the sanction of non-proliferation against North Korea's nuclear program. However, by making a military assistance treaty with a rogue State that invented a nuclear weaponry system, Russia chose to give up its dignity and authority as a permanent member of the UNSC. If South Korea takes subsequent reaction as self-defense to start a nuclear weapon program against North Korea, Russia does not have any right to raise a veto if it were to be a fair and consistent rule-taker of its precedence. Even the stakes of other permanent members in the UNSC have been thrown away on the street because of the Russia and North Korea Treaty in 2024. It serves its own interests without considering its previous attitudes against such a peace wrecker.

5. The Trap of Non-reciprocity with the Third State

The third concerns Article 5 of the Russia-North Korea treaty in 2024. This clause embraces vivid exclusivity not to make any agreement and not to take part in any actions with third States directed against the two Parties on all comprehensive areas like the sovereignty, security, territorial integrity, right to free choice, and development of political, social, economic, and cultural systems and other vital interests of the other party. This clause ramps up significant political and legal burdens on each other.

When it comes to the relationship between Russia and South Korea before the Russian attack on Ukraine in 2022, Russia put the shackles on its feet voluntarily, not making any agreement or any actions to give favors to South Korea. Suppose South Korea requests Russia's termination or nullification of this comprehensive partnership treaty to re-open constructive ties with Russia. In that case, Russia should strive to sort out this burden with North Korea. If Russia entered into any positive relationship with South Korea, which might degrade any fundamental interests of North Korea, Russia would be in a position against this treaty, which may be the exact trap invented but irresistible by North Korea.

A similar clause was included in the Soviet-DPRK Treaty in 1961. However, this clause in 2024 elaborates with more concrete limitations not to take any agreement or actions against the other party. Since South Korea and the Soviet Union agreed to normalize diplomatic relations on September 30, 1990, the treaty in 1961 was contradictory between Russia and South Korea. When President Kim Young-Sam of South Korea visited Moscow on June 1–3, 1994, the Russian counterpart Boris Yeltsin promised to either repeal or drastically revise the Soviet-DPRK Treaty in 1961[13] to free Russia from the obligation of an automatic involvement in any war

13 Russia notified the termination of the Soviet-DPRK Treaty in 1961 on 7 August 1995; it was terminated one year later, on 10 September 1996.

waged by North Korea.[14] This new treaty, with a comprehensive partnership with an immediate military assistance clause, meant the revival of the Soviet-DPRK Treaty in 1961. Given that Russia would want to regain normal ties with the third State, a similar process should be reiterated to nullify or terminate this Russia-DPRK Treaty in 2024.

6. China, Unexpected Remoteness as a Third Party

- ***China Saved North Korea at the Sacrifice of Taiwan***

When the Russia-DPRK Treaty in 2024 was publicly announced, the most bewildered party might have been China. As for the influence over political stability in the Korean Peninsula, it is not too much to say that China has been the greatest guardian of North Korea. In respect to political and economic support by China for North Korea, it should be mentioned that the Chinese military intervention in the Korean War. China lost almost 1 million soldiers during the war, which was the most significant number of casualties compared with those of South Korea, North Korea, and UN troops.[15] If it were not for the Korean War on 25 June 1950, China was supposed to take over Taiwan thanks to the exclusion from the Acheson Line Declaration.[16] China became involved in unwanted wars with unpredictable consequences by losing the momentum to take over Taiwan in advance.[17] After all, for over 70 years, China never had another chance to reunify Taiwan with mainland China.

- ***Automatic Military Assistance Treaty in 1961***

Regarding the military assistance clause in the Russia-DPRK treaty in 2024, North Korea has another similar treaty on automatic military assistance with China. North

14 Jae-Nam Ko, "New Direction of Korean-Russian Relations: Toward a Comprehensive Partnership", Institute of Foreign Affairs and National Security, October 1994, www.ifans.go.kr

15 The Korean War lasted for three years, one month, and two days, from 25 June 1950 to 27 July 1953. First, there were approximately 138,000 South Korean deaths, 450,000 wounded, and 609,000 casualties, including the missing, 520,000 North Korean fatalities and injured, and 800,000 including the missing, 58,000 UN deaths, 480,000 wounded, and 546,000 including the missing and prisoners of war, and 136,000 Chinese deaths, 208,000 wounded, and 973,000 casualties including the missing, prisoners of war, and non-combat casualties. VOA Korea, "Statistics Related to the Korean War", 24 June 2011, www.voakorea.com/a/article-625-124496254/1348359.html

16 Acheson Line refers to the U.S. Far East defense line for Northeast Asia announced by the U.S. Secretary of State on January 12, 1950. According to this declaration, South Korea, Taiwan, and the Indochina Peninsula were excluded from the U.S. defense line, which gave China, Russia, and North Korea sufficient perception of those areas as not strategically important. Miles Maochun Yu, "Green, Yellow, or Red-What Color was Dean Acheson's Speech?", Military History in the News, Hoover Institution, 9 March 2017, www.hoover.org/research/green-yellow-or-red-what-color-was-dean-achesons-speech

17 Ian Easton, "The Koran War Saved Taiwan from the Clutches of Chairman Mao", *The National Interest*, 10 April 2020, www.nationalinterest.org/blog/buzz/korean-war-saved-taiwan-clutches-chairman-mao-142852?page=0%2C1

Korea and China signed a treaty on 11 July 1961, which contained "the obligation of immediate military assistance in a state of war" and the obligation "not to enter into any alliance against the other Contracting Party." This treaty was agreed with precisely the abovementioned obligations just five days after the conclusion of the Soviet-DPRK Treaty in 1961.

The two military assistance treaties are still contradictory regarding the obligation not to enter into any alliance against other Contracting Parties. Does North Korea identify the two counterpart States with the same political and economic interests in the Korean Peninsula? The two military assistance treaties established the triangle coalition against the U.S. and South Korea with firm legal obligations. According to the logical analysis of this obligation, China, Russia, and North Korea should not enter into any alliance or any agreement or action against their fundamental interests, which may have a particular risk of endangering their interests in each other. Ironically, there were two discrepancies between China and Russia. The first was from the famous ideological disagreement, the Sino-Soviet Conflict.[18] The second was from their deep-rooted entanglement in their border dispute.[19] Even though China and Russia had incongruous interests in each other, they had kept their military assistance treaties with North Korea for a long time after 1961. In this respect, it is fair to assess North Korea managed the two treaties cautiously and neutrally.

When international criticism was at its peak due to the nuclear weapon program, China did not escape the relief of food supply for the famine of North Korea, and it provided even crude oil. Since the termination of the Soviet-DPRK treaty in 1961, China has been the only guardian to embrace the obligation of automatic military assistance to North Korea, which could be political leverage in the negotiation of North Korea's nuclear program, since nominally China consistently opposed the development of nuclear weapons by North Korea; South Korea tended to lean over China with such backgrounds.

- ***China's Grudge Against North Korea***

Even though China has continued to support food and energy relief since the sanctions of the UNSCRs against North Korea, nowadays Russia and North Korea look like best friends ever since revamping up the dead clause of military assistance in the Soviet-DPRK Treaty in 1961. It is noteworthy that Beijing urged President

18 This concerns disagreement on their ideologic issues since the 20th Congress of the Communist Party of the Soviet Union in 1956. It originated a significant split of the Communist States into pro-Soviet and pro-Chinese factions.

19 The border demarcated in the 19th century between the Qing dynasty and the Russian Empire by unequal treaties became the origin of their border conflict. The most volatile moment occurred in March 1969, which had been compromised with a ceasefire and returned to *the status quo ante bellum*. However, their sour relations have remained and continue to be inconclusive until now. After this conflict, China sought a *rapprochement* with the U.S. as a counterbalancing strategy in 1972.

Putin not to visit Pyongyang straight after meeting President Xi in May of 2024.[20] Despite China's apparent woe on official rapprochement between Moscow and Pyongyang, the new comprehensive partnership treaty cast enough questions on the return for China's 60 years of aid from food, fuel, and money.[21] Furthermore, China has kept its opposing tones on North Korea's nuclear program and continuous missile tests. However, it has not supported additional sanctions against North Korea in the UNSC since the ICBM test on 24 March 2022 for improving relations with appeasement policy.[22] Until now, China is known as North Korea's biggest trade partner and, without doubt, has the most leverage over Kim Jong-un's regime.[23] Notwithstanding, North Korea chose to hedge its bets against absolute dependency on China, which might be understood as a step of giving China a kind of betrayal or humiliation.

7. Why is North Korea Changing its Partner?

- ***China, White Elephant to North Korea***

Given North Korea's substantially dependent relationship with China, a somewhat sudden rapprochement between Russia and North Korea caused China to keep its distance from the two states. From a realistic international perspective, North Korea's value to China is a kind of buffer zone from the large U.S. military base supported by South Korea. Meanwhile, for its validity to be realized as valuable, China should have control over North Korea. Otherwise, the ungrateful and shameless attitude of North Korea toward China will derogate China's dominance in the regional and global competitiveness of hegemony.

For the pursuit of independence from any other power, given that North Korea would consider too much dependence on China as a hindrance to undermine the stability of Kim's regime with its nuclear weapons program and ICBM program,[24] it is natural that North Korea should hedge its bet with other balancing powers like Russia and Iran.[25] As for the survival of Kim's regime, dependence on China

20 BBC, "China Is the True Power in Putin and Kim's Budding Friendship", 19 June 2024, https://www.bbc.com/news/articles/c1vv196pe3eo

21 KBS, "Chinese Media Criticizes, 'Where Did the Aid to North Korea Go?'", 12 October 2014, https://news.kbs.co.kr/news/pc/view/view.do?ncd=2946684

22 UN, "Security Council Fails to Adopt Resolution Tightening Sanctions Regime in Democratic People's Republic of Korea, as Two Members Wield Veto", 26 May 2022, https://press.un.org/en/2022/sc14911.doc.htm

23 Clara Fong and Eleanor Albert, "The China-North Korea Relationship", Council on Foreign Relations, 7 March 2024, https://www.cfr.org/backgrounder/china-north-korea-relationship

24 Alan Soderman, "China Supported Sanctions on North Korea's Nuclear Program. It's also Behind their Failure", *AP News*, 3 November 2023, https://apnews.com/article/china-north-korea-sanctions-6e69cd6c0c17fba261f62ea8e5bc25c5.

25 Kim Tong-Hyung, "North Korea Sends a Delegation to Iran in a Growing Effort to Break Its Diplomatic Isolation", *AP News*, 24 April 2024, https://apnews.com/article/north-korea-iran-diplomacy-military-cooperation-russia-f82461908cb59a15a634747e9ab48f6c; Christy Lee, "US and EU Eye

would be interpreted as a double-edged sword. As much as Kim's regime has poured their budget into the nuclear weapons program, the incremental scarcity of food and energy forced North Korea to be more dependent on China. That means China has increased its leverage on North Korea. Therefore, superficially, the relationships between China and North Korea might be considered inseparable, "as close as lips and teeth." However, that made North Korea more vulnerable to strategic choices in China. Since the 2017 nuclear test, the strategic goal of China has been clearly defined as the status quo in the Korean Peninsula rather than the two Koreas' reunification. North Korea's propulsion to more active nuclear weapons and long-range missile development was an obstacle to China's plans for regional and global paradigm. North Korea is not even a member of the "One Belt and One Road Initiative" of China's grand plan. It is also understandable why North Korea endeavors to diversify risk regarding political and strategic relations with Russia instead of China. At that point, the phrase, "Japan is our enemy of 100 years, China is our enemy of 1,000 years"[26] is often heard in North Korea. It tells us the reality of regional politics surrounding the Korean Peninsula.

- ***Quid pro quo between Russia and North Korea***

Meanwhile, what is the reason for the sudden rapprochement between Russia and North Korea? Since the termination of the Soviet-DPRK Treaty in 1961, their relationship had changed into the "Treaty of Friendship, Good-Neighborliness, and Cooperation" in 2000. In 2024, it is significant for North Korea that Russia vetoed a UN resolution renewing the mandate of the UN Panel of Experts (PoE).[27] Thinking over the previous Russian support towards sanctions against Kim's regime, such a turnaround means North Korea would get free from such global monitoring systems, which have finally failed.[28] Furthermore, Putin was quoted as saying that North Korea has its own "nuclear umbrella" and Pyongyang has not asked Moscow for any help thereon.[29] This can be a giant stride for supporting the international status of North Korea, such as isolated sanctions in the UNSC. The most formidable

North Korea-Iran Military Cooperation", *Voice of America*, 1 May 2024, https://www.voanews.com/a/us-and-eu-eye-north-korea-iran-military-cooperation/7593077.html

26 Bruce W. Bennett, "North Korea, and China Aren't the Allies You Think They Are", RAND, 27 September 2023, https://www.rand.org/pubs/commentary/2023/09/north-korea-and-china-arent-the-allies-you-think-they.html

27 The PoE's mandate expired at the end of April 2024. It had been established under UNSCR 1874 and made up of a group of seven experts who had monitored the enforcement of international sanctions on North Korea's nuclear and ballistic missile programs, including nuclear activities in Yongbyon; arms embargo; and, most recently, 58 suspected cyberattacks on cryptocurrency companies. Victor Cha and Ellen Kim, "Russia's Veto: Dismembering the UN Sanctions Regime on North Korea", CSIS, 29 March 2024, https://www.csis.org/analysis/russias-veto-dismembering-un-sanctions-regime-north-korea

28 UN News, "Russia Vetoes DPR Korea Sanctions Resolution", 28 March 2024, https://news.un.org/en/story/2024/03/1148121

29 Kelsey Devenport, "North Korea, Russia Strengthen Military Ties", *Arms Control Today*, https://www.armscontrol.org/act/2024-07/news/north-korea-russia-strengthen-military-ties

gift for North Korea is the clause of "immediate military assistance," which can be returned alive despite some limitations of automatic military assistance.

In turn, what could Russia acquire equivalent to such a promise? Since August 2023, a large amount of ammunition has been transferred from North Korea to Russia, which would seriously affect Russia's Ukraine invasion.[30] In addition, multiple news reports have reported that North Korea agreed with Russia to dispatch its troops or workers to support Russia's war against Ukraine.[31]

8. Final Remarks

- ***Who Would be the Winner: North Korea?***

Surrounding the Korean Peninsula, global powers wrestle with each other for their purpose. As mentioned, while China has kept its diverse aid policy for North Korea to secure the buffer zone for the status quo, Russia tried to intervene in this situation for the incumbent necessity for a massive ammunition barter with a long-vacant clause of military assistance for North Korea. During the endless provocation of a nuclear weapons program, even though North Korea had received much economic support from China, it did not want to be swayed by China as the only predominant guidance. It was completed for the triangle alliance of China-Russia-North Korea against the U.S.-South Korea-Japan. However, the triangle embraces an uncalculated loss of stakes in the Korean Peninsula between China and Russia. China should divide its stakes with Russia even at the cost of a substantial aider position; instead, Russia should guarantee its military commitment to protect North Korea in the uncertain instability in the Korean Peninsula, which North Korea has long pursued. Given that further assistance measures like the dispatch of regular troops of North Korea in the Russian Territory would be taken, this means North Korea completed two blood alliances, including China. Thanks to the Russia-DPRK Treaty in 2024, Russia cannot deny a nominal commitment to North Korea in international relations. North Korea succeeded in paving the way from isolation caused by continuous sanctions of the UNSC by taking the middle post between China and Russia, who might even consider North Korea as a sour candy but cannot spit it out of their mouths for the time being.

- ***Who Would be the Loser?***

With the sudden rapprochement with North Korea and Russia, China is the uneasiest State. As China requested Putin not to visit Pyongyang directly after the visit of Xi in Moscow, it wanted to manage the balance of power as the status quo in the

30 Al Jazeera, "North Korea sent Russia Millions of Munitions in Exchange for Food: Seoul", 28 February 2024, https://www.aljazeera.com/news/2024/2/28/n-korea-sent-russia-millions-of-munitions-in-exchange-for-food-says-seoul.

31 Reuters, "South Korea Says North Korea Troops Dispatch to Russia Is 'Grave Security Threat'", 18 October 2024, https://www.reuters.com/world/south-korea-says-north-korea-troop-dispatch-russia-is-grave-security-threat-2024-10-18/

Korean Peninsula. But Russia received a mass of ammunition from North Korea and probably expected to locate the troops of North Korea in Ukraine. China will not provide such support for Russia, but North Korea can do it. Hence, in terms of *quid pro quo*, Russia guaranteed military assistance in the Korean Peninsula at the request of North Korea. For the time, China will lose its monopolistic dominance over North Korea in the issue of nuclear weapons and missile programs; furthermore, where in case of war Chinese troops would get into the war automatically, then North Korea will call for Russian military assistance. The redeeming point is that the primary trade partner with North Korea could not be changed to Russia instead of China. China will hold onto the leash of North Korea and manipulate its trading terms in both visible and invisible ways. This new rapprochement of the Russia-DPRK Treaty in 2024 will allow China to delve into which measures should be exerted over North Korea regarding majorly dependent economic border trade. Who would be the last loser? Even though not determined, their futures will depend on the follow-up of North Korea's juggling the tri-angle alliance. What is true is that North Korea is taking a risk in gambling with its destiny.

References

Al Jazeera (2024), "North Korea Sent Russia Millions of Munitions in Exchange for Food: Seoul", 28 February 2024, https://www.aljazeera.com/news/2024/2/28/n-korea-sent-russia-millions-of-munitions-in-exchange-for-food-says-seoul

BBC (2024), "China Is the True Power in Putin and Kim's Budding Friendship", 19 June 2024, https://www.bbc.com/news/articles/c1vv196pe3eo

Bennett, Bruce W. (2023), "North Korea, and China Aren't the Allies You Think They Are", RAND, 27 September 2023, https://www.rand.org/pubs/commentary/2023/09/north-korea-and-china-arent-the-allies-you-think-they.html

Bowen, Andrew S. et al. (2024), "Russia-North Korea Relations", CRS Reports, 10 September 2024, https://crsreports.congress.gov/product/pdf/IF/IF12760

Brannikova, Anasticia (2019), "United States-DPRK Relations: Is Normalization Possible?", Center for Strategic and International Studies (CSIS).

Cha, Victor and Kim, Ellen (2024), "Russia's Veto: Dismembering the UN Sanctions Regime on North Korea", CSIS, 29 March 2024, https://www.csis.org/analysis/russias-veto-dismembering-un-sanctions-regime-north-korea

Devenport, Kelsey (2024), "North Korea, Russia Strengthen, Military Ties", Arms Control Association, July–August 2024, https://www.armscontrol.org/act/2024-07/news/north-korea-russia-strengthen-military-ties

Easton, Ian (2020), "The Koran War Saved Taiwan from the Clutches of Chairman Mao", *The National Interest*, 10 April 2020, www.nationalinterest.org/blog/buzz/korean-war-saved-taiwan-clutches-chairman-mao-142852?page=0%2C1

EEAS (2024), "Sanctions: Joint Statement on DPRK-Russia", 31 May 2024, www.eeas.europa.eu/eeas/sanctions-joint-statement-dprk-russia_en

Fong, Clara and Albert, Eleanor (2024), "The China-North Korea Relationship", Council on Foreign Relations, 7 March 2024, https://www.cfr.org/backgrounder/china-north-korea-relationship

Gibson, John S. (1957), "Article 51 of the Charter of the United Nations", *India Quarterly* 13, no. 2.

KBS (2014), "Chinese Media Criticizes, 'Where Did the Aid to North Korea Go?'", 12 October 2014, https://news.kbs.co.kr/news/pc/view/view.do?ncd=2946684

Kim, Tong-Hyung (2024), "North Korea Sends a Delegation to Iran in a Growing Effort to Break Its Diplomatic Isolation", *AP News*, 24 April 2024, https://apnews.com/article/north-korea-iran-diplomacy-military-cooperation-russia-f82461908cb59a15a634747e9ab48f6c

Ko, Jae-Nam (2014), "New Direction of Korean-Russian Relations: Toward a Comprehensive Partnership", Institute of Foreign Affairs and National Security, October 1994, www.ifans.go.kr

Lee, Christy (2024), "US and EU Eye North Korea-Iran Military Cooperation", *Voice of America*, 1 May 2024, https://www.voanews.com/a/us-and-eu-eye-north-korea-iran-military-cooperation/7593077.html

Presidential Press and Information Office (2000), "A Russian-North Korean Summit Was Held in Pyongyang", 19 July 2000, http://en.kremlin.ru/events/president/news/38435

Reuters, "South Korea says North Korea Troops Dispatch to Russia Is 'Grave Security Threat'", 18 October 2024, https://www.reuters.com/world/south-korea-says-north-korea-troop-dispatch-russia-is-grave-security-threat-2024-10-18/

UN (2022), "Security Council Fails to Adopt Resolution Tightening Sanctions Regime in Democratic People's Republic of Korea, as Two Members Wield Veto", 26 May 2022, https://press.un.org/en/2022/sc14911.doc.htm

UN News (2024), "Russia Vetoes DPR Korea Sanctions Resolution", 28 March 2024, https://news.un.org/en/story/2024/03/1148121

U.S.A. gov (2006), "Russian Federation: New Rules for Special Operations Abroad (LL file No. 2007-03469)", December 2006, https://tile.loc.gov/storage-services/service/ll/llglrd/2019669411/2019669411.pdf

VOA Korea (2011), "Statistics Related to the Korean War", 24 June 2011, www.voakorea.com/a/article-625-124496254/1348359.html

Yu, Miles Maochun (2017), "Green, Yellow, or Red-What Color was Dean Acheson's Speech?", Military History in the News, Hoover Institution, 9 March 2017, www.hoover.org/research/green-yellow-or-red-what-color-was-dean-achesons-speech

9 China vs the West: Militaries on a Collision Course?

Asia vs the West – Economies Moving in Opposite Directions?

*Ryszard Zalski**

1. Introduction

In this chapter, the author will use the term "the West," meaning both the US and the EU. The aim of the chapter is to present two tendencies happening at the same time. Those vectors are going in opposite directions.

On one hand, we have the CCP's aggressive behavior and specific warfares directed both at regional neighbors and against Western countries.

On the other hand, we observe Western weakness in response to such provocations. Neither the US nor its Asian allies respond to PLA's regular provocations in the air and on the high seas. Western militaries choose the moral high ground.[1]

We observe such a submissive behavior not only in the case of the supreme military power like the US, but also with some of the US' allies – like Australia, Taiwan and Japan.

An exception here is the 2023/24 posture of the Philippines, whose military forces stood up to the aggression of the Chinese Coast Guard and recorded and published it. This Filipino behavior has forced the Chinese Communist Party (CCP) to explain their attacks on the Filipino forces and to issue repeated statements denouncing both Philippines' defense as well as the support it receives from other countries.

So, it's only recently that the countries mostly attacked by China – Taiwan, Japan, the Philippines and India – began mutual cooperation, exercises and exchanges.

Here are a few examples:

- American-Filipino bases access agreements
- Philippine-Japanese mutual access agreement
- Vietnam and Japan strengthening security ties (defense equipment and technology transfers)
- India-Japan 2+2 foreign and defense ministers' meeting

* Journalist, Independent researcher, Taiwan.

1 During interviews on my YouTube channel Studio Asia (www.youtube.com/@studio_asia) I asked numerous guests with military backgrounds about the reasons for such passive behavior. I was given this exact reason – "professionalism and moral high ground of Western military services."

DOI: 10.4324/9781003545750-11

- AUKUS
- ASEAN's first-ever joint military drills

2. Regional Cooperation

This regional cooperation is an example of the hub and spokes theory – the hub being the US military and spokes its cooperating regional allies and partners. This cooperation includes supporting each other with military equipment. The reason for the mushrooming cooperation and exchanges is the unspoken Lord Voldemort in the region, that one big neighbor who has territorial issues with almost everyone.

Due to the absence of a decisive response from the Biden administration, regional countries had to take the initiative and start cooperating with each other.

Other challenges to those China-related developments in Asia are both China's involvement in Russia's aggression to Ukraine and in the conflict in Gaza, as well as summer 2024 joint Sino-Belarussian forces exercises on the Baltic Sea. The Chinese government is also increasingly present in Latin America. The CCP is taking a very active approach in shaping the global security situation and challenging the US wherever possible.

At the same time, the West is moving in the opposite direction from China. Frequent visits by European leaders and Biden administration officials in Beijing in 2023/24 make it clear that keeping up the dialogue is very important to the Americans.

However, it is far less important to the Chinese side and gives it a leverage to be used against Western leaders – a possible concession from the CCP to meet or not to meet a Western official. Additionally, CCP leadership can show its displeasure with a Western country's policy by denying them a meeting with Xi Jinping, at the same time allowing Western business leaders visiting China to meet the chairman.

3. Don't Ask, Don't Tell

Another area where the CCP's policy is superior to the West's is in making thorny topics disappear from public discourse.

The only government that tried to take up the origin and CCP's responsibility for the global spread of the Wuhan virus was Australian Prime Minister Scott Morrison's administration in July 2021. The result were tariffs on major Australian exports to China. They came at a huge cost to the Australian economy, but over time the country recovered from them.[2]

Another topic which has been removed from public discussion by the Xi regime was the content of the famous Spy Balloon discovered over the US in January 2023.

2 Jeffrey Wilson, *Australia Shows the World What Decoupling from China Looks Like* (03.08.2024) "Foreign Policy": https://foreignpolicy.com/2021/11/09/australia-china-decoupling-trade-sanctions-coronavirus- geopolitics/

After Secretary Blinken's visit to China, he dismissed the topic in an interview and the Biden administration let it disappear.

Neither American nor EU governments follow up on the topics of the illegal Chinese police stations. They were simply shut down, and as in the aforementioned cases, didn't come up in bilateral relations again.

In the following section, I will discuss growing Western economic dependence on Asian manufacturing.

4. The Dependence

The obvious question is – why are Western corporations and governments so dependent on the Chinese market?

The first world leader who began challenging China's aggressive behavior was President Donald Trump.

Initially criticized and ridiculed, over time he was proven right – so much so that parts of his policy towards China were taken over by the Biden administration.

Since the outbreak of the Wuhan virus during Trump's term and with the Russian aggression on Ukraine during Biden's administration, there is no excuse for anyone to dismiss Western dependence on totalitarian regimes. And yet, both the corporate and political worlds are still involved in cooperation with Russia and China. The reasons for this dependence on Russia's resources and China's manufacturing base is that Western democracies don't really have a choice. Their dependency on those dictatorships has been self-inflicted over the last few decades. The reasons are leftist policies leading to the fostering of the social welfare state, constantly rising production costs and proliferation of regulations for more and more industries. As a result, the EU had to rely on cheap gas from Russia, cheap labor from China and military protection from the USA.

All those reasons have been pointed out by former president Trump, who was ridiculed for it during his time in office.

Leftist and populist policies implemented by the EU have made it to a large extent impossible for many companies to compete with Asian manufacturers.

Endless restrictions and regulations, the promotion of values over business and recent green policies have made the EU uncompetitive. It's better in the case of the US, although American industries are also heavily reliant on Asian manufacturing.

The West has simply out-taxed and out-regulated itself from the global marketplace. To be more precise, Western voters for decades have supported leftist and socialist policies. Some of their elected representatives have been conveniently blaming Asians for stealing Western jobs. Other politicians have been lobbying for and promoting closer cooperation with the CCP. There were only a few who talked about the dangers of such dependency on the CCP. The ones calling for restrained money printing, deregulating industries and fiscal reforms exist on the fringes of Western politics.

Those decade-long developments led the West to the current situation, where businesses and huge parts of manufacturing are forced to shut down their operations and production. The only option is to move them to Asia. The West also lacks the necessary manpower and talent with knowledge and experience how to operate modern industries.

It's even worse – Western economic weakness also affects its military capabilities. Here are three examples of such a situation:

- The US is preparing to service its naval assets in Japan and Korea, among others, due to lack of its own resources and personnel
- The AUKUS project [3]
- Dependence on Asian semiconductor manufacturers both in terms of facilities and the know-how, i.e. engineers (Taiwanese specialists are being given green cards for the whole family and moved to the Arizona factory)

Social spending has risen globally in recent decades, but in the West much more than in Asia – both as a percentage of the GDP as well as in terms of population covered with it.[4]

The government spending as ratio of the GDP in 2022 for Europe is in the 50–60% range, for the US 30–40% and for Asia 10–30%.[5]

Asian economies are less regulated and have a more committed and diligent workforce. Governments not only provide less social welfare and are less ideological than the EU and current Biden administration. By ideological, I mean they don't promote socially divisive gender ideology or industry-restricting green policies.

Asian employees work much more overtime than their Western counterparts and sacrifice more of their private life for their companies. This different approach to work ethic and dedication is described in detail in Chris Miller's *Chip Wars*.

This brings us to the next chapter, where I will discuss one of the most essential modern industries, which is heavily dominated by Asian manufacturers.

5. Global Competition

Semiconductors are an example of an industry where many developed Western and Asian countries are competing with still-developing Asian countries. I will now discuss the reasons Asian countries are attracting more investment than well-established First World economies.

3 Josh Luckenbaugh, *JUST IN: Navy Investing in Industrial Base to Fix Sub Schedule, Cost Overruns* (17.08.2024) "National Defense Magazine": https://www.nationaldefensemagazine.org/articles/2024/10/2/navy-investing-in-industrial-base-to-fix-sub-programs-cost-schedule-challenges. Stew Magnuson, *Special Report: Sub Deal Poses Questions About Shipyard Capacity* (17.08.2024) "National Defense Magazine": https://www.nationaldefensemagazine.org/articles/2023/2/16/sub-deal-poses-questions-about – shipyard-capacity

4 *World Social Protection Report 2024–26: In figures* (20.08.2024): https://www.ilo.org/resource/article/world-social-protection-report-2024-26-figures

5 *Government spending as a share of GDP, 2022* (20.08.2024): https://ourworldindata.org/grapher/historical- gov-spending-gdp; *Social Protection Statistics – Social Benefits* (20.08.2024): https://ec.europa.eu/eurostat/ statistics-explained/index.php?title=Social_protection_statistics_-_social_benefits

Both the US and the EU are trying very hard to get back into the technological race, which they used to lead.

As of mid-2024, the EU isn't able to attract substantial investment into the chip manufacturing industry. One example is the Intel semiconductor assembly and test facility near Wrocław, Poland,[6] worth around €4 bln, which was announced in 2023 and as of now is put on hold. Another facility is being planned near Magdeburg, Germany, with construction beginning planned for 2025 and worth over €30 bln. There are also factories planned in France, Italy and Ireland – totaling around €80 bln.

However, as of the end of summer 2024, due to financial problems Intel is laying off employees and possibly cutting off some investments. Therefore, the future of some of those plants is uncertain.

I would like to present Malaysia as a country aiming to become a global semiconductor hub and targeting to attract $100 bln of investment in this industry

While it already accounts for over 10% of the world's testing and packaging, "Malaysia is seen as well placed to grab further business in the semiconductor sector, as Chinese chip firms diversify outside of China for assembling needs."[7]

Vietnam is in a similar situation. It has been profiting from both Chinese and foreign companies escaping American sanctions on Chinese chip manufacturers. In recent years, this country has become a hub for semiconductor production. And so, as a result of the US Chips Act, its government is planning to invest in Vietnam's semiconductor industry in a bid to diversify supply chains and reduce dependency on China.

However, the total amount of the investment "appropriated under the CHIPS Act of 2022 provides the Department of State with $500 million ($100 million per year over five years, starting in Fiscal Year 2023)."[8] The US government increasingly sees Vietnam as a hub for diversifying its supply chains and an alternative to the Chinese manufacturing base.

Now, let's compare the CHIPS Act subsidy with investments by the major players in this industry.

The subsidy war has already begun. TSMC alone is investing in its three semiconductor plants in the US 65 mld $.[9]

> Speaking at "Vietnam Semiconductor Summit" in Hanoi on Sunday, he [Robert Li, Vice President of U.S. Synopsys] said building a foundry could

6 *Investment Near Wrocław, Poland, Will Help Create a First-of-Its-Kind End-to-End Leading-Edge Manufacturing Semiconductor Value Chain in Europe.* (27.09.2024): https://www.intc.com/news-events/press-releases/detail/1627/intel-plans-assembly-and-test-facility-in-poland

7 *Malaysia Targets Over$100 bln in Semiconductor Industry Investment* (13.08.2024) "Reuters": https://www.reuters.com/world/asia-pacific/malaysia-pm-says-targeting-over-100-bln-investment-semiconductor-chips-2024-05-28/

8 *Department of State Allocating $100 Million in FY 2023 for CHIPS Act Projects* (15.09.2024) "State": https://www.state.gov/department-of-state-allocating-100-million-in-fy-2023-for-chips-act-projects/

9 *TSMC Arizona and U.S. Department of Commerce Announce Up to US$6.6 Billion in Proposed CHIPS Act Direct Funding, the Company Plans Third Leading-Edge Fab in Phoenix* (20.08.2024) "TSMC": https://pr.tsmc.com/english/news/3122

> cost as much as $50 billion, and would entail competing on subsidies with China, the U.S., South Korea and the European Union which have announced spending plans on chips between $50 and $150 billion each."

As Zachary Abuza, a professor at the National War College in Washington, DC stated, there are still many problems ahead of Vietnam's semiconductor industry:

> When companies look at Vietnam, it looks really good on paper but when they actually have to go through and look to see if there is sufficient electricity, what's the infrastructure and most importantly, what are the human resources like . . . I don't think Vietnam is going to be the producer that it thinks it is.[10]

The last example of an Asian economy trying to establish itself in the flourishing semiconductor industry is Indonesia. It's entering a highly competitive market dominated by a number of established players. This process requires not only substantial investments to attract significant foreign companies; it also means finding its own niche to use strengths, which are "[Indonesia's] abundant raw materials. The country is rich in silica sand, a critical component in the production of silicon wafers and, consequently, in semiconductors."[11] Since 2022, President Widodo's administration has been implementing a downstreaming policy for silica sand. It involves limiting exports and enhancing domestic processing capabilities, as done in the case of nickel, which included even banning its exports.

So, all three countries – Indonesia, Malaysia and Vietnam find themselves in the same niche. Like Vietnam, Indonesia faces various difficulties – i.e. lack of talent.

In the next section, I will introduce recent developments of the semiconductor industry in the US.

6. Recent Initiatives in the US

Apart from supporting manufacturers in Asia, the US government is also helping both American and foreign companies who are planning to boost their production in the US: the former being Intel and the latter TSMC.

Let's start with the taxpayer money spent on domestic companies. The funding for projects boosting US production comes from the CHIPS and Science Act passed by Congress in 2022 with more than $52 billion planned.

"Commerce Secretary Gina Raimondo told reporters she wants to see 20% of these advanced chips made in the United States by 2030."[12] "The company will

10 *Vietnam's Bid to Exploit US-China Chip Tensions Confronts Labour Hurdles* (10.08.2024) "Al Jazeera": https://www.aljazeera.com/economy/2024/3/4/as-vietnam-bids-to-become-chip-leader-energy-and-labour-woes-stand-in-the-way

11 *Indonesia's Bold Bid to Become a Semiconductor Hub* (13.08.2024) "The Diplomat": https://thediplomat.com/2024/08/indonesias-bold-bid-to-become-a-semiconductor-hub/

12 *Biden Is Giving Intel $8.5 Billion for Big Semiconductor Projects in 4 States* (15.09.2024) "NPR": https:// www.npr.org/2024/03/20/1239533039/biden-chips-arizona-intel

build two new plants in each of Chandler, Ariz., and New Albany, Ohio, and will modernize a fifth existing plant in Arizona."[13]

Subsidies are also intended for foreign companies locating their production on American soil. I mentioned TSMC's investment of more than $65 billion in three labs in Phoenix, Arizona, which will manufacture the world's most advanced semiconductors. At the beginning of April 2024, the Biden-Harris administration signed with a TSMC subsidiary a non-binding preliminary memorandum of terms to provide up to $6.6 billion in direct funding under the CHIPS and Science Act.[14] The US government plans to support TSMC financially with $11.6 billion, including $6.6 billion in grants and up to $5 billion in loans.

Drawing on my own professional experience in recent years with hundreds of Taiwanese semiconductor engineers, I can attest not only to their professional expertise, but also to a level of commitment and dedication to their companies which is very difficult to find among Western employees. They often work 10 hours a day or more. In some cases, they are available (on their phones) at night. Even women endure mental and physical abuse in form of yelling and disrespectful remarks from their superiors.

7. Recent Initiatives in the EU – Too Little, Too Late?

Not to be outdone, the EU's own European Chips Act entered into force in September 2023 and was billed as a €43 billion subsidy plan aimed at boosting Europe's share of the global chip market to 20% by 2030. However, the German think-tank interface found that Europe may not be on track to meet that goal and has not had 15% of the global market over the past 40 years. This is one of the reasons why at the beginning of September 2024, Europe's main computer chip industry group, European Semiconductor Industry Association (ESIA), called on the European Union to draw up a revamped "Chips Act 2.0" support package plus name an envoy to lead the sector. The group also demanded the EU Commission's chip policy should feature fewer export restrictions, focus on those areas where European companies already had advantages and award aid faster.[15]

European dependence on other parts of the world became apparent during the time of the Wuhan virus.

> Reportedly, the U.S. automotive industry lost production of some four million vehicles due to chip shortages in and after 2020, while in Europe, a senior

13 *Biden Is Giving Intel $8.5 Billion for Big Semiconductor Projects in 4 States* (15.09.2024) "NPR": https:// www.npr.org/2024/03/20/1239533039/biden-chips-arizona-intel

14 *Biden-Harris Administration Announces Preliminary Terms with TSMC, Expanded Investment from Company to Bring World's Most Advanced Leading-Edge Technology to the U.S.* (12.08.204) "Commerce": https://www.commerce.gov/news/press-releases/2024/04/biden-harris-administration-announces-preliminary-terms- tsmc-expanded

15 *Semiconductor Body Calls for EU 'Chips Envoy', More Support* (15.09.2024) "Yahoo": https://finance.yahoo.com/news/european-semiconductor-industry-group-esia-141920617.html?guccounter=1

German official observed in 2023 that "we lost 1–1.5 percent of our GDP in 2021 because of a lack of semiconductors – or about €40 billion.[16]

As of September 2024, a European Semiconductor Manufacturing Company (ESMC) semiconductor fab[17] is under construction in Dresden. It will be the first to produce so-called high-performance chips in the EU (although it's planned to be operating at full capacity by 2029). Europe holds 9% of the global chip manufacturing market (down from ca. 44% in 1990), whereas Taiwan holds a 60% share of the overall fab market and manufactures almost 90% of the world's most advanced chips. The EU Chips Act aims to increase Europe's share to 20% of the global chip industry by 2030.[18]

8. The Gap

The gap between Asian vs Western capabilities becomes more obvious with the following data:

1. The West mostly focuses on manufacturing chips, forgetting the other part – namely assembly, testing, and packaging (ATP). If the Western chips still need to be sent to Asia for ATP after manufacture and then sent back for consumption, the supply chains just doubled in length. Add to this that of the almost 500 assembly and test facilities worldwide, 65 are in the Americas and only 24 in Europe.[19]
2. Although a Dutch company, ASML, is the world's only producer of the EUV lithography tools needed to fabricate the most advanced chips, not a single European chipmaker is yet capable of using them.[20] Europe doesn't have cutting-edge chip designers and electronic design automation (EDA) software tool providers.
3. Both the founder of TSMC Morris Chang and the current chairman and CEO CC Wei stated on numerous occasions that both the US and the EU chips will be more expensive and therefore less competitive than the Taiwanese ones.[21]

16 *A World of Chips Acts: The Future of U.S.-EU Semiconductor Collaboration* (14.10.2024) "CSIS": https:// www.csis.org/analysis/world-chips-acts-future-us-eu-semiconductor-collaboration

17 European Semiconductor Manufacturing Company (ESMC) is a joint venture between TSMC, Robert Bosch GmbH, Infineon Technologies AG and NXP Semiconductors N.V. Note – European partners will hold only a 30% stake, the rest will remain in Taiwanese hands.

18 *Europe Is Convincingly Pursuing a Path to Semiconductor Sovereignty* (14.10.2024) "Eetimes": https://www.eetimes.eu/europe-is-convincingly-pursuing-a-path-to-semiconductor-sovereignty/

19 *The Global Semiconductor Talent Shortage* (11.09.2024) "DeLoitte": https://www2.deloitte.com/us/en/pages/technology/articles/global-semiconductor-talent-shortage.html

20 Arrian Ebrahimi, *Groundbreaking Chip Sovereignty Europe's Strategic Push in the Semiconductor Race* (10.11.2024): https://www.ifri.org/en/memos/groundbreaking-chip-sovereignty-europes-strategic-push- semiconductor-race

21 Matthew Connatser, *TSMC Confirms It'll Dig into Dresden for Chip Giant's First Fab on Euro Soil* (16.10.2024) "The Register": https://www.theregister.com/2024/07/30/tsmc_breaks_ground_dresden/

9. Workforce

Still, there is one area where both Western and Asian companies have similar problems: the lack of qualified engineers. If the semiconductor sector does not become more attractive, the resulting talent gap for engineers will be massive: more than 100,000 each in the United States and Europe and upwards of 200,000 in Asia–Pacific (excluding China). We should note here that major disparities exist among countries in Asia–Pacific. For instance, India is a potential net exporter of engineering talent, while other countries, such as Japan and South Korea, face severe shortages.[22]

According to a survey "Challenges in advanced computing and functionalities" from May 2024 – "Electrical/Electronic Engineering is the most common and sought after background to work in semiconductors, followed by physics and Computer science." So are other skilled construction workers (like pipefitters, welders, electricians, and carpenters).

Not only that – but the industry is also staring down a wave of impending retirements. One-third of semiconductor employees in the United States are aged 55 or older. The European Union fares better, with one-fifth of the workforce in this demographic, but it also has a significant proportion of engineering and manufacturing employees close to retirement age.[23]

> With an estimated more than two million direct employees worldwide in 2021, Deloitte predicts that more than one million additional skilled workers will be needed by 2030, equating to more than 100,000 annually. For context, there are fewer than 100,000 graduate students enrolled in electrical engineering and computer science in the United States annually.[24]

With expanding Diversity, Equity and Inclusion (DEI) plus Environmental, Social and Governance (ESG) policies, the West keeps limiting its industrial and manufacturing development. At the same time, those policies are much less or not at all implemented in their Asian competitors.

10. Conclusions

China's military aggression (in the air and on the high seas) and unfair trade practices (subsidies, IP theft, corruption) towards the West remain without a proper

22 *How Semiconductor Companies Can Fill the Expanding Talent Gap* (12.10.2024) "McKinsey": https://www.mckinsey.com/industries/semiconductors/our-insights/how-semiconductor-companies-can-fill-the- expanding-talent-gap

23 *How Semiconductor Companies Can Fill the Expanding Talent Gap* (12.10.2024) "McKinsey": https://www.mckinsey.com/industries/semiconductors/our-insights/how-semiconductor-companies-can-fill-the- expanding-talent-gap

24 *The Global Semiconductor Talent Shortage* (10.10.2024) "Deloitte": https://www2.deloitte.com/us/en/pages/ technology/articles/global-semiconductor-talent-shortage.html

response. If there is any trade reaction at all, then it's rare situations like the recent tariffs on EVs. However, those tariffs don't help to increase Western competitiveness; they are more a sign of helplessness and are buying the West some time.

Apart from lack of reaction, China's bold behavior is also the result of both PRC's and Asia's rising manufacturing prowess and the West falling behind.

Western governments are trying to revive manufacturing with more subsidies, stimuli and money printing. However, Western problems are: 1. structural – rising taxation and inflation, expanding social welfare programs; 2. ideological – under the current von der Leyen EU leadership and under the Biden administration (environmental and leftist policies constraining companies' development).

Even recent electoral wins of EU rightist parties won't change much, since those wins are not substantial enough to influence parliaments. Also, those parties focus more on politics and immigration than difficult and long-term fiscal and economy reforms.

Both systems are moving in opposite directions, with Asia producing and developing modern industries, often with GDP growth in the 3–7% range. The EU's growth is much lower and restricted by increasing regulations.[25]

References

Average Annual Growth Rate of Gross Domestic Product in the European Union from 1996 to 2024 (15.10.2024) "Statista": https://www.statista.com/statistics/1070317/eu-gdp-growth-rate/

Biden Is Giving Intel $8.5 Billion for Big Semiconductor Projects in 4 States (15.09.2024) "NPR": https://www.npr.org/2024/03/20/1239533039/biden-chips-arizona-intel

Biden-Harris Administration Announces Preliminary Terms with TSMC, Expanded Investment from Company to Bring World's Most Advanced Leading-Edge Technology to the U.S. (12.08.2024) "Commerce": https://www.commerce.gov/news/press-releases/2024/04/biden-harris-administration-announces-preliminary-terms-tsmc-expanded

Connatser, Matthew, *TSMC Confirms It'll Dig into Dresden for Chip Giant's First Fab on Euro Soil* (16.10.2024) "The Register": https://www.theregister.com/2024/07/30/tsmc_breaks_ground_dresden/

Department of State Allocating $100 Million in FY 2023 for CHIPS Act Projects (15.09.2024) "State": https://www.state.gov/department-of-state-allocating-100-million-in-fy-2023-for-chips-act-projects/

Ebrahimi, Arrian, *Groundbreaking Chip Sovereignty Europe's Strategic Push in the Semiconductor Race* (10.11.2024): https://www.ifri.org/en/memos/groundbreaking-chip-sovereignty-europes-strategic-push-semiconductor-race

Europe Is Convincingly Pursuing a Path to Semiconductor Sovereignty (14.10.2024) "Eetimes": https://www.eetimes.eu/europe-is-convincingly-pursuing-a-path-to-semiconductor-sovereignty/

The Global Semiconductor Talent Shortage (11.09.2024) "DeLoitte": https://www2.deloitte.com/us/en/pages/technology/articles/global-semiconductor-talent-shortage.html

Government Spending as a Share of GDP, 2022 (20.08.2024): https://ourworldindata.org/grapher/historical-gov-spending-gdp

25 Average annual growth rate of gross domestic product in the European Union from 1996 to 2024 (15.10.2024) "Statista": https://www.statista.com/statistics/1070317/eu-gdp-growth-rate/

How Semiconductor Companies Can Fill the Expanding Talent Gap (12.10.2024) "McKinsey": https://www.mckinsey.com/industries/semiconductors/our-insights/how-semiconductor-companies-can-fill-the-expanding-talent-gap

Indonesia's Bold Bid to Become a Semiconductor Hub (13.08.2024) "The Diplomat": https://thediplomat.com/2024/08/indonesias-bold-bid-to-become-a-semiconductor-hub/

Investment Near Wrocław, Poland, Will Help Create a First-of-Its-Kind End-to-End Leading-Edge Manufacturing Semiconductor Value Chain in Europe (27.09.2024): https://www.intc.com/news-events/press-releases/detail/1627/intel-plans-assembly-and-test-facility-in-poland

Luckenbaugh, Josh, *JUST IN: Navy Investing in Industrial Base to Fix Sub Schedule, Cost Overruns* (17.08.2024) "National Defense Magazine": https://www.nationaldefensemagazine.org/articles/2024/10/2/navy-investing-in-industrial-base-to-fix-sub-programs-cost-schedule-challenges

Magnuson, Stew, *Special Report: Sub Deal Poses Questions About Shipyard Capacity* (17.08.2024) "National Defense Magazine": https://www.nationaldefensemagazine.org/articles/ 2023/2/16/sub-deal-poses-questions-about-shipyard-capacity

MalaysiaTargets Over $100 bln in Semiconductor Industry Investment (13.08.2024) "Reuters": https://www.reuters.com/world/asia-pacific/malaysia-pm-says-targeting-over-10 0-bln-investment-semiconductor-chips-2024-05-28/

Semiconductor Body Calls for EU 'Chips Envoy', More Support (15.09.2024) "Yahoo": https://finance.yahoo.com/news/european-semiconductor-industry-group-esia-141920617.html?guccounter=1

Social Protection Statistics – Social Benefits (20.08.2024): https://ec.europa.eu/eurostat/statistics-explained/index.php?title=Social_protection_statistics_-_social_benefits

TSMC Arizona and U.S. Department of Commerce Announce Up to US$6.6 Billion in Proposed CHIPS Act Direct Funding, the Company Plans Third Leading-Edge Fab in Phoenix (20.08.2024) "TSMC": https://pr.tsmc.com/english/news/3122

Vietnam's Bid to Exploit US-China Chip Tensions Confronts Labour Hurdles (10.08.2024) "Al Jazeera": https://www.aljazeera.com/economy/2024/3/4/as-vietnam-bids-to-become-chip-leader-energy-and-labour-woes-stand-in-the-way

Wilson, Jeffrey, *Australia Shows the World What Decoupling from China Looks Like* (3.08.2024) "Foreign Policy": https://foreignpolicy.com/2021/11/09/australia-china-decoupling-trade-sanctions-coronavirus-geopolitics/

A World of Chips Acts: The Future of U.S.-EU Semiconductor Collaboration (14.10.2024) "CSIS": https://www.csis.org/analysis/world-chips-acts-future-us-eu-semiconductor-collaboration

World Social Protection Report 2024–26: In Figures (20.08.2024): https://www.ilo.org/resource/article/world-social-protection-report-2024-26-figures

10 China and the Qing Court – Fostering the Sphere of Influence with an Ancient Strategy

*Cho Wong**

1. Introduction

When President Xi Jinping visited Moscow in March 2023, he muttered the following words as he bade farewell to President Putin: "Change is coming that hasn't happened in a hundred years, and we are driving this change together".[1]

What President Xi meant by that was open to interpretation. However, it shows that he is very confident that China will, with the help of Russia, drive a new world order with fellow totalitarian countries and have a bigger say in world affairs.

In fact, this popular quote by President Xi was first mentioned by Li Hongzhang,[2] a Qing Court (QC) mandarin who had experience in dealing with the west. He said, "China has encountered a powerful enemy (meaning the western powers) that has not been seen in thousands of years, and China is in a major change that has not been seen in the past three thousand years".[3]

Towards the end of the Qing Dynasty, not only China was facing strong sea power from foreign countries; the real change internally was the introduction of the concepts of democracy, science and ultimately, modernisation. These were the real threats to the government then, and their first reaction was to counter them with nationalism.

To quote the Greek historian Herodotus, "To understand a people requires understanding their history".[4] This chapter attempts to explain why President Xi and some of his people resent the west. (Some, however, given the chance, would vote with their feet and go and live in the west.) Xi and his ruling party, the Chinese Communist Party (CCP), are also facing foreign and internal threats. According to

* Warwick University, UK.

1 This conversation was recorded by journalists on 22 March 2023 when President Xi Jinping was bidding farewell to President Putin at the steps of the Kremlin. People speculated that the two leaders were plotting something together to change the world.

2 Li Hongzhang (15-02-1823 to 07-11-1901) was the Chancellor of the QC during the reigns of Emperor Tonzhi and Guangzu. Neither of the emperors had real power. Empress Dowager Cixi was the true agent (15-02-1823 to 07-11-1901).

3 Alice E. Neve Little, *Li Hung-Chang: His Life & Times*, London: Cassell & Company, 1903.

4 Raymond Kierstead, *Herodotus and The Invention of History*, reed.edu, 01-09-2011.

DOI: 10.4324/9781003545750-12

the political line of the party, nationalism is often used to unite people, especially in times of crisis.

In addition, Alfred Adler[5] and the school of Individual Psychology proposed that individuals often develop certain feelings of inferiority or self-pity, and overcoming these feelings can lead to heightened self-esteem and personal growth. "Self-pity becomes self-esteem" aligns with his theories on overcoming inferiority complexes and striving for personal development. This is the root of the Little Pinks and the Fifty-cent Gang, which will be discussed.

2. The Qing's Rule on the Middle Plain

The Qing dynasty (1644–1912) was founded by Huang Taiji[6] in 1636 with its capital in Shenyang. He came through the Great Wall and overthrew the Ming Court in 1644 and moved its capital to Beijing. They were Manchurians and considered barbarians from the north by the Ming Chinese. The fall of the Ming Dynasty was a bitter blow to the Ming Chinese's pride and was considered a national humiliation.

2.1 The Heyday of the Qing's Rule and its GDP

According to British economist Maddison,[7] the total GDP of the Qing Dynasty in 1820 was US$228.6 billion, 32.9% of the world.[8] The population during Emperor Qianlong's[9] rule reached 300 million, the highest in history. As a result of economic growth, the nation felt more powerful, and the QC extended its territories significantly.

At the time, the Dzungar Khanate,[10] a Mongol state established in the 17th century, was the last great nomadic empire in Eurasia. It controlled a significant territory across modern-day Xinjiang, parts of Mongolia, Kazakhstan, Kyrgyzstan, spanning Central Asia. It rivalled both the Qing Dynasty in China and the Russian Empire.

The QC began its campaign to conquer the Dzungar Khanate. Decisive battles occurred between 1755 and 1759, leading to the annexation of the region known as Xinjiang ("New Frontier") into the Qing Empire. Not long after, the Qing army also gained control over Tibet in the early 18th century. These conquests were part

5 Alfred Adler (07-02-1870 to 28-05-1937) was an Austrian medical doctor, psychotherapist, and founder of The School of Individual Psychology.

6 Huang Taiji (28-11-1592 to 21-09-1643), the Manchu leader who disposed the Ming Dynasty and established the Jin Dynasty. Also known as Abahai and Emperor Taizong of Qing.

7 Angus Maddison, British economist (06-12-1926 to 24-04-2010) was an expert on quantitative macro-economic history.

8 *China's Economic Rise: History, Trends, Challenges, and Implications for the United States*, every-CRSReport.com, 12-07-2006.

9 Qianlong (25-09-1711 to 07-02-1799) ascended the throne in 1735. He was the fourth emperor of Qing to rule over China.

10 Dzungar Khanate (1634–1758) was a Tibetan Buddhist nomadic empire on the Eurasian Steppe in Central Asia.

of the QC's broader efforts to secure its borders and establish control over important buffer regions.[11]

Similarly, Taiwan was not part of China until 1683. The Ming Emperor Hongwu (1328–1398) listed 15 countries that he considered independent: Korea, Japan, Okinawa, Taiwan, North Vietnam, Cambodia, Thailand, South Vietnam, Sumatra, Java, Malaya, South Vietnam, North Sumatra and Brunei.[12] A "sea ban" (Haijin) policy was enforced at the time whereby most private maritime activities and foreign trade were restricted. This was aimed to:

- combat piracy and costal raids by the Japanese wokou (pirates);
- centralise economic power by restricting sea trade;
- isolate and limit foreign influences which might disrupt Chinese culture and social order (sound familiar?);
- and to prioritise agricultural development over commerce and maritime ventures.

When the QC defeated the Ming, Ming loyalist Zheng Chenggong resisted the Qing army from the southeastern coast of China. In 1661, he and his army fled to Taiwan and defeated the Dutch who occupied Taiwan By 1662, the Dutch surrendered, thus ending their 38-year rule on the island. Zheng set up the Kingdom of Tungning in Taiwan, and the intention was to use it as a base to hopefully reclaim the mainland from the Qing Dynasty.[13]

In 1662, the QC banned all its coastal ports from trading externally. Residents along the coast were ordered to move 30 to 50 miles inland. Ultimately, in 1683, the QC defeated Zheng's grandson and annexed Taiwan. The maritime ban set up by the Ming Dynasty was also abolished.

In 1874, some people from Okinawa arrived in Taiwan and were killed by the natives there. The Japanese government, on behalf of the victims, asked the QC to investigate. The reply was that the natives were not considered as Qing's citizens and therefore not within the scope of Qing's rule. In a sense, the QC did not consider Taiwan as part of its territory.

2.2 Western Understanding of the Faraway Middle Kingdom

Adventurers and traders from the west brought back stories and valued goods from the mysterious country in the east. During the early Ming dynasty, European knowledge of China was very limited. The tales of Marco Polo's (13th century) travels were often regarded with scepticism, but nevertheless his accounts were

11 This was the first time Xinjiang and Tibet was included into "Greater China", not as often claimed by CCP's foreign office spokespersons: "These territories have always been an indivisible and a sacred part of China since ancient time".

12 Maria Lim, "The Country Without Conquest", *Journal of the British Association for Chinese Studies*, Vol. 2, bacsuk.org.uk, Huang-Ming Zuxum.

13 Known as the Mudan Incident, in September 1872. Wikipedia.org.

significant. During the 16th century, Portuguese explorers such as Jorge Álvares[14] reached China, and Macau was established as the first European settlement. Towards the end of the period, Metteo Ricci[15] and other Jesuit missionaries began to arrive in China. Details of Chinese society, culture and technology became better known as a result of their work in Beijing and their scholarly exchanges.

Global trade became more important at the height of Ming Dynasty due to the European aristocracy's indulgence in Chinese imports such as porcelain china, tea and silk, especially when the desire for these items became popular for the emerging middle class throughout Europe.

During the early Qing period (17th – 18th centuries), Jesuit missionaries continued their efforts in providing detailed and often admiring accounts of Chinese culture, society and achievements. The Jesuits' integration into Chinese society and their work as QC's astronomers and mathematicians impressed many in Europe and presented China as a land of great sophistication and knowledge.

2.3 The Middle Kingdom's Insistence on Using the Imperial Tributary System

Although the QC was fascinated by western knowledge, the idea that China was the centre of the world persisted. Traditionally, the Imperial Tributary System[16] was a Chinese diplomatic and trade practice that reached its peak during the Qing Dynasty. This was a framework for China's interaction with neighbouring countries and exhibited the hierarchical nature of Sino-centric worldviews.

The tributary system was based on a Confucian worldview in which China, or the "Middle Kingdom", was at the centre. Neighbouring countries were considered lesser, yet respected, participants in this order. The Chinese Emperor was seen as the "Son of Heaven", with a mandate to rule all "under Heaven" (Tianxia). Tributary states were required to recognise the superiority of the Chinese emperor. Regular missions to the Chinese court to offer tribute had to be made symbolically. In return for their tribute, these states received protection, favourable trade terms, gifts and recognition from the QC.

This exchange helped to maintain peace and stability in the region, promoting trade and diplomatic relations. Tributary missions involved delegations from these states travelling to Beijing, where they would perform rituals of submission and present local products and treasures. Traditionally, delegates from these missions had to wait until "summoned" by the emperor, and they had to kow-tow to the Son of Heaven as part of the protocol. In return, the emperor would bestow lavish gifts and confer titles on the visiting dignitaries. Perhaps this system was an inspiration of President Xi's Belt & Road Initiative and his often-quoted saying, "a community with a shared future for mankind".

14 Jorge Álvares (died 08-07-1521) was a Portuguese explorer.

15 Matteo Ricci (06-10-1552 to 11-05-1610) was an Italian Jesuit priest and one of the founding figures of the Jesuit China missions.

16 Everett Munez, *Tributary System*, britannica.com.

3. The Beginning of the End of the QC

3.1 Desire of the West to Open Up the Eastern Market

With the high demand for tea, porcelain and silk, more trading vessels from Europe visited China, and it was important for western traders to establish trading posts along its coast. However, the QC still wanted to maintain control of how and where these tradings were conducted. They feared that if it was a free-for-all, western influence would seriously undermine the imperial system and the culture which had been maintained for thousands of years.

Between 1757 and the mid-19th century, the QC channelled all foreign trade to Guangzhou (Canton). Foreign traders could only conduct business with a designated group of Chinese merchants – the Hongs.[17] This enabled the QC to limit western access to China and let the government control trade more efficiently and also monopolising the profits. (This is very similar to the CCP's early system of foreign trade restrictions only through designated State-Owned Enterprises). They continued to view foreign trade as part of the tributary missions and expected the traders to respect Chinese terms and superiority.

Foreign merchants were heavily regulated, and they were only allowed to reside in specific areas during the trading season. The trouble was that the QC believed that they had a self-sufficient economy and were not that interested in western goods.

3.2 Huge Deficit of the Balance of Trade Between East and West

The QC imposed duties and taxes on all imported and exported goods which contributed to the state's coffers. Western traders had to pay their Chinese counterparts in silver. In the beginning, there was plenty of silver (founded in Central America after European colonisation there). However, the trading nations' deficit became serious during the 18th and early 19th centuries, as the Chinese viewed imported textiles as inferior and there was very little interest in other imported goods.

By the end of the 18th century, it was estimated that the British East India Company was exporting 6 million taels of silver annually to China. Between 1800 and 1825, over £3 million Chinese goods were imported by Britain, again paid in silver.[18]

The imbalance in trade led to a depletion of silver in Europe, and the overexploitation of silver mines in the Americas led to huge environmental and human costs. In addition, the strain on silver reserves in Europe caused deflationary pressures and therefore concerns in European economies. The US' independence also played a part in restricting the shipping of silver from the New World back to Europe.

17 *Canton System*, britannica.com.

18 *The British Intra-Asian Trade with China 1800–1842*, HKU Scholars Hub, hub.hku.hk.

3.3 Problems with Chinese Currency's Dependence on Silver

Initially, the influx of silver helped bolster the Chinese economy as it facilitated trade and commerce. However, the negative effect was inflation, and the economy became increasingly dependent on silver for trade and tax collection. Regional imbalances and tensions grew as coastal cities grew wealthy leaving the poorer provinces inland behind. (Sound familiar?) Ultimately, this social imbalance and inflation caused unrest and dissatisfaction in the population, leading to revolts and protests.

It had become non-economically viable for western traders to ship silver to China to pay for desirable goods to be shipped back. Something had to give.

3.4 Opium as the Commodity that Breaks the Deadlock

To balance trade, the British East India Company started to ship Indian-produced opium to China (mainly by smuggling). Opium poppies had been used in traditional Chinese medicine for centuries.[19] They were mostly cultivated in Yunan. However, locally produced opium could not compete with the imported counterpart as it was not as strong. The widespread import of opium as a recreational drug began in the early 19th century. It is important to understand that taking opium at that time was not considered immoral.

Back in the UK, opium was also still legally obtainable as a recreational drug. King George III (1760–1820) and King George IV (1820–1830) were known to be opium takers.[20] It was not until 1914 that opium was outlawed in Britain.

As a consequence, the power of the QC, its reserves and the population's addiction to opium created an opportunity for fundamental changes.

3.5 The Opium Wars

The First Opium War (1839–1842) was a conflict as a result of the QC's restricted trade practices (Guangzhou/Canton was the only place allowed for foreign activities, via destinated Chinese importers), and the imbalance of trade. In 1839, Lin Zexu[21] was appointed by the QC to oversee the end of the opium trade. Lin used strong measures, including confiscating and destroying large quantities of opium from British merchants (Jardines, for example). William Jardine reported it to then-Foreign Minister Palmerston, saying that the Chinese wanted to bar imported opium so that they could monopolise the trade domestically. The British Parliament,

19 Jose A. Canton-Alvarez, *A Gift from the Buddhist Monastery: The Role of Buddhist Medical Practices in the Assimilation of the Opium Poppy in Chinese Medicine During the Song Dynasty (960–1279)*, Cambridge University Press, 09-11-2019.

20 "George IV: The Rehabilitation of Old Naughty", *The Guardian*, 28-08-2011.

21 Lin Zexu (30-08-1785 to 22-11-1850) was Qing's Governor General in Guangdong.

with the authorisation of Queen Victoria, ordered the British navy to retaliate.[22] QC lost, and the Treaty of Nanjing was signed in 1842. Hong Kong was ceded to Britain, and more ports were open for foreign trade.

The Second Opium War (1856–1860) occurred due to the confiscation of a vessel called Arrow, which was registered under a British flag. Qing officials claimed that the vessel, which was docked in Whampoa, did not have the correct papers. The Captain of the Arrow lied to the British Ambassador in Guangzhou (Harry Parkes) that the Qing soldiers seized the vessel and destroyed the British flag.[23] Qing's Commissioner refused to apologise. At similar time, French preacher Auguste Chapdelaine[24] was executed in Guangxi because he was preaching without permission. The British and French joined forces and attacked Guangzhou. Other countries, such as Russia and the US, also attacked Tientsin/Tianjin.

The Treaty of Tientsin was signed in 1858, granting the foreign traders more freedom in trading in more ports and allowing foreign legations in Beijing.

However, when British representative Sir Harry Smith Parkes and his team (39 people altogether) visited Beijing to exchange contracts, they were captured by the QC, imprisoned and tortured, contrary to the agreed terms of safe conduct. They were kept in a small, cramped space, suffered beatings and deprived of food and water. Twenty-one of them, including high-ranking officials and soldiers, died as a result.[25]

This led to the British force entering Beijing and burning down the Summer Palace. The QC had to sign the Treaty of Peking, in which Qing agreed to rectify the Treaty of Tientsin and conceded Kowloon to the British.

4. Qing's Fight Back and Loss

4.1 Introducing Western Science to Level Up

By now, the QC recognised the gap between the east and west. Efforts were made to introduce western science and technology by translating western scientific texts on mathematics, astronomy, engineering and medicine into Chinese; establishing institutions such as Tongwen Guan (translation schools) in Beijing to teach western science and languages to train up officials and scholars in western knowledge; sponsoring students to study in the US and Japan in subjects such as engineering and military science, with a view that they could bring home new knowledge. Western military technology and training methods were also adopted by the government.

22 B. Cassan, *William Jardine: Architect of the First Opium War*, Eastern Illinois University.

23 Justin Pollard and Stephanie Pollard, "The Arrow Incident", *History Today*, Vol. 69, 10-10-2019.

24 Auguste Chapdelaine (died 29-02-1856) was a French Christian missionary of the Paris Foreign Missions Society. His Chinese name was Ma Lai.

25 *Harry Smith Parkes*, Military-history.fandom.com.

4.2 Boxer Rebellion and Qing's Reliance on Them

The Boxers[26] (Yihequan or Righteous and Harmonious Fists) were a grassroots movement by Chinese people who were anti-foreign, anti-colonial and anti-Christian. In the beginning, they were also anti-Qing! They believed that their martial arts practices enabled them to be invulnerable to western weapons. They targeted foreign nationals, foreign legations and local Chinese who had converted to Christianity. They blamed the QC and foreigners for all the problems faced by China. (As in the present day, citizens always blame foreigners for hardships because they are easy targets.)

At the time, because of high inflation, economic difficulties, natural disasters, resentment towards foreign influence and the inequality in special privileges granted to foreigners under the various treaties, the movement gained significant support, especially in Shandong and other northern provinces.

Within the power corridors of the QC, there were plots and counter plots. Empress Dowager Cixi's[27] son Emperor Tongzhi[28] ascended to the throne aged 5 in 1861. The Empress managed the state's affairs on his behalf. However, he died in 1875, aged 18. Cixi played an important role in installing her nephew, Guangxu,[29] as the new emperor at the age of 4, with Cixi actually ruling the country. When Guangxu was 27, he orchestrated a reform (known as the Hundred Days' Reform)[30] in 1898 with a view to modernise education, military, economy and government institutions and, using today's words, to "make Qing great again!" His key goal was also to gain back power from Cixi. This was supported by the reform-minded officials and foreigners in Beijing. They believed a modern China would benefit global trade.

However, Cixi and her conversative followers saw the reform as a threat to their power and influence. In September 1898, Cixi orchestrated a coup and placed Emperor Guangxu under house arrest. Many reformist leaders were executed. The foreign powers, supportive of Guangxu, asked one of their doctors to see Guangxu to make sure he was in good health. Cixi was displeased, but owing to foreign influence, she could not do anything. Secretly, she was plotting for the replacement of Guangxu by Pujun, her nephew and a member of the imperial family.

Meanwhile, anti-foreign activities of the Boxers attracted her attention. On the 7th of June 1900, she invited them to enter Beijing. The Boxers caused chaos, including killing foreign ambassadors, burning churches and killing preachers. On the 10th, they surrounded the embassy district. The foreign powers held an emergency meeting in Tianjin and decided to form an army of 8 nations (the Eight Nation Alliance) to go to Beijing to deal with the Boxers.

26 *Boxer Rebellion*, britannica.com, 09-07-2024.

27 Empress Dowager Cixi (29-11-1835 to15-11-1908), *Cixi Biography & Facts*, britannica.com, 14-08-2024.

28 Emperor Tongzhi (27-04-1856 to 12-01-1875).

29 Emperor Guangxu (14-08-1871 to 14-11-1908).

30 *Hundred Days of Reform*, britannica.com.

Cixi's chief of- staff lied to Cixi that he received an official document from the foreign forces demanding Cixi release Emperor Guangxu and return him to his throne. Cixi was furious and on 21st June 1900, after an emergency meeting with her officials, she issued an "Imperial Declaration of War to All Foreign Nations",[31] officially declaring war against Britain, the US, France, Germany, Italy, Japan, Russia, Spain, Belgium, Holland and the Austro-Hungarian Empire.[32]

The key reasons behind her decision to gamble were rooted in a complex mix of internal and external pressures. Then, China was facing significant internal unrest and widespread dissatisfaction with the QC, stemming from economic hardship, corruption and foreign intervention. What better than to switch people's focus onto waging war with the "foreign devils"?

Foreign powers had been carving out spheres of influence in China, imposing unequal treaties, humiliating and weakening China's sovereignty. The Boxer Movement's aim to expel foreign influence and missionaries resonated with many Chinese, including some in the QC. Empress Cixi was under substantial pressure from conservative elements who supported the Boxers' anti-foreign stance. They saw the Boxers as a potential ally in resisting foreign domination. By aligning with the Boxers and declaring war, Cixi saw an opportunity to harness the nationalist sentiments to rally the populace and potentially regain control over her nation's sovereignty.

The war, however, resulted in devastating losses for China. The Eight-Nation Alliance overwhelmed Chinese forces and captured Beijing. In the aftermath, the QC was forced to sign the Boxer Protocol in September 1901, which imposed severe penalties, including large indemnities and further concessions to the foreign powers.

5. Unequal Treaties Leading to National Shame

The "unequal treaties"[33] refer to a series of agreements that the QC was forced to sign with Western powers, including Japan, during the 19th and early 20th centuries. These treaties were characterised by terms that are one-sided, heavily favouring the foreign powers and undermining the sovereignty of the QC. The key ones were:

1842 The Treaty of Nanking: as mentioned earlier, this was a result of the First Opium War with Britain. It ceded Hong Kong to the British, opened 5 ports, Canton (Guangzhou), Amoy (Xiamen), Fuzhou, Ningpo (Ningbo) and Shanghai to the British trade and granted extraterritorial rights to British citizens. In addition, 21 million silver dollars were paid to the British for the costs of the war and for the confiscated opium.

31 Sean McGuffin, *The Boxer Rebellion 1899–1901*, ODUMUNC, 2017

32 Yet, it was Cixi who declared war first.

33 Xavier Lacroix, *Unequal Treaties with China*, Digital Encyclopaedia of European History, ehne.fr, 22-06-2020

1844 The Treaty of Wanghia: signed with the US, granting them the same rights as the British.

1844 The Treaty of Whampoa: signed with France, granting them similar privileges as the British and the US.

1858 The Treaty of Tientsin: as mentioned earlier, this was the result of the Second Opium War and a set of treaties signed with Britain, France, Russia and the US. Opium trade was legalised and the right of foreign nationals, such as the right to travel inside China, was expanded. More open ports such as Dailian, Zhenjiang and Qingdao were added. The foreign powers were promised the right to establish legations (embassies) in Beijing.

1860 Convention of Peking: these agreements concluded the Second Opium War after the QC refused to implement the Treaty of Tientsin. Kowloon Peninsula was conceded to the British, and land was promised to the establishment of foreign legations.

1895 The Treaty of Shimonoseki: this was the result of the First Sino-Japanese War. The QC conceded Taiwan and the Pescadores Islands to Japan, recognised the independence of the Korean Peninsula and provided a large indemnity.

1898 The Second Convention of Peking: the New Territories, adjacent to Kowloon and Hong Kong Island, were leased to the British for 99 years until 1997.

1901 The Gengzi Treaty (the Boxer Protocol or the Treaty of Beijing): as mentioned earlier, this was signed following the Boxer Rebellion. This treaty included provisions related to reparations, military presence and certain territorial concessions as a result of the engagements by the Eight-Nations Alliance against the QC.

China was required to pay a large indemnity (totalling 450 million taels of silver) to the 8 foreign powers to compensate for damages incurred during the Boxer Rebellion.

The treaty also formalised the right of foreign powers to establish legations in Beijing with extraterritorial rights, meaning foreign nationals were subject to their home country's laws rather than Chinese law.

Foreign troops were permitted to occupy certain areas in Beijing and other locations, and the military presence in China was increased under the pretext of maintaining order.

(In fact, the US used their Gengzi indemnity to build QingHua University[34] in Beijing and sponsored Chinese scholars to study in the US. This was rarely mentioned by the CCP.)

These treaties significantly increased foreign control over Chinese territory through spheres of influence, extraterritorial rights and economic concessions. The Qing government effectively lost significant control over its sovereignty and

34 History-School of Humanities and Social Sciences, Tsinghua University, rwxy.tsinghua.edu.cn/shssen/About/History

trade, and foreign intervention in domestic affairs increased dramatically during this period.

This was a critical phase in the history of foreign relations in China, leading to further pressures and changes leading up to the eventual fall of the Qing Dynasty in 1911.

In terms of territories lost, here is a summary of the major foreign powers involved and the specific territories or rights they received:

Russia: control over Port Arthur (Lüshunkou) and Dalian (Dalny) on the Liaodong Peninsula. It also secured rights for railway construction and development in northeastern China, particularly in Manchuria.

Britain: continued its control over Hong Kong and extended its influence over the southern China. It also acquired certain railway concessions and rights in North China, similar to the privileges secured during earlier treaties.

France: retained control over Guangzhou Bay (now part of Guangdong Province) and expanded its interests in southern China.

Germany: kept the leased territory of Qingdao (Tsingtao) in Shandong Province and secured economic concessions and rights to build infrastructure.

Japan: acquired significant influence over Shandong Province, including rights to develop railways and other industries and extended its interests in Manchuria through economic and military influence.

United States: it did not receive territories in the same manner as the European powers. Instead, it secured the Open Door Policy, which emphasised the importance of maintaining equal trading rights for all countries in China and preventing any single power from monopolising trade.

Italy: acquired some minor concessions but did not receive significant territorial gains compared to the other powers. It received certain rights but did not secure vast territories or significant economic positions in China.

In terms of territory, Russia gained the most:

Outer Manchuria:

The Treaty of Nerchinsk (1689): This established the border between the QC and Russia, effectively recognising Russian claims to certain territories in Siberia west of the Amur River.

The Treaty of Aigun (1858): This treaty further delineated the border, conceding land east of the Amur River (also known as the Heilongjiang River in China) to Russia, which included the region now known as Primorsky Krai.

The Treaty of Peking (1860): This treaty confirmed the cession of the territory east of the Amur River, and also granted the Russians access to Vladivostok on the Pacific coast, solidifying their foothold in the area.

Parts of Mongolia: The previous treaties also impacted areas in Outer Mongolia, although the QC maintained nominal control until the independence movement in the early 20th century led to Mongolia's declaration of independence in 1911.

Port Arthur (Lüshunkou) and Dalian: Following the Boxer Rebellion and the Boxer Protocol (1901), Russia gained a strong military presence and ultimately leased Port Arthur and the surrounding territory (including Dalian) on the Liaodong Peninsula. This was further solidified after the Treaty of Shimonoseki in 1895 but was temporarily reversed due to Japan's influence in the region.

The series of unequal treaties with Russia led to significant territorial losses for the QC particularly in the northeastern regions, which later became vital to Russian expansion into Asia. These treaties not only altered China's borders but also had long-lasting impact on its sovereignty and territorial integrity.

Incidentally, Jiang Zemin, who was General Secretary of the CCP, signed off several agreements[35] to resolve longstanding border disputes between China and Russia. Russia kept Heilongjiang (Amur) River Region, notably Bolshoy, Ussuriysky Island (Heixiazi Island in China) and Damansky Island (Zhenbao Island). We have to realise that when the CCP keep saying territories are sacred and non-divisible, there is flexibility built in. Russia is treated differently.

Japan also made gains on territories from the QC.

Treaty of Shimonoseki (1895): Taiwan (Formosa) was ceded to Japan, marking the beginning of Japanese rule over Taiwan, which lasted until the end of WW2. Pescadores Islands (Penghu) were also ceded to Japan, along with Taiwan.

Liaodong Peninsula: Although Japan initially gained control over this territory, it was forced to return it to China due to international pressure (notably from Russia and France). However, Japan later regained control of the peninsula, including Port Arthur (Lüshunkou) and Dalian, after their shock victory over Russia in the Russo-Japanese War (1904–1905).

Korea: While not directly ceded as a territory, Korea was recognised as a Japanese protectorate as part of the concessions in the treaty. This laid the groundwork for Japan's subsequent annexation of Korea in 1910.

During World War I, Japan presented the "Twenty-One Demands"[36] to China, which included various concessions that would effectively give Japan control over several areas:

Shandong Province: Japan sought to retain the rights it gained in the Treaty of Shimonoseki, along with further control over economic and political aspects of the province, which had previously been under German control. This included the special rights and privileges to operate in the region and significant influence over Shandong's administration. These agreements led to significant territorial losses for China and a considerable increase in Japanese influence within the region, heralding a period of imperial expansion for Japan in East Asia.

35 The Treaty of Good-Neighbourliness and Friendly Cooperation Between the PRC and the Russian Federation was a 20-year strategic treaty signed by Jiang Zemin and Vladimir Putin on 16-07-2011. On 28-06-2021, Russia and China extended the treaty for another 5 years, wikepedia.org.

36 *Twenty-one Demands*, britannica.com

Apart from the land ceded, the QC had also lost economic control and vast foreign reserves. Local governments were forced to set low import tariffs, which were beneficial to foreign traders and harmful to the local economy. Victorious powers often demanded large cash indemnities. The erosion of political and judicial sovereignty significantly weakened local governments and created an environment of internal unrest and rebellion.

The humiliation and suffering caused by these treaties catalysed a surge of nationalist sentiment and efforts to modernise and reform. The ideas of Nationalism and Modernisation had spread. This eventually contributed to the fall of the Qing Dynasty and the emergence of the Republic of China.

All these unequal treaties were a symbol of the "Century of Humiliation" China endured and remain a sensitive topic in China's historical memory.

6. CCP's Clever Use of National Shame to its Advantage

As mentioned before, nationalism in China is a result of a very complex matrix, originating from the start of the Qing Dynasty.

First, when the Ming Dynasty fell, most people were anti-Qing. This was due to the Qing warriors being considered "barbarians from the north of the Great Wall – the Jins";[37] these people were not Hans (the majority in China). After the reign of QC began, most anti-government activities went underground. They included sending secret messages organising uprisings written in small pieces of paper then stuffed inside mooncakes to avoid detection. Secret societies such as the White Lotus Society and the Ming Society were set up to sabotage the QC. Their slogan was "Overthrow the Qings and Resurrect the Mings". These secret societies became the present-day Triads.

At the peak of the Qing Dynasty, the economy was doing very well. Exports of Chinese products propelled the national GDPs, improved the living standard and XinJiang (New Territories) were added to the map of China. Most people then forgot about the anti-Qing sentiment.

However, the opium wars and the foreign powers' forceful opening of the Chinese market had exposed the weakness of the QC and broken the dream of "China is the centre of the world". People began to realise how backwards China was in terms of science and technology. There were several conflicting ideas on how China could catch up with the west:

- Learning western science and technology only but Confucian philosophy was still the mainstream in governance systems;
- Believing that the Confucian philosophy was out of date and China should import ideas and knowhow from the west wholesale.

37 *Jin Dynasty, China-Mongolia [1115–1234]*, britannica.com

When the CCP came to power, they chose the latter, bringing Marxism and Leninism into China. At the time, ordinary Chinese were tired of the civil wars caused by warlords fighting each other after the collapse of the QC; internal conflicts between leaders of the Republic of China in the mainland; and by Japan's invasion of China during WW2. The gap between the haves and the have-nots was enormous, and a lot of politicians were corrupt.

The CCP used the slogan of "Serving the People", together with clean government, guerilla warfare and the ideology of freeing the poor from capitalists. At first, they were defeated and chased by the Nationalist Party (Kuomintang/KMT) led by Chiang Kai-shek.[38]

Chairman Mao[39] led his Red Army on a military retreat which covered about 6,000 miles to Yan'an (described by the CCP as the 28,000-mile Long March). The Long March (1934–1936)[40] is often romanticised as a heroic journey symbolising resilience and determination. It played a crucial role in solidifying Mao's leadership within the CCP, and ultimately it helped the Party to regroup and gain support from the peasants.

Owing to the corruption within the Republic of China (RoC) government, infiltration of the CCP in various ranks inside the Nationalist Party and ultimately arms embargo by the Americans against Chiang Kai-shek, the nationalists were defeated by Mao and fled to Taiwan. Today, the Republic of China remains in existence despite the claim by the CCP that Taiwan is "a sacred and inalienable part of China".

CCP's propaganda machine kept reminding citizens that "Without the Communist Party there will be no New China." Chairman Mao said, "The Chinese people have stood up[41] (against foreign meddling)" when he made his first speech during the founding ceremony of the People's Republic of China in Tiananmen Square on October 1, 1949. In reality, the country was very, very poor by then after the harsh period since the fall of the QC.

6.1 The CCP Against the "Elites"

It was relatively easy for ordinary Chinese citizens to blame the dire state on the old government which was made up of, in their eyes, the elites who were educated and/or supported by the west. During Mao's reign, he regularly directed or encouraged people's revolts against the elites. He also managed to include his enemies, within and outside the CCP, into these groups of elites to be punished or eliminated.

38 Chiang Kai-shek (1877~1975) led the Kuomintang (Chinese Nationalist Party) for 5 decades and was head of Republic of China government between 1928 and 1949, bbc.co.uk/history/historicfigures/chiang_kaishek.shtml

39 Stuart Reynolds Schram, *Mao Zedong*, Britannica.com, 05-09-2024

40 Long March, 15-10-1934 to 10-1935, britannica.com

41 *The Chinese People Have Stood Up! 21-09-1949, Opening Address by Mao Zedong, Chairman of the CCP at the First Plenary Session of the Chinese People's Political Consultative Conference*, china.usc.edu

For example:

The Three-anti Campaign (1951) – it aimed to combat corruption, waste and corruption within the CCP, the government and the military. It mainly targeted party members and officials.

The Five-anti Campaign (1952) – bribery, theft of state property, tax evasion, cheating on government contracts and stealing state economic information were targeted. The campaign primarily focused on business owners and the middle class.

Socialist Transformation of Agriculture and Industry (1953–1956) – it aimed to transform agriculture through communes and to nationalise industry and commerce. The goal was to steer China's economy towards socialism.

First Five-Year-Plan (1953–1957) – this comprehensive plan aimed at economic development, focusing on heavy industry, infrastructure and the collectivisation of agriculture was implemented in 1953. It was a carbon copy of Soviet-style centralised planning.

Cultural and Thought Reform – these were efforts to reform education and promote ideological conformity within arts and culture.

The Anti-Rightist Campaign (1957) – it was a political campaign initiated by Mao after he encouraged intellectuals to criticise and offer suggestions to improve the government and the CCP's practices. This period, known as the Hundred Flowers Campaign, triggered many people to open their hearts. The criticisms proved more intense and widespread than anticipated and as a result, the Anti-Rightist Campaign was used to suppress dissent. Hundreds of thousands of intellectuals, academics and party members were persecuted, many of whom were subjected to public criticism, imprisonment or forced labour. It stifled intellectual freedom and political discourse in China for a long period.

The Great Leap Forward[42] (1958–1962) – it was a social and economic campaign that Mao initiated. The aim was to transform China rapidly from an agricultural society to a socialist society by means of rapid industrialisation and collectivisation. Communes, large collective farms intended to consolidate resources and labour to improve output, were established.

In an effort to boost steel production, Mao started the "Everyone to refine steel" movement. Small, local furnaces were constructed in backyard settings. People even donated their pots and pans in an effort to help. However, the quality of steel produced was very poor, and these efforts diverted attention and labour away from cultivating the land.

Agricultural policies implemented during the period were radical and scientifically unsound. For example, birds were considered pests for consuming grains and therefore had to be eliminated. Predictably, the harvests followed were devastated by all kind of insects because there were not enough birds to control their population.

42 *Great Leap Forward, 1958–1960*, britannica.com

On the whole, the campaign was a big disaster. The mismanagement, coupled with exaggerated production reports, led to widespread famine and it was estimated that 15 to 45 million people perished as a result. Mao's position within the CCP was weakened.

The Cultural Revolution[43] (1966–1976) – it was a follow-through of the disastrous Great Leap Forward that had caused mayhem and put Mao in a awkward position. It was not in his blood to admit mistakes or failures. His position as the Great Leader was in danger. He launched the Cultural Revolution to impose his orthodoxy within the CCP and to reserve and enforce communism in the country by removing capitalist, traditionalist and cultural elements from the Chinese society. He blamed these people for resisting his goal to make China a communist utopia.

The movement began in May 1966, when Mao aimed to reassert his control over the Communist Party and the country, fearing that China was moving away from socialist ideals. He called for a purge of elements he considered "counter-revolutionary" and promoted fervent support for his leadership and ideology.

One of the most visible aspects of the Cultural Revolution was the rise of the Red Guards. These were groups of young people, mainly students, who were mobilised by Mao to attack and criticise intellectuals, traditional customs, "bourgeois" elements and perceived enemies of the state. They played a significant role in spreading chaos and violence throughout the country. Schools and universities were closed, and education was disrupted for a generation. Traditional Chinese culture and historical relics were attacked and destroyed. Books were burned, and many cultural and religious artifacts were vandalised.

The Cultural Revolution was marked by widespread persecution and violence, including public humiliations known as "struggle sessions", where individuals were forced to confess to crimes against the revolution. Many were tortured, imprisoned or killed.

Political leaders deemed insufficiently loyal to Mao, such as Liu Shaoqi[44] and Deng Xiaoping,[45] were purged. Many experienced harsh treatment during the Cultural Revolution. Several prominent figures fell from power, while others rose by supporting Mao's radical agenda.[46]

China's economy was so bad that in the early Sixties, there was an influx of refugees from the mainland to Hong Kong. On the other hand, when people from Hong Kong went back to the mainland to visit their relatives, they would take bags of old clothes and food (even cooking oil) with them. My mother made one of these visits.

43 Kenneth G. Lieberthal, *Cultural Revolution*, britannica.com, 05-09-2024

44 Robert C. North, *Liu Shaoqi*, britannica.com, 10-07-2024

45 *Deng Xiaoping*, britannica.com, 07-09-2024

46 This was the time when President Xi's father, Xi Zhongxun, one of the Vice Premiers in the CCP, was persecuted and sent to the countryside for re-education. He was later rehabilitated and held significant positions again after the end of Cultural Revolution. Zi's childhood suffered as a result.

During the Cultural Revolution, Mao also started anti-Confucianism and anti-Lin Biao[47] campaigns, reflecting the broader goals of the movement to purge traditional values and reinforce Mao's ideology.

6.2 Anti-Confucianism Campaign

Confucianism emphasising moral values, social harmony and respect for hierarchy and tradition was seen by Mao and the CCP as part of the "Four Olds" that needed to be eradicated. Mao believed that Confucian values were antithetical to the socialist ideals that the Communist Party aimed to promote. The anti-Confucianism campaign sought to challenge and dismantle the influence of Confucian thought in Chinese society. This involved critiquing Confucian teachings and promoting revolutionary values that aligned with Marxist and Maoist ideals. The campaign led to attacks on traditional educational systems and practices, as well as an embrace of criticisms against Confucian scholars and their influence on Chinese society. The emphasis was on revolutionary culture over traditional values.

It is very remarkable that now President Xi uses Confucianism as a model to present a highly orderly and cultured China to the world.

6.3 Anti-Lin Biao Campaign

Lin Biao was Mao's designated successor and a prominent military leader. He played a key role in the Cultural Revolution and was instrumental in promoting Mao's ideas through the publication of the "Little Red Book"[48] (Quotations from Chairman Mao Zedong). In 1971, Lin Biao was implicated in an alleged coup attempt against Mao. The circumstances surrounding his death in a plane crash raised many questions and fuelled speculation regarding his political ambitions and betrayal.

Following Lin Biao's downfall, the Communist Party launched a campaign to denounce him and his deeds. This included a propaganda campaign that painted Lin as a traitor and counter-revolutionary. The campaign served to reinforce Mao's authority and to clarify the political landscape following Lin's exit. Lin Biao's fall was significant because it indicated that even those within the highest ranks of the Party were not secure from purges and highlighted the intensity of factional struggles during the Cultural Revolution.

Both the anti-Confucianism campaign and the anti-Lin Biao campaign were integral to the Cultural Revolution's broader efforts to reshape Chinese society, eliminate perceived counter-revolutionary influences and consolidate Mao's power.

The Revolution effectively ended with Mao's death in 1976 and the arrest of the "Gang of Four".[49] It is believed that the turmoil and violence associated with

47 Edward J.M. Rhoads, *Lin Biao*, britannica.com

48 *Who, What, Why: What Is the Little Red Book?* bbc.co.uk/news/magazine-34932800, 26-11-2015

49 *Gang of Four*, britannica.com

the Revolution resulted in the deaths of anywhere from hundreds of thousands to possibly over two million people. In addition to direct deaths, the upheaval caused severe psychological, cultural and economic damage that lingered in Chinese society for decades.

6.4 Opening up for Foreign Investment by Deng

Deng Xiaoping returned to power in China in the late 1970s, after the end of the Cultural Revolution and the death of Mao Zedong in 1976. Deng gradually consolidated his power and became the paramount leader of China by 1978.

Once in power, Deng implemented a series of economic reforms that marked a significant shift from the Maoist policies of the past. These reforms are often referred to as "Reform and Opening Up", and they aimed to modernise China's economy by introducing elements of a market economy while maintaining the political framework of the Communist Party's rule.

For example:

Introduction of Market Reforms – Deng's government introduced market-based economic reforms, which included decentralising economic decision-making and allowing local governments and enterprises more autonomy in production and pricing.

Household Responsibility System – This policy replaced collective farming practices with a system where individual farmers could lease land, make their own production decisions and sell surplus produce for profit. This significantly increased agricultural productivity and farmers' incomes.

Special Economic Zones (SEZs) – Deng established Special Economic Zones in coastal areas, such as Shenzhen and Zhuhai, to attract foreign investment, technology and managerial expertise. These zones offered tax incentives and more flexible economic policies, serving as a testing ground for market-oriented economic reforms.

Opening to Foreign Investment – The Chinese government actively sought foreign investment and technology transfers by opening up to international businesses. Joint ventures with foreign companies became more common, providing capital and expertise that helped modernise Chinese industries.

Reforms in Industry – The reforms expanded beyond agriculture to encompass industrial sectors, encouraging state-owned enterprises to increase efficiency and productivity. Some inefficient enterprises were closed or restructured.

Focus on Education and Technology – Recognising the need for modernisation, Deng emphasised the importance of education and scientific advancement. Investment in education, science and technology became a priority, aiming to equip China's workforce with skills necessary for a modern economy.

Deng Xiaoping's policies played a pivotal role in transforming China from a largely agrarian economy to one of the world's largest economies. His pragmatic approach

("Once you open a window for fresh air, it is inevitable that you will let in some flies"; "It doesn't matter whether the cat is white or black in colour, it is a good cat if it catches mice")[50] set the stage for rapid economic growth and integration into the global economy, leading to significant improvements in living standards for millions of Chinese people. The first group of foreign investors in China came from Hong Kong, Taiwan and overseas Chinese entrepreneurs.[51]

However, with economic growth came corruption. Officials were using their power and authority to get involved in business and trade. Deng began the Anti-Spiritual Pollution Campaign, aimed at combating the influence of western ideas and capitalists' values which were seen as threats to the socialist ideology and social fabric of China. Censorship and restriction in literature, arts and the media were introduced. Eventually, these restrictions were dissipated in order to balance ideological control with ongoing economic reforms. Worsening inequality led to student protests, which ultimately led to the Tiananmen incident on 4th June 1989.

Jiang Zemin came to power as the General Secretary of the Communist Party of China in 1989, a position he held until 2002. Jiang was also the Chairman of the Central Military Commission from 1989 to 2004 and served as the President of China from 1993 to 2003.

Hu Jintao succeeded Jiang Zemin as the General Secretary of the Communist Party in 2002, serving until 2012. Hu became the President of China in 2003 and held the position until 2013. He was also the Chairman of the Central Military Commission from 2004 to 2012.

Their appointments marked significant developments in China's political landscape, with both leaders playing key roles in the country's economic growth and international engagement during their respective tenures.

6.5 WTO Membership

On 11th December 2001, China joined the World Trade Organisation (WTO). Joining the WTO was crucial for China to integrate with the global economy, benefiting from reduced trade barriers and access to international markets. China had also signed up to follow global trade rules and standards. This event accelerated China's economic growth and cemented its role as the world's factory.

Both Jiang and Hu adopted the so called "quietly, quietly, make some money" or "Hide one's capabilities and bide one's time" approach. They were both friendly to the west and encouraged foreign investors to set up manufacturing facilities in China to utilise the abundance of cheap labour during China's urbanisation. It is fair to say that between Deng's Open Door Policy in 1975 and Wu's retirement in 2013, both China and the CCP enjoyed a honeymoon period.

50 In quotes: Deng Xiaoping, *China Daily*, 20-08-2014

51 This period of growth in China is often referred as a miracle by the leaders of the CCP. To be fair, China came from a very low economic base before it was opened up. The success was mostly due to the entrepreneurship of the Chinese people and reduced interference from the government.

However, WTO membership and freeing the economy did not bring political reform. The only significant reform was Deng's directive that the top position of President of the PRC would be limited to 2 5-year terms. The governance would be "collective". This was to avoid the recurrence of personality cult and one-man-rule seen during the Mao period.

On 15th November 2012, Xi Jinping was appointed as the General Secretary of the CCP as well as the Chairman of the Central Military Commission. The latter position enabled him to control the People's Liberation Army. Xi was formally elected as the President of China on 14th March 2013. Hence, he has become the paramount leader of China overseeing political, military and government functions.

He inherited substantial foreign exchange reserves. By the end of 2012, China's reserves were approximately U$3.31 trillion, the largest in the world at the time. The amount reflected the country's significant trade surplus, direct foreign investment and other capital inflows contributing to its economic strength and ability to engage in international financial markets. In 2013, China's GDP per capita reached U$6,900.

6.6 The China Dream

Xi began promoting the concept of the "China Dream" shortly after he assumed office as the General Secretary of the CCP. It represents his vision for national rejuvenation, prosperity and a stronger role for China on the global stage. There are several goals, including improving living standards, achieving economic growth and fostering a sense of national pride and unity among the Chinese people. The "Hide one's capabilities and bide one's time" approach was replaced by Xi's "Making enemies on all sides, yet exuding authority from all directions"!

As China has become the world's second-biggest economy, its ambition is to be appreciated and respected by the rest of the world, particularly by its neighbouring countries. Xi's diplomats have started to use a more aggressive and assertive foreign policy approach. The name "Wolf Warrior Diplomacy" was coined after a popular Chinese action film, "Wolf Warrior 2", released in 2017, which features a character embodying nationalism and a strong defence of Chinese interests.

Chinese diplomats and officials have become more vocal and forceful in defending China's interests, often pushing back against criticism from other countries. The approach emphasises national pride and encourages a more robust portrayal of China on the global stage. Chinese diplomats have increasingly utilised social media platforms to communicate and engage with both domestic and international audiences, often responding directly to foreign criticisms. The approach is marked by a willingness to confront perceived slights or challenges to China's sovereignty and international standing, seen in various instances involving territorial disputes, human rights issues or trade matters.

Overall, "Wolf Warrior" diplomacy reflects a broader trend of heightened Chinese nationalism and a shift away from the more cautious, low-profile diplomacy of previous decades. It aligns with Xi's vision of a stronger, more influential China on the international stage.

Xi's vision has given ordinary Chinese citizens a vehicle to vent the long period of national humiliation, from the foreign powers bullying the QC, to the deaths and destruction during the civil war between KMT and CCP with the Japanese invasion in between, to Mao's various campaigns to the end of the Cultural Revolution.

The rise of nationalism has also helped build an image that China should become the centre of the world again (as in the Qing Dynasty), and regain its "lost" territories during the QC. It includes reciting its legitimacy in ruling Xinjiang, Tibet and Hong Kong, plus the belief that its neighbours (once Qing's tributaries) such as the Philippines, Vietnam, Cambodia and Thailand should "look up" to China. In terms of territories, the belief is that the South China Sea is rightfully China's territory and should become China's inner sea. This belief is imprinted in the so-called "Nine-Dotted Lines".

6.7 Re-establishing People's National Self-Belief in Difficult Times

In 2013, Xi launched the Belt and Road Initiative (BRI). As we know, it is a global development strategy that aims to enhance connectivity and cooperation between Asia, Europe and Africa. Some say that it is a great global vision. Some say that it is to buy influence from less developed countries. As of 2023, various reports indicated that China may have pledged around U$1 trillion in total funding to cover investments and many infrastructure projects, trade and development.

That was in the good old days, when China was riding high on the waves, foreign direct investment was huge, jobs were plentiful and people genuinely felt good about being Chinese. At the time, Alibaba, Tencent and other property development companies such as EverGrande were the darlings of the stock market.

This was also reflected in record numbers of Chinese going overseas for their holidays and record spending. China became the top nation in overseas travelling and expenditure. However, the bubble began to burst during and after Covid. With the confirmation that China was no longer the largest population, Mr Xi entering into his third term by changing the constitution and controlling everything and the introduction of harsh but vague laws in national security, foreign investors became spooked.

The property market and the rise in property prices has become unsustainable. The number of apartments/flats completed and under construction can house the total population of the US. With job losses increasing (the government stopped reporting youth unemployment figures in June 2024 until they redefine the criterion), house prices began to collapse. This has brought down the whole property development sector. The private tutoring sector disappeared as Mr Xi dislikes pupils spending too much time after school at lessons. The tech sector suffers as Mr Xi accuses them of "disorderly expanding business", especially when Alibaba tried to expand into internet banking business, which would have been devastating for the state-owned banks which are less nimble.

To divert attention, CCP continues to whip up nationalism, first boycotting South Korean products, followed by Japanese goods (as protests on the discharging of nuclear-contaminated water) and Taiwanese agricultural products.

The weak domestic consumption, coupled with the CCP's insistence on focusing on manufacturing rather than service industries, has led to over-production in steel, electric vehicles, solar panels, batteries etc. The QC's tactics of exporting, exporting and exporting is used by dumping excess production overseas to earn foreign income to compensate for the loss in foreign reserves during Mr Xi's reign. Another tactic of replacing imports by domestic production (as in the case of opium by the QC) is also high on the agenda, especially now that high-tech chips and other equipment face export embargo by western countries.

With Mr Xi's China Dream, there is a re-emergence of the mentality of the Tributary System, with a network of loose international relations centred around China to facilitate trade and foreign relations but acknowledging China's hegemonic role within a Sinocentric world order.

7. Conclusions

One has to look at the history of modern China to understand why people behave the way they behave now. Chinese in the mainland have undergone generations of "national insults" from foreign forces. Rather than blaming the incompetence of the QC, the warlords, the leaders of ROC and CCP, it is easier to channel the blame towards foreigners who always want to exploit China.

Most of the population has a chip on their shoulder, a kind of post-traumatic stress disorder after the suffering and sacrifices they and the older generation have had to make to allow China to be economically successful. They have had to give up their freedom of speech and expression, keep quiet or tell good stories of China. In return, the governing party promises them a better life. Political reform has never been on the agenda.

The government, through propaganda and education, has planted the seed that foreign countries will never forget to take advantage of China. A popular slogan, "The American imperialists will never cease their attempts to destroy China", is cited often by Chinese leftists. This produces a group of "fifty-cents" (allegedly, people were paid 50 cents by the government for each anti-western post they make on the internet) and "little pinks" (who will criticise anyone online who dares to defame China). They have very thin skin (so called "heart-of-glass" which can be broken easily) when they come across the opposite opinions. No one seems to appreciate how difficult it would be for a foreign occupier to run a country as big as China with its 1.4 billion inhabitants.

CCP's number one task is to continue to rule China come what may. With modern electronic surveillance systems and the policies of encouraging people to spy on each other (back to the Cultural Revolution days), it is not easy for the grassroots to organise protests. No one wants to risk harassment and worse, imprisonment or even disappearance.

It is Mr Xi's desire to rule the CCP and the CCP to rule the country. The CCP's reign is in fact a continuation of the old, traditional Chinese feudal dynasty system. In the traditional way, each dynasty was ruled by emperors sharing the same surname (a continuation of a family). Since the CCP took over China, the rulers were not of the same surname. Rule-by-Surname has been replaced by Rule-by-Party.

Chairman Mao, the first ruler, was at the top job for 27 years (1949–1976) with mixed results. After Mao, it was agreed that there would be a limit to 2 5-year terms for each successor, until Mr Xi changed the constitution to allow him a third term.

An interesting contrast is the Kims in North Korea, where they have successfully merged the system of Rule-by-Surname and Rule-by-Party.

7.1 Looking into the Future

The lives of mainland Chinese citizens have always been in the hands of the rulers.

One can see a patten in the feudal dynasty system. When the country was in chaos, a "hero" would appear and defeat the old rulers and set up a new dynasty. He would be clever, strong and would be supported by most people who were looking for a period of relative peace and calm. They would feel blessed in having a good ruler who would bring prosperity. The population would grow.

The throne would then be passed on within the family until a new emperor felt the need to conquer more land to feed the growing population as well as his own ego; or to teach the foreign intruders a lesson by raging war against them. Tax had to go up to feed the army. People's lives would get worse.

Unfortunately, when an incompetent emperor was in charge, with questionable mandarins and yes-men in place, corruption would spread and chaos would return. Then another revolution would happen and a change of dynasty would follow, and the cycle would carry on.

Even under the Rule-by-Party system, the lives of citizens still depend on how capable the ruler is. It is commonly agreed that previous leaders Deng Xiaoping, Jiang Zemin and Hu Jintao implemented policies which helped China to catch up and became the second-largest economy of the world.

However, if the performance of that ruler is below par, Chinese citizens do not have the power to vote anyone or the ruling party out of the government.

People ask, "Will there be a change of dynasty once again?"

In theory, it is very difficult for people to rise up and start a new revolution under CCP's 24/7 digital surveillance.

However, there are some "what if" scenarios:

- Xi's health may deteriorate;
- Xi may underestimate the west's commitment to protect Taiwan and start an invasion assuming that the west will not retaliate militarily (yet Mr Xi may be right in this assumption);
- It may come to a point whereby Chinese citizens feel that their sacrifices in giving up political and other personal freedoms no longer give them the expected standard of living in return. In other words, the social contract is not fulfilled. Chaos may come back (time for a change of dynasty?);
- CCP's own hierarchy may feel that their interests and benefits are under threat with Mr Xi's continuous anti-corruption campaigns or if the Chinese economy worsens, which threatens their personal wealth. Revolution may start from within the Party.

If Mr Xi can manage the downturn of China's economy in the short term and if he wants to continue for a fourth term as CCP's General Secretary, he will need another excuse or to make another promise. Taking Taiwan by force will be the obvious one. With his third term ending in October 2027, the period leading up to that date could be a critical time.

Looking back at history, at the end of the rule by the QC, various attempts were made to elevate China into the modern era. However, a change of dynasties has not succeeded in changing mainland China into a modern democracy. The main reason could be that emphasis was mainly made in saving the nation (from further humiliations) by scholars rather than enlightenment of the people. Without going though enlightenment, citizens do not have the understanding and appreciation of personal liberty, free speech, free expression and the concept of universal value and rule of law. Only with universal education among all citizens without biased propaganda or brain-washing can members of society have full participation in making China a modern, rule-based and reliable associate of the world.

References

bbc.co.uk

Britannica.com

Dr. Gavin S.H. Chiu, *The History and Political Economics Not Taught in Text Books*, Good Time Publishing, 2021, ISBN 978-988-74521-6-4

Immanuel C.Y. Hsu, *The Rise of Modern China*, Oxford University Press, 1990, ISBN 0-19-505567-4

Stephen Y.Y. Shiu, *Confession of a Previous China Supporter*, Y.Y. Shiu Publishing, 2023, ISBN 978-626-01-1651-4

Stephen Y.Y. Shiu, *The Disappeared 80 Years in Modern Chinese History*, Hong Kong New Media Limited, 2015, ISBN 978-988-14176-8-8

11 India's Growing Role

Balancing Between the East and West

*Pooja Bhatt**

1. Introduction

Geopolitics is witnessing a complex interplay of relations where geopolitics, economics, and strategic relations have divided the world into the East and the West. These bifurcations emerge from the cultural and civilizational aspects that have led to the formation of two world orders. Eastern cultures seem to have philosophical underpinnings, such as Buddhism, Taoism, and Confucianism, that have translated into these societies' value systems, perceptions, problem-solving, and other structural workings (Pae 2020). On the other hand, the Western world, typically associated with Europe and North America, often represents a different socio-economic and political vision for the world order envisioned from the values of democracy, equality, justice, capitalism, and so on. Therefore, the economic development, political systems, and social values between these two might be geographical and continue to demonstrate differences in cultural and ideological understanding of issues. While the West has traditionally dominated the global order due to its economic, military, and multilateral dominance, the East has not only revived itself in the past few decades as the region and also the geopolitics. Replacing the traditional ideological and military competition between the capitalist US and communist/ Marxist USSR, China has now emerged as a new global competitor to the US with its economic, military, and institutional might.

In recent years, these global-level shifts have also been accompanied by another structural change: the rise of India as a nation. A postcolonial third-world country with low developmental figures, India has emerged as the world's fifth-largest economic and fifth-largest military power. In addition to a growing financial, manufacturing, and demographic powerhouse, India is one of the agenda-shaping nations between East and West, the Global North and Global South. In addition to its relative growth, there has been a general awareness in the leadership towards becoming a voice of the Global South's underdeveloped and developing nations, which are often underrepresented on the international platform. Therefore, New Delhi is walking on a tightrope to seek economic development for the GS countries and representation at the multilateral level while retaining its strategic autonomy.

* Associate Professor, Jindal School of International Affairs, OP Jindal Global University, India.

DOI: 10.4324/9781003545750-13

2. The Proverbial East-West Rivalry

The US-China competition might have an ideological underpinning, but it is towards the same goal of becoming a global superpower. The clashing aspirations have taken the form of competition and even conflict, but not without global ramifications. After being the only pole of superpower for several decades, the US has been receding in its relative economic and military aspects for several domestic and international reasons. The overstretched budgets and global international economic and military commitments have led to significant backfires in domestic politics. As the US political and diplomatic outreach was being reshaped in every region in the last few years, the Chinese presence has seen an upswing in its political, military, economic, technological, and multilateral aspects. Beijing now rivals the US in every aspect, leading to a new East-West rivalry where China threatens US supremacy in geopolitics.

While the US and China remain the major trading and diplomatic partners, the economic and military Cold War between the two superpowers has made countries manage their relations with the two deftly. At the same time, Chinese military aggressiveness in the South China Sea and the Taiwan Strait has intensified, turning the region into a geostrategic hotspot. While various countries are responding to the Chinese threat at the bilateral and domestic levels, the area has seen overt militarization of the nations. The ideological conflict between the US and China has now transformed into a trade war and protectionism, a technology war, and military competition. This competition-conflict dynamics has severely impacted global international trade, security, and multilateral cooperation. On the other hand, it has compelled nations to seek alternate ways of collaboration to achieve security development and to face common challenges.

3. India's Rising Regional and Global Position

India's role on the global stage has evolved significantly since its independence in 1947. Initially adhering to a policy of non-alignment during the Cold War, India sought to maintain equidistance from the Eastern bloc led by the Soviet or USSR and the Western bloc led by the United States. This non-aligned stance allowed India to cultivate relationships with a diverse range of countries, positioning itself as a leader in the Global South.

However, the end of the Cold War ushered in a new era of globalization and economic interdependence. India began to pivot towards the West, particularly as economic reforms in the 1990s opened its markets. The liberalization of the Indian economy spurred domestic growth and made India an attractive destination for Western investment and technology. As a result, India has increasingly partnered with Western powers, particularly the United States, while maintaining robust ties with its Eastern neighbors. Another crucial factor in the partnership is the shared vision backed by similar values on various regional and global issues. Belief in the multilateral institutions based on equality amongst nations, peaceful dispute resolution, adherence to the rule of law, freedom of access to the global commons including seas and space the waters, and transparent economic processes, resilient supply chains, and sustainable and high-quality infrastructure development are some of these values where India finds itself aligned with the Western world order.

As of 2024, it is the world's third-largest military expenditure, second-largest armed force, fifth-largest economy by GDP nominal rates, and third-largest economy in terms of purchasing power parity. However, its position in the past few decades has manifested in growing regional and global ambitions. India has full diplomatic relations with over 200 states, including Palestine, the Holy See, and Niue. India is a prominent regional power and a potential superpower. The nation's aversion to bloc politics to alliance formation has continued since the Cold War era. Transformed into what is referred to as Strategic Autonomy, the pursuit of national interest and development over alliances remains central in India's foreign policy approach. On the other hand, India had pursued partnerships with countries of differing socio-political status.

While the core of Indian foreign policy still follows the Non-Aligned Movement, there has been a shift towards multi-alignment (Raghavan 2017). India is a member of several global and regional multilateral organizations, such as the United Nations, World Trade Organization, International Monetary Fund (IMF), G7, and the G-20, widely considered the primary economic locus of emerging and developed nations. India has been influential in other international organizations, such as the East Asia Summit, the Asian Development Bank, BRICS, the Shanghai Cooperation Organisation, and the IBSA Dialogue Forum. India is also a member of the Asian Infrastructure Investment Bank and is a primary investor in regional developmental projects. As a former British colony, India is a member of the Commonwealth of Nations and maintains relationships with other Commonwealth countries.

4. Bridge Between the East and the West

Recent times have seen the East-West divide further widening with the Russian war against Ukraine, the Chinese aggression against Taiwan, the Philippines, and Vietnam in the South China Sea, as well as the Israel-Palestine crisis. The West, led by the US, has supported the smaller nations against the aggressor. During these difficult geopolitical times, India refused to vote against aggressors such as Russia (The Hindu 2023) and Israel (The Hindu 2024) at international platforms such as UNSC, which was followed by Western sanctions that would have directly impacted the people instead of the leadership. Instead, it abstained from voting, condemned the act, and sought a peaceful resolution of disputes (MEA 2024). This diplomatic stand can be consistent with India's posture, which shames the act rather than the aggressor. At the same time, Indian leadership offered to be a peacebuilder and negotiator between the warring parties in Ukraine and Russia (Economic Times 2024). However, on the Israel-Palestine issue, while India has consistently supported nations' solutions and condemned the violence, due to its relationship with both countries, it has overtly refrained from any further intervention. Taking each case as unique, New Delhi has advocated for peace without aggravating the scenarios.

5. Norm Taker to Norm-maker

At the multilateral level, the UN, WTO, G20, G7, BRICS, SCO, and others have been the institutional litmus test for India, where it has been constantly trying to include the voices of underrepresented as well as balancing between the haves and the have-nots. Within BRICS, it has emerged as a voice for the Global South and also acts as a mediator between other influential members like China and Russia on one side. New Delhi simultaneously leveraged the group to promote regional economic and geopolitical interests globally. India has been instrumental in pushing for initiatives like the New Development Bank, demonstrating its role as an agenda-shaper within the bloc.

On the other hand, as one of the later entrants as members of the China-led Shanghai Cooperation Organization (SCO) alongside Pakistan and Iran, India's primary focus at the SCO has been to eradicate terrorism and terrorist groups as a prevalent threat to the region. Its presence has also tried to revive SCO's mandate of promoting connectivity and socio-economic development in Eurasia. According to scholars, New Delhi seeks to reconfigure the SCO platform into a "development-focused entity rather than one with an anti-Western agenda" (Pant 2024).

The recent rise of the Quad (or Quadrilateral Security Dialogue), involving India, the United States, Japan, and Australia, underscores India's commitment to strengthening its ties with like-minded areas, particularly in the Indo-Pacific region. However, this partnership ranges from ensuring a free and open maritime domain and countering China's growing influence to looking at developmental cooperation in various emerging regional threats such as maritime threats of piracy, natural disasters, supply chain disruptions, cybersecurity, etc. The Quad's Wilmington Declaration 2024 highlights Global Goods, demonstrating that India has been more than a "weak link" in the quadrilateral. However, given that most of these initiatives aim to build an alternative to Chinese actions in the region, the challenge for the group lies in promoting regional stability while engaging in competitive diplomacy.

6. Economic Dynamics

India's economic aspirations are at the heart of its diplomatic strategy. As one of the world's fastest-growing economies, India seeks to position itself as a global manufacturing hub and a significant player in international trade. This ambition requires carefully balancing attracting Western investment and fostering trade relations with Eastern economies, particularly China and the ASEAN countries.

India occupies a unique but complex position in the East-West geoeconomic competition. The emergence of the Indo-Pacific as a geostrategic hotspot to its economic and demographic relevance has sharpened the competition between the US and China. India's strategic location, growing economic importance, and military capacity in the Indo-Pacific region make it necessary to balance the competing interests of the two superpowers. India's economic growth is tied to both East and

West. Still, its foreign policy reflects a balancing act between deepening ties with the two economic powers while preserving longstanding relationships with Russia and managing challenges posed by China.

India's economy is deeply integrated into the global system. It shares significant trade relations with the West (US, Europe) and the East (China, South Korea, Japan, ASEAN, etc.). China continues to be one of India's largest trading partners, but a large trade deficit besides trust and security deficit also marks trade relations. The US is also an important partner, and the growing trade and investment ties with the West have increased India's economic importance globally.

As demonstrated by BRI, India's economic growth is increasingly tied to access to Western markets, technology, and capital and the need to counterbalance China's economic unilateralism in Asia. However, in recent years, India has attempted to play the role of a balancer in geopolitics in the following ways:

First is the emerging supply chain bifurcation, which emerges as one of the striking spaces where India manages its relations between the West and the East. The trade war between the US and China and the broader strategic shift towards "decoupling" have opened new avenues for India to position itself as an alternative manufacturing hub. Countries now seek to diversify supply chains away from China, which has led to more foreign investment in India and other Asian economies, particularly in sectors like electronics, pharmaceuticals, and automobiles.

Second, India relies on energy imports, much of which comes from the Middle East and Russia. Despite deepening India-US bilateral relations and the US-led sanctions on Russia, India has also maintained its energy ties with Moscow, particularly in the context of the Russia-Ukraine war. To circumvent the crude oil payment via dollars due to US sanctions, India made payments in Rupees for the Russian crude oil. India's longstanding relationship with Russia complicates India's relations with the US and its allies. However, Indian leadership has maintained that the country's stance is characterized by pragmatism, balancing its national interests with broader strategic considerations.

The third area where India carefully manages its relations between the East and the West is defense and technology cooperation. India-US defense and technology cooperation has come a long way since the US sanctions against New Delhi in the 1998 nuclear weapons test. The two countries understand the growing risk of Chinese hostility in the region. While India is developing its defense production through Indigenous production under Atmanirbharta (Self-reliance), it is aware of the benefit of collaboration with like-minded partners such as the US in technology transfer and even joint production. Similarly, New Delhi and Washington sought to deepen relations in the Critical and Emerging technologies field, and the two sides signed the iCET Agreement (The White House 2023). The two countries have transcended their relations to the trilateral and plurilateral formats with other like-minded countries in fields of supply chain resilience, such as under QUAD and the US-India-ROK Trilateral Technology Initiative, to name a few. Other areas where the US and India see strength in working together are cybersecurity, space cooperation, telecommunications, clean energy, maritime security, infrastructure development, and so on (MEA 2024).

7. India as a Global Leader in Climate Action and Disaster Resilience

Towards its role as a solution provider to the most pressing issues of our times, i.e., clean energy, climate change, and disaster management, India spearheaded two critical ideas that shaped an intergovernmental organization with global support. The first is the International Solar Alliance, which India, in collaboration with France, has been promoting to increase the use of solar energy through a dedicated framework of the wider community (investors, scientists, industry, governments, etc.) since 2015. As of 2024, over 150 countries have signed the Framework of Cooperation to mobilize the effort against climate change. Another initiative by India that found global support is the Coalition for Disaster Resilient Infrastructure (CDRI). It was announced in 2019 by PM Modi at the UN Climate Action Summit that it would provide resilient and sustainable infrastructure to the world's most vulnerable regions in Africa, Asia, and small island developing nations (SIDS). The CDRI is an international partnership between governments and other agencies that promotes disaster resilience. As of 2024, 40 countries are members of CDRI, highlighting the global commitment to India-led action towards clean energy research and funding.

8. Voice of the Global South

Besides becoming a third pole in East and West ideological and cultural competition, India has also attempted to bridge the divide between the affluent Global North and the resource-rich but underdeveloped Global South. India's presidency of the G20 Economic Fora in 2022–23 provides an unprecedented opportunity to shape multilateral agenda-making from business-centric to people-centric policies. The Global South's aspirations, issues, and problems have long been underrepresented on multilateral platforms. At the same time, India, through its experience with other multilateral organizations such as BRICS and IBSA, understands that the Global South is not coherent but shares a similar agenda. This experience led New Delhi to undertake a unique approach of collaborating with over 130 countries of the Global South (and some from the North) in its first purely online Leaders-led meeting in three successful annual meetings called the Voice of the Global South Summit since 2023 (MEA 2024). The virtually organized VOGSS has been a unique initiative that began as an extension of Prime Minister Shri Narendra Modi's vision of One Future ("Sabka Saath, Sabka Vikas, Sabka Vishwas aur Sabka Prayas") and is underpinned by India's philosophy of Vasudhaiva Kutumbakam, or the "World is one Family" (MEA 2023). VOGSS envisages bringing together countries of the Global South to share their perspectives and priorities on a common platform across a whole range of issues.

The outcomes of these meetings provided important feedback for India's G20 presidency, where issues such as climate change and finance, trade equity, disaster relief, women empowerment, education, healthcare, and so on became pillars of the G20 agenda. Indian efforts fructified bringing the developing countries' concerns, priorities, and interests to the international stage for discussion and action at G20. In other words, India successfully brought the efforts of the Global North and the aspirations of the Global South nations together by transforming into the voice of the developing and underdeveloped.

9. *Vasudhaiva Kutumbakam* - World as Family

Another decisive unifying contribution by India has been the concept of Vasudhaiva Kutumbakam. While this Sanskrit phrase has been a part of Indian philosophy since ancient times, the unifying impact of the idea was further explored during India's G20 presidency. The theme encouraged the multilateral community to seek progress and growth as one universal family, transcending borders, languages, and ideologies. This was translated into India's call for human-centric progress and a "people-driven movement" by building all-inclusive themes on education, healthcare, women empowerment, clean energy, and traditional values as guiding forces (MEA 2023).

With an astute understanding of the ever-changing nature of global partnerships in the emerging multipolar world, India also embraces the role of *Vishwamitra* (world's friend). India's External Affairs Minister, S Jaishankar, summarizes the importance of maintaining varying degrees of bilateral relationships for all: "Some friends may also be more complicated than others. They may not always share the same culture of mutual respect or ethos of diplomatic etiquette. We have, from time to time, seen comments on our domestic issues" (Hindustan Times 2024).

10. Cultural Diplomacy

Cultural ties play a crucial role in India's international relations. Since times immemorial, the soft power of Indian culture, including its traditions, arts, and spirituality, has fostered goodwill in both Eastern and Western countries. Being the cradle of Yog, Buddhism, traditional and holistic lifestyles and well-being approaches, even ancient knowledge of science, math, and other discourses continue to attract its admirers. India's diverse cultural heritage resonates with a global audience, enhancing its diplomatic outreach. Initiatives like the International Day of Yoga reflect India's ability to promote its cultural values while engaging with the world. Diwali has become another globally celebrated festival because of the vast spread of the Indian diaspora and its appeal. Indian music and cinema have their followers all over the world. At the same time, the current global order is in a fragile, bifurcated state, recognizing cultural diplomacy as a bridge between countries, cultures, and values.

PM Modi stated that protecting the environment is part of India's cultural heritage. Therefore, India must take the lead in countering this challenge and work towards a change in global attitudes towards the challenges of climate change. He said Indian culture was replete with illustrations that indicated "prakriti-prem" or "love for nature (PMO 2015)."

Additionally, India's diaspora is vital in strengthening ties with both regions. Indian communities abroad foster cultural and economic links, bridging India and the host countries. This cultural diplomacy enhances India's global image and helps maintain its position as a significant player in international affairs.

India's position between the East and West is fraught with geopolitical challenges. The rise of China as a dominant power poses a significant threat to India's regional aspirations. The border disputes, particularly in the Himalayas, reflect the historical tensions between the two nations. India must navigate these challenges carefully, fostering defense partnerships with Western nations while engaging in dialogue with China to manage conflicts.

Moreover, India's relations with Pakistan further complicate its balancing act. The longstanding rivalry with Pakistan, particularly over the Kashmir issue, necessitates a careful approach. While India seeks to enhance its defense capabilities through Western alliances, it must also strive for regional stability by addressing its bilateral relations with Pakistan and exploring avenues for peace.

11. Conclusion

This chapter overviews India's growing role as a balancing power between the East and West. Contrary to being a swing state or weak link, its policies are marked by *realpolitik*, adhering to its strategic foresight and adaptability. It finds its partnership with the West on the issues where Global Goods and Commons are concerned; on the other hand, its relations with the East have emerged from security and economic aspects. But as a friend to both, New Delhi's approach to building a world of harmony amidst the differences. As it continues to navigate the complexities of international relations, Indian political leadership remains vigilant in addressing regional tensions while pursuing its economic and strategic interests. By leveraging its cultural strengths and fostering collaborative partnerships, India can position itself as a key player in shaping the future of global governance, ensuring it finds solutions in this rapidly fragmenting world. In doing so, India can embody the essence of a 21st-century partner that champions managing relations with nations based not only on national interests but on achieving regional growth and global stability. New Delhi's foreign policy has been earmarked with cooperation, inclusivity, and a balanced approach to diplomacy. As global tensions escalate, India's role will face a constant challenge in shaping the contours of international geopolitics and economics, finding East and West meeting points and keeping its strategic autonomy intact.

References

"Can India Broker Peace with Russia-Ukraine? How New Delhi is Positioning Itself as Ajit Doval Meets Vla." (2024). *The Economic Times*. https://economictimes.indiatimes.com/news/defence/can-india-broker-peace-between-russia-ukraine-how-new-delhi-is-positioning-itself-as-ajit-doval-meets-vladimir-putin/articleshow/113311966.cms?from=mdr

"English Translation of Prime Minister's Closing Remarks at the Concluding Leaders' Session of the 2nd Voice of Global South Summit." (2023). *Ministry of External Affairs,*

Government of India. https://www.mea.gov.in/Speeches-Statements.htm?dtl/37297/English_translation_of_Prime_Ministers_Closing_Remarks_at_the_Concluding_Leaders_Session_of_the_2nd_Voice_of_Global_South_Summit

Haidar, S. (2024). "India Didn't Sign Letter of Support by 104 Nations for U.N. Secretary-General After Ban by Israel." *The Hindu*. https://www.thehindu.com/news/international/104-countries-issue-letter-of-support-for-un-secretary-general-after-israel-ban-india-stays-out/article68746578.ece

Harsh Pant. (2024). "India's Balancing Act in the SCO." *Observer Research Foundation*. https://www.orfonline.org/research/india-s-balancing-act-in-the-sco

"Human-Centric Globalisation: Taking G20 to the Last Mile, Leaving None Behind -Narendra Modi." (2023).

Johny, S. (2023). "Positing India's Stand on the Ukraine War." *The Hindu*. https://www.thehindu.com/opinion/lead/positing-indias-stand-on-the-ukraine-war/article66573033.ece

"Joint Fact Sheet: The United States and India Continue to Expand Comprehensive and Global Strategic Partnership." (2024). *Ministry of External Affairs, Government of India*. https://www.mea.gov.in/bilateral-documents.htm?dtl/38323/Joint+Fact+Sheet+The+United+States+and+India+Continue+to+Expand+Comprehensive+and+Global+Strategic+Partnership

Pae, H.K. (2020). The East and the West. In: *Script Effects as the Hidden Drive of the Mind, Cognition, and Culture. Literacy Studies*, Vol. 21. Springer, Cham.

PM to Heads of Indian Missions. (2015). Press Information Bureau, Govt of India. https://www.pmindia.gov.in/en/news_updates/pm-to-heads-of-indian-missions/

"Question No-710 Conflict between Israel and Palestine." (n.d.). *Ministry of External Affairs, Government of India*. https://www.mea.gov.in/rajya-sabha.htm?dtl/37581/QUESTION_NO710_CONFLICT_BETWEEN_ISRAEL_AND_PALESTINE

Raghavan, P.S. (2017). "The Making of India's Foreign Policy: From Non-Alignment to Multi-Alignment," *Indian Foreign Affairs Journal*, 12/4: 326.

The Hindustan Times. (2024). "'India Positioning Itself as Vishwamitra': Jaishankar on the Multipolar World." https://www.hindustantimes.com/india-news/india-positioning-itself-as-vishwamitra-jaishankar-on-multipolar-world-101730563212605.html

The White House. (2023). "Fact Sheet: United States and India Elevate Strategic Partnership with the initiative on Critical and Emerging Technology (iCET)." https://www.whitehouse.gov/briefing-room/statements-releases/2023/01/31/fact-sheet-united-states-and-india-elevate-strategic-partnership-with-the-initiative-on-critical-and-emerging-technology-icet/

12 Impact of the Korean Wave – Values and Culture Shaping Intercultural Approach in Southeast Asia and Pacific

*Lidia M. Wisniewska**

1. Introduction

The Korean Wave, also known as Hallyu, has become a global cultural phenomenon, originating in South Korea[1] and spreading across Asia and beyond. The public face of Hallyu is often attributed to the late 1990s and early 2000s, with the release of several influential Korean movies and TV dramas. Nevertheless, the actual origins of the Korean Wave can be traced back to earlier factors that set the stage for its emergence.

Conversely, Hallyu is predominantly conceptualized within academic discourse and popular culture journals as a conduit for disseminating Korean culture, and as a nationalistic strategy. Nevertheless, insufficient attention has been devoted to the actual impact of the Korean Wave on Asian, Pacific, and South Korean societies, particularly in terms of its influence **with** the global culture[2] contained within the

* Research Professor at CENTRUM Cátolica Graduate Business School, Lima, Peru & Pontifical Catholic University of Peru, Lima, & Society for Intercultural Education, Training and Research (SIETAR Europa, SIETAR France, SIETAR Polska), France.

1 The author of this chapter spent a period of three years in South Korea (2011–2013). During this time, she worked at the Chonnam National University in Gwangju in the framework of the POSEIDO international project, which aimed to facilitate the internationalization of higher education and research in the Asian region and beyond. During that period, she also conducted research for her doctoral dissertation, which examined the professional practices of internationalization in universities and the impact of Korean culture on these strategies. Her research aimed to identify how internationalization and local culture can foster intercultural competencies on Korean campuses. She maintained contact with colleagues in Korea, Southeast Asia, and the Indo-Pacific, traveling to these regions annually, as well as developing collaborations through the Society for Intercultural Education, Training, and Research (SIETAR) networks.

2 "Global culture" -1)"*Still others define global culture as an interconnectedness across local cultures comprised of cosmopolitan elite who travel around the world and appreciate diversity.*" Reyes, V., Investigation global culture, its creation, structure and meaning. In: *Globalizing Cultures, Theories, Paradigms Actions*, Mele, V., & Vujnovic, M. (eds.). Brill, 2016, p. 24.2) Some authors identify "global culture" and globalization with Americanization.Shimemura, Y., Globalization vs. Americanization: Is the world being Americanized by the dominance of American culture, *Comparative Civilizations Review*, Vol. 47, Issue 47, 2022. https://scholarsarchive.byu.edu/ccr/vol47/iss47/7?utm_source=scholarsarchive.byu.edu%2Fccr%2Fvol47%2Fiss47%2F7&utm_medium=PDF&utm_campaign=PDFCoverPages

DOI: 10.4324/9781003545750-14

Korean Wave. A similar question can be posed regarding the impact of the Korean Wave on the national culture of South Korea. A number of traditional elements of Korean culture are evident within the Hallyu, including a focus on harmony, Confucian values, cuisine, architectural styles, the Korean language, a sense of affection and loyalty, Korean etiquette, and so forth. Conversely, a multitude of global cultural elements are discernible in the vast majority of media pertaining to the Korean Wave. Such elements as interculturality, immigration, feminism, equality, inclusion and belonging, feminization, gender identities, lesbian, gay, bisexual, transgender (LGBT) identities, the model of success and lifestyle, social justice, and school harassment and bullying are all present in the Korean Wave media (throughout K-dramas, K-music groups and idols). These elements of national and global culture are brought into closer proximity through the "Korean face," which facilitates the dissemination of these aspects of global culture to other Asian societies.

In examining the historical, social, political, and economic factors that have contributed to the emergence and evolution of the Hallyu, it becomes evident that some lessons were taken from the Western champion of soft power,[3] the USA. The process of self-identification of the Korean Wave with the force of Americanization is underway. Undoubtedly, the cultural diplomacy[4] represents the most effective strategy employed by the Korean government to enhance the country's regional and global image, and in turn, facilitate its societal advancement and growth. A positive image of the country exerts a significant influence on potential consumers' perceptions and preferences.

The term "Korean Wave," or "Hallyu," is used to describe the global popularity and dissemination of South Korean popular culture. The term "Hallyu" (한류) is believed to have originated in China in the late 1990s. This term is translatable literally as "Korean Wave" or "Flow of Korea." In 1999, Chinese journalists first employed this term to describe the rising prominence of Korean entertainment and culture in China. The term encompasses a multitude of aspects of Korean popular culture, including K-pop music, K-dramas (television series), Korean films, Korean fashion, Korean beauty products and trends, Korean cuisine, Korean language and literature, Korean online games and technology, Korean lifestyle, Korean idols, fandoms, and numerous other elements of this omnipresent and successful strategy.

3 "Soft power" represents the non-coercive criteria of power, generally of a State, in particular among these criteria cultural influence. This concept was defined by the American geopolitician Joseph Nye in 1990 as "*the ability to seduce and attract*"; the concept of soft power puts into perspective the notion of power in a non-conventional framework. Nye, J., *Bound to Lead: The Changing Nature of American Power*, New-York, 1990.

4 Cultural diplomacy – takes a promotion and advocacy approach and uses cultural products as foreign policy tools in the interest of promoting state priorities. According to Michael Walter, cultural diplomacy is a type of soft power that includes the "exchange of ideas, information, art, language and other aspects of culture among nations and their peoples in order to foster mutual understanding." Waller, M. J. (ed.), Cultural diplomacy, political influence, and integrated strategy. In: *Strategic Influence: Public Diplomacy, Counterpropaganda, and Political Warfare*, Washington, DC: Institute of World Politics Press, 2009, p. 74.

The Korean Wave is frequently delineated into distinct generations. The initial phase, designated as Hallyu 1.0, commenced in the late 1990s and was primarily concerned with the dissemination of Korean television dramas and films throughout the Asian region[5] (China, Japan, Vietnam, Cambogia, Thailand, Philippines, etc.). The second generation of the Korean Wave, also known as Hallyu 2.0, originated in the mid-2000s and was characterized by the global dissemination of K-pop through social media and online platforms. The third generation of the Korean Wave (Hallyu 3.0) was identified and defined in the mid-2010s, while the current fourth generation emerged around 2020 and is notable for its high level of activity in both online and offline contexts. For example, the group *Tomorrow X Together* draws a parallel between the phenomenon of growing pains and the emergence of a horn on the head. In contrast, the *NewJeans*[6] K-pop group (comprising five girls) engages in the act of stoning nostalgia, which has the effect of rendering the experiences of Millennials more peculiar.

The Hallyu is a topic of frequent discussion in numerous academic journals and popular cultural periodicals. It is employed as a conduit for disseminating Korean culture, thereby serving as a nationalistic strategy. The objective of this study is to elucidate the multifaceted impact of the Korean Wave on Asian and Pacific societies and their cultures, as well as on South Korean society. What elements of traditional Korean culture are being disseminated through this phenomenon, and what elements of global culture are spread by the Korean Wave? How is this impact occurring, and which elements of global culture are being brought into closer proximity to other Asian and Pacific countries through the "Korean/Asian" face of this phenomenon?

2. The Korean Wave and the Factors of its Emergence

The phenomenon of the Korean Wave was principally driven by economic factors, with political and social considerations also exerting an influence. At the time, Korea's reputation in the region was marred by a number of negative factors, including: the legacy of violence and poverty resulting from the Japanese occupation of 1910, the internal conflict that followed that occupation, the democratic movements of the 1980s, the negative perception of traditional society about the impact of the American presence, and the Asian economic crisis of the 1990s.

The circumstances were particularly challenging. The Korean government implemented substantial reforms that facilitated the dissemination of ideas and the movement of people. In the early 1990s, the prohibition on overseas travel for Korean nationals was lifted. In 1996, the government initiated a process of media liberalization, which entailed the elimination of censorship. Moreover, the

5 Glodev, V., Wijaya, G., & Ida, R., The Korean wave as the globalization of South Korean culture, *WACAANA Jurnal Ilmiah Ilmu Komunikasi*, Vol. 22, Issue 1, pp. 108–120, June 2023.

6 Vick, M., NewJeans makes history as the first K-pop girl group to perform on 'Dick Clark's Rockin' New Year's Eve, *The Messenger*, January 11, 2024.

restructuring of the Korean *chaebols*[7] (such as Samsung[8] and LG), was accelerated by the aforementioned liberalization and extended into the entertainment and cultural business sectors.[9] In a discussion with his advisors, the Korean president Kim Young Sam was informed that the revenue generated by a single American film equaled that of 600,000 Korean-made cars. The promotion of the U.S. economy gained through the dissemination of a favorable image of the United States was acknowledged. This prompts the question of whether the same process could be applied to Korea. In other words, could the process of Koreanization, occurring both domestically and beyond national frontiers, be a viable alternative to Americanization?

The crisis of 1997 prompted Korea to undertake a comprehensive reassessment of its existing corporate culture.[10] As a result, Koreans began to ascribe greater value to their own culture. This resurgence of Korean culture enabled South Korea to cultivate a distinctive modern culture that was different from that of Japan or the West. The Korean Ministry of Culture made a significant investment in the entertainment industry. In a relatively short period of time, a total of 300 cultural technology departments were established at various national universities and provided with financial support. The liberalization of the media, the education of young Koreans abroad, the liberty of speech, and the support of restructured chaebols all contributed to the creation of modern, innovative movies that retained a visible Korean identity and cultural aspects.[11]

The Korean Wave has had a notable impact on the South Korean economy. In 2004, the Hallyu phenomenon accounted for 0.2% of South Korea's gross domestic product (GDP), or approximately $1.87 billion. By 2019, the estimated impact of Hallyu on the Korean economy was $12.3 billion. In 2019, the total value of Hallyu reached $95.935 billion, contributing to an 87.6% increase in tourism export growth compared to 2018.[12] These numbers also impact the image of an idea and its perception by the Asian region and globally.

Hallyu has become a significant element of South Korea's soft power strategy, enabling the country to exert cultural influence at the regional and global levels. This cultural influence has contributed to an improvement in South Korea's international image and reputation, facilitating engagement in diplomatic discussions and negotiations. The popularity of Korean cultural products has contributed to the

7 Chaebols – "rich family" or "financial clique" is a large industrial South Korean conglomerate run and controlled by an individual or family. A chaebol often consists of multiple diversified affiliates, controlled by a person or group.

8 Samsung was founded in 1938 as a trading company. In 1969 the company ventured into the electronic industry, with its first product a black-and-white television.

9 Katawa, T., & Asano, Y., 1994 a big year for South Korea's Kim, *The Daily Yomiuri*, February 24, 1994. http://www.lexisnexis.com/hottopic/? (Accessed November 10, 2024).

10 Burton, J., "A wonder tiger reluctant to change its stripes" Jon Burton explains the cultural barriers to economic reform in crisis-torn South Kore, *Financial Times*, November 29, 1997.

11 Truong, B., *The Korean Wave: Culture Export and Implications*, Spring 2014.

12 Truong, *The Korean Wave.*

strengthening of bilateral relations, particularly with other Asian countries, such as Japan, China, and Southeast Asian countries. Despite historical tensions, the popularity of Korean dramas and K-pop in Japan has facilitated the fostering of more positive people-to-people relations. However, it is important to acknowledge the movements in countries like Japan or Cambodia, which were created in response to the aforementioned factors (to criticize and limit the influence of the Korean Wave in their society, especially among young generations).

The Korean government has employed the use of Hallyu as a cultural diplomacy tool on numerous occasions. Korean cultural centers have been established in numerous countries with the objective of promoting the Korean language and culture. Furthermore, Korean diplomatic missions frequently organize concerts featuring K-pop music and film festivals as part of their public diplomacy initiatives. Hallyu has also facilitated economic diplomacy. The popularity of Korean products associated with Hallyu (e.g., cosmetics, fashion) has improved trade discussions and agreements. As reported by US News, Korea's global cultural influence ranking increased from 31st in 2017 to 7th in 2022.[13]

The growing interest in Korean culture and the marketing of its society have resulted in an increase in educational exchanges, with a corresponding rise in the number of international students opting to pursue their short-term or long-term studies in South Korea. The popularity of Korean-language programs has contributed to an increase in cultural understanding.

The concept of "soft power" can be understood through the lens of ecomaps, which illustrate the multiplicity of faces associated with it. The manner in which the Korean Wave exerts soft power in an international context differs from the manner in which historically imperialist countries do so, as observed by Hyeri Jung.[14,15] The perception of Korean popular culture as less threatening is shaped by the country's historical lack of invasion or colonization of other nations.[16] Moreover, additional authors[17] and interviews conducted by the author of this chapter corroborate the notion that Korea has been perceived as a sub-empire and a relatively minor power. This suggests that the Korean Wave may be able to establish a niche for itself and be perceived as less threatening. Concurrently, Korean culture has the potential to serve as a cultural mediator amidst the backdrop of a rapidly evolving global cultural landscape.

13 Yoon, Y.-S., Korea cultural wave puts Korea 7th in world cultural power, *Business Korea*, September 11, 2023. https://www.businesskorea.co.kr/news/articleView.html?idxno=118177.

14 Jung, H., *Transcultural Media and the Soft Power of the Korean Wave: A Reversed Ethnographic Approach to U.S. Fan's Reception of Korean Popular Culture*, Dissertation, University of Texas at Austin, 2017. https://repositories.lib.utexas.edu/server/api/core/bitstreams/89ac9a42-1106-4b2f-8d0b-c66108d01aed/content

15 Yoon, T.J., & Jin, D.Y. (ed.), *The Korean Wave Evolution, Fandom, and Transnationality*, Lanham, Boulder, New York, London: Lexington Books, 2017, p. 235.

16 Hong, E., *The Birth of Korean Cool: How One Nation is Conquering the World Through Pop Culture,* New York, NY: Picador, 2014.

17 Ryoo, W., Globalization, or the logic of the cultural hybridization: The case of the Korean wave, *Asian Journal of Communication*, Vol. 35, Issue 3, pp. 137–151, 2009.

The Korean Wave functions as a mediator in the West, particularly in the USA, but also in Asian countries. Here, the global American intercultural paradigm, which emphasizes diversity, equality, inclusion, and belonging, as well as gender aspects, has taken on a Korean face (an Asian face). This has been facilitating the introduction of these concepts into Asia-Pacific countries. The social modernity with previosly mentioned concepts, that would likely not be accepted at the same pace if it were presented with "Western faces," advances in the form of innovation and progress with a Korean (Asian) face through other Asian and Pacific countries. This impact is felt in popular culture unconsciously through the presence of music, dance, fashion, images, screens, and movies, as well as idols' stories, fandoms practices, and the use of Korean cosmetics and Korean beauty salons, which have proliferated in Singapore, Thailand, Vietnam, and other countries. Moreover, the elements of the Korean cultural strategy are pervasive across various facets of life, including cuisine, music, television, film, beauty, education, tourism, and dramas. It is almost challenging to avoid being immersed in this wave of influence.

3. How the Impact of the Korean Wave is Happening – Social Learning Theory and Proximity Theory

The theoretical framework selected for the analysis of the impact of the Korean Wave on society and culture draws upon the disciplines of education studies, cultural studies, and diplomacy. It employs a multi-disciplinary approach, integrating insights from the theory of impact, social learning theory (also known as social cognitive theory), vicarious learning theory, and proximity theory, with a particular focus on the Asia-Pacific region.

The social learning theory, and its subsequent iteration, the social cognitive theory, as postulated by Albert Bandura, posits that individuals learn through the observation, imitation, and modeling of others' behavior.[18,19] Vicarious learning is a process through which individuals can gain new behaviors and knowledge by observing and emulating the actions and experiences of others. The source of learning can be found in a variety of media, including films, television series, literature, and comics (manhwa,[20] manga). Additionally, the lifestyle and work of idols can serve as a source of inspiration and knowledge.

In alignment with Bandura's theory, individuals develop sophisticated forms of social conduct through direct experience or observation and modeling of others, or through vicarious learning. The tenets of social learning theory are based on three fundamental assumptions. Firstly, it is assumed that the behavior in question must be learned. Secondly, the theory posits that the learning of actions occurs via

18 Bussey, K., & Bandura, A., Social cognitive theory of gender development and differentiation, *Psychological Review*, Vol. 106, pp. 676–713, 1999.

19 Grusec, Joan E., Social learning theory and developmental psychology: The legacies of Robert Sears and Albert Bandura, *Developmental Psychology*, Vol. 28, Issue 5, pp. 776–786, 1992.

20 Manhwa (만화) is Korean version of comics. Technically and aesthetically, manhwas are no different from manga. They are printed in black and white.

observation of a model. Thirdly, the social diffusion of ideas, values, and behaviors is facilitated by symbolic modeling via the media. Consequently, the theory underscores the pivotal role of the family, subculture, and mass media as conduits of social learning in the absence of tangible, quantifiable rewards.[21]

Bandura's theory of observational learning and modeling posits that individuals acquire knowledge through observation of the behaviors, attitudes, and consequences of others. In the context of the Korean Wave, consumers across Asia and the Pacific observe Korean pop culture with great regularity, including K-dramas, K-pop, fashion, and lifestyle trends, through a variety of media channels. Such cultural products function as exemplars, exhibiting behaviors, styles, and values that audiences may imitate or adopt.

Bandura's theory of social learning postulates that children learn behaviors by observing others, both directly in real life and vicariously through the media. Indeed, the most effective method for teaching a child a specific behavior is to demonstrate the desired behavior and have the child model it, as is commonly observed in the context of television. Additionally, cognitive processes, such as attention and retention, are implicated in the interpretation, storage, and recall of behavior.[22] Moreover, adolescents are in the process of developing into adults, learning from other individuals who are regarded as role models. Another form of modeling can be observed in the formation of a specific concept of success, which is analogous to the concept of success in American culture. This concept of success is manifested in various ways, including a particular lifestyle, the possession of expensive goods such as cars and clothing, a specific hairstyle, and so on. The Korean Wave provides an illustrative example of this phenomenon, whereby a significant number of adolescents aspire to emulate Korean stars by following them as a model. The notion of success according to Korean perception is not merely about achieving 100% in any given situation; rather, it is about recognizing that any score below 100 represents a missed opportunity.[23] The notion of hard work and perfection is instilled at an early age in Korean society, with children as young as six or even younger already contemplating their future plans for university. Frequently, children embark on the arduous journey to become K-pop stars from an early age. Their parents, in turn, begin to envision the prosperity that these K-models have achieved, overlooking the prevalent realities of Korean society, which are reflected in the growing number of suicides.[24] Is the K-model worthy to be followed?

21 Bussey & Bandura, Social cognitive theory of gender development and differentiation.

22 Strasburger, V.C., Children, adolescents, and the media, *Current Problems Pediatric Adolescent Health Care*, February 2004.

23 We can find the singular voices already which criticize this kind of Korean approach, being conscious about its impact on the health population. PSY Gangnam Style (강남스타일), K-pop the most viewed YouTube video in the world, created in 2012, already contains the critic of artificial lifestyle of the riches part of the Korean society (Consulted, 15/11/2024 https://www.youtube.com/watch?v=9bZkp7q19f0)

24 South Korea has the fourth-highest suicide rate in the world and the highest among OECD countries. Mitsanas, M., & Lee, Ch., *How Data Restrictions and Funding Constraints Hamper South*

The appeal of Korean celebrities can be attributed to a multitude of factors, including their outward attractiveness and charismatic personalities. The strategic use of social media and online platforms represents a crucial element in the efficacy of this marketing strategy. Additionally, the aforementioned factors contribute to the overall appeal of these celebrities, with a particular focus on their physical attributes, including their faces, silhouettes, skin, and hairstyles. Korean fashion is strongly influenced by physical marketing and the Korean Wave.

The capacity of the Hallyu to retain its audience is demonstrated by the repeated exposure to Korean content which is high-quality. The emotional engagement of the audience with the storylines and characters is a significant factor. It is also important to note that the role of memorable music and visual aesthetics are also very influencing. Individuals with an affinity for Korean culture frequently emulate observed behaviors through the adoption of Korean fashion styles, the acquisition of knowledge regarding the Korean language and cultural practices, and the emulation of K-pop dance moves and music styles.

The motivation to engage with and adopt elements of Korean culture can be attributed to several factors, including the perceived prestige and modernity associated with Korean products. The visibility of Korean products on the global stage has reinforced their prestige in the Asia-Pacific region as well, thereby reinforcing the desire for cultural connection and identity with them as a result of Asian effects of creativity. In Vietnam and Thailand, among others, a strong identification with the K-Wave phenomenon was observed, particularly among those seeking to emulate a wealthy and successful lifestyle. This suggests that it is possible to model oneself on the Korean ideal of success. Conversely, the glamorous aspects of Korean life are predominantly depicted in K-Wave, frequently deviating from the realities of the Korean society. In order to afford the premium quality Korean products that are widely available in competitive markets, individuals must be willing to invest significant time and effort, often working long hours under considerable pressure.[25]

The influence of peer groups and social media communities has facilitated the pervasiveness of the Korean Wave across various domains of life, including formal (e.g., education) and informal (e.g., fashion) realms. The phenomenon has also integrated elements of Korean popular culture (characterized by a unique blend of tradition and modernity) with appealing cultural products that reflect a synthesis of Eastern and Western influences. This synthesis is increasingly perceived as

---

Korea's Suicide Prevention Efforts, June 12, 2024. https://time.com/6982596/south-korea-suicide-prevention-centers-data-funding-insufficient/ (Consulted November 12, 2024).

25 The observations and interviews presented in this chapter were conducted by the author during her stay in South Korea, primarily in Gwangju, with additional research conducted in Seoul, Busan, and other cities. These findings are based on the author's experiences during multiple travels within Korea and conversations with individuals from diverse social classes and professional backgrounds. She has been observing Korean society since 2011, when she was awarded a Korean Government Scholarship to leave and study in Korea. This enabled her to become involved in both Korean academic culture and society culture.

a form of global culture. This "hybrid culture"[26] has a resonance with audiences across Asia and the Pacific, who share similar cultural backgrounds and aspire to modernization. The success of the Korean Wave as a form of soft power illustrates the capacity of social learning to influence not only individual behaviors but also broader societal trends and international relations.

The pervasive integration of Korean cultural elements through social learning has precipitated a surge in tourism to South Korea, a concomitant rise in demand for Korean products and services, and a proliferation of cultural and economic exchanges between South Korea and other countries. This phenomenon has been observed particularly between China, Japan, Vietnam, and South Asian countries. However, research on the Pacific region has yielded less information on this subject.

While the Korean Wave has been largely successful in spreading through social learning mechanisms, it is important to note the potential for cultural homogenization and the loss of local traditions. The necessity for critical media literacy to counterbalance the impact of foreign cultural products and the function of government policy and media regulation in influencing cultural flows is evident when examining the influence of the Korean Wave on Asian and Pacific societies and their cultures, as well as on Korean culture and Koreans themselves. It is necessary to pose a number of questions, including the following: What is genuinely Korean about the Korean Wave, and what has been influenced by Americanization or the globalization of American culture?

The phenomenon of social modeling manifests at both the collective and individual levels. Modeling represents a significant social mechanism through which behavioral patterns, social roles, and socio-structural arrangements are replicated across generations. Nevertheless, modeling is a factor in both cultural evolution and cultural transfer. When individuals are exposed to models whose styles of thinking and behavior differ, observers rarely pattern their behavior exclusively after a single source. Furthermore, they do not typically adopt all the attributes of even their preferred models. Rather, observers typically combine various aspects of different models into new amalgams that differ from the individual sources. As a result of the variability in the characteristics, different observers create new blends of characteristics.

In conclusion, Bandura's social learning theory provides a valuable lens through which to understand the influence of the Korean Wave on Asian and Pacific cultures. Through the use of observational learning and modeling, Korean popular culture has effectively influenced behaviors, attitudes, and cultural trends throughout the region, demonstrating the power of media in shaping social and cultural landscapes.

26 *Hybrid culture* – results from the blending of two or more distinct cultures, creating a new, unique cultural identity. The United States and Australia serve as first examples of hybrid cultures at the national scale.

4. Influence of Korean Wave on Pacific Area

In the context of the contemporary global environment, which is characterized by rapid change and interdependence, the importance of soft power is becoming increasingly evident. However, it is also clear that the concept of *smart power*, as proposed by Nye,[27] represents a potentially powerful and visionary approach to foreign policy.[28] South Korea seems to be on that path.

To illustrate the influence of the Korean Wave on the Pacific area, one might cite a few examples from the television series, including one of the big hits of the K-dramas, titled "*Winter Sonata*" (2002),[29] as well as "*Jewel in the Palace*," and, most recently, "*Parasite*", which was awarded at the Cannes Festival. From the Korean pop music genre, which has achieved global recognition, the 2012 PTS featured PSY and his internationally celebrated song, "Gangnam Style" should be mentioned. The impact of South Korean culture, particularly in regard to regional trends (also global), is discernible in a multitude of economic domains, including fashion, cuisine, language, culture, cosmetics, and more.

The current state of affairs in South Korea and Pacific region can be characterized as one in which the younger generation (born after 2000) is shaped by the cultural patterns originating from South Korea. These influences in literature can be identified with the following labels: cultural diplomacy, soft diplomacy, cultural aggression, or "kimchi diplomacy."[30]

There has been a notable increase in cultural awareness about Korean culture and society, which has contributed to the formation of a positive image that has replaced the previously held perception of Korea in the 1990s. The popularity of K-dramas has facilitated the integration of traditional culture and Confucianism into the modern Asian/Korean context and in the regions. This illustrates that the notion of an "American world" as a paragon of cleanliness, affluence, and development is not exclusive to the United States. Asian countries can also be perceived in a similar light. The protagonists of Korean television series, or K-dramas, and K-pop stars are held in high regard by the wider Southeast Asian public.

It is evident that the proximity of external appearance and culture is instilling a sense of self-belief and national pride among the younger generation in Korea and also in the Pacific region. They perceive that they can emulate the Korean standard of fashion and modernity. Such individuals demonstrate an appreciation for Korean culture, perceiving it as an exemplification of the Asian experience. Such

27 Nye, J., Power and foreign policy, *Journal of Political Power*, Vol. 4, Issue 1, 2011.

28 Kim, M., The growth of South Korean soft power and its geopolitical implications, *Journal of Indo-Pacific Affairs*, October 31, 2022. https://www.airuniversity.af.edu/JIPA/Display/Article/3212634/the-growth-of-south-korean-soft-power-and-its-geopolitical-implications/

29 *Winter Sonata* 겨울연가 produced in 2002, south Korean television drama series, starring Bae Yong-joon. The series had huge commercial success, extensively viewed in Japan, China, the Philippines, Malaysia, and Nepal.

30 The Kitchen Sisters, *Kimchi Diplomacy*. https://kitchensisters.org/hiddenkitchens/kimchi-diplomacy/

individuals exhibit pride in their Asian identity, a sentiment that has been kindled by the Korean image.

A preference for Korean dramas over Thai dramas is evident among Thai viewers. Similar situations were observed in other countries of the region. This leads to the question of why this is the case. This is due to the fact that they are wholly distinct from Taiwanese dramas and films. The tone is optimistic, the narrative is linear, and the central character progresses through challenges while advancing towards a resolution. The plot of the drama is relatively straightforward and portrays a romantic and positive relationship, which is perceived as a positive model for young people.

The content of K-dramas reflects contemporary societal issues, which viewers may perceive as offering potential guidance on solutions to those issues. It offers a moment of introspection on analogous problems or dilemmas they encounter in their professional or personal lives. To illustrate, they advance the promotion of a healthy diet, reproductive health, the position of women in the family and society, and present potential solutions to the issues that arise. The impact of K-dramas on Korean women in Korea, in diaspora, and on other Asian women, particularly in Singapore and Bangkok, is considerable. The viewers identify with the history and actors of the K-dramas, particularly with regard to the position of women in society and the family. The K-dramas, while they consider the traditional values, also support gender equality. Additionally, K-dramas are set in educational institutions and address contemporary issues affecting young people, including harassment, suicide, overwork, and matters pertaining to the LGBT+ community. The Korean drama *Extraordinary Attorney Woo*[31] offers a redefinition of the meanings of disability and masculinity, providing potential models and visions of these concepts within the region.

Conversely, specific elements within Korean dramas have been the subject of substantial criticism, particularly among younger viewers. Such portrayals include those of alcoholism and the effects of plastic surgery. The consumption of alcohol is a significant aspect of Korean culture, observed frequently in professional and academic contexts (reflected in K-dramas), including interactions between professors and students. The feminization of the male form in Korean style and its subsequent dissolution is another important aspect which is seen. The spread of Korean culture throughout Southeast Asia and the Pacific has been significant and can play an important role in perceptions of masculinity and femininity in these societies, especially by contrasting them with traditional gener roles.

The promotion of plastic surgery and fashion has contributed to the emergence and proliferation of the concept of the "Korean style" among both female and male populations. Some observers have noted the feminization of the male form in Korean style and its subsequent dissemination throughout Southeast Asia and the Pacific.

31 Extraordinary Attorney Woo, *Emphasis on the extraordinary*. https://lstitt.medium.com/extraordinary-attorney-woo-emphasis-on-the-extraordinary-c14ea6524381 (Consulted November 10, 2024).

In terms of education and its impact, it is important to consider the role of Korean-language learning and education. The growing popularity of K-dramas has resulted in a notable increase in the number of individuals who have been motivated to learn the Korean language. Consequently, there has been a notable increase in interest surrounding Korean-language courses and resources, both abroad and in Korea. The motivation to comprehend the dialogue without relying solely on subtitles was a significant factor. This is associated with the accessibility of brief Korean-language curricula, although the option of pursuing studies at a Korean university is also a possibility. It is of particular interest to note that demographic shifts are prompting higher education institutions to attract a growing number of international students in order to prevent the closure of Korean universities. This aspect of the relationship between the Korean Wave and the internationalization strategy of higher education is of significant importance and should not be overlooked.[32]

It is not uncommon for popular Korean dramas to feature scenes set in locations within South Korea. This has stimulated interest among tourists from Oceania and Southeast Asia in visiting South Korea and exploring these picturesque destinations. Moreover, Korean tourism boards have been instrumental in the promotion of these locations. A review of the literature and statistical data on the subject revealed that women are particularly drawn to the locations depicted in television programs and films. Additionally, the wedding preparation and photography quality are appealing factors for young couples. A variety of services can be recommended in the absence of a definitive plan. Therefore, the newlyweds take with them the most significant day of their lives, which they have prepared and celebrated in a manner that is both traditional and reflective of the globalized Korean culture. The weddings are not conducted in accordance with traditional Korean ceremonies; however, within the context of Korean services, the possibilities for this day are limitless.

The popularity of Korean beauty products, skincare routines, and clothing styles in Southeast Asia has increased as a consequence of the influence of K-dramas. In Bangkok, it is exceedingly uncommon to find a beauty salon or cosmetic shop that does not carry Korean cosmetics. Moreover, nearly all beauty salons have names associated with Korea in some way. The manner of application of these cosmetics is also significantly influenced by the prevalence of internet tutorials prepared by Koreans. In this way, the influence of Korean beauty practices extends beyond the moment of contact between Korean women and their beauty salon staff. It also brings the long Korean protocol of caring for their face and body into their daily practice.

K-dramas frequently examine universal themes such as love, family, friendship, and the presence of cross-cultural storytelling. These universal storylines resonate with audiences in Southeast Asia and Oceania, contributing to a broader appreciation of cross-cultural engagements, meetings, and marriages. Furthermore, some

32 Keyston Education Group, February 26, 2024. https://www.keg.com/news/k-pop-your-way-in-attracting-students-with-korean-language-buzz

individuals engage with these programs throughout their lives, acquiring Korean language skills and forming expectations about their future romantic partners. These expectations are often romanticized, with visions of a "prince and a princess" as depicted in K-dramas. The appeal of the series lies in its simplicity and ease of viewing, with minimal cognitive effort required.[33]

K-dramas have contributed to the growth of online communities and fan groups in Thailand and Bangkok, where enthusiasts engage in discussions about their preferred shows, share fan art, and participate in fan clubs and events through social media platforms.

Additionally, K-dramas have exerted an influence on local entertainment, prompting the incorporation of analogous content and themes in regional Southeast Asian entertainment. It is possible that content creators may seek to capitalize on the popularity of K-dramas by including similar elements in their own productions.

Some K-dramas have begun to incorporate international and multicultural perspectives, which can contribute to discussions about diversity and representation in Southeast Asian media and entertainment. Also, mixed international and intercultural weddings have taken place. The presence of Lisa[34] (born in Thailand) in the K-pop group is a noteworthy inclusion in the South Korean girl group BlackPink. It exemplifies cultural and international egalitarianism towards others and leaves a positive image of Korea and its open attitude towards intercultural collaboration. On the other hand, it is giving an example of high-quality activities enriched by cultural diversity.

5. Conclusion

In light of the growing significance of globalization and global culture, coupled with the intensifying polarization and regionalization, there is a pressing need for a long-term national strategy that employs a discerning and intelligent approach. The objective of this chapter is to direct the reader's attention to the growing importance of South Korea and the Indo-Pacific region, which is assuming an increasingly prominent role on the global stage.

We are currently witnessing a period of intense international and global collaboration, yet concurrently, an intensification of competition for resources and markets. In this context, the role of cultural diplomacy as a means of exerting soft power is becoming increasingly apparent. Nevertheless, it is clear that the concept

33 Some of the opinions gathered during interviews with Chinese and Taiwanese young professionals. (Informal interviews between 15 May 2023 and 30 September 2024.)

34 Lisa held the record for the most-subscribed female K-pop soloist on YouTube with her channel Lilifilm Official, which had 8.24 million subscribers; Caprio, J., 5 times Blackpink's Lisa outdid bandmates Jennie, Rosé and Jisoo, from breaking YouTube records with her debut solo single Lalisa to ranking as 'most popular female K-pop idol'. *South China Morning Post*. Archived from the original on September 15, 2021. September 15, 2021. https://www.scmp.com/magazines/style/celebrity/article/3148791/5-times-blackpinks-lisa-outdid-bandmates-jennie-rose-and (Accessed September 10, 2024).

of hard power cannot be overlooked. The concept of smart power, as proposed by Nye, represents a potentially powerful and visionary approach to foreign policy. It appears that South Korea is pursuing a strategy of disseminating its positive image and cultural influence throughout Southeast Asia, the Pacific region, and beyond.

The Korean Wave has been identified as a form of soft power, a strategy that facilitates public diplomacy through the involvement of cultural diplomacy. It constitutes an important economic asset for South Korea, generating revenue through exports, tourism, and education, slowly and softly changing the image and culture of Southeast Asia and the Pacific. The favorable image of South Korea that has been created through the Korean Wave strategy is contributing to the spread of Koreanization across this region and the wider world. To what extent do the images of South Korea influence perceptions of Korea and Asia beyond the Asiatic continent? It is important to note that the Korean Wave is not merely disseminating traditional Korean culture; it is also serving as a powerful conduit for global Americanized culture, facilitating its reception into Asian and Pacific societies. Indeed, so-called global culture, interculturalism, gender studies, women's empowerment, sexism, social equality, social justice, LGBT rights, multiculturalism, and the environmental movement are more readily accepted and adopted in the Asia-Pacific region, with the Korean face acting as a conduit for their introduction. At the same time, these concepts are perceived as dimensions of progress and innovation for the societies in question.

The pride that many Asians feel when watching Korean cinema is perfectly aligned with the quality, content, and effects of Hollywood films. This phenomenon is influencing Asian and Pacific societies in a way that is contributing to the spread of the Korean Wave. The positive, affluent, attractive, youthful, athletic role models promote a successful Korean lifestyle and society, which makes it desirable and more natural for Asian people to identify with these models, and to perceive the "American dream" as a realistic aspiration, which already was won by Koreans.

The vision and value of "American success" is becoming a tangible concept for Asian groups and actors who share physical and cultural similarities. This is particularly evident in the Asian Pacific region, where the idea of success is becoming increasingly aligned with Western ideals. It is conceivable that the success currently being enjoyed by Korea could be replicated elsewhere, with countries adopting a similar approach to that taken by the Korean Wave.

This could involve emulating aspects of Korean life, including lifestyle, fashion, cuisine, education, and even appearance. Conversely, in this positive aspiration towards a more austere Koreanization, Pacific societies, as well as Koreans themselves, do not perceive a direct correlation or a strong inclination towards emulating American culture, particularly in terms of its more radical aspects, such as physical characteristics like the face, nose, and eyes. It is therefore pertinent to inquire whether the Korean Wave is indeed enhancing the visibility of Korean physical beauty. It is estimated that one in five young girls between the ages of 15 and 20 in Seoul have undergone at least one surgical procedure. This phenomenon can also be observed in other Asian societies where the influence of the Korean Wave is significant, including China, Cambodia, Taiwan, Thailand, Singapore, and others. These individuals often seek surgical interventions in South Korea, making it the leading destination for this type of plastic surgery globally.

The preceding descriptions of the soft cultural influence of South Korea on the Southeast Asia and Pacific region illustrate the significance of the changes that have occurred in this region over the past few years. These changes demonstrate that even a relatively small territorial country can have a substantial impact on the region, the continent, and even the wider world, through the strategic organization of cultural diplomacy. It was observed that Western concepts of global culture are being integrated with the Korean Wave, which is then disseminated throughout the Pacific region. This has led to an increased awareness of global issues, social justice, and other matters. This has resulted in a shift in the mindset of residents in Asia, demonstrating to them that the 21st century is their century.

References

Bussey, K., & Bandura, A., Social cognitive theory of gender development and differentiation, *Psychological Review*, Vol. 106, 1999.

Dator, J., *Jim Dator: A Noticer in Time*, Springer, 2019. https://doi.org/https://doi.org/10.1007/9783-030-17387-6

Glodev, V., Wijaya, G., & Ida, R., The Korean wave as the globalization of South Korean culture, *WACAANA Jurnal Ilmiah Ilmu Komunikasi*, Vol. 22, Issue 1, June 2023.

Grusec, J. E., Social learning theory and developmental psychology: The legacies of Robert Sears and Albert Bandura, *Developmental Psychology*, Vol. 28, Issue 5, 1992.

Hong, E., *The Birth of Korean Cool: How One Nation is Conquering the World Through Pop Culture*, New York, NY: Picador, 2014.

Jung, H., *Transcultural Media and the Soft Power of the Korean Wave: A Reversed Ethnographic Approach to U.S. Fan's Reception of Korean Popular Culture*, Dissertation, University of Texas at Austin, 2017. https://repositories.lib.utexas.edu/server/api/core/bitstreams/89ac9a42-1106-4b2f-8d0b-c66108d01aed/content

Katawa, T., & Asano, Y., 1994 a big year for South Korea's Kim, *The Daily Yomiuri*, February 24, 1994. http://www.lexisnexis.com/hottopic/?

Keyston Education Group, K-pop your way. In: *Attracting Students with Korean Language Buzz,* February 02, 2024. https://www.keg.com/news/k-pop-your-way-in-attracting-students-with-korean-language-buzz

Kim, Y.-H., Checking out fourth-generation K-pop. In: *KOREANA*, Summer 2023. https://www.koreana.or.kr/koreana/na/ntt/selectNttInfo.do?nttSn=118669&bbsId=1119

Mele, V., & Vujnovic, M. (eds.), *Globalizing Cultures, Theories, Paradigms Actions*, Brill: Leiden, 2016.

Mitsanas, M., & Lee, Ch., *How Data Restrictions and Funding Constraints Hamper South Korea's Suicide Prevention Efforts*, June 12, 2024. https://time.com/6982596/south-korea-suicide-prevention-centers-data-funding-insufficient/

Nye, J., *Bound to Lead: The Changing Nature of American Power*, New-York: Basic Books, 1990.

Nye, J., Power and foreign policy, *Journal of Political Power*, Vol. 4, Issue 1, 2011.

Onishi, N., South Korea adds culture to its export power, *The New Your Times*, June 29, 2005.

Ryoo, W., Globalization, or the logic of the cultural hybridization: The case of the Korean Wave, *Asian Journal of Communication*, Vol. 35, Issue 3, 2009.

Shimemura, Y., Globalization vs. Americanization: Is the world being Americanized by the dominance of American culture, *Comparative Civilizations Review*, Vol. 47, Issue 47, 2022. https://scholarsarchive.byu.edu/ccr/vol47/iss47/7?utm_source=scholarsarchive.byu.edu%2Fccr%2Fvol47%2Fiss47%2F7&utm_medium=PDF&utm_campaign=PDFCoverPages

Sooho, S., The evolution of the Korean wave: How is the third generation different from previous ones?, *Korea Observer*, Vol. 51, Issue 1, 2020.

Strasburger, Victor C., Children, adolescents, and the media, *Current Problems in Pediatrics and Adolescent Health Care*, Vol. 34, Issue 2, February 2004. https://www.sciencedirect.com/science/article/abs/pii/S1538544203001652?via%3Dihub

The Kitchen Sisters, *Kimchi Diplomacy*. https://kitchensisters.org/hiddenkitchens/kimchi-diplomacy/

Truong, J. Brian, *The Korean Wave: Culture Export and Implications*, HIST484 Globalization Capstone, Unpublished Undergraduate Paper, Spring 2014.

Vick, M., NewJeans makes history as the first K-pop girl group to perform on 'Dick Clark's Rockin' New Year's eve, *The Messenger*, January 11, 2024.

Waller, M.J. (ed.), *Strategic Influence: Public Diplomacy, Counterpropaganda, and Political Warfare*, Washington, DC: Institute of World Politics Press, 2009.

Yoon, T.J., & Jin, D.Y. (ed.), *The Korean Wave Evolution, Fandom, and Transnationality*, Lanham, Boulder, New York, London: Lexington Books, 2017.

Yoon, Y.-S., Korea cultural wave puts Korea 7th in world cultural power, *Business Korea*, September 11, 2023. https://www.businesskorea.co.kr/news/articleView.html?idxno=118177

Young, Jin D., & Yoon, T.-J., The Korean wave: Retrospect and prospect, *International Journal of Communication*, Vol. 11, 2017.

13 Restoring Indonesia's Global Maritime Fulcrum Vision

The Hedging Narrative that Connects the Indo to the Pacific

*Bagus Jatmiko**

1. Introduction

The Indo-Pacific region has emerged as a focal point of geopolitics, economics, and security contestation, particularly in the maritime realm.[1] With the rise of China and the shifting balance of power, the region has become the meeting point of many powers with embedded national interests, particularly between China and the US, creating new strategic challenges for regional actors. Against this backdrop of great power competition (GPC) in the Indo-Pacific, Indonesia seeks to play a pivotal role in shaping the emerging regional order[2] through many platforms, particularly the Association of Southeast Asian Nations (ASEAN), where Indonesia is a prominent member.

Recognizing the need to navigate the new complex geopolitical dynamics, the administration of President Joko "Jokowi" Widodo has articulated the Global Maritime Fulcrum (GMF) vision as a means to elevate Indonesia's maritime strategic posture.[3] It has the potential to be developed as a hedging narrative to respond to and strategically navigate the geopolitical complexities presented by the battle of narratives from the great power nations.[4] On the one hand, China developed the Belt and Road Initiative (BRI) as a narrative to support its national agenda and promote a fair, open, sustainable, and cooperative approach while refusing foreign

* IDN, Head of Wargaming Center, Indonesian Navy Command and Staff College.

1 Joseph Tertia and Anak Agung Banyu Perwita, 'Maritime Security in Indo-Pacific: Issues, Challenges, and Prospects', *Jurnal Ilmiah Hubungan Internasional*, 14 (2018), 77.

2 Fedro Adasion, 'Indonesia Plays a Pivotal Role in ASEAN in Responding to the US-China Rivalry', *Modern Diplomacy*, 2024 <https://moderndiplomacy.eu/2024/08/21/indonesia-plays-a-pivotal-role-in-asean-in-responding-to-the-us-china-rivalry/> [accessed 2 October 2024].

3 Prashanth Parameswaran, 'Assessing Indonesian Maritime Strategy: Current Evolution and Future Prospects', *Asia Policy*, 15/3 (2020), 113–132.

4 Tangguh Chairil, 'Assessing Indonesia's Maritime Governance Capacity: Priorities and Challenges', *Asia Maritime Transparency Initiative*, 2023 <https://amti.csis.org/assessing-indonesias-maritime-governance-capacity-priorities-and-challenges/> [accessed 23 July 2024]; Khanisa and Faudzan Farhana, eds., *ASEAN Maritime Security: The Global Maritime Fulcrum in the Indo-Pacific* (Singapore, 2022) <https://link.springer.com/10.1007/978-981-19-2362-3> [accessed 23 July 2024].

DOI: 10.4324/9781003545750-15

interference in the case of Taiwan and the South China Sea (SCS).[5] On the other hand, the US established the competing narrative of the Free and Open Indo-Pacific (FOIP) policy along with its regional allies.[6] At its initial stage of inception in 2014, the GMF vision was introduced as the core flagship program of the Jokowi administration as part of his presidential campaign, and it made quite the resonance in the geopolitical discourse. It was widely taken as Indonesia's commitment to take a more active role as a middle power in the region. Moreover, it is considered a relatively ideal narrative strategy by both academics and geopolitical observers to respond to the geopolitical influence both from China and the US and hedge the competing narratives of these great powers, opting more for a more independent and balanced approach.

Unfortunately, in Widodo's second term in office starting in 2019, instead of continuing and developing the implementation of the GMF vision, the administration arguably chose to pivot away from the core maritime themes and geared more toward land-oriented infrastructure development.[7] Moreover, the GMF vision is domestically driven with an inward-looking orientation and mainly focused on domestic economic concerns instead of boosting Indonesia's maritime capabilities to address both internal and external challenges.[8] These moves truncated the GMF into a fleeting vision, particularly after the inauguration of the relocation of the national capital from Jakarta to a place called Nusantara on the island of Borneo, which is located in the center of Indonesia and was perceived to balance the growth between the west and east sides of the country.

This chapter urges critical thinking on perceiving Indonesia's national interest and capabilities through the maritime perspective as a natural approach to presenting a development plan, considering the geographical character of an archipelagic state and, at the same time, a maritime crossroads in one of the busiest shipping routes that link the Indian and the Pacific Oceans. This so-called endowed strategic position should be seen as a strategic leverage point instead of a liability. Hence, the development of a comprehensive maritime narrative and strategy through the restoration and further augmentation of the GMF vision is a dire necessity for Indonesia instead of a distant luxury. The GMF should be seen as the edifice to actualize the potential leverage into a strategic asset, making Indonesia an active key player in the region instead of a calm spectator and an object of the crossroads of

5 Jun Dong, 'China's Approach to Global Security' (presented at the Shangri-La Dialogue 2024, Singapore, 2024) <https://www.iiss.org/en/events/shangri-la-dialogue/shangri-la-dialogue-2024/plenary-sessions/fifth-plenary/> [accessed 8 July 2024].

6 Fadhila Inas Pratiwi and others, 'Global Maritime Fulcrum: Indonesia's Middle Power Strategy between Belt And Road Initiatives (BRI) and Free-Open Indo Pacific (FOIP)', *Central European Journal of International and Security Studies*, 15/3 (2021), 30–54.

7 Dharma Agastia, 'The Global Maritime Fulcrum as a Strategic Narrative: A Critical Examination of Its Emergence, Conveyance, and Decline in Indonesian Strategic Discourse', *Muslim Politics Review*, 2 (2023), 284–317.

8 Edna Caroline, 'Indonesia's Global Maritime Fulcrum: From Hedging to Underbalancing', *Journal of Asian Security and International Affairs*, 8/3 (2021), 413–432.

many nations passing between the two great oceans.[9] Indonesia must respond to the extant strategic narratives and strategies of the great powers aligned with national foreign policy and responsibilities as a prominent country in the region, particularly with the current regional and global environment setting with the presence of great power nations with narratives of their own.

2. Research Purpose, Problem Statement, Importance, and Methods

Indonesia direly needs a comprehensive maritime narrative amidst the geopolitical dynamic in the Indo-Pacific region, particularly with the presence of the Great Power Competition (GPC) between the US and China, along with their strategic narratives. With that purpose, this chapter is working on the problem that Indonesia currently does not have a comprehensive maritime policy that includes the current regional dynamic and development, particularly after the abandonment of the GMF strategy.[10]

Having a comprehensive maritime narrative and strategy that is suitable to the contemporary context of the Indo-Pacific could advance Indonesia's geopolitical power in regional and international platforms. Narrative and strategy refer to the restoration and further augmentation of the GMF vision to be the proper hedging narrative and strategy to equal the extant strategic narratives promulgated by China and the US. This chapter approaches the arguments by explaining the critical points using descriptive analytics frameworks of the extant literature on maritime geopolitics in combination with a constructivist perspective.

Constructivist theory emphasizes the dissemination of ideas, norms, and identity based on the social and cultural contexts that drive state behavior that can be socially constructed and shaped by common perceptions.[11] It argues that a state's intentions, commonly accepted norms, and similar definitions of shared interest by emphasizing the ideational factors can influence collective state behavior at the strategic level. This approach allows policymakers or fellow researchers to comprehend how shared norms, values, and ideas in compelling strategic narratives influence cooperation and the formation of communities with similar interests. Related to the issue of strategic narratives for Indonesia in the Indo-Pacific strategic contexts, constructivism helps mediate the diverging perspectives on emerging

9 Ristian Atriandi Supriyanto, 'The Indian Ocean and Indonesia's Global Maritime Fulcrum: Relevance to ASEAN', *Asean and the Indian Ocean* (2017), 52–61 <https://www.jstor.org/stable/resrep05888.11> [accessed 4 October 2024].

10 Agastia, 'The Global Maritime Fulcrum as a Strategic Narrative', 284–317.

11 Michael L. Barnett, 'Constructivism', in *The Oxford Handbook of International Security*, eds., Alexandra Gheciu and William C. Wohlforth (2018), 0 <https://doi.org/10.1093/oxfordhb/9780198777854.013.7> [accessed 24 June 2024]; Maysam Behravesh, 'The Relevance of Constructivism to Foreign Policy Analysis', *E-International Relations*, 2011 <https://www.e-ir.info/2011/07/17/the-relevance-of-constructivism-to-foreign-policy-analysis/> [accessed 4 July 2024].

issues by promoting common and shared understanding that can be extended to other countries in the region to inform them about the strategic stance that Indonesia has and, further, to influence their decisions and actions to be expected align with Indonesia's respective national interests.

3. GMF Evolution as National Maritime Strategy

The GMF vision's initial purpose is to elevate Indonesia's strategic location as an important fulcrum between the Indian and the Pacific Oceans with the leverage of geographical position along with its resources. GMF was driven by the idea that Indonesia, as an archipelagic state as a matter of fact, had not pivoted its national development strategy on its distinct geographical character as a predominant maritime nation and the biggest archipelagos nation in the world. In his inaugural speech, Jokowi pledged that his administration would focus on the maritime domain during his leadership by stating that Indonesia "has long turned its back on the oceans, straits, and bays."[12] Furthermore, Jokowi briefly introduced the GMF vision as Indonesia's maritime strategy in his speech at the 9th East Asia Summit in Nay Pyi Taw, Myanmar,[13] highlighting the intended strategic shift in Indonesia's foreign policy. The speech emphasized the importance of maritime cooperation for regional security, stability, and economic prosperity and the intention to enhance its influence in regional and global affairs.

In the initial GMF vision and strategy, maritime development had both domestic and foreign policy elements.[14] Moreover, it is meant not just to have an economic agenda but also security and politics while heavily relying upon the dynamics of regional and global environments.[15] The vision was initially built on five core pillars, that is: (1) maritime culture, (2) maritime infrastructure and connectivity, (3) protection of maritime resources, (4) maritime diplomacy, and (5) maritime defense. Further, in 2017, it was expanded into seven pillars, consisting of: (1) maritime culture, (2) marine resources and human resources, (3) maritime defense, security and safety, (4) ocean governance and institutions, (5) maritime economy, infrastructure, and prosperity, (6) marine spatial management and environment, and (7) maritime diplomacy.[16,17] With the focus on these pillars, Indonesia expected to actualize a strong and sovereign maritime nation that could provide a positive

12 Cabinet Secretary, 'Joko Widodo's Inaugural Speech 2014 in Front of Legislative Members', 2014 <https://setkab.go.id/pidato-presiden-joko-widodo-pada-pelantikan-presiden-dan-wakil-presiden-republik-indonesia-di-gedung-mpr-senayan-jakarta-20-oktober-2014/> [accessed 4 October 2024].

13 Cabinet Secretary, 'Joko Widodo's Presidential Speech at the 9th East Asia Summit in Nay Pyi Taw, Myanmar', 2014 <https://setkab.go.id/en/pidato-presiden-ri-joko-widodo-pada-ktt-ke-9-asia-timur-di-nay-pyi-taw-myanmar-13-november-2014/> [accessed 4 October 2024].

14 Caroline, 'Indonesia's Global Maritime Fulcrum', 413–432.

15 Khanisa and Farhana, *ASEAN Maritime Security*.

16 Chairil, 'Assessing Indonesia's Maritime Governance Capacity'.

17 Tukul Adi, 'Maritime Culture Empowerment under Indonesian Ocean Policy', *Journal of Ocean & Culture*, 1 (2018), 102–117; Chairil, 'Assessing Indonesia's Maritime Governance Capacity'.

contribution to regional and global peace and security. Moreover, this national vision had the original intention of collectively transforming Indonesia into a pivotal maritime power, enhancing its strategic influence, and fostering stability and cooperation.

The GMF vision is similar to those visions espoused by China's BRI, India's Act East policy, the Quad's FOIP, and the US rebalancing strategy that act as strategic narratives containing their respective interest in the Indo-Pacific region. Likewise, the vision defines Indonesia's strategic geopolitical and geoeconomic objectives while expanding its bargaining power in the region and avoiding becoming entangled in the power competition between the bigger powers, particularly China and the US. This vision supposedly reaffirms Indonesia's stance in the regional and global communities on what Indonesia believes to be its rights within the corridor of international treaties and customary law. It also acts as a strategic response to any intolerable aggressive behavior by other nations trying to encroach on territorial sovereignty.

The GMF, though distinct and driven by Indonesia's national interests, was initially envisioned by Jokowi to strengthen Indonesia's role as a hub connecting the Indian and Pacific Oceans that intersect with the strategic narratives of the great powers. From the perspective of the GMF, Indonesia implicitly provides an alternative narrative focused on regional balance, inclusivity, and non-alignment, one that is not overtly aligned with either China or US interests but rather pivoted more into safeguarding its autonomy and promoting regional stability. With this narrative, Indonesia is expected to emerge as a mediator and balancing actor amidst the regional competition. By promoting this strategic narrative in the region, Indonesia could reinforce its prominence within ASEAN while forwarding its centrality role in Indo-Pacific issues. In general, GMF's vision could contribute to shaping the narrative of autonomy and regionalism in the Indo-Pacific. It would provide regional countries, particularly the low and middle powers, with a framework to navigate the complex geopolitical dynamics while safeguarding their respective interests.

However, the implementation of the GMF vision into an actual strategy has been inconclusive.[18] The programs under the umbrella of the GMF seemingly pivoted more to domestic economic concerns and inward-looking instead of boosting both internal and external capabilities to address various emerging maritime challenges. It arguably suffered from endogenous flaws that derailed the vision from its initial political course[19] and lacked practical elaboration and guidelines for implementation. Moreover, the vision was a half-baked idea. While promising, the vision was incomplete, which does not inspire confidence regarding its long-term feasibility as a development agenda.[20] Hence, despite the initial rhetorical enthusiasm from

18 Caroline, 'Indonesia's Global Maritime Fulcrum', 413–432.

19 Agastia, 'The Global Maritime Fulcrum as a Strategic Narrative', 284–317.

20 Donald E. Weatherbee, *Understanding Jokowi's Foreign Policy*, 12 (2016) <https://www.degruyter.com/document/doi/10.1355/9789814762601/html> [accessed 4 October 2024].

the government and some of the maritime stakeholders, the GMF has not transformed into an actual sound strategy that can be implemented to address all the challenges mentioned in its pillars.[21] Moreover, the consequences derived from the GMF vision demand more of Indonesia's active "presence" in both oceans, Indian and Pacific, which has failed to be fulfilled by the Indonesian government through its institution. This failure then gives the impression that Indonesia's enthusiasm for linking the Indian to the Pacific Oceans, as has been said in the GMF vision, is merely a superficial one, only to showcase one of its key pillars, maritime diplomacy.[22] In the end, the GMF vision arguably has died as Indonesia's national maritime vision, let alone a sound grand strategy.[23] Nevertheless, the emergence of GMF has provided a framework for the long-term development of a national strategic maritime narrative and strategy.

These critiques, admittedly, are legitimate and should be taken into account in building a more comprehensive narrative and strategy. All the challenges, mostly endogenous, have impeded the continuation of the GMF vision and its actualization into a practical strategy that the operators can implement on the field. Moreover, the Jokowi administration's approach to the GMF as Indonesia's strategic maritime narrative was partial and biased, derailing the GMF's initial goals into more of a land-oriented and economic development, which attenuates the core maritime themes of the narrative.[24]

This chapter argues for the importance of the continuation of the GMF vision as a national strategic maritime narrative and strategy. For that reason, it is crucial to restore and then improve the extant GMF to acknowledge its shortcomings, such as the failure to address regional geopolitical dynamics and causes and the drivers of maritime insecurity. Subsequently, the GMF can be then formulated into a more comprehensive maritime strategy that recognizes all aspects of the maritime domain, including external and internal factors that cause maritime regional dynamics. Most importantly, the implementation of the narrative into a sound strategy should be free from mere rhetoric for political agenda.

4. Improving GMF as a Comprehensive Maritime Strategy

The restoration and the continuation of the GMF vision may not be sufficient when the old perception and implementation pattern are still being used both by the government and maritime stakeholders. This chapter argues that the GMF vision still needs improvement as a comprehensive strategic narrative, particularly in

21 Supriyanto, *The Indian Ocean and Indonesia's Global Maritime Fulcrum*, 52–61.

22 Adelle Neary, 'Jokowi Spells out Vision for Indonesia's "Global Maritime Nexus"', *CSIS Commentary*, 2014 <https://www.csis.org/analysis/jokowi-spells-outvision-indonesia%E2%80%99s-%E2%80%9Cglobal-maritime-nexus%E2%80%9D>

23 Evan Laksmana, 'Indonesia as "Global Maritime Fulcrum": A Post-Mortem Analysis', *Asia Maritime Transparency Initiative*, 2019 <https://amti.csis.org/indonesia-as-global-maritime-fulcrum-a-post-mortem-analysis/> [accessed 5 October 2024].

24 Agastia, 'The Global Maritime Fulcrum as a Strategic Narrative', 284–317.

capturing all the dynamics in the Indo-Pacific region, including the internal and external aspects of Indonesia. Hence, it is important to improve the GMF vision as a national strategic narrative that is able to acquire the complexity of the region and a proper response to the narratives of the great powers in the region in balancing the rhetoric constellation to tone down the battle of narratives. The most important thing is that the GMF vision can be actualized as a practical strategy to be implemented to get the results done by taking the following steps.

This chapter considers the maritime analysis frameworks introduced by Bueger and Edmunds[25] as the fundamental structure to be adopted in improving the GMF. These frameworks provide the foundation to build a strong maritime narrative by considering the important aspects both at the macro and micro levels of the domain, internal and external factors of the countries, contributing to the holistic understanding of the issues in the regional maritime domain. Moreover, they provide valuable starting points in making sense of the complexity of the maritime domain, particularly with the presence of the GPC, which is significant in improving GMF into a comprehensive strategic maritime narrative. A holistic comprehension of the maritime domain complexity is profoundly fundamental in building a strong narrative and a sound strategy in a predominant maritime region, such as the Indo-Pacific. Unfortunately, policymakers and stakeholders lack awareness in understanding of the complexity of the maritime domain in the region, where such awareness should be paramount.[26]

The development of GMF as a comprehensive maritime policy narrative consists of several important aspects and considerations that are elaborated as follows: First, the framework prioritizing adherence to law and the significance of complying with international regulations and treaties. The incorporation of legal frameworks within policy formulation provides foundational principles, legitimate bases, and mechanisms for cooperation or resolving disputes with international recognition and justification for claims made by states that buttress a rules-based maritime order. However, policymakers must recognize the limitations and deficiencies inherent in the law. The law is often inherently state-centric, with states either favoring legal uncertainty or manipulating the law for their own benefit.

The second framework underscores the perception of how states put their prioritization and interests to make sense of the state's behavior. It comprises two focal points: the first is the state's approach that predominantly depends on its national power to interpret international law, which is commonly disregarded while

25 Christian Bueger and Timothy Edmunds, *Understanding Maritime Security* (Oxford, New York: Oxford University Press, 2024).

26 Bueger and Edmunds, *Understanding Maritime Security*; Jonathan D. Caverley and Peter Dombrowski, 'Too Important to Be Left to the Admirals: The Need to Study Maritime Great-Power Competition', *Security Studies*, 29/4 (2020), 579–600; Ariel González Levaggi, *Great Power Competition in the Southern Oceans: From the Indo-Pacific to the South Atlantic*, Palgrave Studies in Maritime Politics and Security (Cham, 2023) <https://link.springer.com/10.1007/978-3-031-36476-1> [accessed 8 July 2024]; Jon D Harbaugh, 'A Constructivist Approach to Great Power Maritime Relations in the South China Sea', Final Paper, *Naval War College*, 2022.

emphasizing its national interest. This phenomenon, known as "lawfare" or "legal statecraft," is evident in the South China Sea conflict, where China asserts its unilateral claim to the territory based on its distinct interpretation and justification of the international laws of the sea. Second, the emphasis is on following international regulations, identities, and networks anticipated to unite states together to counterbalance a formidable adversary, which is the case with the US and its alliances and partnerships. This framework most accurately delineates the present dynamic of global geopolitics, particularly the GPC, emphasizing the interests of the great powers and the reactions of the lesser powers. Nonetheless, acquiring the intricate specifics of maritime security concerns is challenging due to the elevated abstraction at the strategic level of states. Hence, the development of maritime security policy must recognize the GPC along with its intricacies and its potential impact on the formulation of the end policy.

The third framework asserts that the importance of having interpretation and meaning in both discourse and practice is crucial for the formulation of comprehensive maritime policy. For instance, the countries in the SCS would perceive maritime security as a facet of national security issues, encompassing arms proliferation and interstate conflicts under the framework of sea power. While a maritime concept generally encompasses all facets, certain aspects may necessitate greater prioritization than others. Despite the various results due to the different interpretations and contexts, incorporating an intuitive articulation of maritime domain concerns that is updated with the current dynamics is essential for the formulation of a comprehensive maritime security policy, as it acknowledges the diverse perspectives shaping the analytical process.

The last framework emphasizes the significance of identifying the causes and underlying factors of maritime insecurity as an essential approach to addressing its potential root causes effectively. Identifying the core causes of maritime insecurity necessitates the examination of various aspects, including regional context, geographic location, and cultural influences, which are essential for offering significant insights to policymakers. This perspective is valuable in understanding the factors associated with blue crime or maritime terrorism, which delineates seven fundamental causes: geographic location, insecure maritime environment, inadequate law enforcement, economic disparity, cultural acceptance and legitimation, crime-enabling skills, and the presence of organized crime.

Despite the valuable contribution these frameworks may provide, the policymakers and stakeholders should also acknowledge their limitations and use them more as guidance instead of a strictly followed standard operating procedure. Moreover, the interpretation and implementation of these frameworks require careful consideration, particularly in relation to the specificity of the issues at hand, such as those technicalities and specific matters faced by the operators in the field.

5. Discussion

The GMF vision should be the core of Indonesia's overall foreign policy. The policy should be established on the natural geographic characteristic of the world's largest archipelago and profoundly maritime nation. Moreover, the GMF should also be articulated into a sound strategy to ease the practical implementation through the initial implementation of the government organizations and subsequently to the rest of the national maritime stakeholders. Henceforth, the GMF vision should relate to and address the issue discussed in the previous maritime analysis frameworks.

Based on the discussed theoretical frameworks, this chapter then elaborates on their intertwining relationships with the existing pillars of the GMF concept. The relationship between the GMF pillars and the theoretical maritime analysis frameworks is essential for understanding whether Indonesia's GMF vision can effectively address both national and global maritime challenges, as discussed in the frameworks. From these relationships, this chapter expects to comprehend both the significance and the shortcomings of the GMF concept in responding to imminent maritime issues.

The maritime culture, as the first pillar, emphasizes Indonesia's maritime identity and history to promote awareness of Indonesia's maritime heritage and foster a maritime culture that encourages the population to view the sea as a vital element of national life (e.g., promoting maritime-based sports, celebrating maritime-based culture ceremonies, and endorsing national maritime heritage). It can then be related to the frameworks of states' interests, particularly Indonesia's national interests, to strengthen national identity, which is considered to be critical in advancing its strategic interest in the Indo-Pacific region. Moreover, it can foster a national mindset that supports sovereignty and the protection of maritime territories. This pillar also can support the development of national resilience and soft power in regional and global forums, reinforcing Indonesia's role as a leader in the region. Nevertheless, this pillar may have a limited direct impact on international law in the short term. However, in the long term, a strong maritime culture could encourage active participation in shaping international law and aligning local cultural perspectives with global standards.

The second pillar, marine and human resources, focuses on optimizing maritime resources (fisheries, marine energy) and developing human capital in the maritime domain. This pillar could address the maritime insecurity framework by acknowledging and solving the causes and drivers at the micro level through effective management and ensuring the human capital required for a secure maritime economy, such as government support on maritime-oriented training and education. Meanwhile, the primary challenge of this pillar is the necessity for maritime resources and human capital exploitation to comply with the international regulations on sustainable resource management, which is often violated by the stakeholders in the maritime domain.

Maritime defense, security, and safety, as the third pillar, prioritizes the safeguarding of Indonesia's territorial waters from threats such as piracy, terrorism, illegal, unreported, and unregulated (IUU) fishing, smuggling, and trafficking. This pillar specifically addresses maritime insecurity directly, as the threats are part of the aspects of insecurity in the maritime domain. Hence, the GMF's focus on maritime security directly addresses these insecurity drivers. Moreover, security and safety aspects are the core interests with significant contributions to national security. Strengthening maritime security also supports sovereignty, freedom of navigation, and territorial integrity, aligning with national interests. Maritime security and safety must operate within the scope of international frameworks like the United Nations Convention on the Law of the Sea (UNCLOS), regional security agreements, and multilateral cooperation on law enforcement. Hence, through this pillar, Indonesia seriously intends to integrate the compliance of international laws and regulations into its national strategy to maintain legality and cooperation. Nevertheless, the challenges in articulating regional and global events through the perspective of maritime security and safety without becoming entangled in the GPC tensions are daunting.

The fourth pillar is the ocean governance and institution that focuses on building effective governance structures and institutions to manage maritime affairs, including regulatory bodies and maritime legal frameworks. From the description, this pillar directly addresses the international law and regulation framework. Governance and institutions are crucial for ensuring compliance with international maritime law. Strong governance systems can arguably improve the international maritime laws and regulations implementation and enforcement. Moreover, effective maritime governance is directly tied to national interests in maintaining control over maritime territories, ensuring lawful resource exploitation, and preventing violations of sovereignty. Meanwhile, this pillar has the primary challenge in addressing maritime insecurity since weak institutions are often linked to maritime insecurity, as ineffective governance can lead to lapses in enforcement. Hence, the success of this pillar depends on how well Indonesia can establish resilient and accountable institutions that are adaptable to evolving maritime security threats.

Maritime economy and infrastructure, as the fifth pillar of the GMF, aims to develop Indonesia's economic ecosystem, including ports, shipping lanes, and logistics, as well as boost maritime trade. It addresses the state's interests in building a strong economy and infrastructure that serves national economic interests, enhancing trade connectivity, and boosting national competitiveness in maritime commerce. This pillar addresses maritime insecurity through the focus on the underdeveloped infrastructure that influences local and regional economic development. This study contends that economic inequality is arguably one of the causes of maritime insecurity. Hence, without proper regulation and management of the economy and infrastructure aspect, it is very likely that maritime insecurity will increase due to the vulnerabilities caused by poorly maintained maritime infrastructure or limited surveillance capability. This pillar may have issues with complying with the international regulations and requirements as promulgated by international standardization institutions because non-compliance with such regulations might threaten further national maritime development. Moreover, the maritime economy strategy is highly vulnerable to geopolitical shifts. It is crucial for the government to effectively manage the relationship between the maritime economy pillar and the geopolitical dynamics to mitigate any unwanted impacts due to the geopolitical dynamics.

The sixth pillar, marine spatial management and environment, emphasizes the sustainability of maritime spaces and the protection of marine environments, addressing the risks of pollution, overfishing, and habitat destruction. This pillar specifically focuses on the maritime insecurity aspect due to the degradation of the environment that is also recognized as the cause of insecurity, as it leads to resource scarcity, economic instability, and conflict over dwindling resources. This GMF pillar aligns with addressing such drivers by focusing on environmental conservation and spatial planning. This pillar also addresses international law, regulation, and treaties due to the compliance requirements with international environmental regulations, which are required to address environmental challenges. However, this pillar may have the challenge of keeping the balance between short-term economic gains and long-term sustainability. It is not easy to maintain the balance between these two aspects, particularly when the government is compelled to find more income from natural resource extraction that may bypass environmental protection (e.g., government decision to reopen sea sand export that is considered to be harmful to the environment).

Maritime diplomacy, the seventh pillar, emphasizes advancing Indonesia's maritime diplomacy to foster cooperation, resolve disputes, and influence maritime policy at regional and global levels. This pillar addresses international law, regulations, and treaties with the crucial role of ensuring Indonesia's effective engagement in any international negotiations, compliance with treaties, and resolving maritime disputes peacefully. This GMF pillar helps Indonesia align with global maritime norms while pursuing its national interests. It directly addresses the interests of the state by influencing projection on global platforms, advocating for its interests in international negotiations (e.g., UNCLOS disputes), and building alliances that support its maritime objectives. However, this pillar may be challenged in interpreting the regional and global events due to the intensification of competition between the great powers in the Indo-Pacific. The government must increase diplomatic efforts to smartly balance the relationship between competing great powers in the Indo-Pacific while maintaining autonomy in its maritime policies.

In general, the GMF pillars provide a solid framework for addressing many of the issues highlighted by the theoretical maritime analysis frameworks. Each pillar has direct relevance to specific components of international law, state interests, maritime insecurity drivers, and global strategic shifts. However, the success of these pillars in addressing maritime challenges depends on how effectively Indonesia integrates them into broader regional and international frameworks, navigates great power competition, and balances short-term interests with long-term sustainability. Moreover, the GMF pillars not only address current maritime challenges but also provide a platform for Indonesia to assert its leadership in the Indo-Pacific. By aligning these pillars with international law, strategic interests, and evolving security threats, the GMF can contribute more significantly to Indonesia's role as a pivotal maritime power.

6. Conclusion

This chapter has elaborated on the importance of restoring and then improving the GMF vision as Indonesia's comprehensive maritime narrative and grand strategy as a response to the competing strategic narratives of the great powers in the Indo-Pacific region. Despite the government's abandonment of the GMF as a national maritime vision and grand strategy, its establishment has laid the path for a long-term strategic framework. Moreover, as a matter of fact, some maritime institutions and experts, such as the Navy, Coast Guard, and maritime academics and observers, still express and depict the GMF in their discourse with the purpose of reviving it from the graveyard. Its importance and significance are arguably undeniable to support Indonesia's regional and global agenda by forwarding a comprehensive strategic narrative as part of the hedging strategy, which could mediate the different interests of many regional state actors, particularly the great powers, the US and China. The hedging strategy refers to a strategic approach adopted by states, particularly middle and small states, to enable them to navigate complex geopolitical situations involving great powers nations.[27] Essentially, it involves diversifying partnerships and avoiding exclusive reliance on any single power, thereby mitigating risks and maximizing options in an uncertain geopolitical environment. Moreover, the further impact of the GMF could echo and influence other middle-power countries[28] to act more freely and avoid getting trapped in the middle of the GPC in the Indo-Pacific while forwarding cooperation for a more conducive strategic environment and still keeping national interests at their course.

However, this chapter acknowledges the shortcomings of the extant GMF that is lacking in addressing several aspects of the maritime domain, particularly in capturing the regional and global geopolitical dynamics within the concept. This proposition is arguably due to the GMF never having a well-developed vision or strategy to begin with. It was not supported by profound and comprehensive research and development as the backbone of the GMF formulation. Nevertheless, the GMF is derived from a logic and philosophy that is sound and suitable for Indonesia, the world's largest archipelagic state. Hence, restoring and improving the GMF as a comprehensive strategic narrative and strategy is a logical and strong premise that should be maintained.

Most importantly, the inclusion of all internal and external policies or aspects must be incorporated into a single grand strategy that can then be implemented by different ministries or other governmental bodies instead of being developed and implemented separately, which will risk putting the whole focus of the maritime narrative and strategy in disarray. This notion suggests that the government leadership plays a crucial role from the formulation through the implementation of the vision and strategy to ensure its success. Moreover, the government should specifically acknowledge this specific shortcoming in the effort to restore and improve

27 Cheng-Chwee Kuik, 'Shades of Grey: Riskification and Hedging in the Indo-Pacific', *The Pacific Review*, 36 (2022), 1–34.

28 Middle power countries are those sovereign states that face constraints in projecting their power and often prioritize securing their sovereignty and territorial integrity but still hold a significant degree of influence on the global stage. Thomas Wilkins, 'Middle Power Hedging in the Era of Security/Economic Disconnect: Australia, Japan, and the 'Special Strategic Partnership', *International Relations of the Asia-Pacific*, 23/1 (2022), 93–127.

the GMF as the national maritime vision and strategy. The reluctance of the stakeholders to take part in executing the GMF hindered the optimum implementation of the strategy. Moreover, the government's lack of enthusiasm for continuing the GMF vision concept by dropping it halfway through the first administration term and completely abandoning it in the second term, replacing it with inland-oriented economic and infrastructure development and the ultra-ambitious mega-project of the national capital relocation, has completely dissolved the GMF from the government official discourse and documents and it only remains as a mere idea and cliches.

These arguments are the segue to the main issue when it comes to the GMF discourse: its continuity. Despite the obvious importance of GMF vision as a national strategic maritime narrative, or what remains of it, to respond to the great powers' narratives and strategies being developed in the Indo-pacific region, the primary concern is whether the figures in the succeeding administration will have the conscience and the vision in perceiving Indonesia as a maritime nation and a vital player in the Indo-Pacific maritime environment. Whether the succeeding administration will restore and then improve the initial GMF vision, embracing all of its lackings into a more comprehensive strategic narrative that could respond to the great powers narrative in the Indo-Pacific region, as proposed by this chapter, remains to be seen. However, looking at the possible inclination of the succeeding administration under Prabowo Subianto as the elected president, which tends to have land-oriented characteristics, the likeliness of restoring GMF's vision, let alone improving it, has a very slim chance. Hence, in the absence of the executive leadership's political will to prioritize the maritime domain and its grand strategy, the discourse may still be alive among maritime institutions, stakeholders, academics, and observers. However, the opportunity to extend and actualize Indonesia's national agenda and interests in the maritime domain through a comprehensive maritime narrative and strategy will be missed in vain.

7. Acknowledgment

This chapter acknowledges the LPDP (Indonesia Endowment Fund for Education Agency) for funding the author's PhD program.

References

Adasion, Fedro, 'Indonesia Plays a Pivotal Role in ASEAN in Responding to the US-China Rivalry', *Modern Diplomacy* (2024) <https://moderndiplomacy.eu/2024/08/21/indonesia-plays-a-pivotal-role-in-asean-in-responding-to-the-us-china-rivalry/> [accessed 2 October 2024].

Adi, Tukul, 'Maritime Culture Empowerment under Indonesian Ocean Policy', *Journal of Ocean & Culture*, 1 (2018), 102–117.

Agastia, Dharma, 'The Global Maritime Fulcrum as a Strategic Narrative: A Critical Examination of Its Emergence, Conveyance, and Decline in Indonesian Strategic Discourse', *Muslim Politics Review*, 2 (2023), 284–317.

Barnett, Michael L., 'Constructivism', in *The Oxford Handbook of International Security*, ed. by Alexandra Gheciu and William C. Wohlforth (2018), <https://doi.org/10.1093/oxfordhb/9780198777854.013.7> [accessed 24 June 2024].

Behravesh, Maysam, 'The Relevance of Constructivism to Foreign Policy Analysis', *E-International Relations* (2011) <https://www.e-ir.info/2011/07/17/the-relevance-of-constructivism-to-foreign-policy-analysis/> [accessed 4 July 2024].

Bueger, Christian, and Timothy Edmunds, *Understanding Maritime Security* (Oxford, New York: Oxford University Press, 2024).

Cabinet Secretary, 'Joko Widodo's Inaugural Speech 2014 in Front of Legislative Members' (2014) <https://setkab.go.id/pidato-presiden-joko-widodo-pada-pelantikan-presiden-dan-wakil-presiden-republik-indonesia-di-gedung-mpr-senayan-jakarta-20-oktober-2014/> [accessed 4 October 2024].

Cabinet Secretary, 'Joko Widodo's Presidential Speech at the 9th East Asia Summit in Nay Pyi Taw, Myanmar' (2014) <https://setkab.go.id/en/pidato-presiden-ri-joko-widodo-pada-ktt-ke-9-asia-timur-di-nay-pyi-taw-myanmar-13-november-2014/> [accessed 4 October 2024].

Caroline, Edna, 'Indonesia's Global Maritime Fulcrum: From Hedging to Underbalancing', *Journal of Asian Security and International Affairs*, 8/3 (2021), 413–432.

Caverley, Jonathan D., and Peter Dombrowski, 'Too Important to Be Left to the Admirals: The Need to Study Maritime Great-Power Competition', *Security Studies*, 29/4 (2020), 579–600.

Chairil, Tangguh, 'Assessing Indonesia's Maritime Governance Capacity: Priorities and Challenges', *Asia Maritime Transparency Initiative* (2023) <https://amti.csis.org/assessing-indonesias-maritime-governance-capacity-priorities-and-challenges/> [accessed 23 July 2024].

Dong, Jun, 'China's Approach to Global Security' (presented at the Shangri-La Dialogue 2024, Singapore, 2024) <https://www.iiss.org/en/events/shangri-la-dialogue/shangri-la-dialogue-2024/plenary-sessions/fifth-plenary/> [accessed 8 July 2024].

González Levaggi, Ariel, *Great Power Competition in the Southern Oceans: From the Indo-Pacific to the South Atlantic*, Palgrave Studies in Maritime Politics and Security (Cham, 2023) <https://link.springer.com/10.1007/978–3–031–36476–1> [accessed 8 July 2024].

Harbaugh, Jon D, 'A Constructivist Approach to Great Power Maritime Relations in the South China Sea', Final Paper, *Naval War College* (2022).

Khanisa, and Faudzan Farhana, eds., *ASEAN Maritime Security: The Global Maritime Fulcrum in the Indo-Pacific* (Singapore, 2022) <https://link.springer.com/10.1007/978-981-19-2362-3> [accessed 23 July 2024].

Kuik, Cheng-Chwee, 'Shades of Grey: Riskification and Hedging in the Indo-Pacific', *The Pacific Review*, 36 (2022), 1–34.

Laksmana, Evan, 'Indonesia as "Global Maritime Fulcrum": A Post-Mortem Analysis', *Asia Maritime Transparency Initiative* (2019) <https://amti.csis.org/indonesia-as-global-maritime-fulcrum-a-post-mortem-analysis/> [accessed 5 October 2024].

Neary, Adelle, 'Jokowi Spells out Vision for Indonesia's "Global Maritime Nexus"', *CSIS Commentary* (2014) <https://www.csis.org/analysis/jokowi-spells-outvision-indonesia%E2%80%99s-%E2%80%9Cglobal-maritime-nexus%E2%80%9D>.

Parameswaran, Prashanth, 'Assessing Indonesian Maritime Strategy: Current Evolution and Future Prospects', *Asia Policy*, 15/3 (2020), 113–132.

Pratiwi, Fadhila Inas, Irfa Puspitasari, Indah Hikmawati, and Harvian Bagus, 'Global Maritime Fulcrum: Indonesia's Middle Power Strategy between Belt and Road Initiatives (BRI) and Free-Open Indo Pacific (FOIP)', *Central European Journal of International and Security Studies*, 15/3 (2021), 30–54.

Supriyanto, Ristian Atriandi, 'The Indian Ocean and Indonesia's Global Maritime Fulcrum: Relevance to Asean', *Asean and The Indian Ocean* (2017), 52–61 <https://www.jstor.org/stable/resrep05888.11> [accessed 4 October 2024].
Tertia, Joseph, and Anak Agung Banyu Perwita, 'Maritime Security in Indo-Pacific: Issues, Challenges, and Prospects', *Jurnal Ilmiah Hubungan Internasional*, 14 (2018), 77.
Weatherbee, Donald E., *Understanding Jokowi's Foreign Policy*, 12 (2016) <https://www.degruyter.com/document/doi/10.1355/9789814762601/html> [accessed 4 October 2024].
Wilkins, Thomas, 'Middle Power Hedging in the Era of Security/Economic Disconnect: Australia, Japan, and the "Special Strategic Partnership"', *International Relations of the Asia-Pacific*, 23/1 (2022), 93–127.

Part III

International Arrangements

14 Embracing India's Strategy in the Indo-Pacific

Emphasis on the Quad and Beyond

*Simran Walia**

1. Introduction

One of the most significant geopolitical developments of the last 15 years has been the transformation of the term "Indo-Pacific" from a term of art in marine biology to a region of current strategic concern. At first, New Delhi was more wary, even though the US and Japan were among the nations who embraced the formulation, mostly because they wanted to include India in the Asia-Pacific security framework.

However, the Indo-Pacific idea was adopted in response to China's expanding influence in South Asia and the Indian Ocean, and it has since become a pillar of India's foreign policy. India's approach, which demonstrates strategic adaptability in a shifting geopolitical landscape characterized by differing agendas among key players, entails working pragmatically on specific concerns with a variety of established friends and new partners.

India temporarily withdrew from the wider region after the 1962 conflict with China, but as its economy began to liberalize, it introduced the "Look East" strategy in 1992 to strengthen its economic and cultural ties with Southeast Asia. The policy changed to "Act East" in 2014, adding a maritime security component and expanding its purview to encompass East Asia. To improve marine security, encourage sustainable development, and strengthen collaboration among Indian Ocean littoral governments, India started the Security and Growth for All in the Region (SAGAR) project the following year. These initiatives, which prioritize commerce and connectivity, are forerunners of India's Indo-Pacific strategy.

India's evolving views on the Indo-Pacific concept were not just a response to what China was doing. Former Japanese Prime Minister Shinzo Abe introduced the idea of the "confluence of the two seas" in a parliamentary speech during a 2007 trip to India, highlighting the interconnectedness of the Pacific and Indian

* Associate Fellow & Ph.D. Candidate. Ms. Simran Walia is a Research Analyst at Manohar Parrikar Institute of Defence Studies and Analyses (MP-IDSA), New Delhi, India and is Pursuing PhD in Japanese Studies from Jawaharlal Nehru University, New Delhi.

DOI: 10.4324/9781003545750-17

oceans.[1] His subsequent efforts to promote a "free and open Indo-Pacific" complemented India's Act East Policy and matched India's aspiration for an inclusive regional architecture. Preserving the openness and inclusivity of the Indo-Pacific region is India's top goal. The idea of a "free and open Indo-Pacific," where all nations respect international law and enjoy freedom of navigation, is supported by New Delhi. Because of the region's importance as a hub for international trade and energy resources, India is concentrating on enhancing marine domain awareness and protecting vital sea routes in addition to connectivity projects to strengthen trade and investment ties.

Four pillars support India's Indo-Pacific strategy:

- Utilizing issue-based relationships to work with nations to address common challenges. This entails taking an active part in security discussions, "mini-laterals," and regional forums. As of right now, India's main regional allies are the US, Japan, Australia, and France.
- Staying away from what Modi called "alliances of containment." India will engage with partners to promote common principles rather than forcing them to take sides in a conflict (such as China v. India or the US v. China).
- Accepting regional order through evolution as opposed to revolution. India supports the acceptance of new concepts that are freely developed by international law and respect for sovereignty rather than being unilaterally imposed because it is aware that norms and laws in the Indo-Pacific are likely to change over time.
- Acknowledging regional organizations and associations as a crucial component of the future order. In addition to working with organizations like the Quad, IORA, and the Bay of Bengal Initiative for Multi-Sectoral Technical and Economic Cooperation (BIMSTEC), among others, India supports ASEAN's relevance in the changing Indo-Pacific regional architecture.

The fundamental concept of the balance of power theory is that nations will join an alliance system against a dominant or hegemonic power that poses a threat to the other nation's security. In an anarchic world where the security of an individual is guaranteed by itself, nations resort to external alignment to safeguard their security. They also enhance their relative power to maintain their security, which is key in the structural framework of international politics. Through balancing, nations try to uphold the status quo against a power that can have a potential impact on their security. The significance of this theory is one of the oldest in the field of international politics, stretching from Kauṭilya in ancient India to Thucydides in ancient Greece. However, the relevance and significance of the balance of power have amplified with the rise of China and the coming of the great-power politics in the Indo-Pacific.

1 Centre for Air Power Studies, New Delhi, India & Jawaharlal Nehru University, New Delhi, India Abe, Shinzo, *"Confluence of the Two Seas" (speech, Parliament of the Republic of India, 22 August 2007)*. https://www.mofa.go.jp/

China's increasing influence in the Indian Ocean is balanced by India's geographic and geopolitical prominence in the Indo-Pacific. India's security concerns, which are mainly focused on China's encirclement policy through port facilities in India's neighbourhood, especially Gwadar and Hambantota, and the desire to preserve and protect free and open sea lanes of communications against worries about China's chokepoint in the South China Sea and growing maritime presence in the Indian Ocean under the pretence of antipiracy operations, are the main drivers behind the need for such a counterbalance. In contrast to the Asia-Pacific architecture, the Indo-Pacific structure offers New Delhi a chance to transcend its longstanding designation as a middle power. India's entry into the League of Great Powers, especially the US and Japan, and its development of strong strategic ties with Washington and its regional allies serve to further support this. India's ambitions to become a great power and its capacity to project power in the Indo-Pacific and beyond are greatly enhanced by this.

New Delhi's primary goal in the Indo-Pacific is to protect India's interests and solidify its position in the Indian Ocean. The maritime lanes of the Indian Ocean are essential to India's economic growth and energy security. India's security and attempts to exert influence overseas may be threatened by threats in this area.

Keeping the Indo-Pacific region open and inclusive is India's top objective. A "free and open Indo-Pacific" where all nations respect international law and enjoy freedom of navigation is a concept that New Delhi supports. India has prioritized improving marine domain awareness and protecting vital sea lanes, along with connectivity activities to strengthen trade and investment links, due to the region's importance as a conduit for global trade and energy supplies.

2. India and the QUAD in the Indo-Pacific Dynamics

India has been a vocal supporter of a Free and Open Indo-Pacific. The ASEAN nations, the US, and Australia have all stated that they believe India ought to have a bigger role in the region. With the ten ASEAN nations bridging the two big oceans, India views the Indo-Pacific as a geographical and strategic region. The core tenets of India's Indo-Pacific vision are "inclusiveness, openness, and ASEAN centrality and unity." According to India, the Indo-Pacific region comprises the Pacific Island nations and extends from the eastern coast of Africa to Oceania, or from the African coast to the American coast.

In addition to hosting the Indian Ocean Naval Symposium, India has been an active participant in various mechanisms, including the Mekong Ganga Economic Corridor, the Bay of Bengal Initiative for Multi-Sectoral Technical and Economic Cooperation (BIMSTEC), the East Asia Summit, the ASEAN Defence Ministers Meeting Plus, the ASEAN Regional Forum, and the Indian Ocean Rim Association (IORA). India is attempting to engage with the Pacific Island nations through the Forum for India-Pacific Islands Cooperation (FIPIC).

India does not view the Indo-Pacific region as a club with a few number of members or as a strategy. Maintaining regional security requires communication, a shared rules-based order, unhindered trade, freedom of navigation, and the resolution of conflicts in conformity with international law. To prevent any one state from controlling the Indo-Pacific area or its waterways, India believes that it should cooperate with other like-minded nations to govern a multipolar regional order based on rules. For example, although India has consistently emphasized the importance of ensuring freedom of navigation and overflight in the South China Sea, a more assertive stance is currently being adopted, with the SCS being referred to as "the global commons," wherein "the interests of no third party should impinge" and all disputes should be resolved in conformity with international law.

Through its relations with important nations in the area, India is putting its Indo-Pacific policy into effect. Quad Framework is one such example, along with ASEAN and many other emerging minilateral platforms and frameworks.

3. Background of the Quad

When the Indian Ocean tsunami, one of the greatest natural disasters in history, killed over 200,000 people across 14 nations in 2004, the Quad framework was established. Numerous nations united to offer immediate humanitarian aid in response to the startling death toll. A tsunami "core group" comprising India, Japan, the United States, and Australia started providing aid to the impacted nations by donating more than 40,000 troops, humanitarian responders, helicopters, cargo ships, and aircraft.[2] "India's full capabilities came as a surprise to the world, highlighting India's strength, leadership abilities, and commitment to the Indo-Pacific," said former Foreign Secretary Shyam Saran.

As the humanitarian aid effort came to a close in the middle of January 2005, the leaders began to envision a new version of the Quad framework. Shinzo Abe, the prime minister of Japan at the time, put forth an "arc of freedom and prosperity" in 2006 that supported democracy, freedom, human rights, and the rule of law. Manmohan Singh, the prime minister of India at the time, travelled to Tokyo that same year. In a joint statement, the two nations said they were excited to start a conversation with "like-minded" nations in the Indo-Pacific area. America's involvement in the Quad conversation was indicated in 2007 by US Vice President Dick Cheney. Abe visited India that same year and delivered a lecture on the "confluence of the two seas," which provided the Quad with ideological support.

Two Malabar naval exercises were conducted in 2007. Japan participated in the US-India drill and it expanded to include Singapore and four navies, making it a multilateral exercise. But when China began to dispute the exercises, the alliance broke up. India's standing in the Quad was further weakened when communist parties in India started to demonstrate against the maritime drills. Another reason for India's reluctance was its concern that competition with China might prevent it from joining the Nuclear Suppliers Group (NSG). Additionally, India lacked

2 Grossman, Marc, The Tsunami Core Group: A Step toward a Transformed Diplomacy in Asia and Beyond, *Security Challenges*, *1*(1), 11, 2005.

Australian backing, mostly because of China, and its main motivator, Shinzo Abe, quit as Prime Minister.

However, increasing Chinese aggression forced India to quicken the Quad's pace. The Quad was revived as Quad 2.0 in 2017 when the presidents of the Quad countries convened in the Philippines during the ASEAN summit, following a lapse of almost eight years. The rise of China, the expansion of India's economic and strategic influence, and – above all – the growing significance of the Indian Ocean as a strategic trade corridor that transports nearly two-thirds of the world's oil shipments and a third of bulk cargo have all contributed to the need for a change in the security architecture from the Asia-Pacific to the Indo-Pacific in the twenty-first century. These elements have contributed to the re-establishment of the Quad and the rise of regional stakeholders demanding an open and free Indo-Pacific. The Association of Southeast Asian Nations (ASEAN) centrality, rule of law, sustainable and transparent infrastructure investment, freedom of navigation and overflight, mutual respect for sovereignty, and peaceful dispute resolution are the foundations of the member states' shared Indo-Pacific vision, which is based on their dedication to preserving an Indo-Pacific that is free, open, inclusive, peaceful, and prosperous and is based on a rules-based international order.

Notably, the group raised the conversation to the level of secretary of state or foreign minister in 2019. After COVID-19 emerged as a major concern, the group was renamed "Quad Plus," which included three more Indo-Pacific nations – South Korea, Vietnam, and New Zealand – as well as a few outside parties: Brazil and Israel. The logic of convergent security concerns under the pandemic and collaboratively examining a path forward is what motivates this growth. Furthermore, with each member facing increased tensions with China, the China issue has dominated the Quad's political and security discussions. For example, since 2018, Washington and Beijing have been at odds over a bilateral trade war and subsequent diplomatic repercussions. Since April 2020, India and China have maintained a military presence at the Line of Actual Control. On June 15, a violent clash in the Galwan Valley claimed the first lives in over 45 years.

Several defence, trade, and foreign policy disagreements have become the heart of Canberra's rapidly deepening diplomatic rift with Beijing. Similarly, China's increasing assertiveness in the East China Sea has exacerbated Japan's already escalating tensions with China.

India, which had previously been a reluctant member, started to take the initiative. For instance, Australia started asking India to rejoin the Malabar exercises in 2017, and India eventually agreed in 2020. Additionally, border disputes – the Doklam incident in 2017 and the Galwan Valley confrontation in 2020 – pushed India to take an active role by showcasing its production capacity, supply chain, technology, and pharmaceutical knowledge at the 2021 Quad virtual and in-person summit. Despite these unilateral actions by China, the Quad has in theory maintained that it is not hostile to any nation; yet, China's growing expansionist plans are a manifestation of the Quad's growing anti-China stance. As mentioned, China is no longer an unknown danger.

India's participation with the Indo-Pacific region is facilitated by the Quad cooperation with the US, Japan, and Australia. It enables India to work with other states to address concerns regarding China as a political deterrent. The focus of economic cooperation is on common concerns on China's involvement in the global manufacturing supply chain, which puts the Quad nations at risk of trade pressure. India's concerns about China's growing technology prowess, especially in telecommunications, are addressed by the quad collaboration on cybersecurity threats and technological security. The Quad members' combined military capabilities are improved through joint military exercises.

By offering a forum for multilateral projects that support regional peace and prosperity, such as vaccine diplomacy, alternative debt financing, emerging technologies, infrastructure development, maritime security, humanitarian aid, and the fight against illegal fishing, the Quad also helps to advance a positive agenda for the Indo-Pacific.

New Delhi has the highest level of strategic confidence in Tokyo among its Quad partners. Both countries are dedicated to maintaining the rules-based international order from a geopolitical standpoint. Japan and India share a commitment to promoting economic growth and development, as seen by their significant investment in India, especially in important infrastructure projects. Over the years, the two nations have launched numerous collaborative projects, but because their bureaucracies find it difficult to work together, their implementation has been delayed.

Perhaps India's most significant bilateral relationship is its strategic cooperation with the United States, which is its largest export market, second-largest defence supplier, and preferred partner for joint military exercises. India's adversaries are effectively offset by the growing strategic collaboration between the US and India, primarily through defence cooperation. The two have been able to put aside their Cold War differences because they have similar worries about China, terrorism, and Indo-Pacific security. The pace at which the two nations strengthen their partnership has occasionally been hampered by notable disagreements over free trade, climate change, relations with Russia and Iran, and longstanding misgivings about the US's reliability held by some Indian elites, but the general direction of the two nations' relationship is clear. In some ways, the relationship between the US and India is the opposite of that between Japan and India in that trust has grown slowly despite notable accomplishments.

While Indo-Australian relations are no longer marked by "mutual indifference," they still don't have the same depth and scope as India's alliances with the other Quad countries. India probably voted against Chinese and Russian attempts to sabotage the AUKUS accord at the International Atomic Energy Agency because both countries are concerned about maritime security, regional stability, and revisionist powers in the Indo-Pacific. However, major divisions have not been resolved by shared concerns about China. While Australia depends on US dominance for its national security, India aspires to a multipolar world. Given its meagre navy budget, Australian strategists doubt India's strategic importance in the area, while Indian strategists believe Australia is less important than the US or Japan.

Additionally, India has expanded its bilateral relations with the Quad countries and gone beyond the Quad. India has a mutual logistical assistance agreement and an information-sharing arrangement with Australia. In addition, both nations have had discussions on defence strategy and marine security and have taken part in bilateral military drills like AUSINDEX (Australia India Exercise) and AUSTRA HIND. Japan and India have taken part in bilateral military drills like Dharma Guardian and JIMEX (Japan-India Maritime Exercise). The General Security of Military Information Agreement (GSOMIA) and reciprocal supply and service agreements are among the agreements that both countries have signed. Through accords like the Communications Compatibility and Security Agreement (COMCASA), the Logistics Exchange Memorandum of Agreement (LEMOA), and the General Security of Military Information Agreement (GSOMIA), India has strengthened its defence ties with the United States. Both nations have participated in bilateral military drills like Tiger TRIUMPH, COPE INDIA, YUSH ABHYAS, and VAJRA PRAHAR, as well as cooperative peacekeeper training.

Furthermore, the Quad has given its members a chance to engage in other arrangements with "like-minded" countries. Australia, India, and Japan, for instance, have declared their plans to start a supply chain resilience project. Additionally, India has collaborated on COVID-19 projects with the US, South Korea, Israel, Brazil, and the UK. There is also a trilateral among India, Japan and the US, wherein these three nations cooperate to secure the Indo-Pacific region and counter China's expansionist behaviour.

4. Effectiveness of the Quad

India is still a quiet participant in the conventional security arena, even with its stronger ties to the Quad. All of the Quad's members are directly threatened by China's growing influence in the Indo-Pacific, but India has felt uneasy portraying the Quad as an anti-China alliance. Rather, New Delhi consistently asserts that the group is "standing[ing] for something" rather than "standing against something or somebody."

India, and thus the Quad, opposes a robust military alliance and instead favours non-traditional security concerns, such as collaboration on cutting-edge technology, humanitarian and disaster relief, maritime domain awareness, and vaccine diplomacy. This enables New Delhi to diversify its relationships through several alliances, maintain decision-making autonomy, avoid securitization, and influence the area.

India continues to establish adaptable ties with nations, including some that are hostile to the Quad, as the Quad develops a more ambitious agenda that includes collaboration in STEM research, regional infrastructure development, and climate change. When New Delhi, along with other Quad members, declined to denounce Moscow's invasion of Ukraine while simultaneously asserting that "the use or threat of use of nuclear weapons is inadmissible," it demonstrated India's complicated relationship with the Quad.

As a major participant and middle power, India must actively engage in alliances to counterbalance China's increasing assertiveness, despite its previous non-alignment. This is because of the escalating geopolitical tensions in the Indo-Pacific region. As a result, India asserts that it has adopted a multi-aligned approach by moderating in the Shanghai Cooperation Organization, the BRICS, the G20, the G7, and the Quad. According to the State of Southeast Asia 2023 poll, India's approval rating increased from 5.1% in 2022 to 11.3% in 2023, propelling it from the bottom to third place as a trusted partner in the area. Given its difficulties in enforcing international law, as demonstrated by its reactions to incidents like the 2021 coup in Myanmar and the Russia-Ukraine conflict, it is imperative to assess India's changing foreign policy.

China's increasing influence in the Indo-Pacific, especially its Belt and Road Initiative (BRI), which has resulted in the construction of port facilities in India's neighbours, can be offset by India through the Quad, creating a feeling of encirclement in New Delhi. India can transcend its status as a middle power and expand its influence outside of the Indo-Pacific region with the help of the Quad. India's participation in the Indo-Pacific is further enhanced by its Act East Policy and Extended Neighbour Policy. With the Quad as a backdrop, India's bilateral ties with "like-minded" nations can be further reinforced through defence linkages, weapons exchange agreements, intelligence sharing agreements, and much more.

At the group's last summit of his term, held in Wilmington, Delaware, on September 21, 2024, former US President Joe Biden boldly declared, "The Quad is here to stay." Due in large part to the fact that their security environment has gotten much worse since 2008, quad participants are standing pat. In addition to China's growing aggressiveness in the Indo-Pacific, North Korea is also becoming more aggressive and developing a nuclear program. In addition to ongoing Chinese patrols around the disputed Senkaku Islands (called the Diaoyu in China) in the East China Sea, Japan is becoming increasingly alarmed about a Taiwan Strait crisis that could affect its southwestern Ryukyu Islands.

It's safe to assume that the four Quad participants' security relations are at an all-time high. This is encouraging because it shows that the Quad is more than just a short-term, fair-weather project like it was the first time. Instead, the agreement is a tool that complements and enhances the hard security lines that these nations have already established with regard to China.

The Quad's exceptional growth in the number of mutual international challenges it tackles today compared to its early years is another factor contributing to its likelihood of survival. Delivering disaster relief and humanitarian aid to Indonesia and 13 other nations impacted by the 2004 Indian Ocean earthquake and tsunami was the responsibility of the original Quad, which was formerly known as the Tsunami Core Group and included the same participating nations. However, the Quad had changed dramatically by 2006, and members were already defending their conversations by claiming that they weren't intended to oppose China.

There are perhaps certain challenges too. New Delhi must make sure that the Quad is not relegated to an anti-China bloc since there is a chance that tensions with China could be rekindled on several fronts. Since China and India are both members of global organizations like the Shanghai Cooperation Organization (SCO) and Brazil, Russia, India, China, and South Africa (BRICS), regulating China through the Quad might jeopardize India's participation in other organizations.

Disagreements among the members of the Quad may intensify as world problems continue to escalate. As Russia intensifies its assault in Ukraine, India, and the other Quad countries continue to divide as New Delhi tries to stay neutral and uphold its longstanding strategic alliance with Moscow. The group may also experience other crises. A potential Chinese attack on Taiwan serves as a prime illustration. India would adamantly try to stay out of such a battle, and New Delhi has probably been the only one to keep the Quad's public remarks from specifically mentioning the need to preserve peace and stability in the Taiwan Strait. The Wilmington Proclamation does not refer to Taiwan.

It's also possible that other minilaterals – small groups working together on a specific set of challenges – will eventually push the Quad out. In the South China Sea, the United States has another minilateral agreement with Australia and Japan in addition to the Quad and AUKUS, and it has also negotiated separate arrangements with the Philippines. Then there's the "Squad," a new quartet that shares many of the Quad's members, with the exception that India has been replaced by the Philippines.

A number of suggestions for improving the Quad's future and preventing reversals, such as: increasing collaboration on space and maritime domain awareness. A hybrid organization might be one approach, maintaining the flexible and ad hoc aspect of minilaterals but having a governing body with legal constraints to direct implementation and hold member countries responsible for advancement.

Restricting the size and scope of the projects the Quad is working on could be another strategy. This would enable nations to prioritize their most pressing concerns while determining the viability and financial resources for a solution. Lastly, stringent information-sharing procedures, such as implementing standardized forms for information exchange, may be necessary to increase India's credibility within the Quad.

By taking such actions, a framework that enables more effective contributions from all member countries – including India – will be developed.

5. Conclusion

The Indo-Pacific framework has become a defining feature of India's foreign policy, despite early hesitancy. Although China's increasing military and economic engagement in South Asia and the Indian Ocean sparked its adoption, the Indo-Pacific idea has given India a strategic framework for its larger foreign policy goals.

New Delhi's support for a regional order based on norms, encouragement of economic integration, and initiatives to improve maritime security are proactive changes in foreign policy rather than a reaction to a changing world. New Delhi's strategy is to engage in issue-based cooperation with longstanding allies or new partners as needed, embracing strategic flexibility in a changing geopolitical environment where the agendas of important actors differ. The Indian Ocean is New Delhi's primary geographic priority, in contrast to its Quad partners. As a result, countries like the UK that have strategic interests in the IOR have unrealized opportunities to strengthen their ties with India. The Quad places a strong emphasis on fostering economic friendship and trust. This approach adds new protections to non-member countries, including ASEAN countries, while combining current security measures.

Unlike previous security-focused mini-laterals that are constrained by operational and physical limitations, the Quad places a strong emphasis on extended maritime domain awareness. The Indian Ocean continues to be the Quad's primary geo-security area, and the Indian Navy, with assistance from the US, Japan, and Australia, is essential to strengthening cooperative capabilities and facilitating prolonged maritime operations.

The Quad's strength is rooted in its market economies, pluralistic cultures, and democratic politics – all of which serve as stabilizing forces in a world that is prone to instability. Resonant and aligned cooperation is ensured by the range of Quad members' services and capabilities across several disciplines, which offers a credible and robust alternative to China's or any one Quad member's solutions.

References

Abe, Shinzo, *"Confluence of the Two Seas" (Speech, Parliament of the Republic of India, 22 August 2007)*. https://www.mofa.go.jp/

Bajpaee, Chietigj, Has India Defanged the Quad?, *The Interpreter*, June 21, 2024. https://www.lowyinstitute.org/the-interpreter/has-india-defanged-quad

Deb, Urmika, India in the Quad: Insider or outlier?, *The Strategist*, April 02, 2024. https://www.aspistrategist.org.au/india-in-the-quad-insider-or-outlier/

Jash, Amrita, The Quad Factor in the Indo-Pacific and the Role of India, *Journal of Indo-Pacific Affairs*, March 08, 2021. https://www.airuniversity.af.edu/JIPA/Display/Article/2528182/the-quad-factor-in-the-indo-pacific-and-the-role-of-india/

Kuo, M. A., The Origin of Indo-Pacific as a Geopolitical Construct, *The Diplomat*, *25*, 2018.

Ladwig, Walter, *The Indo-Pacific in Indian Foreign Policy*, RUSI, April 30, 2024. https://rusi.org/explore-our-research/publications/policy-briefs/indo-pacific-indian-foreign-policy

Malhotra, Aditi, Engagement, not Entanglement: India's Relationship with the Quad, *Georgetown Journal of International Affairs*, May 01, 2023. https://gjia.georgetown.edu/2023/05/01/engagement-not-entanglement-indias-relationship-with-the-quad/

Medcalf, R., Reimagining Asia: From Asia-Pacific to Indo-Pacific. In: Rozman, G., and Liow, J. (eds.), *International Relations and Asia's Southern Tier*. Asan-Palgrave Macmillan Series. Springer, Singapore, 2018. https://doi.org/10.1007/978-981-10-3171-7_2

Ministry of External Affairs, Government of India, *Annual Report 2019–20*. New Delhi: Ministry of External Affairs, Government of India. http://www.mea.gov.in/Uploads/PublicationDocs/32489_AR_Spread_2020_new.pdf

Ministry of External Affairs, Government of India, *Indo--Pacific Division Briefs*, 2020. https://mea.gov.in/

Ministry of Foreign Affairs of the People's Republic of China, *Foreign Ministry Spokesperson Wang Wenbin's Regular Press Conference on September 29, 2020*, September 29, 2020. https://www.fmprc.gov.cn/

Pant, Harsh, *India and the Quad: Chinese Belligerence and Indian Resilience*. Observer Research Foundation, March 20, 2022. https://www.orfonline.org/research/india-and-the-quad

Rajagopalan, Rajeshwari, Beyond the Quad: BoomingSecurity Cooperation Efforts in the Indo-Pacific, *The Diplomat*, January 14, 2023. https://thediplomat.com/2023/01/beyond-the-quad-booming-security-cooperation-efforts-in-the-indo-pacific/

Roy-Chaudhury, R., and de Estrada, K. S., India, the Indo-Pacific and the Quad, *Survival*, *60*(3), 181–194, 2018. https://doi.org/10.1080/00396338.2018.1470773

Sullivan de Estrada, K. India and Order Transition in the Indo-Pacific: Resisting the Quad as a 'Security Community', *The Pacific Review*, *36*(2), 378–405, 2023. https://doi.org/10.1080/09512748.2022.2160792

Vashisht, Pankaj, Indo-Pacific Strategies: What Do They Entail for India?, *Journal of Indo-Pacific Affairs*, April 24, 2023. https://www.airuniversity.af.edu/JIPA/Display/Article/3371487/indo-pacific-strategies-what-do-they-entail-for-india/

15 ASEAN Centrality

The Indispensable Myth

*Jeffry A. Hollman**

1. Introduction

In the world of international relations, one concept reigns supreme: sovereignty. As defined by Merriam-Webster, sovereignty is "supreme power especially over a body politic" and "freedom from external control or autonomy."[1] Both definitions are instructive as we explore the concept of ASEAN Centrality and its viability as a method for securing the collective interests of South-East Asian nations. However, the latter definition features more prominently in the discourse between nations as they seek to reconcile their national interests with those of their neighbors, allies and competitors. In an era of Great Power Competition, national sovereignty is frequently challenged, especially for smaller nations trying to improve their position in the global order.

One way to guard one's sovereignty is to join forces with other nations, through alliances, treaties, defense and trade agreements, and other multi-lateral associations, organizations and institutions. In South-East Asia, one such grouping is the Association of South-East Asian Nations or ASEAN. Established in 1967 by the Foreign Ministers of Indonesia, Malaysia, the Philippines, Singapore and Thailand, ASEAN sought to foster

> cooperation in the economic, social, cultural, technical, educational and other fields, and in the promotion of regional peace and stability through abiding respect for justice and the rule of law and adherence to the principles of the United Nations Charter.[2]

Though many contend the Association was founded to deter expansionist aggression and protect its member countries from becoming proxies in the Cold War,[3]

* Colonel, U.S. Indo-Pacific Command (USINDOPACOM) J34.

1 Definition of Sovereignty, *Merriam-Webster Dictionary*. https://www.merriam-webster.com/dictionary/sovereignty

2 ASEAN Website, *The Founding of ASEAN*. https://asean.org/the-founding-of-asean/

3 Ao, T., The Discord over Sabah between Malaysia and the Philippines, *Indian Council of World Affairs*, 27 August 2020. https://www.icwa.in/show_content.php?lang=1&level=3&ls_id=5311&lid=3744

DOI: 10.4324/9781003545750-18

it was equally focused on averting internal division and disputes. In fact, just prior to its establishment, ASEAN members Indonesia, Malaysia and the Philippines were involved in a heated dispute over ownership (or sovereignty) of Sabah.[4] Though they agreed to disagree on the matter and move forward in the spirit of cooperation, this seed of sovereignty would remain ever-present and challenge the Association's attempts to deal with both internal and external matters in a cohesive and unified manner.

Fast-forward to 2008; ASEAN had grown to ten member nations (adding Brunei, Cambodia, Lao, Myanmar and Vietnam) and took the next formal step in documenting its structure, purpose and goals by publishing the ASEAN Charter. According to their website, the ASEAN Charter became "a legally binding agreement among the 10 ASEAN Member States." It was also "registered with the Secretariat of the United Nations, pursuant to Article 102, Paragraph 1, of the Charter of the United Nations."[5] However, despite it having a "legal personality,"[6] it does not restrict or subvert member nation sovereignties, nor does it require all disputes to be worked through the Association's legal mechanisms.[7] This is important to note, as it paves the way for *Sovereignty* to undermine *Centrality*.

As previously mentioned, the impotence of *Centrality* threatens the Association's ability to mediate both internal and external disputes. The territorial identity of Sabah exemplifies an internal challenge, while overlapping claims in the South China Sea represent both types of challenge: internal disputes among ASEAN claimants and external disputes between individual member nations and China. An additional dynamic surfaces with external disputes, specifically when not all member nations have a vested interest in the particular dispute, but we will explore that further later in the chapter.

The purpose of this chapter is to explore the ASEAN concept of *Centrality* in relation to a growing focus on the primacy of sovereignty and territorial integrity. While revered by member nations and external supporters alike, ASEAN Centrality has struggled for legitimacy as it pertains to matters involving individual national sovereignty, and the territories and resources over which that sovereignty extends. *Centrality* is best understood by considering the past, present and future of this foundational concept, using disputes surrounding overlapping claims in the South

4 Sabah is currently a Malaysian State. In the early 1960s, it gained independence from Britain through a referendum by which the people voted to become part of Malaysia. Both Indonesia and the Philippines objected, as they considered North Borneo (its former colonial name) to belong to them as part of their respective sovereign territories. Indonesia would eventually relent and give up their claim, but the Philippines persisted and to this day contend Sabah belongs to them. In the mid-1960s, Thailand tried to mediate the dispute and all parties agreed to put it on the back burner in the spirit of cooperation. It was out of this contentious quarrel that ASEAN was born.

5 ASEAN Website, *Significance of the ASEAN Charter*. https://asean.org/asean-charter/

6 A High-level Legal Experts Group (HLEG) was appointed at the 41st ASEAN Ministerial Meeting in Singapore, to address three key issue areas: (1) legal personality of ASEAN, (2) dispute settlement and (3) privileges and immunities.

7 ASEAN Protocol on Enhanced Dispute Settlement Mechanism, *Article 1: Coverage and Application, Paragraph 3*. https://asean.org/asean-protocol-on-enhanced-dispute-settlement-mechanism/

China Sea as the most recent and poignant example of its limitations and viability as a unifying force in South-East Asian geopolitics.

2. A Concept is Born

I'd venture to guess most people have never heard the word *Centrality*, nor do they know what it means. Personally, I had never heard the word until I started to pay attention to Indo-Pacific geopolitics and became acquainted with ASEAN. A Google search for the term brings up the usual definitions and meanings, along with references to network theory, nodal analysis and various graphical representations. The most useful definition for our purposes defines the term as "the fact of being the main or most important part of something."[8] ASEAN Centrality then is the most important aspect of the organization. But what does it mean to the ten member nations that enshrined this concept into their legally binding, UN-registered charter?

According to the Lowy Institute, the publication of the ASEAN Charter in 2008 marked the first mention of the word *Centrality*;[9] however, a search of the ASEAN website shows the term first used at the 39th ASEAN Ministerial Meeting in Kuala Lumpur in July of 2006.[10] Deferring to the charter as the authoritative source on the matter, *Centrality* is defined in the context of the Association's purpose as the primary driving force in its dealings with external partners.[11] In part, that means ASEAN should engage with external partners with a united voice, leveraging their collective power and position to reap benefits and secure favorable outcomes for all members of the Association. In many cases this makes sense; however, as mentioned previously, it does not preclude individual member nations from working with external partners outside of ASEAN. In fact, the charter calls upon all members to respect the fundamental importance of sovereignty, territorial integrity and non-interference in the internal matters of other member nations.[12] It is this caveat that dooms *Centrality* from the very start, and why the concept has struggled for relevance since its inception. One particular example lays bare the failure of *Centrality* in ASEAN affairs: the still-to-be-concluded Code of Conduct (COC) in the South China Sea.

Although the first official Declaration on the Conduct (DOC) of Parties in the South China Sea was released in 2002, the game board had been re-arranged by

8 Definition of Centrality, *Cambridge Dictionary*. https://dictionary.cambridge.org/us/dictionary/english/centrality#google_vignette

9 Yaacob, R., The translator: "ASEAN Centrality," *The Interpreter, The Lowy Institute*, 4 April 2024. https://www.lowyinstitute.org/the-interpreter/translator-asean-centrality

10 ASEAN Website, *Joint communique of the 39th ASEAN ministerial meeting (AMM) Kuala Lumpur, 25 July 2006*, 12 October 2012. https://asean.org/joint-communique-of-the-39th-asean-ministerial-meeting-amm-kuala-lumpur-25-july-2006/

11 ASEAN Charter, Chapter 1, Article 1, January 2008.

12 ASEAN Charter, Preamble and Chapter 1, Article 2, January 2008.

Beijing much earlier.[13,14] Regardless, the Declaration was a necessary first step to get disputants to agree to resolve overlapping claims peacefully and respectfully. A quick review of the three-page document clearly shows China has not acted in good faith, nor has it nurtured the foundation required to facilitate conclusion of a binding COC. Three glaring examples support this claim, standing in stark contrast to the peace-loving language sprinkled throughout the Declaration. The first is in reference to Paragraph 2 of the DOC, whereby all parties declared they would commit "to exploring ways for building trust and confidence . . . on the *basis of equality* and *mutual respect* (emphasis added)."[15] Perhaps the most blatant illustration of the PRC's disregard for this particular commitment occurred in 2010 at the 17th ASEAN Regional Forum, when China threw a tantrum directed at the U.S., Vietnam and Singapore, stating, "China is a big country and other countries are small countries, and that's just a fact."[16] The second is in reference to Paragraph 4, whereby all parties agreed to "resolve their territorial and jurisdictional disputes by *peaceful* means, *without resorting to the threat or use of force* (emphasis added)."[17] While there are literally dozens of examples of China's disregard for this element of the DOC, the most recent one is particularly heinous. On the morning of September 29th 2024, two Chinese Coast Guard vessels encircled and attacked Vietnamese fishermen,[18] similar to an attack three months earlier on Filipino soldiers attempting to resupply their outpost on the BRP Sierra Madre.[19] The third and final example is in reference to Paragraph 5, whereby all parties consented to "exercise self-restraint in the conduct of activities that would complicate or escalate disputes and affect peace and stability including, among others, *refraining from action of inhabiting on the presently uninhabited islands, reefs, shoals, cays, and other features* (emphasis added)."[20] Fast-forward to 2015, when China constructed a small structure on stilts at Mischief Reef, claiming it was intended as a shelter for fishermen to take refuge in during inclement weather. However, throughout 2015

13 Ott, M., The South China Sea in strategic terms, *The Wilson Center*, 14 May 2019. https://www.wilsoncenter.org/blog-post/the-south-china-sea-strategic-terms

14 In 1974, China evicted the Vietnamese from an outpost in the Paracels, and in 1995, China occupied Mischief Reef, which was clearly within the Philippine Exclusive Economic Zone (EEZ).

15 Declaration on the Conduct of Parties in the South China Sea, signed by all ASEAN members and the People's Republic of China (PRC), in the Kingdom of Cambodia, 4 November 2002.

16 Pomfret, J., U.S. takes a tougher tone with China, *The Washington Post*, 30 July 2010. https://www.washingtonpost.com/wp-dyn/content/article/2010/07/29/AR2010072906416.html?sid=ST2010072906761

17 Declaration on the Conduct of Parties in the South China Sea, signed by all ASEAN members and the People's Republic of China (PRC), in the Kingdom of Cambodia, 4 November 2002.

18 Hai, A., Vietnam protests Chinese attack on fishing vessels in South China Sea, *Voice of America*, 3 October 2024. https://www.voanews.com/a/vietnam-protests-chinese-attack-on-fishing-vessels-in-south-china-sea/7808763.html

19 Aljazeera News, *China Coast Guard accused of behaving 'like pirates' in South China Sea*, 20 June 2024. https://www.aljazeera.com/news/2024/6/20/china-coast-guard-accused-of-behaving-like-pirates-in-south-china-sea

20 Declaration on the Conduct of Parties in the South China Sea, signed by all ASEAN members and the People's Republic of China (PRC), in the Kingdom of Cambodia, 4 November 2002.

and into 2016, China embarked on a massive land reclamation project, turning a small shack on stilts into a sprawling military base.[21,22]

These are just a few of the reasons why ASEAN and China have been unable to transition the DOC of 2002 into a binding COC some 22 years later. But there are other reasons why the disputes have lingered so long: internal division within ASEAN on whether to press China on the issue. A lack of unity on the issue is one obvious factor contributing to the impasse. This lack of unity can be attributed to the fact that not all ASEAN members have a vested interest in the matter. In fact, exactly half of ASEAN's members have no stake in the South China Sea whatsoever, except perhaps that freedom of navigation should be preserved.[23] However, each of them *do* have stakes in their bilateral relations with China and therefore refrain from taking sides (i.e., supporting the collective claims of other ASEAN members in dispute with China). This reality took center stage in 2012 when ASEAN failed to issue the customary joint communique at the body's Regional Forum, the first time in its 45-year history.[24] The sticking point? Cambodia's insistence that language concerning South China Sea disputes be removed and handled bilaterally, in accordance with China's preference.[25] So it would seem ASEAN Centrality has not delivered on its promise to secure a brighter future for its 10 member nations. As political tensions in the Indo-Pacific continue to rise, it is unlikely this "most important" concept will prevail.

3. Centrality in 2024

Though *Centrality* has suffered numerous defeats at the hands of *Sovereignty*, it remains a faint and distant rallying cry for member nations and external powers alike. For 57 years it has refused to be silent, finding its way into joint communique after joint communique. Any external power seeking to court the Association wisely pays homage to the sacred principle, for fear of offending or alienating the organization. Yet despite its many failings, the spirit of ASEAN Centrality has been invoked several times this year, primarily by member nations seeking to calm the turbulent waters lapping at their shores.

A review of this year's headlines reveals two particular approaches in the quest to salvage *Centrality*. The first suggests the concept should serve as a unifying

21 Mollman, S., Photos: How a "fishermen's shelter" on stilts became a Chinese military base in the South China Sea, *Quartz Daily Brief*, 15 December 2016. https://qz.com/863811/mischief-reef-how-a-fishermens-shelter-on-stilts-became-a-chinese-military-base-in-the-south-china-sea

22 RFA Staff, New photos show China's artificial islands are highly developed military bases, *Radio Free Asia*, 31 October 2022. https://www.rfa.org/english/news/southchinasea/china-artificial-islands–10312022043801.html

23 Singapore, Thailand, Cambodia, Lao and Myanmar do not have disputed claims in the South China Sea.

24 BBC News, *Asean nations fail to reach agreement on South China Sea*, 13 July 2012. https://www.bbc.com/news/world-asia-18825148

25 Epstein, A., ASEAN still torn over security challenges, *Geopolitical Intelligence Services*, 2 October 2024. https://www.gisreportsonline.com/r/asean-issues/

force to advance the interests of multiple member nations. The champion for this strategy is the Philippines, who has stepped up coordination and cooperation with the Vietnamese Coast Guard in an attempt to push back against China's aggressive and coercive activities within their respective Exclusive Economic Zones (EEZ). Chester Cabalza, president and founder of Manila-based think tank International Development and Security Cooperation, told Inquirer.Net that this approach would standardize and promote ASEAN Centrality.[26] In the same article, geopolitical authority Don McLain Gill surmised that the initiative would make it more difficult for China to drive a wedge between the two ASEAN members, both of which had been recipients of recent Chinese aggression in the South China Sea.[27] As they say, there is strength in numbers, especially when it comes to taking on an assertive global power like China. Most recently, Philippine President Ferdinand "Bongbong" Marcos Jr. confirmed he had raised the issue at the 44th and 45th ASEAN Summit and Related Summits.[28] His calls for renewed attention on the still-to-be-concluded COC were met with derision and defiance by Chinese Premier Li Qiang, who attempted to deflect the issue and instead blame everything on the meddling of outside forces. While not specifically naming the United Sates, Li's reference is one used frequently by Beijing to refer to Washington and its Allies.[29] Li's toxic reaction came across in true "Wolf Warrior" fashion and does not bode well for any near-term progress on a COC, let alone a binding one.

The other approach is a favorite of the so-called "non-aligned" members, who view *Centrality* through a very different lens. Their view argues that only issues common to all members should be championed by the Association, so as not to damage the interests of individual nations. The most obvious example of this view has already been discussed: ASEAN's failure to issue a joint communique at their 2012 Regional Forum. Including language on South China Sea disputes was not in Cambodia's best interest, not only because they were not a party in the dispute, but also because doing so would have damaged its relations with China. This outcome was not surprising, and Cambodia is not the only member who stands to lose in a tug of war with China. Economic repercussions are the biggest factor. For instance, at the recent 44th and 45th ASEAN Summit and Related Summits, China and ASEAN continued negotiations to upgrade their free trade agreement (FTA), with a goal of creating what Li Qiang referred to as an "ultra large-scale

26 Mendoza, J., 'Revolutionary': Vietnam coast guard sets first-time drills with PCG, *Inquirer.Net*, 5 August 2024. https://www.inquirer.net/410498/revolutionary-vietnam-coast-guard-sets-first-time-drills-with-pcg/

27 Mendoza, Revolutionary.

28 Bajo, A., Marcos raises South China Sea issue in ASEAN Summit, *GMA News Online*, 9 October 2024. https://www.gmanetwork.com/news/topstories/nation/923125/marcos-raises-south-china-sea-issue-in-asean-summit/story/

29 Ng, E., and Saksornchai, J., China defiant over South China Sea skirmishes in ASEAN talks and blames meddling by foreign forces, *AP News*, 10 October 2024. https://apnews.com/article/asean-laos-china-south-china-sea-myanmar-ad1f39ff6d0bc353f07598b06bf214b7

market."[30] To emphasize the importance of this FTA, it is worth noting that China is ASEAN's top trading partner and third-largest source of foreign investment. In the 14 years since the FTA's inception, trade has nearly tripled from $235.5 billion to $696.7 billion.[31] So it's easy to see why *Centrality* struggles for relevance, at least on controversial topics like the South China Sea.

4. Future Considerations

At this point, you might be wondering how *Centrality* might regain its place as a driving force in ASEAN's relations with external powers. How might ASEAN leverage both *Sovereignty* and *Centrality* to maximize benefit for its 10 member nations? One way would be to collectively agree that the two concepts are not mutually exclusive. While breaking with the majority may preserve certain national interests, it does so at the expense of solidarity and collective benefit. In the case of a binding COC, it comes at the expense of much-needed regional security and stability. If Cambodia is afraid of the consequences of angering its largest trading partner, investor and creditor, it's up to the other nine member nations to say, "We've got your back." And together they can wage war in the court of public opinion, which in the case of the South China Sea is clearly on their side.[32] Any retribution imposed by an external power could be exposed in the media and amplified by ASEAN and its fellow member nations. As a collective, they could dissuade the retaliatory behavior by imposing costs of their own. Though I'm sure it would hurt economically, other external supporters could pitch in to mitigate the damage and further compel the aggressor to relent. Similar to how Taiwan enlisted both domestic and external support to blunt the effects of China's pineapple ban[33] or how Lithuania has survived China's weaponized trade tactics,[34] ASEAN's more vulnerable members could take refuge within the organization's collective power and influence. As we have seen in recent years, China's economic instruments are not invincible, especially when their opponents band together and push back.

Another way ASEAN could leverage both concepts to its maximum benefit would be to reinvent *Centrality*, with the intent of strengthening its power as a foundational driving force. The term itself has been used *ad nauseam* for almost 20 years now. While members and external powers alike pay homage to the concept at every opportunity, most people have lost sight of what it truly means. It

30 Ng and Saksornchai, China defiant over South China Sea skirmishes in ASEAN talks and blames meddling by foreign forces.

31 Ng and Saksornchai, China defiant over South China Sea skirmishes in ASEAN talks and blames meddling by foreign forces.

32 In 2016, the Philippines brought their South China Sea dispute to the Hague's Permanent Court of Arbitration, which invalidated Beijing's claim and ruled in their favor. Beijing refused to accept the ruling and to this day shows no signs of negotiating on the matter.

33 McDonald, T., China and Taiwan face off in pineapple war, *BBC News*, 19 March 2021. https://www.bbc.com/news/business-56353963

34 Dempsey, J., China's bullying of Lithuania Spurs European unity, *Carnegie Europe*, 18 January 2022. https://carnegieendowment.org/europe/strategic-europe/2022/01/chinas-bullying-of-lithuania-spurs-european-unity?lang=en

doesn't help that its definition is sparse and somewhat ambiguous: the primary driving force in ASEAN's dealings with external partners. Perhaps ASEAN needs to convene a special session dedicated to defining what *Centrality* is and (just as important) what it isn't, along with common, agreed-upon expectations for how it will guide the Association's pronouncements and proceedings. This could be incorporated into an update to their charter or as a new standalone agreement. Once the 10 member nations are able to better define the concept, the next task would be to sell it both internally (whole of government, constituents, etc.) and externally (global and regional powers, other multi-lateral bodies, etc.). Finally, ASEAN needs to find ways to publicize and celebrate true examples of ASEAN Centrality, extolling its virtues in detail and telling the story of its exponential benefits for the peoples of South-East Asia and beyond.

5. Conclusion

However effective such tactics might be in boosting the reputation and efficacy of *Centrality*, the concept will always be vulnerable to manipulation, pressure and competing interests. Sovereignty will remain an "easy button" for any nation seeking to avoid geopolitical consequences contrary to its national interests. Only by reinventing the term can ASEAN hope to harness the power of *Centrality* and wield it for the mutual benefit of its members and other like-minded partners. Collective security and stability in the region are vital to preserving peace and prosperity for South-East Asia. Disregard for international law and freedom of navigation in the global commons threatens more than just sovereignty and access to resources; it also threatens economic development, social elevation and human progress. Mustafa Kemal Atatürk once said, "Sovereignty is not given, it is taken." For *Centrality* to survive (and thrive) will require a similar commitment. No external power is going to willingly compromise on its own national interests if ASEAN does not demand it as a prerequisite to doing business. There is indeed strength in numbers, but only if those numbers are united in a common cause.

References

Aljazeera News, *China Coast Guard accused of behaving 'like pirates' in South China Sea*, 20 June 2024. https://www.aljazeera.com/news/2024/6/20/china-coast-guard-accused-of-behaving-like-pirates-in-south-china-sea

Ao, T., The discord over Sabah between Malaysia and the Philippines, *Indian Council of World Affairs*, 27 August 2020. https://www.icwa.in/show_content.php?lang=1&level=3&ls_id=5311&lid=3744

ASEAN Charter, Chapter 1, Article 1, January 2008.

ASEAN Charter, Preamble and Chapter 1, Article 2, January 2008.

ASEAN Protocol on Enhanced Dispute Settlement Mechanism, *Article 1: Coverage and application*, Paragraph 3. https://asean.org/asean-protocol-on-enhanced-dispute-settlement-mechanism/

ASEAN Website, *Joint communique of the 39th ASEAN ministerial meeting (AMM) Kuala Lumpur, 25 July 2006*, 12 October 2012. https://asean.org/joint-communique-of-the-39th-asean-ministerial-meeting-amm-kuala-lumpur-25-july-2006/

ASEAN Website, *Significance of the ASEAN Charter*. https://asean.org/asean-charter/

ASEAN Website, *The founding of ASEAN*. https://asean.org/the-founding-of-asean/

Bajo, A., Marcos raises South China Sea issue in ASEAN summit, *GMA News Online*, 9 October 2024. https://www.gmanetwork.com/news/topstories/nation/923125/marcos-raises-south-china-sea-issue-in-asean-summit/story/

BBC News, *Asean nations fail to reach agreement on South China Sea*, 13 July 2012. https://www.bbc.com/news/world-asia-18825148

Declaration on the Conduct of Parties in the South China Sea, *Signed by all ASEAN members and the People's Republic of China (PRC) in the Kingdom of Cambodia*, 4 November 2002.

Definition of Centrality, *Cambridge dictionary*. https://dictionary.cambridge.org/us/dictionary/english/centrality#google_vignette

Definition of Sovereignty, *Merriam-webster dictionary*. https://www.merriam-webster.com/dictionary/sovereignty

Dempsey, J., China's bullying of Lithuania Spurs European unity, *Carnegie Europe*, 18 January 2022. https://carnegieendowment.org/europe/strategic-europe/2022/01/chinas-bullying-of-lithuania-spurs-european-unity?lang=en

Epstein, A., ASEAN still torn over security challenges, *Geopolitical Intelligence Services*, 2 October 2024. https://www.gisreportsonline.com/r/asean-issues/

Hai, A., Vietnam protests Chinese attack on fishing vessels in South China Sea, *Voice of America*, 3 October 2024. https://www.voanews.com/a/vietnam-protests-chinese-attack-on-fishing-vessels-in-south-china-sea/7808763.html

McDonald, T., China and Taiwan face off in pineapple war, *BBC News*, 19 March 2021. https://www.bbc.com/news/business-56353963

Mendoza, J., 'Revolutionary': Vietnam coast guard sets first-time drills with PCG, *Inquirer.Net*, 5 August 2024. https://www.inquirer.net/410498/revolutionary-vietnam-coast-guard-sets-first-time-drills-with-pcg/

Mollman, S., Photos: How a "fishermen's shelter" on stilts became a Chinese military base in the South China Sea, *Quartz Daily Brief*, 15 December 2016. https://qz.com/863811/mischief-reef-how-a-fishermens-shelter-on-stilts-became-a-chinese-military-base-in-the-south-china-sea

Ng, E., and Saksornchai, J., China defiant over South China Sea skirmishes in ASEAN talks and blames meddling by foreign forces, *AP News*, 10 October 2024. https://apnews.com/article/asean-laos-china-south-china-sea-myanmar-ad1f39ff6d0bc353f07598b06bf214b7

Ott, M., The South China Sea in strategic terms, *The Wilson Center*, 14 May 2019. https://www.wilsoncenter.org/blog-post/the-south-china-sea-strategic-terms

Pomfret, J., U.S. takes a tougher tone with China, *The Washington Post*, 30 July 2010. https://www.washingtonpost.com/wp-dyn/content/article/2010/07/29/AR2010072906416.html?sid=ST2010072906761

RFA Staff, New photos show China's artificial islands are highly developed military bases, *Radio Free Asia*, 31 October 2022. https://www.rfa.org/english/news/southchinasea/china-artificial-islands–10312022043801.html

Yaacob, R., The translator: "ASEAN centrality", *The Interpreter, The Lowy Institute*, 4 April 2024. https://www.lowyinstitute.org/the-interpreter/translator-asean-centrality

16 Latin America

The Forgotten Coast of the Indo-Pacific?

*Juan Pablo Toro**

1. Introduction

The total coastline of the eleven Latin American countries that border the Pacific extends approximately 29,500 kilometers, constituting a large part of the eastern margin of this ocean. The countries that stand out for their populations and economies include Mexico, Colombia, Peru and Chile,[1] which have been united since 2011 in a free trade bloc called the Pacific Alliance.[2] They all have the United States and China as their main trade partners in the exchange of goods and services. Consequently, their prosperity depends on shipments crossing these waters without major setbacks. The navies of these countries[3] regularly participate in naval exercises such as RIMPAC[4] or UNITAS[5] to contribute to the stability of the Pacific Ocean, while at the same time carrying out maritime interdiction operations to confront challenges such as drug trafficking and illegal, unregulated and unreported fishing that occurs not only in their jurisdictional waters, but also in the enormous exclusive economic zones that they must monitor.[6] In recent years, the concept of the Indo-Pacific has become more widely used among chief naval officers and scholars of security studies in the Western Hemisphere to refer to the interconnected

* AthenaLab executive director.

1 Economic Commission for Latin America and the Caribbean (ECLAC). *Preliminary Overview of the Economies of Latin America and the Caribbean 2023*, December 14, 2023. https://repositorio.cepal.org/entities/publication/642af810–0aea-4997-add6–6c0437dafdac

2 Pacific Alliance, *Potential Productive Linkages between the Countries of the Pacific Alliance and China, Korea, Japan and Thailand*, 2019. https://www.subrei.gob.cl/estudios-y-documentos/otros-documentos/detalle-otras-fichas-y-reportes/potenciales-encadenamientos-productivos-entre-los-países-de-la-ap-y-mercados-de-china-japón-corea-y-tailandia

3 International Institute for Strategic Studies. *The Military Balance 2022*, London: International Institute for Strategic Studies, 2022.

4 J.P. Toro, Una mirada al interior del ejercicio Rimpac desde la participación de la Armada de Chile, *El Mercurio*, September 15, 2018, p. D13.

5 J.P. Toro, Coaliciones marítimas para aguas agitadas, *El Mercurio*, August 31, 2024, p. A6.

6 Y. Loaiza, *Se inició en Ecuador el mayor ejercicio militar de América contra la pesca ilegal*, June 24, 2024. https://www.infobae.com/america/america-latina/2024/06/24/se-inicio-en-ecuador-el-mayor-ejercicio-militar-de-america-contra-la-pesca-ilegal/

DOI: 10.4324/9781003545750-19

nature of a maritime system that includes the Indian Ocean.[7] Authors have examined whether these Latin American countries with extensive projection into the Pacific are or should be considered an integral part of a broader strategic framework.[8] Mexico, Colombia, Peru and Chile, countries who are currently discussing this nomenclature, broadly consider that their liberal democracies and open economies need free trade sea routes. It happens that they also have a history of privileged security ties to the United States.

The Pacific and Indian Oceans have always been interconnected for sailors. Ferdinand Magellan and Sebastián Elcano blazed a trail 500 years ago, and later in the 16th century trade route between the coasts of the Americas and Southeast Asia were opened by way of the "Manila Galleon" (also known as the "Nao de China" or "Acapulco Galleon"), a ship that sailed between present-day Mexico and the Philippines.[9] Therefore, when we talk about the Indo-Pacific today, it is not that geography has changed; instead, we are witnessing a reconstruction of geopolitical interests driven by competing nations trying to dictate where the power struggles lay.[10] "How leaders define regions can affect their allocation of resources and attention; the ranking of friends and foes; who is invited and who is overlooked at the top tables of diplomacy," holds Medcalf.[11]

The term "Indo-Pacific" already appears in several official documents from different countries in the Americas, Asia and Europe, highlighting its relevance as a strategic framework,[12] severely criticized by China, which sees it as yet another maneuver by Western nations to dilute or contain its emergence as a global player.[13] However, there are real justifications for its use as either a place or an idea, following Medcalf's thesis.[14] As a place, the concept is explained by the existence of two oceans connected through of a series of straits (Malacca, Sunda, Lombok) that complement each other in connecting the Americas, Europe, the Middle East and Asia. This gives rise to an interconnected maritime system (trade, diplomacy

7 J.P. Toro, El Indo-Pacífico y su proyección hacia América Latina: La vía japonesa, in J. Sahd, N. Albertoni, & D. Rojas (eds.), *América Latina y su proyección en el Asia-Pacífico*, Santiago de Chile: Centro de Estudios Internacionales de la Universidad Católica, 2022, pp. 105–122.

8 J.P Toro, Chile en el escenario geopolítico actual: Destino Indo-Pacífico, in P. Vera & R. Ortiz (eds.), *América Latina en la nueva geopolítica global*, Lima: Centro de Estudios Estratégicos del Ejército del Perú, Willam J. Perry Center for Hemispheric Defense Studies, Strategic Studies Institute U.S. Army War College, 2024, pp. 207–221.

9 P. Gordon & J.J. Morales, *The Silver Way: China, Spanish America and the Birth of Globalisation, 1565–1815*, Hong Kong: Penguin Book, 2017.

10 R. Kaplan, The *Revenge of Geography: What the Map Tells Us About Coming Conflicts and the Battle Against Fate*, New York: Random House Trade Paperbacks, 2014, p. 29.

11 R. Medcalf, *Indo-Pacific Empire: China, America and the Contest for the World's Pivotal Region*, Manchester: Manchester University Press, 2020, p. 5.

12 B.J. Cannon & K. Hakata, *Indo-Pacific Strategies. Navigating Geopolitics at the Dawn of a New Age*, London: Routledge, 2023.

13 Tien-Sze Fang, China's foreign policy transformation and its implications for the Indo-Pacific, in B.J. Cannon & K. Hakata (ed.), *Indo-Pacific Strategies. Navigating Geopolitics at the Dawn of a New Age*, London: Routledge, 2021, p. 129.

14 Medcalf, *Indo-Pacific Empire.*

and infrastructure), where what happens in one part affects another. As a region, the Indo-Pacific encompasses the world's most populated country (China), the largest democracy (India), the country with the highest number of Muslim inhabitants (Indonesia) and more than half of the Earth's population. In the commercial sphere, its shores contain ten ports among those with the greatest cargo movement, and 60% of global trade is shipped along Asian maritime routes. Its importance in terms of security lies in the fact that it includes seven of the ten largest armed forces in the world (China, India, Russia, the United States, Japan, Pakistan and Indonesia), and six countries that possess nuclear weapons (China, India, Pakistan, Russia, the United States and North Korea). From a battlefield perspective, it is a predominantly air, navy, space, and cyber environment.

The most relevant issue, as Jaishankar explains, is not the relative size of the Indo-Pacific, but the fact that those who use the concept agree in assigning it special priority as an area of interest.[15] Is the Indo-Pacific particularly relevant in Latin America? Official documents were reviewed to determine whether Mexico, Colombia, Peru and Chile are considered (or consider themselves) Indo-Pacific countries.

2. A Review of National Policies

Australia's foreign policy white paper, "A stable and prosperous Indo-Pacific", mentions Japan, Indonesia, India, the Republic of Korea and the United States as bilateral partners, while also incorporating Southeast Asia (mainly Singapore and Malaysia). The Pacific coast of Latin America is not considered within this geographic area.[16] For Canada, one of the latest countries to publish an Indo-Pacific strategy, the Indo-Pacific represents important opportunities, but also challenges due to China's assertive and coercive attitudes.[17] Government policy placed forty nations within the region, excluding any mention of the southeastern quadrant of the Americas. In fact, it does not involve Latin America at any point in its strategy. France, in its strategy on the Indo-Pacific, includes many countries, even mentioning

15 S. Jaishankar, *The India Way. Strategies for an Uncertain World*, Uttar Pradesh: HarperCollins, 2020, p. 182.

16 Australian Government, Department of Foreign Affairs and Trade, Indo-Pacific Partnerships. *Foreign Policy White Paper*, n.d. https://www.dfat.gov.au/sites/default/files/minisite/static/4ca0813c-585e-4fe1–86eb-de665e65001a/fpwhitepaper/foreign-policy-white-paper/chapter-three-stable-and-prosperous-Indo-Pacific/Indo-Pacific.html

17 The forty nations mentioned in the text include: Australia, Bangladesh, Bhutan, Brunei, Cambodia, Democratic People's Republic of Korea (DPRK), India, Indonesia, Japan, Laos, Malaysia, Maldives, Mongolia, Myanmar, Nepal, New Zealand, the Pacific island countries (14), Pakistan, People's Republic of China (PRC), Philippines, Republic of Korea (ROK), Singapore, Sri Lanka, Taiwan, Thailand, East Timor and Vietnam. See Government of Canada, *Canada's Indo-Pacific Strategy*. Global Affairs Canada, February 29, 2024. https://www.international.gc.ca/transparency-transparence/Indo-Pacific-indo-pacifique/index.aspx?lang=eng

Antarctica within its geographic frame of reference.[18] This can be attributed to the fact that it has island territories in the region, such as Reunion in the Indian Ocean or Tahiti in Polynesia. However, it is not totally clear if France considers the Pacific coast of Latin America, despite its size, an integral part of the Indo-Pacific, as the following image reflects. This situation has been even questioned by French analysts, who have called for its correction "as soon as possible".[19]

Following France's lead, the European Union has published its own strategy towards the Indo-Pacific. It focuses primarily on enhancing relations and cooperation in this vast region, which includes Southeast Asian countries, Australia, India, Japan, New Zealand, the Republic of Korea, the United Kingdom and the United States. The strategy focuses on issues such as security, trade, investment and environmental challenges, among others. It does not include Latin America as part of the Indo-Pacific.[20]

The case of South Korea, on the other hand, is different. In its 2022 "Strategy for a Free, Peaceful, and Prosperous Indo-Pacific Region", in addition to highlighting its relations with the United States, India, Australia, New Zealand, France, Germany, the United Kingdom and Southeast Asia, it mentioned Latin America and the Pacific Alliance made up of Chile, Colombia, Mexico and Peru. This reflects Seoul's aim towards not only expanding economic and commercial relations, but also collaborations on various other global affairs, such as in renewable energies.[21] It is also worth analyzing the case of Japan, since the concept of the Free and Open Indo-Pacific originated in this country and was later adopted by other nations. In its document "New Plan for a 'Free and Open Indo-Pacific (FOIP)'", updated in 2023, Latin America and the Caribbean are mentioned for the first time, in the context of Tokyo's efforts to support countries such as Ecuador and Guatemala. Japan's commitment is placed on the rule of law and inclusive economic order, where areas such as digital trade, food security, maritime cooperation and connectivity are the most critical.[22]

Finally, the US strategy promotes an alignment with its traditional partners in the Indo-Pacific, but there is no mention of the Latin American countries of the

18 Ministry of Europe and Foreign Affairs of France, *France's Indo-Pacific Strategy*, 2022. https://www.diplomatie.gouv.fr/IMG/pdf/en_dcp_a4_indopacifique_022022_v1–4_web_cle878143.pdf

19 Institut français des relations internationales, Replacer l'Amérique du Sud sur la carte française de l'Indo-Pacifique. Convergences politiques, économiques et pistes de coopération, *Céline Pajon*, February 02, 2024. https://www.ifri.org/fr/notes/replacer-lamerique-du-sud-sur-la-carte-francaise-de-lindo-pacifique-convergences-politiques

20 European Commission and High Representative of the Union for Foreign Affairs and Security Policy, *The EU Strategy for Cooperation in the Indo-Pacific*, 2021. https://www.eeas.europa.eu/sites/default/files/jointcommunication_2021_24_1_en.pdf

21 Government of the Republic of Korea, *Strategy for a Free, Peaceful, and Prosperous Indo-Pacific Region*, 2022. https://www.mofa.go.kr/eng/wpge/m_26382/contents.do

22 Ministry of Foreign Affairs of Japan, *New Plan for a "Free and Open Indo-Pacific (FOIP)"*, pp. 6–7, 2023. https://www.mofa.go.jp/files/100477660.pdf

Pacific coast, including of its neighbor Mexico. The strategy goes on to promote strong alliances with a handful of key allies:

> Our approach, therefore, draws from and aligns with those of our closest friends. Like Japan, we believe that a successful Indo-Pacific vision must advance freedom and openness and offer 'autonomy and options.' We support a strong India as a partner in this positive regional vision. Like Australia, we seek to maintain stability and reject coercive exercises of power. Like the ROK, we aim to promote regional security through capacity-building. Like ASEAN, we see Southeast Asia as central to the regional architecture. Like New Zealand and the United Kingdom, we seek to build resilience in the regional rules-based order. Like France, we recognize the strategic value of an increasing regional role for the European Union (EU). Much like the approach the EU has announced in its Strategy for Cooperation in the Indo-Pacific, American strategy will be principled, long-term, and anchored in democratic resilience.[23]

3. A Regional Perspective: Chile, Colombia, Peru and Mexico

It seems quite clear that the countries on the Western coast of the Indo-Pacific have a rather limited vision of this region, which does not reach the coasts of the Americas, but does reach those of Africa. In addition, when reviewing documents from Chile, Colombia, Mexico and Peru, there are rather sporadic references to considering themselves part of the Indo-Pacific, and there is nothing resembling a strategy (or at least a strategic orientation) that positions them as an integral part of the macro region.

In the case of Chile, the adoption of the Indo-Pacific concept is most evident in the area of security and defense and is aligned with the military priorities the United States has constructed as part of its military-to-military relationship with the country. There are also mentions in the economic sphere, with an emphasis on relations with India. Without a doubt, the most important document is Chile's National Defense Policy 2020, which includes a complete section on the Indo-Pacific, in which it is described as a vital area for national development and prosperity.[24] It also identifies potential risks and conflicts in the region, such as "threats to free navigation along air and sea routes that are vital for trade". Given that freedom of navigation in the Indo-Pacific is considered part of Chile's defense policy, the document urges Chile to increase its participation in bilateral and multilateral bodies on issues related to security.

23 United States Government, *Indo-Pacific Strategy of the United States*, p. 7, 2022. https://www.whitehouse.gov/wp-content/uploads/2022/02/U.S.-Indo-Pacific-Strategy.pdf

24 Ministerio de Defensa de Chile, *Política Nacional de Defensa 2020*, Santiago de Chile: Ediciones Ministerio de Defensa, 2021, p. 36.

Recently, Chile joined the Indo-Pacific Land Power Conference in 2021, whose purpose was none other than "preserving a free and open Indo-Pacific through strength and preparedness." In a panel discussing extreme cold weather/mountaineering operations in the Indo-Pacific, then-Commanding General of the US Army Alaska, Major General Peter B. Andrysiak, referred to the importance of the Arctic, stating that "we are re-building knowledge and proficiency to operate in extreme cold weather, mountainous, and high-latitude environments", also underscoring that

> to compete in the Arctic and globally, we will work with Indo-Pacific and Arctic allies and partners. We are expanding partnerships with Norway, Sweden, Finland, and Denmark; re-invigorating partnerships with Japan, Canada, India and Mongolia; and expanding training and educational opportunities with Korea, Nepal, and Chile.[25]

Likewise in 2021, authorities from Chile's Undersecretary of Defense participated in the Chile-US Working Group for Cooperation in the Indo-Pacific, and in 2019, the country went to the Indo-Pacific Chiefs of Defense Conference. Foreign Affairs ministers and other authorities have referred to the Indo-Pacific in a more economic sense, but since President Gabriel Boric took office in 2022, there has been no record of its use in documents and speeches, without any public explanation in this regard.

As for Colombia, an official document from 2022 mentioned the concept with the aim of deepening bilateral relations with the countries of the Pacific Rim, particularly those of Southeast Asia, leading to the promotion of a series of concrete diplomatic actions.[26] Vice President Marta Lucía Ramírez called for deepening ties with India to produce vaccines against COVID-19, with the purpose of "strengthening our country's political and commercial investment in the Indo-Pacific", since the region promised "many opportunities for growth and wealth creation".[27] However, once left-winger Gustavo Petro came to the presidency in 2022, references to the Indo-Pacific disappeared.

Peru's National Center for Strategic Planning published an interesting study titled "Peru in the Indo-Pacific region: Strategic proposals to strengthen commercial development",[28] which examines the trade balance with the region, aiming to

25 Infodefensa, *Chilean Army Presents Cold Weather Experience at Indo-Pacific Land Power Conference*, May 31, 2024. https://www.infodefensa.com/texto-diario/mostrar/2954668/ejercito-chile-expone-experiencia-clima-frio-Indo-Pacific-land-power-conference-2021

26 Ministry of Foreign Affairs of Colombia, *Institutional Action Plan*, 2022. https://www.cancilleria.gov.co/taxonomy/term/8491

27 DNA Web Team, *Colombia's Vice President Calls for Joint Vaccine Production with India, see Opportunities in Indo Pacific*, October 3, 2021. https://www.dnaindia.com/world/report-colombia-vice-president-marta-luc-a-ram-rez-calls-for-joint-vaccine-production-with-india-2913882

28 National Center for Strategic Planning, Platform of the Peruvian State, *Peru in the Indo-Pacific Region: Strategic Proposals to Strengthen Commercial Development*, 2023. https://www.gob.pe/

identify opportunities in export mining, textile, agricultural and fishing products. It also seeks greater access to the areas of knowledge and technology. However, the study only applies its analysis to the countries located between the Pacific and Indian Oceans, thus excluding Latin America for lack of an internationally agreed-upon delimitation. It is important to note that before this report, Peru's only initiative regarding this issue was its participation in the Indo-Pacific Defense Chiefs Conference in 2019.

Finally, in the case of Mexico, the Indo-Pacific is mentioned in various documents that resulted from initiatives aimed at improving economic relations with India and Japan, as well as in an article signed by diplomats in a specialized magazine. A 2020 document from the Ministry of Foreign Affairs, titled "Mexico and India: seven decades of shared experiences",[29] states that it is necessary to relaunch the association between both countries since global economic growth engines have shifted to a broader arc of prosperity in the Indo-Pacific region. It also highlights Mexico's membership in MIKTA (Australia, South Korea, Indonesia and Turkey) and the opportunity for trilateral cooperation in Africa to amplify its potential in the Indo-Pacific region. Some areas of interest in the Indo-Pacific for Mexico are infrastructure, food processing, digital innovation and health.

In an article published in *Foreign Affairs Latinoamérica*, Mexican diplomats Federico Salas Lotfe and Guillermo Chávez argued that the current situation in the Indo-Pacific also represents an unmissable opportunity for their country:

> At first glance, Mexico has the opportunity to be a reference for international value chains through its 14 free trade agreements with 50 countries, and 30 Agreements for the Promotion and Reciprocal Protection of Investments with 31 countries or administrative regions. The most notable pacts are the Mexico, United States and Canada Treaty, and the Comprehensive and Progressive Agreement for Trans-Pacific Partnership, in which Australia, Brunei, Canada, Chile, Japan, Malaysia, Mexico, New Zealand, Peru, Singapore and Vietnam participate. It also has the necessary infrastructure for the transfer of international goods through 11 deep-water ports in the Pacific Ocean.

They also argue that it will be crucial to view Mexico as a hinge country between two antagonistic perspectives and to assume that its insertion in the Indo-Pacific necessarily involves the recognition and opportunities presented by this vast territory.[30] "Therefore, it must design its own strategy under a prism that is both North

---

institucion/ceplan/informes-publicaciones/4591177-peru-en-la-region-Indo-Pacifico-propuestas-estrategicas-para-fortalecer-el-desarrollo-comercial

29 Government of Mexico, *Mexico and India: Seven Decades of Shared Experiences*, 2020. https://www.gob.mx/cms/uploads/attachment/file/600499/Libro_CD04-Mex-India-web-baja.pdf. See page 61.

30 Foreign Affairs Latinoamérica, *Mexico's Insertion in the Indo-Pacific Environment*, 2021. https://revistafal.com/la-insercion-de-mexico-en-el-ambito-del-Indo-Pacifico

American and Latin American and, subsequently, skillfully navigate both currents in a multipolar and interdependent world", the authors said.

4. Conclusion

After analyzing official documents from both sides of the Indo-Pacific (abundant on the Western margins but scarce on the Eastern ones), it seems evident that countries such as Chile, Colombia, Mexico and Peru are not considered an integral part of this broad strategic framework, nor do they themselves seem to be convinced of such. It is true that the concept is "polysemic", as Gonzalez argues,[31] meaning it can reflect many different interests depending on who uses it. Indeed, it is worth exploring the reasons why this happens to be, since Latin American nations have effective connections across the region that date back centuries, but even more importantly, their prosperity and security depend largely on the stability of the Indo-Pacific.

One possible explanation is the fact that these Latin American countries are not used to thinking strategically in general, which would also be the case regarding their eventual positioning in the Indo-Pacific. For this reason, it could be a great opportunity for any of the four nations or, better yet, for the Pacific Alliance bloc to develop a positioning strategy in this region, since it would attract the attention of other partners who apply the same strategic concept and assign it a significant place in their foreign policy. In the best of cases, it could even lead them to redraw their maps. As a coalition, the Pacific Alliance constitutes the eighth-largest economy in the world, contributes 43% of the gross domestic product of Latin America and the Caribbean, attracts 45% of the foreign direct investment flows and adds up to more than 233 million people.[32]

Perhaps most worryingly, by not adopting the Indo-Pacific concept and sticking to the commercially conceived Asia-Pacific concept, these four countries are neglecting a very important dimension of the new geopolitical reality. "The Indo-Pacific is a meaningful geopolitical construct that captures the geographic centrality of the sea – the Indian and the Pacific Ocean – to regional security and the role of naval power in it", as Patalano, Russell and Grant hold.[33] Latin American countries may be overlooking a fundamental area related to maritime security. Notwithstanding, these four countries participate in multinational military exercises in the area and even acquire military equipment from countries such as

31 A. Gonzalez, *From the Indo-Pacific to the South Atlantic: Maritime Strategies of the Great Powers of the 21st Century*, Buenos Aires: Institute of Naval Publications, 2022, p. 212.

32 Pacific Alliance, *What is the Pacific Alliance?* https://alianzapacifico.net/en/what-is-the-pacific-alliance

33 A. Patalano, J. Russell, & C. Grant, Naval power and a framework for regional security in the Indo-Pacific, in A. Patalano, J. Russell, & C. Grant (eds.), *The New Age of Naval Power in the Indo-Pacific. Strategy, Order and Regional Security*, Washington: Georgetown University Press, 2023, p. 5.

Australia,[34] South Korea[35] and India.[36] In addition, they face common challenges such as the impact of illegal, unregulated and undocumented fishing, as well as maritime smuggling of all kinds.

Perhaps in the case of Chile, the discussion on whether it is relevant to use the concept of Indo-Pacific has at least been given some consideration by scholars.[37] One of the most original proposals, though still under development, is the existence of the "Latino Pacífico", a concept that according to its author:

> seeks to sharpen its own focus, which will allow the peripheral position of the region to be reduced. In terms of geospatiality, this concept is rooted in the Pacific Rim of the Americas, positioning itself as a key area of the supply chains of materials and products of the fourth industrial revolution. In functional terms, the Latin Pacific zone is already fundamental in the most pressing global challenges, such as the energy transition, the supply of minerals for electromobility and food security.[38]

When writing about the Indo-Pacific, the greatest difficulty lies in the broadness or lack of definition of the concept from a geopolitical point of view. There is an assumption that it is important, but we do not have a precise notion of where it begins or ends. This chapter has reviewed related perspectives by different actors, to encourage a dialogue or debate that is yet to take place regarding the possible relevance and benefits of integrating the countries of the Pacific coast of Latin America into the Indo-Pacific's strategic framework. It has especially considered those of greater relative weight such as Chile, Colombia, Mexico and Peru, considering that they are liberal democracies that promote a rules-based international order and open economies whose priority security ties lay with the United States. While geopolitical approaches (those that reflect interests rather than locations) are mutable, if these four nations do nothing to modify the current framing, starting by changing the nomenclature, they will continue to be the forgotten coast of the Indo-Pacific. They will lose opportunities and a chance at actively participating in what may be the most relevant geographical hub in the present century, to which they curiously have privileged access.

34 Juan Pablo Toro, Chile to get Australian frigates, *Australian Naval Institute*, April 04, 2020. https://navalinstitute.com.au/14275–2/

35 Park Jae-hyuk, HD Hyundai signs $463 million deal to build 4 warships in Peru, *Korea Times*, April 18, 2024. https://www.koreatimes.co.kr/www/tech/2024/10/129_372877.html

36 Huma Siddiqi, Chile receives Ballistic Helmets and a ship from Indian companies, *Financial Express*, February 25, 2021. https://www.financialexpress.com/business/defence-chile-receives-ballistic-helmets-and-a-ship-from-indian-companies-2201729/

37 See for example a critique by C. Fortin, J. Heine, & C. Ominami, (eds.), *Active Non-Alignment and Latin America: A Doctrine for the 21st Century*, Santiago de Chile: Catalonia, 2021, p. 384.

38 Andrés Bórquez, Mirando a Asia desde el Latino Pacífico, *Diario Financiero*, September 26, 2023, https://www.df.cl/opinion/columnistas/df-conexion-asia-mirando-a-asia-desde-el-latino-pacifico

References

Australian Government, Department of Foreign Affairs and Trade, Indo-Pacific partnerships. *Foreign Policy White Paper*, n.d. https://www.dfat.gov.au/sites/default/files/minisite/static/4ca0813c-585e-4fe1–86eb-de665e65001a/fpwhitepaper/foreign-policy-white-paper/chapter-three-stable-and-prosperous-Indo-Pacific/Indo-Pacific.html

Cannon, B.J., & Hakata, K., *Indo-Pacific Strategies. Navigating Geopolitics at the Dawn of a New Age*, London: Routledge, 2023.

Economic Commission for Latin America and the Caribbean (ECLAC), *Preliminary Overview of the Economies of Latin America and the Caribbean 2023*, December 14, 2023. https://repositorio.cepal.org/entities/publication/642af810–0aea-4997-add6–6c0437dafdac

European Commission and High Representative of the Union for Foreign Affairs and Security Policy, *The EU Strategy for Cooperation in the Indo-Pacific*, 2021. https://www.eeas.europa.eu/sites/default/files/jointcommunication_2021_24_1_en.pdf

Gonzalez, A., *Del Indo-Pacífico al Atlántico Sur. Estrategias Marítimas de las Grandes Potencias del siglo XXI,* Buenos Aires: Institute of Naval Publications, 2022.

Gordon, P., & Morales J., *The Silver Way: China, Spanish America and the Birth of Globalisation, 1565–1815*, Hong Kong: Penguin Book, 2017.

Government of Mexico, *Mexico and India: Seven Decades of Shared Experiences*, 2020. chrome-extension://efaidnbmnnnibpcajpcglclefindmkaj/https://www.gob.mx/cms/uploads/attachment/file/600499/Libro_CD04-Mex-India-web-baja.pdf

Government of the Republic of Korea, *Strategy for a Free, Peaceful, and Prosperous Indo-Pacific Region*, 2022. https://www.mofa.go.kr/eng/wpge/m_26382/contents.do

Fortin, C., Heine, J., & Ominami, C. (eds.), *El No Alineamiento Activo y América Latina: Una Doctrina para el Nuevo Siglo*, Santiago de Chile: Catalonia, 2021.

Institut français des relations internationales, Replacer l'Amérique du Sud sur la carte française de l'Indo-Pacifique. Convergences politiques, économiques et pistes de coopération, *Céline Pajon*, February 02, 2024. https://www.ifri.org/fr/notes/replacer-lamerique-du-sud-sur-la-carte-francaise-de-lindo-pacifique-convergences-politiques

International Institute for Strategic Studies. *The Military Balance 2022*, London: International Institute for Strategic Studies, 2022.

Jaishankar, S., *The India Way. Strategies for an Uncertain World*, Uttar Pradesh: HarperCollins, 2020.

Kaplan, R., *The Revenge of Geography: What the Map Tells Us About Coming Conflicts and the Battle Against Fate*, New York: Random House Trade Paperbacks, 2014.

Medcalf, R., Indo-Pacific Empire: *China, America and the Contest for the World's Pivotal Region*, Manchester: Manchester University Press, 2020.

Ministerio de Defensa de Chile, *Política Nacional de Defensa 2020*, Santiago de Chile: Ediciones Ministerio de Defensa, 2021.

Ministry of Europe and Foreign Affairs of France, *France's Indo-Pacific Strategy*, 2022. https://www.diplomatie.gouv.fr/IMG/pdf/en_dcp_a4_indopacifique_022022_v1–4_web_cle878143.pdf

Ministry of Foreign Affairs of Colombia, *Plan de Acción Institucional*, 2022. https://www.cancilleria.gov.co/taxonomy/term/8491

Ministry of Foreign Affairs of Japan, *New Plan for a "Free and Open Indo-Pacific (FOIP)"*, pp. 6–7, 2023. https://www.mofa.go.jp/files/100477660.pdf

National Center for Strategic Planning, Platform of the Peruvian State, *Perú en la región Indo-Pacífico: Propuestas estratégicas para fortalecer el desarrollo comercial*, 2023. https://www.gob.pe/institucion/ceplan/informes-publicaciones/4591177-peru-en-la-region-Indo-Pacifico-propuestas-estrategicas-para-fortalecer-el-desarrollo-comercial

Patalano, A., Russell, J., & Grant, C. (eds.), Naval power and a framework for regional security in the Indo-Pacific, in *The New Age of Naval Power in the Indo-Pacific. Strategy, Order and Regional Security,* Washington: Georgetown University Press, 2023, p. 5.

Sahd, J., Albertoni, N., & Rojas, D. (eds.), *América Latina y su proyección en el Asia-Pacífico*, Santiago de Chile: Centro de Estudios Internacionales de la Universidad Católica, 2022.
Salas, F., & Chávez, C., La inserción de México en el ámbito del Indo-Pacífico, *Foreign Affairs Latinoamérica*, 2021. https://revistafal.com/la-insercion-de-mexico-en-el-ambito-del-Indo-Pacifico
Vera, P., & Ortiz, R. (eds.), *América Latina en la nueva geopolítica global*, Lima: Centro de Estudios Estratégicos del Ejército del Perú, Willam J. Perry Center for Hemispheric Defense Studies, Strategic Studies Institute U.S. Army War College, 2024.
United States Government, *Indo-Pacific Strategy of the United States*, 2022. https://www.whitehouse.gov/wp-content/uploads/2022/02/U.S.-Indo-Pacific-Strategy.pdf

17 China's Security Engagement in the Indo-Pacific

Lessons from the Shanghai Cooperation Organisation

*Adina Masalbekova**

1. Introduction

The end of the Cold War actively contributed to the debate regarding the end of history – the triumph of Western liberal democracy[1] argued to become a universal ideology. Despite Fukuyama's theorization on the of history being supported by the upsurge of economic liberalization and the rise of global pro-democratic sentiments in the '90s, China's commitment to building communism not only deepened, but Western-style democracy and its values became a threat to this commitment. Having market reforms with a certain level of iron curtains moved aside, China also experienced a democratic outbreak in 1989[2] that was suppressed by the country's authorities. The global decline of communism has not affected Beijing, but rather forced the authorities to identify a new internal threat that has called into question the rule of the Chinese Communist Party.

In the meantime, the post-Soviet space experienced a shocking wave of free market democratization followed by the inflow of new ideas and return of the old beliefs as the Soviet iron walls fell, together with the formation of new nations and territory demarcations. The fall of the Soviet government also created a supremacy void, leading to a number of regional and domestic conflicts. Post-Communist Central Asia's transition to sovereignty involved transnational disputes over demarcation together with the revival of Islamic beliefs, increased civil society and ethnic minority movements. In a culture-historical context, the region of Central Asia extends across the border into China's western region, the Xinjiang Uygur Autonomous Region (XUAR, Xinjiang), with the majority of Turkic ethnic groups populating the region, also referred as East Turkestan by Uyghurs. The gained independence among Central Asian states was therefore linked to increased tensions in Xinjiang caused by Turkic-Muslim ethnic minorities', predominantly Uyghurs, demands for greater political autonomy and independence that continues to this

* University of Central Asia, Kyrgyzstan.

1 F. Fukuyama, Reflections on the End of History, Five Years Later, *History and Theory*, 1995, pp. 27–43.

2 W.Y. Yang & M.L. Wagner, Tiananmen: China's Struggle for Democracy – Its Prelude, Development, Aftermath, and Impact, *Maryland Series in Contemporary Asian Studies*, 1990, Vol. 2, p. 1.

DOI: 10.4324/9781003545750-20

day.[3] China's security concern over its western territory bordering and sharing layered ties with Central Asia – the region experiencing the wide range of issues on its sovereign path – put forward new regional security initiative the Shanghai Cooperation Organisation (SCO) to promote regional peace and stability amid the rapidly changing geopolitical landscape with notable liberal shift. Starting as Shanghai Five with five initial member states, the SCO has been expanding from focusing on the regional cooperation between Russia, China and Central Asia to accepting new member states from South Asia, the Middle East and Eastern Europe, affirming China's role in global governance and pushing its vision for security as an alternative to so-called Western hegemony.

The lack of global attention to the Central Asian region allows China to develop and test its efforts as an influential global leader to gain support favoring China's foreign policy. By emphasizing its non-military bloc positionality in comparison, the SCO is enlarging its geographical scale to gain more supporting voices from its members and dialogue partners for China in the international arena, particularly in the context of the growing escalation in the South China Sea within the Indo-Pacific region.

2. Revisiting Shanghai Confidence-Building Talks

Security developments in the area of the former Soviet Union, particularly those neighboring China's western border, were and still are given little attention and coverage. However, tracking these events is essential to understand the foundation of the SCO that now covers 42% of the world population, together with 23% of the global GDP as of 2024.[4] Thus, the 90s were a time of political instability, economic reforms and continued conflicts in Russia and Central Asia bordering China as Soviet rule fractured: Tajikistan was going through a brutal civil war,[5] while Russian forces were in wars with the Chechen resistance movement fighting for independence for Chechnya; threats of religious radicalization emerged, driven by a revival of religion in the region and the influx of various Islamic movements from abroad;[6] regional stability was also challenged by incomplete border demarcation, which led to frequent disputes between local populations and neighboring states, as well as enabling illegal crossings and smuggling.[7] Sharing a 7,000-km.-long border

3 M. Clarke, China and the Uyghurs: The 'Palestinization' of Xinjiang? *Middle East Policy*, 2015, Vol. 22, Issue 3.

4 Statista, Comparison of the Shanghai Cooperation Organization with Selected Regional International Organizations (2023) *Statista Chart*: https://www.statista.com/chart/32538/comparison-of-the-shanghai-cooperation-organization-with-selected-regional-international-organizations/.

5 T. Epkenhans, *The Origins of the Civil War in Tajikistan: Nationalism, Islamism, and Violent Conflict in Post-Soviet Space*, Lexington: Lexington Books, 2016.

6 J. Engvall, Religion and the Secular State in Kyrgyzstan (10.06.2020) *Silk Road Studies Program*: https://www.silkroadstudies.org/resources/Religion_and_the_Secular_State_in_Kyrgyzstan_-_Johan_Engvall_-_10.06.20_-_FINAL_wCover.pdf.

7 R. Tashtemkhanova, Z. Medeubayeva, A. Serikbayeva, & M. Igimbayeva, Territorial and Border Issues in Central Asia: Analysis of the Reasons, Current State and Perspectives, *The Anthropologist*, 2015, Vol. 22, Issue 3, pp. 518–525.

in the Northwest, where the socio-political developments were rapidly changing and unpredictable, created a new security threat for Chinese leadership from the outside to fuel the Uyghur independence movement in the XUAR.[8]

Throughout the 90s, there were numerous guerrilla operations and even bomb attacks carried out by various groups supporting the movement as an act of protest. Following the March Xinjiang Stability Meeting in 1996, the Chinese government launched a major national anti-crime campaign called *Strike Hard*. The campaign was particularly aimed at combatting separatism and illegal religious activities. The CCP Politburo Standing Committee issued stricter directives to tighten control over the XUAR and suppress subversive activities.[9] At the same time, on April 26, Shanghai hosted a first meeting of the leaders of five states – Russia, Kazakhstan, Kyrgyzstan, Tajikistan and China to address concerns along their shared borders to strengthen joint control over military activities along the border that runs primarily through Xinjiang.

Against the backdrop of this border agreement signed between the states in Shanghai in 1996, they formed a multilateral forum known as the Shanghai Five, based on the Agreement on Confidence-Building in the Military Field in the Border Area (Shanghai, 1996) and the Agreement on the Mutual Reduction of Armed Forces in the Border Area (Moscow, 1997).[10] The group held annual meetings in each member country capital, evolving step by step from an institution of bilateral form to one of a multilateral framework, leading to the Declaration on the establishment of the Shanghai Cooperation Organisation in 2001. The initiative's interest first emphasized combatting separatism, terrorism, religious extremism, weapon smuggling, drug trafficking and illicit migration through data exchange military activities along the border areas. These identified areas of security concerns within the Shanghai summit overlap statement objectives of the "Strike Hard" campaign aimed at the pacification of Turkic Muslim minority in Xinjiang.[11]

Later, the organization's focus opened a window for non-military cooperations around economic, cultural and educational initiatives – valuable for the regional post-Communist socio-economic recovery and international integration as newly formed states. As the topics within the Shanghai Five Group progressed, Russia and China gained support for Russia's position on the Chechen question and China's efforts for national reunification – stressing the importance of adhering

8 S.M. Patrick, *The Uyghur Movement China's Insurgency in Xinjiang*, Monograph of the School of Advanced Military Studies (SAMS), 2010.

9 Rémi Castets, The Uyghurs in Xinjiang – the Malaise Grows: After 11 September 2001, the Chinese Regime Strove to Include Its Repression of Uyghur Opposition Within the International Dynamic of the Struggle Against Islamic Terrorist Networks, *China Perspectives*, 2003, Vol. 49.

10 Nine Countries Currently Enjoy the Status of Full Members of the Shanghai Cooperation Organization (SCO), Including Armenia, Bahrain, Cambodia, and Egypt (27.11.2023) *Shanghai Cooperation Organization*: https://eng.sectsco.org/20231127/1168690.html.

11 P. Pingua, China's Policies for Combating Domestic Terrorism in Xinjiang, *World Affairs: The Journal of International Issues*, 2017, Vol. 21, Issue 3, pp. 62–71.

to the 1972 ABM Treaty,[12] opposed the inclusion of Taiwan in Theater Missile Defense (TMD)[13] and reaffirmed their support for the Nuclear Non-Proliferation Treaty (NPT).[14] Taiwan's ongoing push for independence escalated tensions in the Taiwan Strait, while Western democracies criticized China on the Taiwan question. On the other side of the Shanghai Five border, the Afghan crisis intensified socio-economic tensions in Central Asia, leading to a wide range of threats, including the possible rise of pro-Islamist regimes in Central Asia becoming one of the key concerns to be jointly addressed.

Meanwhile, Russia faced economic and political challenges, needing strong relations with China and its neighbors to counter Western pressures and focus on domestic issues, with the Shanghai Five offering a platform for achieving these goals. The confrontation with so-called Western values was expressed in principles of peaceful coexistence and of opposing to international interference in domestic affairs of sovereign states. In a few years of existence, the Shanghai Five was able to establish various mechanisms such as annual meetings of their defense ministers and foreign ministers, a working group to monitor and supervise the implementation of previous agreements between them as a legal foundation for the Shanghai Cooperation Organisation.[15]

3. The Shanghai Cooperation Organisation – Defining Security Threats in the Region

Uzbekistan's accession to the organization prompted the title change from the Shanghai Five to what is known today as the Shanghai Cooperation Organisation. Uzbekistan does not share a border with China, but occupies a large territory in Central Asia with the largest population, giving the institution considerable weight as a regional actor. The declaration of the SCO once again emphasized their adherence to the purposes and principles of the United Nations Charter, principles of mutual respect for independence, sovereignty and territorial integrity, equality and mutual benefit, resolution of all issues through mutual consultations, non-interference in internal affairs, non-use or threat of use of military force, and renunciation of unilateral military superiority in neighboring areas.[16]

12 Anti-Ballistic Missile (ABM) Treaty Signed Between the U.S.A. and the Soviet Union to Control the Deployment of Missile System: No Longer in Force, *Britannica*: https://www.britannica.com/event/Anti-Ballistic-Missile-Treaty.

13 Deployment of Nuclear and Conventional Missiles for the Purpose of Maintaining Security in a Specific Region, or Theatre, *Britannica*: https://www.britannica.com/topic/ballistic-missile.

14 UN Office for Disarmament Affairs (UNODA), Treaty on the Non-Proliferation of Nuclear Weapons (NPT): An International Treaty to Prevent the Spread of Nuclear Weapons and Weapons Technology, Promote Cooperation in Peaceful Nuclear Energy Uses, and Work Towards Nuclear Disarmament and Complete Disarmament: https://www.un.org/disarmament/wmd/nuclear/npt/.

15 Q. Jia, The Success of the Shanghai Five: Interests, Norms and Pragmatism, *Pacific Symposium of National De*fense University, March 2001, pp. 26–28.

16 Shanghai Cooperation Organization, Declaration on the Establishment of the Shanghai Cooperation Organization (15.06.2001) *World Japan*: https://worldjpn.net/documents/texts/SCO/20010615.D1E.html.

Strengthening regional cooperation and engagement through varying fields covering trade, education and culture, science and technology, energy and environment and others came along as part of the institutional framework aimed at safeguarding regional peace, security and stability.[17] As the world was changing after the end Cold War with the growing liberalization, the Declaration also mentioned the aim towards *new, democratic, just and rational international political and economic order.*[18] With the process of globalization comes the risk of transnational movement spreading into China's territories, creating a risk of potential collaboration (especially in the XUAR) and challenging Chinese leadership. At the time when 9/11 attack pushed the terror discourse[19] and raised Islamophobic sentiments in many parts of the world, the Chinese government succeeded in labeling one of the Uyghurs resistance movements, the East Turkestan Islamic Movement (ETIM), as a terrorist organization internationally. The U.S.-led global military campaign on terrorism served to convince Washington to overlook its longstanding concerns over Chinese human rights abuses in Xinjiang.[20] As the global war on terror was being carried out, the SCO put forward the rhetoric on the *Three Evils Forces* (terrorism, separatism and extremism) to define the country members' joint counterterrorism preventive measures. Following the importance of combating "three evils" in the region, there was an establishment of joint action, known as the Regional Anti-Terrorism Structure, within the SCO framework in 2004.

The structure mandate implied the operation of analytical and legal work and shared database on terrorist, separatist or other extremist groups' activities, including the exchange of information and intelligence collaboration on implementing measures to identify and prevent and suppress offending actions.[21] As Moscow has been an influential actor in the region given the shared Soviet history, the platform is also seen as a tool for Russian-Chinese interests to counterbalance the potential of the Western influence amid the post-9/11 US war in Afghanistan. The US war on terror allowed the region to establish and explore limits of bilateral security ties with Washington resulted in establishments of transit military bases

17 Alyson J.K. Bailes, *The Shanghai Cooperation Organization*, Stockholm: Stockholm International Peace Research Institute, 2007, p. 4.

18 Declaration on the Establishment of the Shanghai Cooperation Organization: https://worldjpn.net/documents/texts/SCO/20010615.D1E.html.

19 D.U. Jamil, Reading Power: Muslims in the War on Terror Discourse, *Islamophobia Studies Journal*, 2014, Vol. 2, Issue 2, pp. 29–42.

20 B. Xu, H. Fletcher, & J. Bajoria, *The East Turkestan Islamic Movement (ETIM)*, Council on Foreign Relations, 2014, p. 4.

21 B. Xu, H. Fletcher, & J. Bajoria, *The East Turkestan Islamic Movement (ETIM)*, Council on Foreign Relations, 2014, p. 4.

in Uzbekistan (2001-2005)[22] and Kyrgyzstan (2001-2014).[23,24] Furthermore, the region brought Western attention with the "Tulip Revolution" in Kyrgyzstan and the Andijan events in Uzbekistan. While the Uzbek authorities were heavily criticized by the UN, the OSCE, the US and the EU with imposed sanctions in response to severe human rights breaches during mass civilian demonstrations in Andijan,[25] the change of power in Kyrgyzstan was contrarily perceived as a democratic revolution.[26] These events and responses to them forced Moscow and Beijing to the organization's internal solidity, shared values, and coordinated responses opposing the imposition of foreign standards and critiquing foreign interference with the pretext of promoting human rights,[27] followed by the pressure to withdraw the US transit base from the region. Popular uprisings and civil society movements advocating for human rights in the region are grouped in the concept of a color revolution that threatens regional peace and stability to the extent of linking them to 'extreme measures' and 'chaos' and 'extremist and terrorist forces'.[28] Nevertheless, the SCO's evolution as a multilateral institute went much further than proposing concepts confronting alleged foreign Western values. The member states increased their efforts to cooperate in the various sectors through the SCO Business Council and the SCO Interbank Consortium,[29] bringing together trade and economy[30] and culture and humanitarian initiatives.[31]

4. The Shanghai Cooperation Organisation – Beyond the Region

The SCO map of political and diplomatic cooperation has been taking further steps by establishing dialogue partners, observer states and membership requests. The inclusion of India and Pakistan to the SCO in the 2017 Astana summit made it the largest regional organization by its member states' share of global GDP in the

22 J.P. Nichol & Foreign Affairs, Defense, and Trade Division, *Uzbekistan: Recent Developments and US Interests*, Congressional Information Service, Library of Congress, May 2005.

23 Eurasianet, US Formally Closes Its Kyrgyzstan Air Base (2021) *Eurasianet*: https://eurasianet.org/us-formally-closes-its-kyrgyzstan-air-base.

24 S. Aris, The Shanghai Cooperation Organisation: 'Tackling the Three Evils'. A Regional Response to Non-Traditional Security Challenges or an Anti-Western Bloc? *Europe-Asia Studies*, 2009, Vol. 61, Issue 3, pp. 457–482.

25 V. Axyonova, The Effectiveness of Sanctions and Regime Legitimacy in Central Asia: Examining the Substance of EU Sanctions Against Uzbekistan, *Europe en Formation*, 2015, Issue 1, pp. 19–35.

26 S.N. Cummings, *Domestic and International Perspectives on Kyrgyzstan's "Tulip Revolution": Motives, Mobilization and Meaning*, Abingdon: Routledge, 2010.

27 J. Yuan, Forging a New Security Order in Eurasia: China, the SCO, and the Impacts on Regional Governance, *Chinese Political Science Review*, 2023, Vol. 8, Issue 3, pp. 422–439.

28 T. Ambrosio, Catching the 'Shanghai Spirit': How the Shanghai Cooperation Organization Promotes Authoritarian Norms in Central Asia, *Europe-Asia Studies*, 2008, Vol. 60, Issue 8, pp. 1321–1344.

29 SCO Secretariat, *Nine Countries Currently Enjoy the Status of SCO Dialogue Partners* (27.11.2023), https://eng.sectsco.org/20231127/1168690.html.

30 SCO Economy, SCO Economic Cooperation, *SCO*: https://eng.sectsco.org/economy/.

31 SCO Culture, SCO Cultural Cooperation, *SCO*: https://eng.sectsco.org/culture/.

strategically critical Eurasia–South Asia region. Contributing to the potential of asserting China's legitimacy as a great power, the expansion aligned with Chinese leadership's geostrategic ambitions to project its influence.[32] Although the membership of India and Pakistan suggested political, economic and security benefits to combat the "3 evils" and promote the organization's recognition, it was challenging to navigate the perennial India-Pakistan conflicts. The accession of politically isolated Iran as an SCO member in 2023 further pushed the SCO map to the greater Middle East.[33] A year later, the map of member states was extended to the West, welcoming its first all-European member – Belarus, which had previously held an observer status. The joint anti-terrorist exercise that took place near Belarus's border with Poland, a member of NATO, following its membership status in July 2024 have garnered significant attention from Western observers, despite previous joint exercises between Minsk and Beijing prior to full membership.[34] As the US-China strategic rivalry continues, the expansion of the SCO around NATO's borders and with NATO member Türkiye as a dialogue partner among the other 14 states, provides a platform for China to challenge the US-led international order. In doing so, China introduced the Belt and Road Initiative (BRI) as an alternative approach to address global connectivity and facilitating the integration of European, Asian and African markets through financing and building transportation networks in developing economies. Amid ongoing tensions in the East China Sea, the BRI is also seen as a Chinese leadership effort toward both ensuring an alternative trade route and securing economic cooperation and along its western borders.[35]

5. Global Security with Chinese Characteristics? Implications for the Indo-Pacific

The growing nature of strategic use of multilateralism is coming to more light in various fields of China's behavior in the beginning of the 21st century, which is also shown in its increasing role in UN peacekeeping operations.[36] In addition, the SCO member states are highly interested in multilateral engagement, particularly in landlocked Central Asia to balance Russian influence in the region, through Chinese investments and development assistance. According to Chinese experts,

32 E. Seiwert, China's Search for Partners with Shared Worldviews: Expanding the "Shanghai Cooperation Organization Family", *Asian Affairs*, 2023, Vol. 54, Issue 3, p. 461.

33 E. Seiwert, China's Search for Partners with Shared Worldviews: Expanding the "Shanghai Cooperation Organization Family", *Asian Affairs*, 2023, Vol. 54, Issue 3.

34 Y. Preiherman, *Belarus Becomes First European Member of Shanghai Cooperation Organization*, Jamestown Foundation: https://jamestown.org/program/belarus-becomes-first-european-member-of-shanghai-cooperation-organization/.

35 S. Azizi, China's Belt and Road Initiative (BRI): The Role of the Shanghai Cooperation Organization (SCO) in Geopolitical Security and Economic Cooperation, *Open Journal of Political Science*, 2024, Vol. 14, Issue 1, pp. 111–129.

36 S. Azizi, China's Belt and Road Initiative (BRI): The Role of the Shanghai Cooperation Organization (SCO) in Geopolitical Security and Economic Cooperation, *Open Journal of Political Science*, 2024, Vol. 14, Issue 1, p. 13.

the SCO played a key role in preventing the Afghan conflict from spreading to the Central Asian region.[37] Considering the possible regional disruption affecting the borders and spreading to Xinjiang, the insurance of regional stability is of importance for Chinese leadership. However, this insurance of stability is described as a concentration on mutual support for the repressive methods followed by these states. From the outside, the organization is often criticized for its lack of democratic credentials, with some labeling it a "dictators' dialogue club", implying its opposition to Western liberal democracy, especially in the fields of cooperation with the latter focusing on fostering the resilience of civil society and independent media and the SCO emphasizing security and economic cooperation than on promoting any specific political model.[38] This focus on fighting the 'extremism', 'separatism' and rejecting foreign 'interference' explains its state-to-state approach, with little transparency and no democratic controls.

This makes the SCO a coalition aimed at regime survival, supporting the status quo. Along with the institute's expansion, many Chinese and international scholars expressed concerns that SCO enlargement might dilute cohesion and hinder efforts to build a common identity due to increased cultural diversity. Scholars had long noted the organization's weak unity, and in 2015, one suggested focusing on mutual respect, cooperation and the "Shanghai Spirit" to solidify a shared identity before expanding further.[39] Later in 2022, the organization's liability and effectiveness was challenged once again amid the Shanghai Cooperation Organization (SCO) summit in Samarkand with the leaders of SCO member states when two member states border disputes resulted in deadly military escalations. Kyrgyz authorities reported that Tajik forces fired mortars targeting areas along the border and reaching as far as Batken city, located approximately 10 km inside Kyrgyz territory.[40] And the elephant in the room within the SCO framework at the moment is the Russian full-scale invasion of Ukraine, or the Special Military operation as Russia frames it, that directly conflicts with the SCO's own principle on *mutual respect for independence, sovereignty and territorial integrity*.

The expanding SCO risks becoming little more than a symbolic platform for friendly leaders, offering membership with minimal obligations while struggling to

37 S. Azizi, China's Belt and Road Initiative (BRI): The Role of the Shanghai Cooperation Organization (SCO) in Geopolitical Security and Economic Cooperation, *Open Journal of Political Science*, 2024, Vol. 14, Issue 1, p. 51.

38 S. Azizi, China's Belt and Road Initiative (BRI): The Role of the Shanghai Cooperation Organization (SCO) in Geopolitical Security and Economic Cooperation, *Open Journal of Political Science*, 2024, Vol. 14, Issue 1, p. 459.

39 S. Azizi, China's Belt and Road Initiative (BRI): The Role of the Shanghai Cooperation Organization (SCO) in Geopolitical Security and Economic Cooperation, *Open Journal of Political Science*, 2024, Vol. 14, Issue 1, p. 460.

40 C. Putz, Kyrgyz-Tajik Conflict Escalates Even Though Presidents Met at SCO (September 2022) *The Diplomat*: https://thediplomat.com/2022/09/kyrgyz-tajik-conflict-escalates-even-though-presidents-met-at-sco/.

demonstrate real-world impact.[41] Sharing informal leadership with Russia, China is the main force behind the SCO development. The organization's framework reflects Chinese values, such as mutual trust and respect for diverse civilizations, seen in the "Shanghai Spirit". Chinese slogans like Xi Jinping's "Community of Common Destiny" and "New Type of International Relations" are incorporated into SCO documents, strengthening China's views on democracy and human rights. Through the SCO, China not only promotes its norms but also amplifies its influence using multilateral platforms.[42] Legal experts argue that the SCO's principles and formulations such as the "Three Evils" framework and its principle of non-interference, undermine and often replace international human rights norms and legal principles developed over decades of effort and lessons. Building their new sovereign state identity and strengthening their independence status in the post-Communist era, Central Asian states became important actors for the Chinese-led multilateral mechanism to test and assert itself as a prominent regional initiative with ongoing enlargement.

6. SCO Expansion Implications for the Indo-Pacific

Accelerated by internal conflicts and scrutiny to address them while maintaining the status quo, China's more proactive role in the multilateral engagement has been shifting from defining regional threats along its borders through creating a regional alliance to challenge the UN system's principle and adherence to human rights and freedom with collected voices through multilateral partnerships. At the same time, Chinese leadership is maneuvering within the existing international system to protect its interests. Despite the UN Office of the High Commissioner for Human Rights (OHCHR) report findings in August suggesting possible crimes against humanity in Xinjiang, the UNHRC voted against discussing the region's human rights situation with all Central Asian states voting in favor Beijing's position on the issue, while other SCO member states did the same or abstained.[43]

In the same year, when the Speaker of the US House of Representatives Nancy Pelosi's trip to Taiwan caused a stormy reaction in the global media with concerns over an escalation of the situation in the Taiwan Strait, the SCO secretary made a statement emphasizing *the principle of "one China"*, opposing any external interference in the internal policies of member states, and advocating the preservation of

41 T. Umarov, Carnegie Endowment for International Peace, SCO Summit: China and Russia (July 2024) *Carnegie Endowment*: https://carnegieendowment.org/russia-eurasia/politika/2024/07/sco-summit-china-russia?lang=en.

42 T. Umarov, Carnegie Endowment for International Peace, SCO Summit: China and Russia (July 2024) *Carnegie Endowment*: https://carnegieendowment.org/russia-eurasia/politika/2024/07/sco-summit-china-russia?lang=en.

43 Al Jazeera, UN Human Rights Council Rejects Debate on Treatment of Uighurs (07.10.2022), *Al Jazeera*: https://www.aljazeera.com/news/2022/10/7/un-human-rights-council-rejects-debate-on-treatment-of-uighurs#:~:text=The%20UN%20Human%20Rights%20Council,to%20%E2%80%9Ccrimes%20against%20humanity%E2%80%9C.

state unity, sovereignty and territorial integrity of the SCO countries, and increasing cooperation in this area between member states in order to ensure peace, security and stability in the Organization's space.[44] Previously, SCO member state leaders have repeatedly expressed their support for Beijing on the Taiwan issue. Despite the SCO objectives and discussions not necessarily (if at all) focusing on the issues in the South China Sea, it is clear that Beijing has been successful to bring its formulations on security threats and concerns into the organization's discourse. Beijing pursuing rapid military modernization, fortifying disputed South China Sea islands, and keeping the possibility of using force to achieve its objectives in Taiwan open, therefore, will likely remain supported by its multilateral partnerships in the evolving debate on the interpretations of customary international law of the sea established within the UN framework.

7. Conclusion

Returning to the debate on *the end of history*, it is certain that the short post-Cold War triumph of Western liberal democracy created not only the multipolarity of powers, but a space to alternative ideas and mechanisms of engagement to grow. The intersection of Chinese domestic security concerns projected into puzzles of security threats in the region, enabling China to create a joint regional discourse leading the narrative and address those threats. Whether it is the relative novelty of the organization's format or the process of integrating young nations into international relations as they keep forming their post-communist identity, the SCO has a number of flaws. One of the more noticeable shortcomings of the SCO is the lack of cohesion among some members beyond the statements and handshakes of country representatives during summits. Moreover, the involvement of Russia, which stood at the origin of the SCO's founding, in the war in Ukraine without a reaction from the SCO structure in practice completely discredits its principles. This lack of response from the SCO structure on conflict escalations within the SCO territory further contributes to the critique of the SCO promoting authoritarian governance. Furthermore, the SCO has been a successful dialogue platform for Beijing to promote its role as an alternative to the West and as a regional and global power, even potentially rivaling Russia.

44 CGTN, Defending One-China: SCO Secretary-General We Support China's Right to Defend Its National Interests (05.09.2022), *SCO*: https://eng.sectsco.org/20220905/CGTNDefending-One-China-SCO-Secretary-General-We-support-Chinas-right-to-defend-its-national-911395.html.

18 Securing International Law Order in the Indo-Pacific

*Joseph Tshilomb Jonathan**

1. Introduction

The Indo-Pacific is a large and diverse region with many latent conflicts. Growing geopolitical rivalries, ongoing militarisation and improved nuclear modernisation could lead to escalation with serious impacts on the Global Economy and Security.[1] In order to equip the readers with appropriate tools for a better understanding of the various aspects characterising the Indo-Pacific Challenges, this chapter has been presented with the following features:

1) Indo-Pacific Region
2) Legal Approach and the United Nations Convention on the Law of the Sea
3) The Case of China and Taiwan
4) The Case of South China Sea
5) The People´s Republic of China versus The Philippines
6) Conclusion with final remarks

2. Indo-Pacific Region

The Indo-Pacific is a maritime region spanning the Indian and Pacific Oceans. This concept has been widely adopted in policy discourse by the United States and its allies, including Australia, Japan, South Korea, India, France, the United Kingdom, Germany and the Countries of the Association of Southeast Asians Nations. Russia and China also have strategic interests in the region. Nevertheless, they generally prefer the older term "Asia-Pacific".[2,3]

* Ph.D. Candidate, Business School, University of Winchester (England).

1 Kenny, Miles, 'The South China Sea', *Britannica.* https://www.britannica.com/editor/The-Editors-of-Encyclopedia-Britannica/4419 (28 November 2024).

2 As the term "Indo-Pacific" has a connotation of geopolitical nature and seems to be associated with 21st Century tensions reflecting maily United States's policy in the Region. Hansong Li, *The "Indo-Pacific": Intellectual Origins and International Visions in Global Contexts*, Published Online, Cambridge University Prees (2021), accessed on the 23rd of April 2025.

3 Teekah, Ethian, 'Indo-Pacific Region', *Britannica.* www.britannica.com/place/Indo-Pacific (28 November 2024).

DOI: 10.4324/9781003545750-21

While there is a broad agreement on the general area of the Indo-Pacific, countries interpret its exact boundaries differently, depending on their own strategic interests.

The increased prominence of the Indo-Pacific concept has been considered by some experts as a response to the rise of China´s power and influence.[4]

3. Economic and Military Significance of the Indo-Pacific

According to a 2022 White House report, the Region is home to half the world's population, nearly two-thirds of the world's economy and seven of the world's largest militaries. The Indo-Pacific is now the centre of global industries including manufacturing, technology, finance, energy, agriculture, fishing and tourism. Moreover, the Indo-Pacific is home to four of of the world's largest economies: the United States, China, India and Japan, As the United States and China compete for economic and geopolitical influence, their different strategies remarkably shape the regional dynamics in the Indo-Pacific, For example, in response to the United States trade within the Indo-Pacific, the Chinese "Belt and Road Initiative" represents a focused effort to extend Chinese economic influence throughout the Indo-Pacific Region.[5]

In spite of the Indo-Pacific significance for the prosperity of each country within it, there are tensions, including territorial disputes in the South China Sea, tensions on the Korean peninsula and across the Taiwan Strait.[6]

4. Legal Approach and the United Nations Convention on the Law of the Sea

The focus in this chapter is placed on the various areas of improvement in legal instruments, namely: Customary Law dealing with the regime of the ocean and the United Nations Convention on the Law of The Sea, 1982, known by the acronym UNCLOS.[7]

Section 1 Legal Approach: The International Ocean Public Order

Scheiber, Nilufer and Moon-Sang Kwon discussed the Ocean Law and engaged themselves in the debates over the 50-year legacy and the emerging issues for the years ahead. The UN Convention on the Law of the Sea, signed in 1982 and

4 Kenny, Miles, 'The South China Sea', *Britannica*. www.britannica.com/editor/The-Editors-of-Encyclopedia-Britannica/4419 (28 November 2024).

5 Rudischauser, W., 'The Indo-Pacific: Confidence-Building in Time of Growing Conflict Potential', *GIGA*, Number 6, ISSN: 1862–359 X (2023).

6 Kenny, Miles, 'The South China Sea', *Britannica*. https://www.britannica.com/editor/The-Editors-of-Encyclopedia-Britannica/4419 (28 November 2024).

7 Couper and Gold, *The Marine Environment and Sustainable Development: Law, Policy and Science*, Digitised Edition, University of Virginia (2007), p. 21.

entering into force in 1994, was the result of a compromise of vital debates on new initiatives for clarification or expansion of the scope of the regime of the Ocean. In this treatise, authors with scientific authority analyse the content of issues related to this regime in developing historical perspectives while analysing present-day issues. The list of treated issues includes the following matters: Controversies on maritime delimitation issues and responses to various challenges brought by dramatic advances in Science and Technology. Most critical in this volume is the discussion of the movement to create a regime a regime for biodiversity in the Area Beyond National Jurisdictions. Eventually, this study offers some perspectives on the effective implementation and judicial interpretations of UNCLOS, Seabed Mining issues, the geopolitics of Marine Protected Areas Declaration as well as the role of The International Maritime Organization, IMO, in responding to climate change. Furthermore, this research offers new knowledge in the field of Ocean Law and Policy since the early period of the industrial revolution and successive waves of revolutionary scientific discoveries and technological innovations which have intensified the global exploitation of Ocean and Coastal Resources. Leading scientists examined the interface of science, technology and Ocean Law historically and from present-time perspectives. Emerging challenges associated with the sustainable and equitable exploitation of the Ocean have been identified. Other issues of relevance were the following: the place of science in dispute on settlement processes, the concurrent uses of the Sea and the importance of the Ocean Governance. Burke developed **The Concept of Classic Public Order of the Ocean**. He promoted the goal of using the Law of Governance of the Sea as a tool in order to improve human dignity; he put forth the idea that the best way to protect the less-developed countries, including Small Islands Nations, within the context of the Law of the Sea was to hold nations to their treaty-based agreements and to require strong evidence of actual state practice before declaring the formation of a customary norm which is usually in favour of developed countries. Burke's argument can be used in solving conflicts of interests between countries in the use of marine resources.[8] **The Concept of Classic Public Order of the Ocean** has been confirmed in the UNCLOS Convention through **the Principle of Mankind Heritage**, which allows all of humanity (with inclusion of developing nations) to benefit both from the preservation of the marine ecosystems and the Ocean's economic resources.

In the Court's meaning, the **International Ocean Public Order** consists of the International Custom Rule that allows States in times of peace to send their warships through straits used for international navigation between two parts of the high seas without the previous authorisation of a Coastal State as long as the passage is innocent. It is also part of the policy which allows co-operation among Governments in the area of governmental regulations and a practice associated with technical matters of all kinds affecting shipping engaged in International

8 Scheiber, H., *Ocean Law Debates: The 50-Year Legacy and Emerging Issues for the Years Ahead*, The Netherlands Brill Academic Publishers (2018).

Trade, and it encourages the general adoption of the highest practicable standards in matters related to maritime safety and efficiency of navigation. In times of peace rather than in war, the principle of the freedom of maritime communication and the obligation for every State not to intentionally allow its territory to be used for acts contrary to the rights of other Nations should be secured.

***Section 2 The United Nations Convention on the Law of the Sea*[9]**

The Law of the Sea process entered into an "era of innovation" in September 1967, and Ambassador Pardo's speech to the UN General Assembly enhanced the UNCLOS process. Three months later a Seabed Committee was established, thereby inaugurating an eight-year period of designing basic rules and regulations for a new Law of the Sea Convention. Among the main issues to be dealt with were the following points: the outer limit of the continental shelf, revenue sharing from resource exploitation beyond 200 miles and the status of oceanic plateaus, ridges, banks and rises. Another issue of relevance was the guidelines for delimiting maritime boundaries between opposite and/or adjacent states. Among the non-jurisdictional issues unresolved in 1975 was the question dealing with compulsory dispute settlement and the question related to the deep Seabed Mining Regime. As with the ongoing UNCLOS process mechanisms for assessing the impact on the interpretation of the Convention's articles, a look at the following aspects is required: 1) new ocean technologies and new ocean uses, including the transfer of technologies to ocean uses by developing countries; 2) the compliance or non-compliance of States with Convention rules and regulations and 3) the implementation of the Convention's action articles calling for cooperation at the sub-regional and regional levels among and between developed and developing nations.[10]

The main provision of the UNCLOS with respect to intervention at Sea is Article 221 of Part XII (Protection and preservation of the marine environment), paragraph 1, which provides that nothing in this Part shall prejudice the right of States, pursuant to international law, both customary and conventional, to take and enforce measures beyond the territorial sea proportionate to the actual or threatened damage to protect their coastline or related interests, including fishing, from pollution or threat of pollution following upon a maritime casualty or acts pertaining to such a casualty which may reasonably be expected to result in major harmful consequences. Article 221 confirms the right of coastal States to take intervention measures at sea.[11]

Aspects of **Customary International Law** have been maintained in the Law of the Sea Convention. The question is whether or not the Intervention Convention provides a complete picture of the present state of public international law for

9 United Nations, 'United Nations Convention on the Law of the Sea' (1982). un.org/depts/los/convention_agreements/texts/unclos_e.pdf (28 November 2024).

10 Couper and Gold, *The Marine Environment and Sustainable Development.*

11 Couper and Gold, *The Marine Environment and Sustainable Development*, pp. 93–107.

the maritime intervention powers of coastal States. Is the Intervention Convention exhaustive in this respect? Does Customary International Law leave room for the taking of intervention measures other than those specified in the Intervention Convention and Protocol? By referring explicitly to both customary and conventional International Law, Article 221 of the Law of the Sea Convention clearly indicates that Customary Law is still applicable, in spite of the existence of the Intervention Convention and Protocol. This means that Customary Law was incorporated in the Intervention Convention and as such should be considered as the basic leading guide on intervention matters by those States which are not a Party to this Convention.[12] With respect to the right of intervention by Coastal States, Customary International Law has its own place beside the Intervention Convention and Protocol in cases of serious maritime incidents not covered by those instruments. Another issue of relevance is whether intervention in such cases is only allowed in case of a threat to a vital ecological interest, similar to that of "The Amoco Cadiz" disaster off the French Coast at Bretagne (1978) following UNCLOS as well as to protect other interests, such as vital economic interests.[13] A restriction to ecological interests would not be applicable because of the fact that vital interests of a Coastal State may obviously be damaged by certain non-pollution incidents. Eventually, it should be accepted that a State, Party to the Intervention Convention and Protocol has the right of intervention vis-à-vis vessels flying the flag of a non-Party. It should be noted that there are conflicting views expressed on this matter. It would be unacceptable if flag States, by not becoming a Party to the Intervention Convention, could offend the legitimate exercise of the right of intervention by Coastal States.

As Ocean and coastal resources will not last forever, there are limits to their availability. There are limits to the extent to which the renewable resources and ecological services of the Ocean can be renewed or maintained.[14] There are obvious limitations of availability to fisheries, use of space, perturbations of habitats and input of pollutants. Therefore,

> The traditional view which considers freedom of the seas with the right of any number of users to exploit a resource as long as they apply some agreed rules should be excluded. There should be provisions under which a user can acquire the right to exclude others from participating directly in the same use. A distinction should be considered between the right of access to a resource and such rights as Free Passage of ships. The following chapter will show how the rules are being applied within the particular cases of the South China Sea (Mainland China versus The Philippines) and the case of Mainland China versus Taiwan.

12 Couper and Gold, *The Marine Environment and Sustainable Development*, pp. 21–25, 93–103.

13 Conan, G., 'The Long Term Oil Spill Effects of the Amoco Cadiz', *Philosophical Transactions of the Royal Society of Biological Sciences*. https://doi.org/10.1098

14 Couper and Gold, *The Marine Environment and Sustainable Development*, pp. 21–31, 91–110.

The Mainland China versus the Philippines and the case of Mainland China versus Taiwan cover the Strait of Malacca which is a major shipping route.

This Region is essential for the prosperity of each country within its range. It is subject to recurrent tensions and violent extremism in South and Southeast Asia.

(Britannica, n.d.)

5. The Case of China and Taiwan

Taiwan, or the Republic of China, is an island separated from Mainland China by the Taiwan Strait. It has been governed independently from Mainland China, which has the official name of the People's Republic of China since 1949, following the end of the Second World War.[15]

China considers Taiwan a renegade province and seeks to unify Taiwan with the People's Republic of China.[16]

Faced with China's military threats and intimidation, the Taiwan government continuously seeks the United Nations' assistance for its recognition as a sovereign State. On the 23rd of August 2022, Taiwan's diplomatic allies issued a joint statement expressing support for Taiwan and advocating peace and stability across the Taiwan Strait. Taiwan repeatedly confirms its national sovereignty and security, exercising restraint and refraining from engaging in disputes. Moreover, it has engaged in pragmatic approaches actively involving participation in the United Nations. It requested that diplomatic allies (Western Countries) speak up for Taiwan at the General Assembly of the United Nations. Taiwan feels the persistent exclusion of its peoples from the United Nations System, advocating the respect of universal values of human rights, which are an important element of the United Nations. The Taiwanese Government hopes to join forces with all the nations of the world in facing global challenges. It believes that Chinese actions undermined peace and stability in the sub-region.[17]

Taiwan claims that China has long pressured the United Nations to adopt an expansive and incorrect interpretation of the United Nations' General Assembly Resolution 2758, which has been the main reason for Taiwan exclusion from the UN System. This resolution does not authorise China to represent Taiwan at the United Nations. Taiwan and China are both independent sovereign States. The UN should ensure that Taiwan is afforded equal rights and due dignity to participate in meetings, mechanisms and activities related to the UN Sustainable Development. Goals and to make contributions. The people of Taiwan aspire to participate in the

15 Center for Prevention Action, *Confrontation Over Taiwan*. org/global-conflict-tracker/conflict/confrontation-over-taiwan (24 November 2024).

16 Teekah, Ethan, 'Indo-Pacific Region', *Britannica*. https://www.britannica.com/place/Indo-Pacific (20 November 2024).

17 Teekah, 'Indo-Pacific Region'.

United Nations' activities. They seek to demonstrate their democratic values and to promote security across the Taiwan Strait. Taiwan seeks to be re-established as a full member State of the United Nations.

Mainland China asserts that there is only "One China" and that Taiwan is part of this "Only One China". The People's Republic of China is the only legitimate Government of China. This Chinese approach is called "The One China Principle" and seeks Taiwan's possible "Unification" with The People´s Republic of China. It claims that Taiwan is bound by the 1992 Consensus reached between representatives of the Chinese Communist Party (CCP) and the Kuomintang (KMT) party which ruled Taiwan at that time. Nevertheless, the CCP and KMT do not share the same interpretation of this consensus, which was never intended, according to Taiwan, to solve the question of Taiwan's legal status. For Mainland China, the 1992 Consensus reflects an agreement that "The two sides of the strait belong to One China and would work together to seek national reunification. For the KMT (Taiwan), that means "One China", different interpretation", with the The Republic of China (Taiwan) standing as the "One China". Taiwan's KMT constitution recognizes China, Mongolia, Taiwan, Tibet and the South China Sea as part of the Republic of China (Taiwan). The KMT does not support Taiwan's independence and has always called for closer ties with Mainland China.[18]

The KMT's chief rival party, the Democratic Progressive Party, DPP, does not accept the 1992 Consensus. At present, the DPP calls for reopening the dialogue with Mainland China to "replace confrontation and promises to maintain the 'cross-strait status quo'". Nevertheless, Mainland China maintains its long-standing proposal for Taiwan, affirming that Taiwan would be incorporated into the Mainland under the formula of "One country, two systems". This is the same formula used for Hong Kong, which was guaranteed the ability to preserve its political and economic systems with a high degree of autonomy.

Such a proposal appears to be unpopular among the Taiwanese peoples. Even the KMT has rejected the "One country, two systems" proposal from Mainland China.

Possible Negative Consequences of the Conflict of China versus Taiwan

Recently, China has deliberately escalated its military intimidation against Taiwan and attempted to unilaterally alter the status quo across the Taiwan Strait. This violated the prohibition on the use of force and the principle of settling disputes by peaceful means as established in the United Nations Charter. China's action arose serious concerns around the globe.

2 There is a risk that Taiwan could be unified with Mainland China by force even if Taiwan aspires to self- determination as a sovereign country. The People's Republic of China has ramped up political and military pressures on Taiwan.

18 Teekah, 'Indo-Pacific Region'.

3 Even if the USA is for the status quo, implying the “One China Policy” and avoidance of Armed Conflicts, it is not excluded that the USA could go to war over the Taiwanese issue.

6. The Case of South China Sea

***Chosen Case:* The People’s Republic of China v. The Philippines**

China claims territories at the Second Thomas Shoul presently belonging to the Philippines. The overall claim of China is related to claims of sovereignty over the sea and the sea’s estimated 11 billion barrels of untapped oil and 190 trillion cubic feet of natural gas. The Chinese claim has led to competing claims from Brunei, Indonesia, Malaysia, the Philippines, Taiwan and Vietnam. The failure of Chinese and Southeast Asian Nations to resolve the disputes diplomatically could undermine International Laws governing maritime disputes and lead to militarisation in the South China Sea.

Chinese Claim

Under International Law, foreign militaries cannot conduct intelligence-gathering activities, such as reconnaissance flights in its Exclusive Economic Zone, EEZ. According to the United States, claimant countries, under the United Nations Convention of the Law of the Sea, UNCLOS, should have freedom of navigation through the Economic Exclusive Zone in the Sea and are not required to notify claimants of military activities.

In July 2016, the Permanent Court of Arbitration at The Hague ruled on a claim brought against China by the Philippines under UNCLOS, ruling in favour of the Philippines on almost every aspect of the claim.[19] However, China refused to accept the court ruling in spite of the fact that the People’s Republic of China is a State party to the treaty establishing the tribunal.[20]

Recent Development of the Case

China has significantly increased the country’s presence in the South China Sea, building military infrastructure comprising naval bases and airstrips on the contested territory. The Chinese also send massive fishing vessels into the EEZs of other countries. China moved an oil rig into Vietnamese water, leading to massive protests in Vietnam.

In addition to that, attempts have been made to block rivals’ efforts including arrests of foreign fishermen and sailors in waters considered to belong to China.

19 International Permanent Court of Arbitration, *The South China Sea Arbitration (The Republic of Philippines v. The People’s Republic of China)*. pca-cpa.org/ar/cases/7/ (24 November 2024).

20 Teekah, ‘Indo-Pacific Region’.

In 2020, tensions appeared with the increase in maritime confrontations between China and the Philippines, prompting joint naval drills between the Philippines and the United States in the South China Sea. In 2023, China revealed a revised map of its territory in the South China Sea, claiming a larger portion of the Sea. A 10th dash was added to include the island of Taiwan and about the entirety of the Spratly Islands being a Chinese territory. This map was rejected by countries in the South China Sea.

It is worth noting the introduction of the Concept of the Transitioning Security Order in the Indo-Pacific, consisting of a set of actionable recommendations for India-EU collaborative security community in the Indo-Pacific.[21]

7. Conclusion

The overall situation in the Indo-Pacific is a complex one. The notion that two nuclear nuclear-armed strategic competitors (the United States and China) should not try to manage their rivalry was unusual even in the days of U.S. diplomat George Kennan and U.S. President Ronald Reagan. The reason for that is because efforts to manage competition make the United States more competitive. Such actions convince the American peoples and U.S. allies and partners that the United States is a responsible actor and that they can confidently rely on Washington´s strategy. Excessively confrontational positions could leave the United States standing alone with limited tools. China is aware of this situation, which is why it often tries to blame tensions on Washington. The current American Government realised a shift in priority to Asia has been considered as a notable success. It is argued that relations with China are steadier than those inherited. There is at least a floor on which more can be done, even though Taiwan remains an obvious source of tension to which both Washington and Beijing are paying far too little attention.

As to the Philippines, the country is a strategic partner to the United States and has concluded a military convention with the U.S. In addition to that, its membership in the United Nations makes it possible to act actively at the international level in order to secure its interests.

In addition to the strategic diplomacy, this work advocates the principle of solving conflicts in the Indo-Pacific by the rules of Law in order to avoid militarisation in the region.

References

Britannica, *Strait of Malacca- Major Shipping Route*, Online Resource, accessed on the 23rd of April 2025.

Center for Prevention Action, *Confrontation Over Taiwan*. org/global-conflict-tracker/conflict/confrontation-over-taiwan (20 November 2024).

21 Krishnamwaty, Rajeshwari and Gheasy, Richard, *The transitioning security order in the Indo-Pacific*. asia.fes.de/news/security-order-indo-pacific (24 November 2024).

Conan, G., 'The Long Term Oil Spills Effects of the Amoco Cadiz', *The Philosophical Transactions of the Royal Society of Biological Sciences*. https://doi.org/10.1098 (28 November 2024).

Couper and Gold, *The Marine Environment and Sustainable Development: Law, Policy and Science,* Digitised Edition, University of Virginia (2007).

Doshi, Rush, 'What Does America Want From China?', *Foreign Affairs*, pp. 174–178 (July/August 2024).

Elder, Danny L., 'Sustainable Use of Marine Ecosystems', *The Marine Environment and Sustainable Development: Law, Policy and Science* (Couper and Gold, Digital Version, University of Virginia, 2007).

International Permanent Court of Arbitration, *The South China Sea Arbitration (The Republic of Philippines v. The People's Republic of China)*. pca-cpa.org/ar/cases/7/ (24 November 2024).

Kenny, Miles, 'The South China Sea', *Britannica* (2024). https://www.britannica.com/editor/The-Editors-of-Encyclopedia-Britannica/4419.

Matheus, Jessica T., 'What Was the Biden Doctrine?', *Foreign Affairs*, pp. 47–51 (September/October 2024).

McLaughin, R., *Technology and New Challenges to Ocean Law,* Brill Academic Publishers (2015).

Rudischauuser, Wolfgang, 'The Indo-Pacific: Confidence-Building in Time of Growing Conflict Potential', *GIGA*, Number 6, ISSN: 1862–359 X (2023).

Scheiber, H., *Ocean Law Debates: The 50-Year Legacy and Emerging Issues for the Years Ahead,* The Netherlands Brill Academic Publishers (2018).

Schneider, M., *Combining Arbitration with Conciliation: Towards an International Arbitration Culture,* ICCA Congress Series No. 8, 57, Albert van den Berg Ed. (1996).

Strong, S. I., 'Beyond International Commercial Arbitration? The Promise of International Commercial Mediation', *HeinOnline,* 45 Wash, UJL 10 (2014).

UN, 'United Nations Convention on the Law of the Sea' (1982). un.org/depts./los/convention_agreements/texts/unclos/unclos_e.pdf

Vierros, M., 'Governance of Marine Areas Beyond National Jurisdictions', *The Magazine of the United Nations,* Liv No. 5, 1&2 (2017).

Wallenfeld, Jeff, 'The South China Sea', *Britannica* (2024). https://www.britannica.com/place/south-china-sea

19 The New South Pacific Diplomacy

*John Wasko**

1. Introduction

Post-World War II major power diplomacy among independent South Pacific nations is outmoded. Modern twenty-first century Pacific diplomacy needs to be reinvented.

The old diplomacy fails to recognize the global significance of military and industrial use of seabed-critical mineral resources present in the South Pacific nations' Exclusive Economic Zones (EEZ).[1]

United States Geological Survey (USGS), Japanese, Chinese, Moana Minerals and Indian research data indicate that billions of tons of subsea Electric Vehicle (EV) battery-critical minerals lie on the deep abyssal open ocean floor in areas under the jurisdiction of the International Seabed Authority (ISA) and within the sovereign EEZ areas of independent South Pacific nations such as Tonga, Papua New Guinea, Solomon Islands, Niue, Nauru, Cook Islands and American Samoa.[2]

The new era of South Pacific diplomatic relations needs to recognize these important physical resource facts and adjust appropriately in several ways: One: South Pacific Island nations can no longer be considered small island land masses

* Executive Director, American Samoa Economic Development Council.

1 Anna Powles, Tess Newton Cain. *Why the Pacific Islands Is Seeing a Rise in 'Defense Diplomacy'*. 2024. United States Institute of Peace. https://www.usip.org/publications/2024/05/why-pacific-islands-seeing-rise-defense-diplomacy

2 James R. Hein, Brandie R. McIntyre, and David Z. Piper. *Marine Mineral Resources of Pacific Islands–A Review of the Exclusive Economic Zones of Islands of U.S. Affiliation, Excluding the State of Hawaii*. 2005. United States Geological Survey Circular. https://pubs.usgs.gov/publication/cir1286

Japan International Cooperation Agency and Metal Mining Agency of Japan. *Ocean Resources Investigation In the Sea Area of SOPAC. Report on the Joint Basic Study for the Development of Resources*. 1991. Japan International Cooperation Agency. https://docs.google.com/document/d/1zo8z_jst9NpR_KgEScHQAGbVkziqON3vUAct7SEuQ2w/edit

Christopher Kelley and Diva Amon. *Deep-Sea Mining Interests and Activities in the Western Pacific*. 2016. Ocean Exploration. https://oceanexplorer.noaa.gov/okeanos/explorations/ex1606/background/mining/welcome.html

Pacific Coastal and Marine Science Center. *Manganese Nodules from the Cook Islands EEZ*. 2015. U.S. Geological Survey. https://www.usgs.gov/media/images/manganese-nodules-cook-islands-eez

DOI: 10.4324/9781003545750-22

jutting out in the South Pacific Ocean dependent on foreign aid for financial sustainability. The World War II concept of "steppingstone" islands and "chain of pearls" defense lines no longer bears the weight of diplomatic significance in the twenty-first century. The South Pacific islands include hundreds of thousands of square miles of sovereign ocean EEZ area. Two: the sovereign EEZ areas, including the mid-equatorial Pacific United Nations Law of the Sea Clarion Clipperton Zone (CCZ), include the critical minerals required to build a global recyclable circular energy loop. The total area of both entities possesses sufficient supplies of critical minerals to end northern hemisphere-originating carbon atmosphere pollution, the main source of planet-threatening climate warming oxygen depletion.

These subsea critical mineral deposits are abundant in base metals used in the manufacture of recyclable EV batteries, industrial magnets, high-strength ferrous metal alloys, smartphones, satellites and computer components. The critical minerals include cobalt, manganese, copper, lithium and rare earth metals.

The global demand for critical minerals is growing exponentially. Terrestrial-based critical mineral mines are currently the major source of raw mineral materials. Terrestrial mines are more than complicated and difficult to develop. The elapsed time from start to productive mining operations usually exceeds ten years. Equally significant, the recovery of useful quality minerals from terrestrial mines continues to degrade. As a direct result, commodity prices of critical minerals escalate.[3]

Critical mineral and rare earth supplies have critical mineral end users seeking new sources for end production products. Until the recent demand surge for critical minerals escalated, the expense of developing new deep sea excavation tools did not justify the investment costs or return on investment. Aggressive seabed mining companies transitioned existing terrestrial land devices to recover deep sea critical mineral ores. Their excavation tools were legacy relatives of terrestrial tracked vehicles; basically, a refit excavator with a dredge device retrofitted to harvest minerals from the seabed floor. Environmentally, the reconfigured tools failed the basic tests of disrupting the deep-sea habitat of many living creatures not yet recorded on ocean taxonomies.

Along with the seafloor dredging devices, a pneumatic suction riser tube was redesigned from the dredging industry. Both reinvented recovery tools were subject to catastrophic single incident failure.[4]

Nevertheless, both private companies and sovereign nations rushed to fill the critical mineral supply void dominated by a handful of critical mineral net exporters such as China, Botswana, Australia and the Democratic Republic of Congo.

3 Richard W. Baker. *The International Relations of the Southwest Pacific: New Visions and Voices*. 1992. East West Center, Honolulu, Hawaii. https://scholarspace.manoa.hawaii.edu/server/api/core/bitstreams/4c539d1f-83ee-4e18-a9b9–02da9f2a9feb/content

Analysis – IEA. *Global Critical Minerals Outlook*. 2024. International Energy Agency. https://www.iea.org/reports/global-critical-minerals-outlook-2024

4 Massachusetts Institute of Technology. *Mining the Deep Sea*. 2020. YouTube Video. https://youtu.be/MWvCtF1itQM?si=_5eFWelzZxy2OAx8

Major auto manufacturers and tech giants such as Amazon, Alphabet, Microsoft and Apple engaged in mineral supply contracts, often relying on Conflict Affected and High-Risk Area (CAHRA) producers. Various corporate Conflict Mineral Reports (CMR), in keeping with the reporting requirements of the Dodd Frank Act, evaded addressing questionable practices that include environmental and human rights issues.[5]

2. Exploration

The International Seabed Authority, an arm of the United Nations, has issued 31 mineral exploration contracts under the principles of the Law of the Sea; Freedom of Access, Sovereign Rights and Common Good. Seventeen of the contracts are positioned in the Clarion Clipperton Zone. ISA has apportioned CCZ seabed mining tracts to South Pacific nations.[6]

Of particular diplomatic interests are the cooperative contracts that unite South Pacific nations, notably Nauru and Tonga, with seabed mining entities. To date, The Metals Company (TMC), a Canada-based company, has completed several exploration surveys, environmental assessments and collection of critical mineral-rich laden polymetallic nodules from the CCZ under the banner of Nauru Ocean Resource Initiative (NORI), a corporate entity wholly owned by TMC.

China, India and Japan have all begun exploratory phases by state-supported mining entities of critical minerals within their territorial waters or seabed plots licensed through the ISA. The Cook Islands have issued exploratory licenses to two private seabed mining companies, Cook Island Consortium and Moana Minerals. The Cook Islands prime minister, Mark Brown, has been adamant that his country's 30-year experience in developing a regulatory mining format for environmentally safe extraction is a verifiable pathway to a second anchor industry in the South Pacific independent nation economically dependent on tourism. The United States of America recently began diplomatic relations with the Cook Islands.

Much of the economic gold rush for seabed critical minerals has originated from years of ocean geological research study. Japan, the USGS, China and Norway have conducted extensive research expeditions in their own territorial waters or in the EEZs of client nations. As the technology advances and becomes more environmentally responsible, the time frame to actual seabed mineral extraction shortens.

NORI, the TMC asset, is scheduled to begin seabed mineral extraction in the ISA CCZ in 2025. Impossible Metals, a Pasadena, California-based high tech company with extensive knowledge and experience in robotics, artificial intelligence,

5 Juliane Kippenberg. *Mining for the Energy Transition Needs to Respect Human Rights*, 2024. Human Rights Watch. https://www.hrw.org/news/2024/07/10/mining-energy-transition-needs-respect-human-rights#:~:text=Human%20Rghts%20Watch%20has%20documented water%20scarcity%20and%20police%20violence

6 International Seabed Authority. *Exploration Contracts*. 2024. https://www.isa.org.jm/exploration-contracts/

solid state sensory devices and remote undersea vehicle operations, has applied to the US regulatory agency, the Bureau of Ocean Energy Management (BOEM), for a license to survey the American Samoa EEZ for critical minerals. Japan, China and India have moved forward in their own critical mineral exploration endeavors.

Without exception, the race to solve the critical mineral demand is growing in importance to a wide and diverse range of interested downstream, midstream, upstream and end users. Unlike China, Japan and India, where sovereign nations own their terrestrial and seabed critical mineral resources, the active downstream mining companies are forced to make cooperative agreements with sovereign nations, mainly in the South Pacific, to access their sought-after mineral resources.[7]

3. History of Exploitation

The presence of natural resources in the South Pacific is not new. The resources have been both a source of revenue for the islands but also a source of foreign exploitation by northern and southern hemisphere powers. The list of exploited South Pacific natural resources is rather extensive and wide-ranging. The first voyagers to arrive in the South Pacific, from Vasco de Balboa (1513) to James Cook (1767), were mainly explorers seeking new trade routes or scouting for economic opportunities for their supportive nation states. Later expeditions began the process of reaping the island's natural riches. Over the ensuing centuries, coral, sandalwood and pearls were misappropriated and carried off to distant markets.[8]

The colonial era of French and British explorers found a rapacious appetite for more barterable and income-producing goods. Timber, ores, fish and agricultural crops devastated natural environments, all in the name of colonial national interests. Eventually human trafficking, a slave trade process called "blackbirding", displaced thousands of islanders sent off to perform menial work tasks in foreign lands. By the 1900s, islanders were relegated to carnival sideshows as "savages" from the "uncivilized islands of the South Pacific".[9]

Even do-gooders brought their brands of cultural misappropriation. Missionaries representing various sects of belief, Congregationalists, Methodists and Catholics imposed Western cultural taboos and beliefs that desecrated thousands of years of cultural customs of Austronesian lineage and history.

7 International Seabed Authority. *Secretary_General_Annual_Report_2023_Chapter4*. 2023. https://www.isa.org.jm/wp-content/uploads/2023/07/ISA_Secretary_General_Annual_Report_2023.pdf

8 James M. Anthony. *Conflict over Natural Resources in the Pacific*. 1986. United Nations University. https://archive.unu.edu/unupress/unupbooks/80a04e/80A04E0e.htm

9 Francis James West and Sophie Foster. *Colonial Rule in the Pacific Islands*. 2024. Britannica. https://www.britannica.com/place/Pacific-Islands/Colonial-rule

Regional Office for Southeast Asia and the Pacific. *Patterns and Prevalence of Trafficking in Persons in the Pacific Islands*. 2023. United Nations Office on Drugs and Crime. https://www.unodc.org/roseap/pacific/2023/10/trafficking-persons-report-pacific-islands/story.htm

The long list of exploitative diversions has left modern South Pacific islanders with a hearty distrust of foreign investors. Since the 1950s, the target of exploitation has been the protein-rich commodity of tuna fish. Multinational agencies such as the Forum Fisheries Agency (FFA) headquartered in Honiara, Solomon Islands, subsidized the American purse seiner fleet consisting of 47 large tuna fishing vessels. The amount of money paid to the island nations was genuinely paltry compared to the retail value of processed fish sold in the American and foreign markets.

Today, wireless cell phone operators have swept into South Pacific regional markets to scoop up data- and voice-based revenues from addicted cell phone users. The iPhone and its imitators have become the twenty-first-century bauble trinket reminiscent of days gone by.

The centuries-old history of exploitation has left South Pacific governments, individual citizens, local entrepreneurs and non-governmental organizations (NGO) somewhat wary of the emerging deep sea mining industry. The concerns of those entities are verifiably justified.

Ninety-nine percent of all carbon pollution originates in the northern hemisphere: China, USA and Europe. Fossil fuel consumption is directly responsible for this destructive state of affairs. With ocean levels rising, low-lying South Pacific islands are most at risk of climate change-based inundation. Pacific islanders are loath to hear "solutions" from the very same people responsible for the inexorably encroaching problem.

In no uncertain terms, South Pacific nations' subsea critical mineral resources hold the real solution to the northern hemisphere's seemingly indifferent attitude toward indigenous island populations.

It is exactly this paradox that gives Pacific islanders pause to wonder if, in the minds of northern hemisphere mining entrepreneurs, critical minerals are merely the next exploitable resource sought by the energy-addicted northern world. The step from colonial rule to modern critical mineral exploitation is very small.[10]

In the midst of the seabed mining entities setting their sights on sovereign critical minerals are the rather ubiquitous "solutions" to rising ocean levels offered by northern hemisphere powers and social influencers. Money for seawalls, "resilience" and climate warming "effects" are band-aid answers to more serious and global environmental damage. International environmental entities such as the Pew Foundation, Greenpeace and the World Wildlife Fund rail on about global warming. Yet none of them are cognizant enough to own up to the very inconvenient apparent fact that collectively they contribute to the problem, not the solution.

South Pacific islanders see this problem-solving anomaly both with disdain and irony. The very same people who have caused the global anthropogenic destruction of the planet are offering seriously nonsensical solutions to the true root causes of

10 Nick Bainton and Emilka Skrzypek. *Pacific Nations Are Extraordinarily Rich in Critical Minerals. But Mining Them May Take a Terrible Toll*. 2022. The Conversation Getty. https://theconversation.com/pacific-nations-are-extraordinarily-rich-in-critical-minerals-but-mining-them-may-take-a-terrible-toll-187172

the problem and, by definition, a tangible threat to South Pacific islanders' way of life and existence.

To South Pacific islanders, the northern hemisphere perception of global warming as an existential global threat seems grossly inadequate at best and socially demeaning at worst. Why, by the reasoning of the average South Pacific islander, should he or she take advice and counsel from a person who drives to work in an internal combustion engine automobile, works in an airconditioned office and chats on a solid-state memory device, and why should they be, in any way, qualified to talk about global warming solutions? It seems ironic to a South Pacific islander that within the borders of their EEZ lies the solution to the very problem caused by the exact same people who are so insistent on entering their South Pacific EEZs to carry off valuable and sought-after critical minerals.

The exploitative cycle is merely starting anew again.

4. The World Has Changed

The last great South Pacific exploitative upheaval was tuna fish. Since then, the world has changed significantly.

Social media, unfettered access to information via the internet and video conferencing applications have made the dissemination of information universal. Today, rare earth metal commodity prices are available at the tap of a button on a smartphone or computer. Competing offers for mining contracts from nation states and private companies are easily shared among government officials and private sector managers. The dark world of "quid pro quo" exchanges is less dark than ever before.[11]

However, the long-established residual effect of South Pacific exploitation courses throughout the business world even today. The standing belief that South Pacific islanders can be cheated out of the true value of their subsea resources is still a predominant notion which drives the profit line on many companies' balance sheets. Critical minerals are just the next item set for exploitation by modern-day pirates.

Very few times in our lives do we own something that other people want. Yet that is exactly the dilemma South Pacific islanders now face. Given the long history of exploitation for short-term gains, the critical mineral-rich nations face new challenges about their economic futures.

In the midst of this dilemma stand the sovereign and global policy makers and regulators. ISA, who control more than 50 percent of the world's ocean seabed and a large volume of seabed critical minerals, have applied international Law of the Sea principles to solving the regulatory issues. In addition to parceling out sectors of the CCZ to individual undeveloped South Pacific Island nations, they have applied well-intended platitudes such as "benefit to all mankind" to their efforts.

11 Pacific Regional DC Hub. *#SwipeUp4Change Hailed as a Success*. 2024. National Determined Contributions, Fiji. https://pacificndc.org/articles/swipeup4change-hailed-success

ISA is understandably pulled in many directions, including the very real overarching need to solve the renewable energy crisis before global warming tips the balance of planet earth survival into the danger zone.[12]

Environmental concerns worry that yet-to-be-discovered deep ocean marine species and the contribution they add to planet survival are threatened by environmentally irresponsible seabed mineral extraction methods. One nation, Nauru, with mining rights and critical mineral resources in the CCZ, has forged ahead in partnership with TMC to soon begin mineral extraction mining. Other nations with mining exploration and extracting contracts in the CCZ are likely to follow Nauru's lead. In the meantime, ISA is still searching for a consensus on mining regulations that satisfies all parties.

The Cook Islands represent the de facto interests of many South Pacific sovereign nations. Thirty years of research and study in their large EEZ has produced an extensive legal framework specifying the ways, means, threats, advantages and benefits of seabed mining. The Cook Islands' conclusion is that local economic benefits and the need to end global warming outweigh the environmental debits of deep-sea environmental concerns.

The Cook Islands' decision to move forward and share their learned knowledge publicly may very well resonate favorably with other South Pacific nations. The northern Cook Islands especially are a collection of low-lying atolls. Global warming and rising sea levels pose a direct threat to their existence. In very pragmatic terms, the Cook Islands have weighed their own physical and economic survival to reconcile the advantages and disadvantages of seabed extraction mining. In practical terms, the Cook Islands have history on their side. In the history of mankind, especially in the nineteenth, twentieth and twenty-first centuries, the universal demand for energy has always outweighed the concerns for the environment. Fracking, whaling, offshore oil and gas drilling, clear-cut timber evisceration, open pit mining, stream tailing pollution and nuclear reactor disasters are the most glaring examples of environmental deprivations.

The Cook Islands have settled on another practical decision. Their lease agreements to date are only exploratory. However, the agreements assure a hefty percentage of mineral revenues to the Cook Islands government. As the Cook Islands Prime Minister, Mark Brown, makes his rounds of conferences and Pacific island meetings, he whispers a gospel of indigenous rights and equity ownership to his South Pacific counterparts. Most recently non-governmental organizations such as the American Samoa Economic Development Council (ASEDC) have taken up a similar clarion call. Between the two agencies, the critical mineral message to South Pacific nations is clear: "don't get ripped off or tricked into giving away your

12 Analysis – IEA. *Key Findings – Introducing the Critical Minerals Policy Tracker*. 2022. International Energy Agency. https://www.iea.org/reports/introducing-the-critical-minerals-policy-tracker
Secretariat of the Pacific Community. *ACHIEVEMENTS OF THE SPC-EU Deep Sea Minerals Project*. 2014. South Pacific Commission. https://dsm.gsd.spc.int/public/files/Deep%20Sea%20Minerals%20Projects%20Achievements%20Brochure_V2.pdf

sovereign riches". This very powerful advice resonates because it unquestionably recalls past colonial, and by extension, exploitation history.

5. World Power Energy Dependence

Foreign powers need also take note. Both ISA, the Cook Islands and ASEDC bring light to the fact that post-World War II diplomacy is anchored in the worn-out theory that Asia Pacific nations form a defense perimeter or military "stepping stones" to form a dual defense barrier and offensive attack line against Japanese forces. That logic no longer applies.

China, the United States of America and Japan are energy-dependent. In order to advance the energy agenda, these energy-dependent nations certainly realize that the seabed critical minerals they pursue all lie within the sovereign EEZs of South Pacific nations. A radical change in their foreign policy will be required in order to access seabed minerals from the island nations at fair and equitable costs. Rather than think of South Pacific independent nations as isolated land masses jutting out of the Pacific oceans, the independent island nations are surrounded by hundreds of thousands of square miles of ocean waters, namely their EEZs. Until the world energy-consuming powers recognize and accept this reality, South Pacific nations are likely to be wary of their neo-colonial intent and negotiate with them at arm's length.

The hope of ISA, Cook Islands, ASEDC and possibly the Pacific Islands Forum (PIF) is that all South Pacific nations will adopt a long-term economically beneficial equity approach to utilizing their seabed critical mineral resources.

While demand for energy seems infinite, the supply of critical minerals, although immense, is finite. The twenty-first-century juggling act for the new coterie of economic influencers will be to dispel short-term gains over the long-term well-being vis-a-vis long-term profit-sharing equity agreements. Nauru learned that difficult lesson with their exhaustible supply of guano fertilizer. Immense profits were realized by Australian mining companies while supplies lasted. When the guano ran out, the fertilizer miners packed up and went home. Nauru was left mostly broke with a mountain of debt for several worthless investments, including real properties and an airline.

6. Trillion-Dollar Enterprise

The threats facing South Pacific nations are large. Several nations, including the Independent State of Samoa, have issued a temporary critical mineral mining moratorium. The moratorium provides the nation with breathing room to sort out the advantages and disadvantages incumbent with their resources.

One specific threat facing all South Pacific nations is financial debt. Many nations such as Fiji pay a high percentage of their annual gross domestic product in order to satisfy annual debt service. In the South Pacific, most bilateral debt is owed to international lenders such as the Asia Development Bank (ADV), the International Monetary Fund (IMF) and the World Bank (WB). However, a substantial bilateral debt amount is owed to countries such as China and Australia

The silent threat to a long-term equity solution is the possibility that China, for example, will barter debt relief or debt forgiveness in exchange for unilateral and unfettered access to EEZ critical mineral-rich resources. Other tempting short-term access for riches proposals from lender nations include infrastructure development, low interest loans, state-owned surveillance systems or simple debt-free cash gifts.[13]

The reality is that subsea critical mineral excavation is a global multi-trillion-dollar enterprise. South Pacific politicians and traditional leaders may easily be persuaded by modern-day trinkets of debt forgiveness or free infrastructure projects in exchange for their riches and the insatiable demand for world energy.

The lessons learned from oil-rich nations offer guidance for independent South Pacific nations. African countries that adapted long-term solutions are reaping the benefits of advanced infrastructure development projects and quality of life improvements for their populations. Nations that pocketed large sums of oil and gas revenues for personal enrichment remain backward and dependent on foreign aid for financial sustainability.

In the South Pacific, there is still no consensus on how each individual nation will allocate their resources. The Cook Islands have made their intentions public and transparent. Their stated goals are long-term and beneficial to the development for the greater good of their population. Other nations have a less beneficial history of general population wealth sharing.

The stark reality is that energy-consumptive nations and private enterprises have their own profit-driven agendas. Both China and the US have bent environmental standards to access energy resources. Terrestrial mining and oil and gas extraction are the most glaring examples.

These threats leave it mainly up to the operations regulators, ISA, NGOs and the independent producer states such as Nauru, Cook Islands and American Samoa, to determine regional frameworks to guide their financial futures. The existing examples of mining operations in island nations such as Papua New Guinea and New Caledonia do not provide great clarity. Indigenous populations have disrupted mining operations, sometimes violently, after seeing their ancestral natural resources carted off while profits remained largely in the hands of foreign mining companies and local governments.

Much of the problem originates from the long and unfortunate history of the islands themselves. Unschooled in and unfamiliar with commercial negotiations and contract management, the island negotiators fall prey to unscrupulous business

13 Ilya Epikhin, Carlo Stella, Amer Hage Chahine, Trung Ghi, Alexey Pankov, Artem Malkov and Marwane Smaiti. *A $20 Trillion Opportunity*. 2024. Seabed Mining. https://www.adlittle.com/en/insights/viewpoints/seabed-mining-20-trillion-opportunity

Michael O'Keefe. *China's Debt Diplomacy in the Pacific, News*. 2018. La Trobe University. https://www.latrobe.edu.au/news/articles/2018/release/chinas-debt-diplomacy-in-the-pacific

Keshmeer Makun. *External Debt and Economic Growth in Pacific Island Countries; A Linear and Nonlinear Analysis of Fiji Islands*. 2021. Science Direct. https://www.sciencedirect.com/science/article/abs/pii/S1703494921000025

motives. Predator businesses normally take advantage of unknowing and far too trusting indigenous civic leaders. While the great dissemination of information, easily researchable commodity prices for example, balances the scales of price negotiation, the traditional strongman position of hierarchical leadership remains subject to abuse.

In fact, present-day demand for critical minerals presents a decision-making ultimatum for many CCZ and EEZ countries. On one hand, the countries have the option of developing an equity plan in which the state or an independent non-governmental community body holds shares in profits and board of director decision-making. Conversely, a moratorium policy defers business like decision-making until greater clarity of the seabed mining industry can be determined. In many ways, a moratorium makes environmental sense. Fast-improving extraction tools such as sensory device robotic extraction undersea vehicles are in design stages to eliminate legacy subsea dredging machines and preserve deep-sea environmental integrity.

7. A Cultural Path – Conclusion

The current decision-making inflection points lay out a cultural path for South Pacific nations. They are faced with an opportunity to reject modern iterations of neo-colonial appropriations. One alternative is to succumb to short-term rewards, even in keeping with cultural norms, that ultimately deprive populations of their ancestral wealth. Or the countries may transition to business protocols and negotiate excavation of their riches to the long-term benefit of both state and the populations.

Influencers and thought leaders such as ISA, Cook Islands and ASEDC hope that their global influence, business acumen and cultural responsibility provide the guidance and framework to build a South Pacific unified policy for the long-term and culturally appropriate critical resource management plan.[14]

The independent South Pacific nations hold the energy transition resource solutions that threaten the survival of Planet Earth due to ongoing environmental fossil fuel consumption abuses. Once the independent South Pacific nations realize the scope of power lying in the depths of their EEZs, they are likely to demand greater diplomatic leverage from major energy-consuming global powers.

14 UN Trade and Development. *Critical Minerals Boom: Global Energy Shift Brings Opportunities and Risks for Developing Countries*. 2024. UNCTAD. https://unctad.org/news/critical-minerals-boom-global-energy-shift-brings-opportunities-and-risks

Jillian Ash. *Social Impacts of Critical Mineral Exploration on Indigenous Peoples' lands: A Case Study from Solomon Islands*. 2024. ScienceDirect. https://www.sciencedirect.com/science/article/pii/S2214790X24000376

Forum Staff. *Critical Minerals: A Resource Race*. 2023. Indo Pacific Defense Forum. https://ipdefenseforum.com/2023/12/critical-minerals-a-resource-race/

James Borton. *Balancing Erosion and Opportunity in Pacific Deep-Sea Mining*. 2024. East Asia Forum. https://eastasiaforum.org/2024/02/28/balancing-erosion-and-opportunity-in-pacific-deep-sea-mining/

Conversely, the first of the major powers to fully accept their energy needs, the resources of the South Pacific nations, adapt a twenty-first century level of respect for the South Pacific populations and resources and are willing to abdicate post-World War II perceptions of the South Pacific island nation states will have grasped a diplomatic foothold required to reverse global warming, assure their own energy requirements, create equity-based wealth in the South Pacific and rescue low-lying nation states globally from the disastrous effects of rising ocean levels.

20 Pacific Island Forum's Strategic Reply to Ocean Change

*Joanna Siekiera**

1. Introduction

In this chapter, the author will deliberately use the term "ocean change" instead of simply "climate change" to emphasize the seriousness of the harmful effects of anthropogenic climate change on the marine environment, especially on the world's largest marine body – the Pacific Ocean.[1] The aim of the chapter is to present the process of establishing a new custom in international law as a result of the actions made by microstates in Oceania. The new international practice consists of depositing maps with lists of geographical coordinates of maritime borders at the United Nations (UN). The geographical scope of the analysis covers the Pacific Islands region, called Oceania. In some contexts, Oceania also includes Australia and New Zealand because of the Pacific Islands communities and indigenous people. Thus, it is important here to distinguish basic terminology. The Pacific islands region is divided into three subregions: Micronesia, Polynesia, and Melanesia. It is crucial to mention that, as the region is indeed diverse and uniquely described and identified based on these sub-regions. Therefore, it also creates differences from a regional perspective. Yet, unification of the region makes it stronger, despite any geopolitical variations and historical disputes.

Although it is common to research climate change effects on various ecosystems on all continents, along with predicting their increasing impact, the literature is indeed modest when it comes to ocean change in Oceania. Is this omission of research because this region is the furthest from the world's decision-making centers, or simply because Oceania's states are not key players in global politics or economies? Perhaps there are not many social scientists, political scientists, or international lawyers specializing in this narrow area of research of legal consequences of ocean change in Oceania. Regardless of the root reason, this lack of

* Assistant Professor, War Studies University, Warsaw, Poland

1 The author sailed across the Pacific Ocean in July and August 2023 during a scientific expedition on board the largest Norwegian training ship, Statsraad Lehmkuhl, on which she was lecturing the law of the sea and sustainable development of the ocean. Therefore, this chapter has not only a theoretical but also a practical dimension, and personal experiences from staying in Fiji, Palau, and Hawaii, which influenced the thoughts presented here.

DOI: 10.4324/9781003545750-23

researched literature needs to be filled in order to help small island states in the Pacific Islands counter the devastating effects of climate change on their lands and seas, to protect their statehood, sovereignty, peace, and stability at the regional and global level, but also to become resilient at any attempts by malicious actors to misuse their fragility and vulnerability.

Although new weather patterns (sudden weather changes, flooding, droughts, etc.) are expected to occur in the future, small island states are already experiencing severe damage and their populations are making serious preparations to protect their statehood and national identity. If meteorological and geological forecasts are to be confirmed, there is a risk of losing their territory, which is one of the key aspects defining statehood.

It is worth emphasizing that long-term energy security decisions made by world leaders, both at the national and global levels, may mitigate or exacerbate climate threats. The least developed countries in Oceania, whose poverty rates are the highest in world rankings, are among the most vulnerable to the effects of climate change. Unfortunately, their voices are not effectively heard at the UN forum. For this reason, without waiting for adopting changes in the international arena like, for instance, an amendment of the UN Convention on the Law of the Sea (UNCLOS),[2] nations living in Pacific Islands Countries decided to legally protect their sovereignty at the regional forum, independently from whatever happens or not at the global forum. It is exactly the low-lying, poor, and underdeveloped or slowly developing island microstates who coined their own name to be used when referring to them: Small Island Developing States (SIDS), and for those exclusively from Oceania: Pacific Small Island Developing States (PSIDS).

Importantly, these groups of states and countries (also called Pacific Island Countries and Territories, PICT, as not all entities in the Pacific have the status of a sovereign state) have contributed the least to global warming (often having a negligible degree of industrialization), although they suffer its greatest impact. The Federated States of Micronesia (FSM), Marshall Islands, Kiribati, and Tuvalu are the most drastic example of this dichotomy. For two decades, FSM has been fighting against strong tides destroying the land, significant flooding of atolls (affecting not only material damage of the coast, but also geochemical changes on the soil, and thus leading to difficulties in harvesting crops and animal husbandry), coastal erosion, destruction of food crops, limiting access to potable water and damage to marine species caused by rising sea temperatures and acidification.[3]

2 UN, Convention on the Law of the Sea, 10 December 1982.

3 For more see: M. Gerrard, G.E. Wannier (eds.), *Threatened Island Nations: Legal Implications of Rising Seas and a Changing Climate,* Cambridge: Cambridge University Press, 2013; R. Warner, C. Schofield, *Climate Change and the Oceans: Gauging the Legal and Policy Currents in the Asia Pacific and Beyond*, Cheltenham: Elgar Publishing, 2012.

2. The Law and the Sea

The Pacific Ocean covers one-third of the Earth's surface. It is home to over 10 million people, spread over 25,000 islands and islets, who proudly call themselves Pasifika or simply "people of the sea".[4] This largest body of water in the world is full of cultural and biological diversity. Pacific Islanders see the ocean not only as their home, but also as the basis of their pure existence in a metaphysical, spiritual sense.[5] Additionally, what is important to food security and thus the survival of the Pacific Islands inhabitants, the main – and sometimes only – source of protein in the region is tuna.[6] Therefore, issues regulated by the Law of the Sea, one of the oldest branches of international law, are of great importance to Pacific Islanders. Those are fishing rights and duties, territorial sea and open ocean zones, and regulations toward public and private entities, to name just a few.

In order to determine and delimit such sea zones under the territorial sovereignty of a given country, it is necessary to use reference points. Yet due to the rising sea level, this solution appears to be strongly disturbed. Indeed, in the field of the Law of the Sea, a fundamental question concerns the measurement of the 200 nautical mile (nm) Exclusive Economic Zone (EEZ) before and after potential changes in the ocean level. Such change could (and already is) result in a reduction of land areas such as islands, atolls, peninsulas of low-lying states, or their deltas. Thus, the reference point will also be moved further landwards, which in turn would reduce the maritime areas. However, what is characteristic for the EEZs of the Pacific Islands is they are many times larger than the land zones constituting the *de jure* reference point for the delimitation of these zones; serving countries for fishing, research, mining, cable laying, tourism, etc. It is the specific archipelagic nature of Oceania that provides them with a disproportionately huge platform (compared to which measures an EEZ of 200 nm). What is more, the ocean is also the basis of the livelihood and history, culture, and identity of the Pacific Islanders.

Ocean change affects sea level, thus contributing to the reduction of land territory and therefore to the reduction of maritime zones. Consequently, there is a general instability in the international legal order. Under the UNCLOS regime, both islands and EEZs are legally defined. The baselines in the Pacific are extremely extensive and disproportionate to the small parts of the landmass of the Islands nations. To illustrate this, an island without a maritime neighbor within a radius of 400 nm can generate 125,664 nm^2 [431,014 km^2] of territorial sea, EEZ, and continental shelf,[7] whereas a "rock" can only generate a claim to a territorial sea of 452 nm^2 [1,550 km^2].

4 E. Hau'ofa, Our Sea of Islands, *The Contemporary Pacific*, 1994, vol. 6, no. 1, pp. 148–161.

5 B.V. Lal, K. Fortune (eds.), *The Pacific Islands: An Encyclopedia*, Honolulu: UH Press, 2000, p. 406.

6 P. D'Arcy, *The People of the Sea: Environment, Identity, and History in Oceania*, Honolulu: UH Press, 2006.

7 C. Schofield, Shifting Limits? Sea Level Rise and Options to Secure Maritime Jurisdiction Claims, *Carbon and Climate Law Review*, 2009, vol. 3, pp. 405–416.

3. Human Security and Climate Resistance

Even the slightest change in land territory can have a significant impact on maritime boundaries and thus cause a threat to state security. Hence the natural, almost automatic association of the statehood and sovereignty of the Pacific Islands Countries with (their) ocean should not surprise us. Without the ocean, Pacific Islanders do not exist and cannot exist – both in the existential and identity sense. Such a close connection of people with the ocean reflects the deeper and embodied relationship of Pacific Islanders with the ocean, land, and all that surrounds them. This unique "Pacific worldview" deals with problems in the "Pacific way", which can be difficult for people from other continents to understand.[8] The resolution to the problem of rising oceans is moving the population, e.g., Fiji or FSM, elsewhere. Pasifika do not want to *be moved*, resulting in existence in a foreign host country, such as New Zealand or Australia. How will the statehood or national heritage be possible, protected, and cultivated? Therefore, the Pacific worldview is expressed currently in the legal struggle to preserve Oceania states' own land and sea territory to preserve their own national identity.

Without going into too much detail about the bio-physical-chemical effects of ocean change, it appears important to point out that ocean change weakens the ability of oceans and coastal areas to provide key services for the populace, such as providing food, storing carbon dioxide, and producing oxygen. Another, lesser known ability of the ocean, unfortunately also strongly damaged by climate change, is the creation of natural, very effective solutions to protect coastlines against erosion and flooding of the land. Examples of these include coral reefs, seagrasses, and mangroves.[9] The International Union for Conservation of Nature issued a report in 2017 which underlines the sustainable management, protection, and restoration of coastal and marine ecosystems that are essential in supporting the continued provision of ecosystem services on which human life and health depend.[10] A low-carbon strategy is essential as never before to maintain both ocean and human health. The health of the inhabitants of Oceania, not only depends directly on the purity of the ocean, specifically its temperature and acidity. In addition, the oceans absorb heat. Since the 1970s, more than 90% of human-induced atmospheric warming has been absorbed by the oceans.[11]

4. Sea-level Rise and Statehood of Pacific Islands

There is a common agreement in scientific research and political activities that the sea level is rising and thus causing a lot of damage to the natural environment, both

8 Thus, a modest attempt to full the academic gap of seeing the law and policies of Oceania through the cultural perspective of Pasifika, in a book by the author: J. Siekiera, *Regional Policy in the South Pacific,* Warsaw: Warsaw University Press, 2021.

9 D. Laffoley, J.M. Baxter (eds.), *Explaining Ocean Warming: Causes, Scale, Effects and Consequences*, IUCN Publications, 2016. https://portals.iucn.org/library/node/46254

10 International Union for Conservation of Nature (IUCN), *The Ocean and Climate Change. Issues Brief*, November 2017.

11 International Union for Conservation of Nature (IUCN), *The Ocean and Climate Change.*

land and maritime. However, it is still uncertain to what extent and how quickly the sea level will rise, causing deadly harm to populations as well as to the existence of states as international legal entities. After all, the ceasing of the existence of a state, according to the international law doctrine, is associated with the loss of one of the key elements of a state (according to the 1933 Montevideo Convention: a permanent population, a defined territory, and government).[12] The situation, especially in the Pacific, may accelerate as four low-lying countries in particular, Kiribati, the Marshall Islands, Tokelau, and Tuvalu, are expected to lose most or even all of their territory by the end of the 21st century.[13]

What is more, flooding, drought, and extreme weather are likely to gradually make coastal areas uninhabitable. Another threat to the security of the PSIDS population will be the socio-economic consequences. Migrations of thousands of displaced people (sometimes called "climate refugees", which is a very popular albeit not a legal term)[14] will be a dramatic consequence of the flooding of urban centers, which are already overpopulated and struggle with high unemployment, especially among young, uneducated people.[15]

Hence, the situation of the population in Oceania is compared to the "front line of global ocean change".[16] The South Pacific region is vulnerable due to three main interrelated factors: smallness,[17] isolation, and fragmentation (the three sub-regions mentioned earlier). While confined land and marine environments are undeniably fragile and ocean-dependent, PSIDS are becoming increasingly vulnerable to multiple threats to both state and human security. These include lack of waste management, land and sea pollution, soil erosion, rapid population growth and overpopulation in coastal areas and capitals, migration (internal, on the islands of one country, and external, international across the Pacific region), dependence on foreign remittances and the continuing post-colonial dependence on foreign aid, drastically changing market prices for goods, and lack of or insufficient infrastructure in Pacific ports and airports.[18]

12 Art. 1 of the Convention on Rights and Duties of States adopted by the Seventh International Conference of American States, December 26, 1933.

13 Gerrard, Wannier, *Threatened Island Nations*; Warner, Schofield, *Climate Change and the Oceans*.

14 There are no legal definitions of "environmental refugees," "climate refugees," or "climate migrants," as the main actors (norm-makers) in international law, states and intergovernmental organizations (IGO), have decided not to codify those terms (yet). Even the main global IGOs dealing with the status of displaced persons – the United Nations High Commissioner for Refugees (UNHCR) and the International Organization for Migration (IMO) – upheld here.

15 R.J. Nicholls, A. Cazenave, Sea-Level Rise and Its Impact on Coastal Zones, *Science*, 2010, vol. 328, no. 5985, pp. 1517–1520.

16 A less-flattering phrase is calling PSIDS "the canary of global warming and rising sea levels" by Phillip H. Muller, former Ambassador of the Marshall Islands to the United Nations. See the foreword to the *Threatened Island Nations*.

17 R. Crocombe, *Asia in the Pacific Islands: Replacing the West*, Suva: University of the South Pacific, 2007, p. 353.

18 J. Siekiera, The Pacific Islands Forum 2015, Port Moresby, in *New Zealand Yearbook of International Law 13*, Christchurch: University of Canterbury, 2015, p. 150.

5. Unprecedented Solution to Unprecedented Problem

PSIDS cannot afford to wait for final and binding political decisions and legal norms made in the international arena, especially in the UN. To secure their legal existence as sovereign states, Oceania states decided to develop legal solutions on their own, at the level that's closer to them – the regional level. As the impact of ocean change is unprecedented, this legal case also requires an unprecedented approach using various legal mechanisms, soft law, and hard law. The physical existence of the countries in the South Pacific, and thus their legal existence, too, is threatened by rising sea levels, which in turn entails other biological, social, and economic consequences mentioned earlier.

It should be emphasized that the loss of part or potentially all of a state territory opens an international discussion on numerous legal dilemmas. At least a few of them can be mentioned here: Can a population without territory still be called a state within the meaning of the Montevideo Convention? Does such a deterritorialized entity still have the rights and obligations of a state, or does it begin to function as a *sui generis* entity, or an *ex-situ* nation,[19] as some lawyers propose? If the baselines for delimitation of the EEZ are changed, will the maritime zones (maritime territory of a given country) also decrease due to the reduction of land territory? Or should we use ambulatory baselines instead of the fixed ones?[20] Would the population of such a sunken state lose their citizenship in the host country, or would they automatically gain a second citizenship? What might be the legal status of such displaced people – would they be referred to as climate migrants? Since there is no international agreement on "climate change refugees" or "climate change displaced persons," should the UN develop such an agreement and seek its ratification? Or perhaps it appears necessary to change the interpretation of international law due to the already over-fragmented legal solutions, including the controversial UNCLOS, which is not always implemented or obeyed. Is it better for PSIDS to create a treaty mechanism, or should they be more flexible and use customary law, which in turn would require a different approach to legal culture?

The aforementioned legal dilemmas only partially illustrate the tragic situation in which the Pacific Island states and territories are currently. Yet, the intention of this chapter is not to look for answers to them, as even the leading politicians and activists disagree on specific solutions. What is more, international decision-makers very rarely consider what Pasifika themselves perceive as the best path for their own region. For this reason, it is exceptionally important to raise awareness of the possible or existing legal consequences of ocean change for the microstates of Oceania while minding the local perspective.

Among the many effects that may arise in the near future, which would be highly devastating for PSIDS, are national claims to maritime jurisdiction. The

19 M. Burkett, The Nation Ex-Situ: On Climate Change, Deterritorialized Nationhood and the Post-Climate Era, *Climate Law*, 2011, vol. 2, no. 3, pp. 345–374.

20 M.R. Wendebourg, Interpreting the Law of the Sea in the Context of Sea-Level Rise: The Ambulatory Thesis and State Practice, *Journal of Environmental Law*, 2023, vol. 35, no. 3, pp. 499–507.

islands face the disastrous prospect of losing their land and therefore maritime territory (delimitated in accordance with UNCLOS) and consequently losing their international legal status as sovereign states. The economic and legal consequence of limiting the EEZs is the loss of the states' sovereign rights to natural resources, which are both migratory marine resources and minerals. The latter include highly valued rare raw materials for the production of batteries in electric cars, as well as possible future weaponry elements.

6. Regional Custom as a New Law

The Pacific Islands Forum (PIF), the most active organization in the Oceania region, issued on August 6, 2021[21] the "Declaration on Preserving Maritime Zones in the Face of Climate Change-related Sea-Level Rise" (hereinafter referred to as the PIF Declaration).[22] PIF member states decided not to wait for global action, nor to seek a universal consensus. From international lawyers' and international relations experts' practice, regional methods turn out to be better, i.e. faster, cheaper, and more effective, than global ones. The innovative approach of the PIF Declaration is embedded in the declarative theory of international law. According to this theory, the declaration of an entity is necessary for establishing and maintaining such a state as a basic and primary unit of international law.[23] The PIF members were particularly clear in the PIF Declaration by announcing their maritime zones established and notified to the UN Secretary-General in accordance with UNCLOS, and thus the rights derived therefrom will continue to apply, without reduction, notwithstanding any physical changes related to sea level rise due to climate change.[24] Additionally, an important message of the document is the call for the UN to consent to a new international custom just recently adopted through the Pacific states' own practice.

Interestingly, on the same day as the PIF Declaration was published, the UN International Law Commission concluded its 72nd meeting.[25] The meeting was historical, as for the first time in UN history, the issue of sea level rise from the

21 The author participated in the 51st PIF Summit in Suva, Fiji, in July 2022. As usual, the key topic was ocean change and preventing its consequences in the region. Compare: *Report Communique of the 51st Pacific Island Forum Leaders Meeting*. https://www.forumsec.org/2022/07/17/report-communique-of-the-51st-pacific-islands-forum-leaders-meeting/

22 *Declaration on Preserving Maritime Zones in the Face of Climate Change-Related Sea-Level Rise*. https://www.forumsec.org/2021/08/11/declaration-on-preserving-maritime-zones-in-the-face-of-climate-change-related-sea-level-rise

23 Such a unilateral act does not finalize the process of self-determination of a state. International recognition by other states is then required. There are several well-known examples of entities that, despite their own declaration and meeting the Montevideo Convention criteria, were not recognized as states.

24 F. Anggadi, Establishment, Notification, and Maintenance: The Package of State Practice at the Heart of the Pacific Islands Forum Declaration on Preserving Maritime Zones, *Ocean Development and International Law*, 2022, vol. 53, no. 1, pp. 19–36.

25 UN, Sea-level rise in relation to international law (28.02.2020) A/CN.4/740.

international law standpoint was analyzed.[26] Yet, the document issued after the meeting did not gain any legal status, *only* an opinion-forming one. It describes the legal and political views on the feasible legal consequences of ocean change by individual states due to their interests. As it can be easily guessed, the states and countries that are not/less exposed to the effects of ocean change were more reluctant to make any changes to UNCLOS or establish new legal solutions in the international arena. In contrast, SIDS requested a quick and effective amendment of the Convention on the Law of the Sea, which would finally cover the legal responses to the destructive effects of sea level rise and introduce legal measures to secure their actual and legal existence.

As this UN document was not intended to resolve any legal dilemmas of ocean change and a possible development of the Law of the Sea, but only to point out the various standpoints of the member states, the PIF heads of state decided to protect their statehood under their own – regional – responsibility. Therefore, in order to prevent the negative consequences of ocean change and thus secure their own maritime territories in a current form, the microstates of Oceania decided to (over)interpret UNCLOS. Art. 76(8) of UNCLOS states: "The limits of the shelf established by a coastal State on the basis of these recommendations shall be final and binding". After depositing maps and lists of geographical coordinates of the baselines along with the external boundaries of maritime zones at the UN Secretary-General, these areas (and declaratively confirmed baselines) are not subject to further review (changes or further proof of legal affiliation) regardless of the future effects of climate change, e.g. flooding of all or part of the territory. The lists of coordinates provided for the delimitation of maritime baselines, limits, and boundaries are open to be checked by the international community. As such, those deposited lists constitute a transparent and reliable source of data in protecting the principles of the law of the sea. Those coordinate lists (satellite data) can also be used and overlaid on electronic maps to inform seafarers, mariners, or researchers.[27]

The depositary authority is the UN Secretary-General through the UN Commission on the Limits of the Continental Shelf (CLCS) in the Division of Ocean Affairs and the Law of the Sea. Currently, 13 Oceania countries, individually or collectively, have submitted their maritime border coordinates: the Cook Islands, Fiji, the Federated States of Micronesia, Papua New Guinea, the Solomon Islands, Palau, Tonga, Tuvalu, Tokelau, and Kiribati, as well as Australia, New Zealand, and France (on behalf of French Polynesia).[28]

26 UN, *Summaries of the Work of the International Law Commission*. https://legal.un.org/ilc/summaries/8_9.shtml

27 C. Schofield, A New Frontier in the Law of the Sea? Responding to the Implications of Sea Level Rise for Baselines, Limits and Boundaries, in R. Barnes, R. Long (eds.), *Frontiers in International Environmental Law: Oceans and Climate Challenges: Essays in Honor of David Freestone*, Leiden: Brill, 2021, p. 190.

28 State on the day of 18/04/2024: UN, *Submissions, through the Secretary-General of the United Nations, to the Commission on the Limits of the Continental Shelf, pursuant to article 76,*

International custom is treated in the doctrine of international law as one of its sources, on an equal footing with international agreements, whose treaty law is more developed and used globally. "International custom, as evidence of a general practice accepted as law"[29] must be based on two elements to be recognized as a source of law: *usus* and *opinio iuris sive necessitatis*. The first element derived from Latin is *usus*. It means the existence of a practice, and therefore the visible application of custom by several states in a stable, continuous manner and towards everyone (*erga omnes*), while not selected entities. Consequently, the second element – *opinio iuris* – refers to the belief in the legal validity of this practice, and therefore the attribution of legal force to the practiced custom, i.e. the norm from which the rights and obligations of individuals arise.

The emergence of a new international custom in Oceania, based on the regional practice of depositing maps and lists of geographical coordinates of maritime boundaries within the UN Division of Ocean Affairs and the Law of the Sea, secures the main aim of international law – ensuring peace and stability in the world.[30] Moreover, given the tragic and state-threatening effects of sea level rise, such an unprecedented legal action at the regional level can help those looking for quick and effective tools in other regions. Such legal stability is indeed necessary in the field of the Law of the Sea, perhaps even more than in other branches of international law, as it is at the sea where the interests of individual states in trade, navigation, and security are most often opposed.

7. Conclusions

At the beginning of the 21st century, in the face of progressive climate change caused by human activity, and in the absence of a sufficient response from legislators, we observe the emergence of a new practice of Oceania states. This regional practice is evolving towards the establishment of international law custom aimed at protecting the statehood and sovereignty of threatened international law entities. The regional practice of the South Pacific states of depositing maritime borders is unprecedented, because the threat of loss of statehood, due not to war, aggression, or the will of the population but to environmental factors, is not regulated by any norm of international law. The stability of land borders, but also maritime borders for islands, low-lying, and deltaic states, plays an important role in maintaining international peace and stability. The right of territorial sovereignty over the territorial sea, the exclusive economic zones and the continental shelf is a priority because states have sovereign rights in this respect in order to search for and

paragraph 8, of the United Nations Convention on the Law of the Sea of 10 December 1982. https://www.un.org/depts/los/clcs_new/commission_submissions.htm

29 Art. 38(1)(b) of United Nations, Statute of the International Court of Justice, 18 April 1946, understood as the unofficial list of international law sources.

30 Art. 1 of the UN Charter, 26 June 1945.

exploit natural resources important for the development of the economy (oil, gas, and other raw materials).

Pacific Island Forum took the most reactive and ambitious line of action. Established in 1971, PIF strengthened collective voice and revealed the Pacific Islanders' commitment to political and economic cooperation. The 2050 Strategy for the Blue Pacific Continent builds on this long history of working together.[31] Documentation was made amid escalating climate change-related impacts and the intensification of geostrategic competition, where those two major facts have been exacerbating the region's vulnerabilities. "Such a strategy is likely to be a significant undertaking if it is to be developed in a way that is robust, comprehensive, and most importantly, owned and driven by the people of the Pacific".[32] According to the 2050 Strategy Implementation Plan, Pacific leadership on global responses to climate change should prioritize the Pacific-led initiatives, yet at the same time rely on international law aid through advisory opinions from the International Court of Justice (ICJ) and International Tribunal on the Law of the Sea (ITLOS).[33]

Therefore, in accordance with the UN Convention on the Law of the Sea, submitting maps together with geodetic data of the continental shelf results in a permanent recording (*declaration*, in legal terminology) of the outer limits of the shelf. Once the information is declared and sent, it "freezes" state borders even despite the effects of sea level rise, submerging land or shrinking it. Through diplomacy by the PIF, the leaders of states and territories in the Pacific encourage the urgent and correct definition of their base points and baselines in order to legitimize their own maritime zones: 12 nm (limit of the territorial sea), 24 nm (contiguous zone) and 200 nm (EEZ).

The emergence of the new custom in international law made in Oceania may inspire states from other maritime regions (e.g. those located in the Indian Ocean or the Caribbean Sea) to follow this pattern, without waiting for the amendment of UNCLOS, ratification of a new law of the sea or recognition of any consensus in the global arena. If this happens, those underdeveloped microstates in the South Pacific, still struggling with the postcolonial legal order, which makes them additionally vulnerable to any foreign influence, would become pioneers in a new chapter in the history of public international law – the effective interpretation of treaty law (UNCLOS) in climate resilience. Such interpretation is aimed at saving statehood and contributing to maintaining stability through close legal cooperation for both human and state security.

31 Pacific Islands Forum Secretariat, *2050 Strategy for the Blue Pacific Continent*, Suva, Fiji 2022, PIF. https://forumsec.org/2050

32 S. Tekiteki, *2050 Strategy for the Blue Pacific Continent & Pacific Roadmap for Sustainable Development*, Suva, Director Governance and Engagement, PIFS, 2020.

33 PIF, *2050 Strategy Implementation Plan 2023–2030, Phase I – 2050 Strategy for the Blue Pacific Continent Setting the Foundations Towards Transformational Change*, Suva, 2020.

References

Anggadi F., Establishment, Notification, and Maintenance: The Package of State Practice at the Heart of the Pacific Islands Forum Declaration on Preserving Maritime Zones, *Ocean Development and International Law*, 2022, vol. 53, no. 1.

Barnes R., Long R. (eds.), *Frontiers in International Environmental Law: Oceans and Climate Challenges: Essays in Honor of David Freestone*, Leiden: Brill, 2021.

Burkett M., The Nation Ex-Situ: On Climate Change, Deterritorialized Nationhood and the Post-Climate Era, *Climate Law*, 2011, vol. 2, no. 3.

Convention on Rights and Duties of States adopted by the Seventh International Conference of American States, December 26, 1933.

D'Arcy P., *The People of the Sea: Environment, Identity, and History in Oceania*, Honolulu: UH Press, 2006.

Gerrard M., Wannier G.E. (eds.), *Threatened Island Nations: Legal Implications of Rising Seas and a Changing Climate,* Cambridge: Cambridge University Press, 2013.

Hau'ofa E., Our Sea of Islands, *The Contemporary Pacific*, 1994, vol. 6, no. 1.

International Union for Conservation of Nature (IUCN), *The Ocean and Climate Change. Issues Brief*, November 2017.

Laffoley D., Baxter J.M. (eds.), *Explaining Ocean Warming: Causes, Scale, Effects and Consequences*, IUCN Publications, 2016. https://portals.iucn.org/library/node/46254

Lal B.V., Fortune K. (eds.), *The Pacific Islands: An Encyclopedia,* Honolulu: UH Press, 2000.

Nicholls R.J., Cazenave A., Sea-Level Rise and Its Impact on Coastal Zones, *Science*, 2010, vol. 328, no. 5985.

PIF, *Declaration on Preserving Maritime Zones in the Face of Climate Change-Related Sea-Level Rise*. https://www.forumsec.org/2021/08/11/declaration-on-preserving-maritime-zones-in-the-face-of-climate-change-related-sea-level-rise

PIF, *Report Communique of the 51st Pacific Island Forum Leaders Meeting*. https://www.forumsec.org/2022/07/17/report-communique-of-the-51st-pacific-islands-forum-leaders-meeting/

PIF, *2050 Strategy for the Blue Pacific Continent*, Suva, Fiji, 2022. https://forumsec.org/2050

PIF, *2050 Strategy Implementation Plan 2023–2030, Phase I – 2050 Strategy for the Blue Pacific Continent Setting the Foundations Towards Transformational Change*, Suva 2020.

Schofield C., Shifting Limits? Sea Level Rise and Options to Secure Maritime Jurisdiction Claims, *Carbon and Climate Law Review*, 2009, vol. 3.

Siekiera J., *Regional Policy in the South Pacific,* Warsaw: Warsaw University Press, 2021.

Tekiteki S., *2050 Strategy for the Blue Pacific Continent & Pacific Roadmap for Sustainable Development*, Suva: Director Governance and Engagement, PIFS, 2020.

UN, *Sea-Level Rise in Relation to International Law*, February 28, 2020, A/CN.4/740.

UN, Statute of the International Court of Justice, 18 April 1946.

UN, *Submissions, through the Secretary-General of the United Nations, to the Commission on the Limits of the Continental Shelf, pursuant to article 76, paragraph 8, of the United Nations Convention on the Law of the Sea of 10 December 1982.* https://www.un.org/depts/los/clcs_new/commission_submissions.htm

UN, *Summaries of the Work of the International Law Commission*. https://legal.un.org/ilc/summaries/8_9.shtml

UN Charter, 26 June 1945.

UN General Assembly, Convention on the Law of the Sea, 10 December 1982.

Warner R., Schofield C., *Climate Change and the Oceans: Gauging the Legal and Policy Currents in the Asia Pacific and Beyond*, Cheltenham: Elgar Publishing, 2012.

Wendebourg M.R., Interpreting the Law of the Sea in the Context of Sea-Level Rise: The Ambulatory Thesis and State Practice, *Journal of Environmental Law*, 2023, vol. 35, no. 3.

Index

Note: Page numbers in **bold** indicate tables in the text.

FSC
www.fsc.org
MIX
Papier | Fördert
gute Waldnutzung
FSC® C083411

Kolibri 360 GmbH
Ferdinand-Jühlke-Straße 7
99095 Erfurt, Deutschland
produktsicherheit@kolibri360.de